FOR LOVE OF COUNTRY

FOR LOVE OF COUNTRY

Confronting Rape and Sexual Harassment in the US Military

TERRI SPAHR NELSON

Second Edition with Special Sections for
Victims of Military Sexual Trauma and Their Loved Ones
and a Guide for Military Leaders

Sugati Publications
www.sugatipublications.com

AUTHOR'S NOTE: Given the sensitive nature of this topic, the author and publisher value the importance of respecting the privacy and confidentiality of the contributors. Therefore, all quotes from victims who participated in this research are anonymous to protect the identity and privacy of the victims, except in the case of Dorothy whose identity is included upon her request.

PUBLISHER'S NOTE: The author and publisher of this book are not dispensing medical, mental health or legal advice or prescribing the use of any techniques as recommended treatment for physical or mental health conditions without the advice of a physician or qualified mental health professional.

Originally published in 2002 by The Haworth Maltreatment and Trauma Press, an imprint of The Haworth Press, Inc. 10 Alice Street, Binghamton, NY 13094.

Transferred to Digital Printing 2008 by Routledge (Taylor & Francis Group), 2008. 2 Park Square, Milton Park, Abingdon, Oxon, OX 14 4 RN 270 Madison Ave, New York, NT 10016

Copyright transferred by Routledge in 2013 upon request by author to Sugati Publications for second edition.

Second Edition ©2015 Sugati Publications.

10 9 8 7 6 5 4 3 2

Library of Congress Cataloging-in-Publication Data
    Spahr Nelson, Terri
    For Love of Country: Confronting Rape and Sexual Harassment in the US Military/
    Terri Spahr Nelson
    Includes bibliographical references
    ISBN 10: 0982580614
    ISBN 13: 9780982580615
    1. United States—Armed Forces—Women. 2. Sexual Harassment—United States. 3. Rape—United States. 4. United States—Armed Forces—Personnel management. I. Title.

Printed in the United States of America. Second Edition.

Publisher: Sugati Publications at www.sugatipublications.com

This book is dedicated to the women and men who were victims of sexual assault or harassment by military personnel. Thank you to those who participated in this study and so courageously spoke about your experiences so that others might learn. Your insights and your words have made a difference. This book is for you.

A special dedication to my parents (2002): For my mom, a cancer survivor for many years, and my dad, a World War II Veteran from the elite First Marines Raider Battalion. You both taught me the true meaning of courage and strength, and the importance of standing up for what you believe.

Acknowledgments

THIS BOOK WOULD be meaningless without the contributions of the women and men who shared their experiences of sexual victimization by military personnel. Their insights and feedback guided me throughout the development of the book. I am truly grateful and honored that they were willing to speak out about something that has touched their lives so significantly. To them, I extend heartfelt thanks.

Many others also made significant contributions— far too many to name individually. To the researchers, the journalists, the military personnel (including the helpful Colonel at the Pentagon), the Judge Advocate, and everyone else who had a part in this book, thank you for your insights. Your contributions are located throughout the book.

Five individuals took additional time to review the manuscript and provide invaluable feedback. To Gloria, Chris, Carl, Dorothy, and Christine, thank you so much for your time, your helpful comments, and your commitment to this issue.

I also want to acknowledge everyone at The Haworth Press who has helped to complete the first edition of the book and Routlege (Taylor and Francis Publishers) who later assumed copyright for continued publication to a wider market. Every person who worked on the project has been so kind and very professional. I especially want to thank Peg Marr, senior production editor, and Dawn Krisko, senior production editor, for their expertise and ongoing support throughout the process, and my editor Robert Geffner for recognizing that this is an important story that needed to be told.

Finally, and from my heart, thank you to my husband and to my son who have been supportive every step of the way during this five-year research study. You have done so much to help me to complete this project, but most important, your support and love have made all the difference.

FOR LOVE OF COUNTRY:

CONFRONTING RAPE AND SEXUAL HARASSMENT IN THE U.S. MILITARY

TABLE OF CONTENTS

Introduction

Second Edition, For Love of Country 2015

THE FIRST EDITION of *For Love of Country: Confronting Rape and Sexual Harassment in the US Military* was a call to action to draw attention to this pervasive problem. That was in 2002—two full years before the Department of Defense had a Sexual Assault Prevention and Response (SAPR) Program and three years before the development of the initial SAPR policies in 2005. Unfortunately, aside from annual statistical data and the addition of several noteworthy policies over the past ten years, the messages in the original publication still hold true today. Despite the significant progress and changes over the past decade, grave and concerning problems persist when it comes to sexual assault in the military.

So why does the US Military remain challenged by this issue after such considerable effort, time and expense? The root of this pervasive problem is twofold: *power failure* and the so-called *zero tolerance policy*.

The underlying premise of the first edition of this book was that leadership failure fueled the systemic crisis of rape and sexual harassment within the Department of Defense (DoD). I defined this leadership dilemma as *power failure*. The term refers to leaders who are steadfastly (and sometimes overtly) unwilling to get on board with the SAPR program and to do what it takes to implement the zero tolerance policy. It was my contention in 2002, and still is today, that such leaders contribute the most toward the problem of sexual harassment and sexual assault in the military.

Leaders who exhibit power failure stand in the way of changing the culture and the climate in the military. Some directly contribute to the problem with their own abusive actions or their failure to act and support SAPR. These leaders ultimately undermine the success of the mission: to eradicate sexual assault and offenders from the ranks through zero tolerance.

Fortunately, there are far more inspiring leaders in the military than those who succumb to power failure. The outstanding leaders understand how sexual assault weakens the military. They are the role models to their junior officers and enlisted Service members by endorsing and supporting the SAPR mission. They can and should be leading the way for this important mission, by doing what the U.S. Military does best: determine the source of a problem and eradicate it.

As I noted in the first edition in 2002, the Department of Defense (DoD) knows how to change an oppressive, destructive culture. They tackled a similar problem in the 1970s with racial discrimination and harassment. Within a decade, the military nearly eliminated blatant and explicit racism and harassment. Slowly, incremental cultural changes occurred resulting in significant and widespread change.

Of course, racism and racial tension are still present in the military. The military is a microcosm of our society and that means some members will bring with them their bias and oppressive ideologies. However, leaders today do not tolerate the overt expression of racism or racial discrimination as they did just a few decades ago. There are policies in place along with effective measures to ensure that Commanders do not allow such abuse or discrimination to surface. If it does however, leaders must act swiftly and do what it takes to address the offense and the offender. Even leaders who may still harbor racial bias or stereotyping will generally not express it as openly due to the cultural shift and the demands for climate change from the top down. The military has effectively implemented zero tolerance of racism. It has not been a widespread, insidious problem in the US Military for some time.

However, many other issues are still very much alive and openly tolerated in the military culture such as homophobia, opposition to women's equality in combat roles, sexual harassment and sexual assault. After a decade of policies, trainings, funding, inquiries by media, advocate groups, Congress and Presidential attention, many would assert that the US Military does not have a zero tolerance policy and in reality, still very much tolerates this crime.

No one truly believes the "zero tolerance" rhetoric when it comes to sexual assault in the military. They have long since been empty words with little, if any, enforcement behind them. Even military leaders who have spoken publicly about zero tolerance (often following a crisis that came to the public's attention) may question the sincerity of their declarations. Every Secretary of Defense for the past 25 years (since the Tailhook scandal in 1991) has proclaimed zero tolerance of sexual harassment and sexual assault in the US Military. Saying it is so has clearly not made a difference in two and a half decades.

Military leaders knew there would be minimal, if any, retributions if they did not pursue a sexual harassment or sexual assault allegation. Until 2014, they also knew that the climate in their unit could exude a lack of respect toward women or about the SAPR program and it would not reflect poorly on them. Now, with the inclusion of sexual assault in the Command Climate Survey, there will be greater oversight and perhaps some self-regulating by leaders who should know better. This is one step in the right direction toward addressing power failure and other underlying systemic challenges, but the climate survey alone will not ensure that leaders do what is right. Enforcement of zero tolerance must occur from the top down—including swift and appropriate action against any leader who fails to act or who acts with disregard to SAPR.

Presumably, most military leaders do understand the negative impact of sexual harassment and sexual assault on command climate and on the mission. These men and women exemplify characteristics of a true leader by demonstrating respect and professionalism and enforcing zero tolerance. These are the leaders we need front and center to support SAPR. We need them to safeguard the integrity of the military by confronting sexism, sexual assault, sexual harassment or any of these issues, they may witness. We need them to be honorable and strong role models for other leaders who may be wavering or may not be fully on board with SAPR. We need our outstanding military leaders working with SAPR, but they must also be empowered to confront the problem of rape and sexual harassment in the US Armed Forces.

Without inspiring and trusted military leaders, the SAPR mission is doomed to fail, the problem will persist, and the cycle will continue. The Department of Defense (DoD) needs all military leaders to commit to zero tolerance—to do whatever it takes to ensure that sexual harassment and sexual assault is not tolerated, accepted, nor condoned in any way. These leaders ultimately will change the culture and climate that still exists in today's military Services. The DoD must call on all military leaders to be partners in the SAPR mission and empower them to act. To assist leaders in responding more effectively to this issue, a guide for military leaders is included in the addendum of this book. Leaders and other professionals are encouraged to use this reference to guide them to be role models for others and to ensure true zero tolerance.

First Edition, For Love of Country 2002

(Before the DoD Sexual Assault Prevention and Response Program Existed)

Preface

Truth has no special time of its own. Its hour is now——always.

—— Albert Schweitzer Nobel Laureate and Missionary

THE UNITED STATES armed forces have taken some serious hits over the last part of the twentieth century. Ironically, these attacks have originated from within. Many contributed to the problem—from the harsh words or judgments toward the victims, to the conspiracies of silence that sealed the truth in the face of injustice. Yet the single greatest contributing reason for the proliferation of this unrest within lies in the hands of the leadership. From the field commanders to the advisors at the Pentagon, they have the power and authority to address this problem or to ignore it.

Unfortunately, far too many service members believe that their leaders have chosen to ignore or minimize sexual violence or harassment in their midst. However, as with the destructive forces of racism and antigay sentiment, this issue will not go away on its own. Just as the Department of Defense attacked racial harassment in the 1970s, sexual violence by military personnel should be fully confronted.

Veterans and active-duty service members are speaking out about the problems of rape and sexual harassment in the U.S. Armed Forces as never before. They want the public to know what has been happening behind the lines. Their personal accounts are the basis for this book—a documentation of the vast problem of sexual abuse in the military.

The service members quoted in this book spoke openly about the military's response to rape and sexual harassment. These service members and veterans exposed multiple counts of power failure by leaders who perpetuated or exacerbated the abuse. They described the loss of military values and the struggles within. They also shared some possible solutions to stop the cycle of abuse. They have provided an inside perspective that has virtually gone unheard of until now.

Given the history of this problem, researching this topic was no easy task. The litany of violence against women by U.S. military service members went on and on. Just when I thought I had all the information I needed, I would receive another letter or phone call from someone who wanted and needed to tell his or her story—another veteran whose life changed because of rape or another parent whose child has not been the same since joining the service. There were certainly no shortage of people who wanted and needed to speak about their experiences with abuse in the military.

I began to question how the military was responding to this pervasive problem in 1996 during the media reports of sexual harassment of trainees at Aberdeen Proving Ground. Although the Army seemed quick to acknowledge the abuses to the public, I knew from my own experiences in the service that there was more to the story. I began sifting through volumes of information—military documents, press releases, official rape reports, news stories, and research studies on the topic—to find out if anyone really knew why this was a continuing problem for the armed services. I realized I was looking for the answers in the wrong places. I needed to hear directly from the women and men who were victimized by their fellow service members.

What started as a national study on the military's response to rape and sexual harassment unexpectedly took on an international focus. I began receiving messages from people at military installations around the world—Germany, Italy, Japan—and across the United States. As the word got out, I heard from former service members (veterans and retirees), from active-duty service members, from Pentagon officials, from advocates, and from experts in the field. I also heard from spouses and parents whose loved ones were raped or sexually harassed while in the military.

In the end, participants in the research study represented each of the service branches and included women and men, officers and enlisted. Their backgrounds, races, and occupations were diverse (from doctors to artillery specialists) as were their ages (from nineteen to sixty-four years old). Some of the respondents had served in wars including those in Korea, Vietnam, and the Persian Gulf. Some had long since retired. Other participants were still on active duty when they contacted me about the study.

Most of the persons who participated in this study were women, although some men did respond. This is consistent with both civilian and military research, which suggests that, overwhelmingly, women are more often the victims of sexual harassment or rape. However, it is important to remember that these types of abuse happen to men as well. Rape and sexual assault can be hurtful and traumatizing no matter what the victim's gender, age, race, or sexual orientation. Having noted this, it is the case that men are more often the offenders or harassers. For simplification in the text, I have referred to victims as females and offenders as males. However, this is neither to minimize nor to deny in any way the extent of sexual assault that men do experience in the military.

Similarly, I have decided to use the term *abuse* as a general description. In some cases, where it is more appropriate to use the terms *sexual harassment, sexual assault,* or *rape,* I have done so. Some professionals in the field prefer to use the word *abuse* to refer only to childhood trauma. Yet, the word *abuse* was oftentimes sufficient to communicate the meaning of the message in this text. However, when addressing only sexual assault, I have used those terms to specify.

Although the women and men in this study spoke out individually, and usually anonymously, they shared a common bond: they were linked by traumas perpetrated against them by U.S. military service members. These women and men told me more about rape and sexual harassment in the military than anyone else or any other research study ever could. Of all the sources of information I encountered, the ones that touched me the most were the messages from the victims themselves. After all, these are their stories.

I listened to what these service members had to say about their victimization and how military leaders responded (or did not respond) in the aftermath of the abuse. I asked them about the types of responses they received from others—which responses were helpful and which were hurtful reactions. I asked them what should be done to address these problems and how the military should help victims of sexual assault and harassment.

Most important, I listened to whatever they had to say. Some were angry; others felt betrayed or deeply hurt by their experiences. Others were still grateful and proud of their time in the service. They relayed their very personal and traumatic experiences in handwritten note cards, typed letters, detailed e-mail correspondences, responses on the research questionnaire, or by phone interview. Countless others have written of their experiences on various Internet Web sites, including those exclusively for military women. Some service members have also shared their experiences with advocacy groups, such as the Miles Foundation or STAMP (Survivors Take Action Against Abuse by Military Personnel). Many just want to talk to someone who will listen and believe them.

I paid very close attention to their individual stories and their accounts of abuse. Then I compiled their messages along with some of the official reports, the statistics, and the press releases. It seemed necessary to include these data to offer a more complete picture of the problem and of some potential resolutions. However, their experiences needed no collaboration. There are times when someone's word is good enough. After five years of research and help from over 200 women and men who shared their experiences and perspectives, it is time to present their side of this story. Their messages do more to substantiate the widespread problems of sexual abuse in the military than any Pentagon report or military survey ever could.

We can and should learn from the insights of those who experienced sexual assault and sexual harassment by military personnel. Maybe then, we will finally learn what we need to do to improve the military's response to the victims, to the offenders, and to this issue. We might also learn how to put a stop to this cycle of abuse. As one veteran and rape victim asked, "Hasn't this gone on long enough?"

Indeed, it has gone on long enough. This enduring problem has cost lives and careers. We cannot afford to lose another life at the hands of continued indifference or power failure. These stories must be told, not to degrade the military, but as a step toward addressing the problem and restoring honor and integrity within the Armed Forces. After all, there is no honor without truth. We owe this much to the women and men who, for love of country, have sacrificed and endured so much.

PART I

An Introduction to the Problem
of Rape and Sexual Harassment
in the U.S. Military

1

WE HAVE MET THE ENEMY AND THE ENEMY IS US

*I was prepared to be a POW (prisoner of war) or worse for my country. I wasn't
prepared to have my superiors and comrades sexually abuse me. I must admit that
a chaplain I told my story to in 1996 said something I had not realized. He said,
"Your comrades were your enemy and you were in a combat zone." I thought that
was rather interesting. I was only nineteen. I just wanted to carry on the tradition
of our family being in the military.*

— NINETEEN-YEAR-OLD FEMALE, RAPED WHILE ON ACTIVE DUTY

WHAT BECAME OF HONOR?

The time is always right to do what is right.

— MARTIN LUTHER KING JR.

SEXUAL ASSAULT AND harassment are deeply rooted in today's armed forces. The problem is
further complicated by a system that has been unable or unwilling to effectively address
this issue over the years. Far too many military leaders have turned their heads to the ongoing abuses and far too many victims were further harmed by a culture that perpetuated and
minimized the abuse. These types of responses represent a breakdown of values, a discon-
nection from the military's true mission and a loss of honor for those involved.

— 3 —

Just half a century earlier my father's generation fought because "it was their duty and it was what needed to be done." They grieved the losses of their fallen friends, brothers, fathers, and husbands. These men and women sacrificed their lives for love of country and for the values in which they believed. They willingly enlisted to be a part of the military to fight for the values upon which our country was founded: freedom and the rights to life, liberty, and the pursuit of happiness. Their patriotism, valor, and honor were certainly something to celebrate. They stood and fought for values that had become distant to us, until the tragedy of international terrorism struck our nation on September 11, 2001.

Something happened to our nation and to our military as a result of the traumas of that day. A renewed sense of patriotism and a newfound unity emerged from the devastation and out of the despair. Many Americans reaffirmed their values and reclaimed their pride. For the military, it meant a call to duty and a recommitment to a higher purpose. For the first time in a long time, enlistees were joining the ranks again because they wanted to serve their country. They wanted to defend the values and the beliefs that so many other men and women before them had protected.

Indeed, most of the men and women in the military today still bring a sense of patriotism, duty, and honor to their roles. However, some service members have brought shame to the uniform and shame to their country. They have been perpetrators of rape and other acts of uncontrolled violence against fellow service members and against civilians. Too often, the behaviors of military personnel at home and abroad have been in the headlines and in the news. The following are examples of lost honor within the ranks of the U.S. armed forces:

1995: Two marines and a sailor are found guilty of kidnapping and raping a twelve-year-old girl in Okinawa.

1996: A Navy lieutenant commander was court-martialed at the Washington Navy Yard on counts of rape, sexual harassment, adultery, and conduct unbecoming an officer for reportedly sexually assaulting a civilian co-worker and creating a hostile work environment with ongoing sexual harassment.

1996/1997: Female students at the Citadel and Virginia Military Institute were victims of repeated sexual harassment and abuse including an incident in which cadets were sprayed with a flammable liquid and their clothes were set on fire.

1997: A former Army drill sergeant at Aberdeen Proving Ground was sentenced to twenty-five years imprisonment, loss of all pay, reduction to lowest enlisted rank, and a dishonorable discharge for being found guilty on eighteen criminal counts including rape, forcible sodomy, communicating a threat, cruelty and mistreatment, and violation of a lawful general order.

1998: The Army's top enlisted soldier, the sergeant major of the Army, faced six accusers in a court-martial for sexual harassment.

1999: A soldier was repeatedly harassed, savagely beaten, and murdered by fellow soldiers at Fort Campbell, Kentucky, because he was thought to be homosexual.

1999: The command sergeant major for U.S. Army Europe and the Seventh Army was reassigned and faced court-martial on charges of forcible sodomy, kidnapping, indecent assault, maltreatment of a subordinate, and fraternization.

2000: A U.S. soldier and member of the international peacekeeping force was accused of raping and murdering an eleven year-old girl in Kosovo. He was the first member of an international peacekeeping mission charged with such heinous crimes.

2001: Three-star general charged with sexual harassment.

2001: Three midshipman football players from the U.S. Naval Academy were allowed to resign from the academy to avoid prosecution on charges of raping a female classmate. The woman was reportedly unconscious at the time of the alleged sexual assaults.

2002: A naval commanding officer of a 300-member flight squad was charged with raping a junior enlisted sailor.

The list goes on and on. Sexual assault, harassment, and other forms of violence by individuals have continued to plague each branch of the service. These criminal acts should be exposed—not to bring discredit to the military, but to strengthen the conviction to confront the problem.

There is no honor to be found in such behaviors, nor is there honor in the men and women who silently stand by and allow the abuses to continue. Likewise, when leaders acquiesce to the abuse or do nothing, they contribute to the problems. When rape and sexual harassment are tolerated, honor, unity, and integrity will suffer.

Codes of Honor and Silence

I will never forget that I am an American, fighting for freedom, responsible for my actions, and dedicated to the principles which made my country free.

— Article VIII, Military Code of Conduct

All recruits take an oath of service upon enlistment. They pledge to a moral code of conduct on the first day of their induction. Some pledge to additional codes of honor as they develop a stronger allegiance to their specific branch of service or to their unit. These become a direct connection to the group's identification and to its values.

Groups become more unified and more cohesive when they have common bonds that may include a shared purpose (mission), shared values, and common goals. Ideally, members will develop a connectedness and a sense of loyalty to their group. We see such camaraderie in college fraternities who refer to a "brotherhood" and in some smaller businesses where employees are considered "family." A connection to a group can be a powerful source of identity. The armed services' need for loyalty and a sense of belonging are no different from any other organization in that regard. Hence, each service branch has its own values, mottoes, and codes in which its members readily identify and often adhere. Sometimes, however, these codes of honor can become barriers.

For example, the motto of the United States Marine Corps, "Semper Fidelis" (Latin for always faithful), is further interpreted as "faithful to my God, country, and the Corps." It is a cherished and respected code used by marines with great pride. However, it is also been used as a shield of silence.

Consider how the honor code may be applied when a marine is accused of beating his wife. Does the Marine Corps have an obligation to protect the service member or his family? Do they refer him for counseling or legal action, or do they acquiesce to the abuse by doing nothing since "he's a good marine and we need to protect our own."

The extent to which the marine code "always faithful" may be applied is ambiguous, at best. A marine who chooses not to report a service member for domestic violence or rape due to a sense of loyalty to the group has done far more harm than good. With that single decision to ignore the crime, the marine has lost some integrity. Moreover, he or she has taken the organization a step away from the values upon which the Constitution was based. Thus, his or her adherence to the code of "Semper Fi" is no longer honorable when compared to a higher standard of valuing human worth.

Similarly, the Air Force Officer Training School's motto "Always with Honor" reflects the ethical and professional standards expected of Air Force officers. As with other codes of conduct, if adhered to earnestly, it can become a rule to live and work by. However, when officers sexually harass their subordinates or opt to disregard abuses in their units, they minimize and devalue their code. How can Air Force personnel put their faith into leaders who disregard their own oath? The loss of honor and respect of military leaders is another step toward the fragmentation of the organization.

A final example comes from "The Articles of the Code of Conduct" for the U.S. armed forces. Article One states: "I am an American, fighting in the forces which guard my country and our way of life." The references to the Constitution and to our basic rights are implicit. A service member who cannot uphold the first article of the Code of Conduct does not deserve to be wearing the uniform. Service members, who abuse their wives or children, rape their colleagues, harm innocent civilians with malicious intent, or murder anyone outside the scope of their role as a soldier in time of war should be court-martialed. They are trained to be soldiers, and it is their job to know how to fight. However, uncontrolled violence should never be tolerated. With every act of homicide, rape, domestic violence, or child abuse, codes of conduct, honor, and integrity are weakened.

The military has faced some difficult social issues in the past, including racial discrimination, the integration of women, and the ongoing debate of accepting homosexuals into the service. It can rise to this challenge as well as strengthen the core values upon which our nation and our military services were founded.

TIMES HAVE CHANGED US

Many of the recruits who are filling the ranks now grew up in the age of modernism, mass media, and mass violence. Many were given mixed messages about human dignity and respect for self and others. They have grown up with movies that glorify violence; video games that equate aggression with power; and music lyrics about rape, murder, and misogyny, particularly violence against women. It is a generation that has grown insensitive to violence in many ways. For some recruits, trauma and violence was a significant part of their lives long before they entered the service. Sadly, the young men and women entering the military today have often witnessed or experienced violence in their homes and their neighborhoods.

The military itself is now a diversified mixture of the new breed of younger-generation soldiers combined with career service members whose knowledge and history are critical to the organization. These career soldiers have seen many changes in the system—changes brought on by the emerging social climate or by new legislation. However, some of these changes are still not readily accepted.

For example, the role of women in the armed forces continues to be a source of conflict. The debate goes on about whether women belong in combat roles and whether women belong in the military at all. In an editorial column by Mona Charen (a political consultant who writes for the Creators Syndicate), Charen stated, "Since the Tailhook imbroglio, the armed services of the United States have leaned so far backward to accommodate women that they are scarcely recognizable as fighting forces" (Charen, 2000, Sec. A). Not everyone agrees that integrating women into the military and taking a serious look at sexual harassment has been a disaster. In fact, we could reasonably conclude that if the military never addressed racial harassment, they would be facing even greater problems today. Likewise, gender and sexual harassment are current social issues that cannot be ignored.

Fortunately, the Department of Defense realized the connection and established clear policies on equal opportunity and harassment. The following is part of the Army's Equal Opportunity Policy taken from Army Command Policy AR 600-20 Section 6.3a:

> *It is the policy of the U.S. Army to provide equal opportunity and treatment for soldiers and their families without regard to race, color, religion, gender, or national origin and to provide an environment free of sexual harassment.* (Department of the Army, 1998)

Despite opposition, there have been changes in military policy. These changes were necessary to keep pace with the social and political advances our nation has experienced. For example, the civil rights legislation in the 1960s necessitated that the military become more unified and racially integrated. Similarly, the inclusion and integration of women into basic training units in the late 1970s was the result of a more progressive sociopolitical climate and a changing world. It eventually led to the development of guidelines for appropriate behavior between males and females. Sexual harassment policies now clearly define behaviors that are inappropriate, whereas two decades ago many soldiers would have viewed sexual overtones in the workplace as a joke.

For example, the popular 1970s' television show *M*A*S*H* often included flirtatious or highly questionable sexual innuendoes between male and female service members. In one episode, an officer pushed one of the nurses onto a desk, laid on top of her, and started kissing and grabbing her. Despite her obvious rejection (kicking and screaming "get off of me") the other men in the room stood by watching and laughing. If this scenario took place in the military today, it would be grounds for sexual harassment charges or possibly sexual assault charges. Times have changed.

Some would argue that the changes in the military have gone too far. Some say you cannot "joke around" anymore because anything can be considered harassment. As political consultant Mona Charen said, "Our women warriors... cannot handle so much as a touch on the upper arm" (Charen, 2000, Sec. A).

Such remarks undermine the real problem and minimize the claims of abuse. Ultimately, the prevalence of these beliefs promotes a resentment of women in uniform. This mind-set serves only to perpetuate the sexual abuse and sexual harassment of women in the armed forces.

The Army recognized that such attitudes and behaviors could foster gender and sexual harassment and impede the organization. Its policy on sexual harassment clearly indicates this:

> *Sexual harassment violates acceptable standards of integrity and impartiality required of all Army personnel. …Sexual harassment is not limited to the workplace and can occur at almost any time. It interferes with mission accomplishments and unit cohesion. Such behavior by soldiers or Army civilians will not be tolerated.* (Department of the Army, 1998, Sec. 6.4)

This type of policy was not necessary when women were not allowed in the military. Thankfully, times have changed and now women, racial minorities, and homosexuals are allowed to serve— though still with some restrictions.

THE TRAUMA OF RAPE FOR SERVICE MEMBERS

> *To take one incident, one trauma, and record it as part of your life. And who could you tell? I went up the line (even the MPs discouraged pressing charges). We were the ones made to feel guilty. We never talked about what was going on. It was an unspoken truth most of us tried to deny. Now the story is being told and we've already paid. How can you make this wrong right?*
>
> —— FEMALE VETERAN AND VICTIM OF RAPE
> AND SEXUAL HARASSMENT IN THE MILITARY, 1998

Rape is a highly traumatic experience for any person. Rape can result in lifelong scars. Unlike combat, there is no sense of pride or duty fulfilled for victims of sexual trauma. To the contrary, these women and men often struggle with feelings of shame and embarrassment from their degrading and humiliating violations. Consequently, many brave and honorable American soldiers are left with psychological wounds in service to our country, regardless of whether they participated in combat.

Despite their traumatic experiences, veterans often take great pride in serving. Many sought a career in the military or desired to carry on a family tradition of service. Although their traumas in war were life changing, it no doubt affords some comfort knowing that their sacrifices were in service to their country. Their efforts were consistent with values of courage and honor. Likewise, it was helpful to have the camaraderie of like-minded patriots, the support of supervisors, and the gratitude of the nation upon their homecoming.

The veterans described in this book left the military forever changed. However, their trauma is compounded by a social climate that prefers not to address, much less celebrate, the sacrifices they made while on active duty. Many of these veterans feel betrayed by the military that they so loved. They feel their sacrifices were for nothing and that others have long since forgotten their battles—especially those committed by their perpetrators.

This book is about a very personal war that has persisted in the U.S. armed forces for some time. As the military was struggling with the values of honor and integrity and the issues of retention and recruitment, it was also losing many excellent soldiers to the enemy within. The women and men who were the targets of uncontrolled sexual violence by U.S. military personnel are now the casualties of this largely ignored war. They have suffered attacks against their bodies, their minds, their careers, and their well-being. After the sexual abuse, many of these service members also had to fight the military to prove their sanity, to save their careers, or to save their lives.

The war within the military and the aftermath of sexual trauma continues every day for thousands of women and men. Veterans of military sexual trauma often must fight their battles alone. They endure shame, humiliation, or further harassment by the leaders and the military they once respected.

Many of these soldiers choose to leave or are forced to leave active duty after the abuse. Some service members remain emotionally battered prisoners of an ongoing war that they will never win. Some of them leave the military as shells of the former patriots who once willingly volunteered to serve our country. Others are discharged from the service, angry, bitter, and wounded from their experiences. Many veterans, however, will leave stronger for enduring the trauma and will go on to meet their goals and beat the demons that once victimized them.

It is estimated that nearly two-thirds of female service members experience unwanted, uninvited sexual behavior in the military (Bastian et al., 1996). To exemplify the magnitude of this problem, consider what would happen if the U.S. armed forces were faced with a problem that affected two-thirds of the male service members. One would hope that there would be an immediate call to action, a stand-down, and nationwide attention to the problem. Those in power would ensure a prompt, corrective response to minimize the numbers affected and immediately attend to the victims' medical and psychological care with all resources available. The problem would be addressed and solved, or at the very least it would receive priority attention and the financial resources necessary to ensure some resolution.

Some might say that sexual assault and harassment in the U.S. military is an epidemic. However, despite the national and international attention to this issue, the war within the ranks continues and the number of casualties increases. In fact, the casualties often include civilians—women and children who become targets of violence by U.S. military servicemen.

Why, then, is this still such a pervasive, ongoing problem? The individuals who share their accounts in this book uncover some of those hidden issues. After more than a decade of studies, senior review panels, and congressional hearings on sexual assault and harassment in the military, it is time to listen with serious intent to the women and men who have been victims. The time has never been better for military leadership to make this ongoing, pervasive problem a true priority.

Women and men abused in the military did not see the enemy approaching. Their peers and their leaders were supposed to be on the same side; they were not supposed to be the aggressors. For military victims of sexual abuse, there is profound truth in the statement, "We have met the enemy and the enemy is us."

A Personal Account of Abuse in the Army

Susan was the victim of repeated sexual harassment in her Army unit. The abuse she encountered included requests and coercion for sexual favors, offers in exchange for sex, harassment regarding sexual orientation, sexually explicit jokes, obscene comments, and sexually explicit materials in the workplace. When Susan reported the sexual harassment, she suffered repercussions and further abuse, this time from her company commander. The commander called her a liar, threatened to kick her out of the military, and referred her for a psychiatric evaluation for making such allegations.

The harasser, according to Susan, "received a slap on the wrist." No charges were brought against him. The Army believed his story over hers. The harassment grew worse. Susan felt betrayed, ashamed, and alone following her report. After that, the climate in the unit was such a hardship for Susan that she eventually attempted suicide. In the end, Susan received the early discharge from the military that her commander had threatened when she first reported the sexual abuse.

Despite the trauma that Susan endured, she still has hope that things will eventually get better for women in the military. She wrote the following summary prior to her discharge from the Army. She was hoping that her feedback could help bring about some change.

Even in the midst of her own pain and an abusive situation, she was trying to make a difference so that other women would not have to go through what she experienced.

I've tried every avenue known to get help. The abuse continues. Just yesterday, I tried to commit suicide. Believe me, it is that bad.

I have no rights here. They step all over me. I know that there are other people out there that have experienced this abuse. This is the very same reason why they feel so confident that they can get away with this.

They tell me that I'm not a team player by coming forward. They're right. I don't want to be part of a team that treats anyone this way. All the documents I'm sending you will probably go unheard. I've been forced to sign letters saying that I lied. That sounds crazy, I know. I wouldn't believe it if I didn't experience this every day.

My battalion is full with women that have similar complaints. They're too afraid to come forward. They've watched what has been done to me. The complaints have been brushed under the rug.

Anyhow, I hope the information I attached is useful. I really want to be a part of making a big difference in the unfair treatment of soldiers. . .

An important note about Susan's story: The harassment she experienced happened in 1999. Her message reiterates the problems of leadership abuse. Susan's story offers a glimpse of the problems that women and men still may encounter when they report sexual victimization. In addition to her letter, Susan sent supplemental information—to verify her efforts to report the sexual abuse, and of her commander's response by sending her to the psychiatric unit. This type of harassment and trauma persists in today's military.

2

THE WEAKEST LINK EXPOSED

This is the worst thing I've ever come across in three decades in the Army.

— MAJOR GENERAL ROBERT SHADLEY (REUTERS NEWS, NOVEMBER 7, 1996)

THE CRISIS SURFACES

One day they are going to find that this was just the tip of the iceberg. When rape victims start talking about what is truly happening in the military, that's when the depth of the problem will really emerge.

— FEMALE VETERAN AFFAIRS SEXUAL TRAUMA COUNSELOR SPEAKING OUT IN THE WAKE OF RAMPANT SEXUAL ABUSE AT ABERDEEN PROVING GROUND, MARYLAND

THE PROBLEMS OF sexual harassment and sexual assault in the U.S. military are epidemic. Reports of abuse continue to flood in as the problem continues to emerge. Surveys of women in the military tell a story of rampant sexual abuse and harassment by their male counterparts amid concerns that the issues are being minimized or ignored by military leaders. According to a 1997 article, "Did We Say Zero Tolerance?" in *U.S. News & World Report* "...18 percent of the Army's women say colleagues have tried to coerce them into having sex and 47 percent say they've received unwanted sexual attention" (Newman, 1997, p. 34). Similarly, a study in 1995 by the Department of Defense found that 72 percent of women and 63 percent of men had experienced "sexist behavior" and that 47 percent of women and 30 percent of men received "unwanted sexual attention" (DoD, 1996).

Each of the service branches has good reason to be concerned about the growing problems of rape and sexual harassment among their ranks. Long before the Tailhook scandal became public knowledge, the Navy Criminal Investigative Services (which includes the Marine Corps) found significant increases in sexual assault cases from 1987 to 1990. Navy authorities were reportedly "concerned about a 55 percent increase in reported rapes at naval bases" (up from 166 in 1987 to 240 reported rapes in 1990). The report also indicated that the Navy was critical of their investigative service for "insensitive treatment of rape victims in many cases" (Schneider and Schneider, 1992, p. xxiv).

Despite concerns expressed by Navy officials in 1990, the problem grew significantly worse. According to information provided by the Office of the Undersecretary of Defense, reported rapes jumped from 240 investigated cases in 1990 to 422 in 1992—a nearly 100 percent increase. In 1996, the numbers of reported rapes were nearly identical to four years earlier. Based on these figures very little has changed in the past decade. This data was provided by the Office of the Undersecretary of Defense and are unpublished. All subsequent Department of Defense data that are not directly cited are from this unpublished data report.

The Air Force, on the other hand, appears to have taken a more proactive stance over the years with regard to prevention programs for sexual assault and harassment. Nonetheless, the numbers of reported rapes still did not change much over a six-year period according to the Department of Defense statistics provided by the Pentagon. The Air Force had 176 rape reports in 1991 and 164 in 1996—only a small change, but the numbers were lower. The biggest difference in the Air Force was in their response to convicted rapists. The average criminal sentence went from 20.28 years in 1991 down to 9 years in 1996. How can the Air Force account for such a dramatic shift in sentencing and punishment for sexual offenders? One would expect the sentencing to increase as public concern and attention to the problem grew.

When the Army found itself in the national spotlight in 1996 with reports of widespread abuse at its training facilities, it took immediate control of the crisis to avert a public relations disaster. The Army held press conferences throughout the investigations, initiated a senior review panel on sexual harassment, conducted studies on sexual assault and gender-integrated training, implemented a toll-free sexual assault hotline, and promptly held court-martials and disciplinary action for all known offenders from the top down.

Nonetheless, despite the Army's efforts, reports of sexual abuse and rape by U.S. Army men continued to surface across the globe. The Army hotline was inundated with over 8,000 calls in less than a year's time (of these, 1,360 calls were labeled "actual allegations" by the Army's Department of Public Affairs) (telephone interview, 1997). In addition to the hotline calls, rape cases that were officially reported for investigation to the Army held steady over a six-year time span from 402 reported rapes in 1991 to 440 in 1996 according to Pentagon records.

Not surprisingly, the problem also surfaced with the Department of Veterans Affairs (VA). Ultimately, it is the VA that ends up providing treatment to many of the rape victims years after their discharge from active duty service. According to 1992 testimony before the Senate Veterans Affairs Committee, an estimated 60,000 to 200,000 women veterans were sexually assaulted while on active duty (Pardue and Moniz, 1996). Clearly, a need exists for such services within the VA due to the high rates of sexual victimization among active-duty service members.

Official confirmations of the prevalence of abuse were also acknowledged in at least two separate Department of Defense surveys. The DoD, in conjunction with the Defense Manpower Data Center, conducted one of the largest studies on sexual harassment in the military in 1995. This survey was a follow-up to a similar, earlier study on the same topic in 1988. The 1995 service wide study on sexual harassment involved three separate surveys. The first survey (Form A, Sex Roles in the Active Duty Military), a replication of the 1988 survey, was a comparison and analysis of improvement over the seven-year period. This survey was sent to over 30,000 personnel for a response rate of 46 percent.

The second survey in the 1995 study (Form B, Gender Issues) was sent to over 50,000 service members with a response rate of 58 percent. The questionnaire included items regarding perceptions of the complaint process, reprisals, training, experiences that occurred outside of the work setting, and an expanded list (from the 1988 study) of potential sexually harassing behaviors. In addition, questions also asked about the service members' perceptions of leadership commitment and efforts to prevent or reduce sexual harassment.

The last survey in the group (Form C) was sent to 9,856 personnel of whom 56 percent participated. This survey was designed to link the results from Forms A and B. It was used "for research purposes" only and was not included in the DoD report made available to the public (Bastian et al., 1996, p. iii).

Over 90,000 active-duty men and women worldwide received surveys, of which 47,000-plus participated. Respondents were from each of the service branches, including Reserve and National Guard members. Some of the major findings of the 1995 DoD study are summarized here and compared in later chapters (Chapters 5, 6, and 9) with the responses from participants in this book. The following is what the Department of Defense discovered about the rates of sexual assault and harassment. Note that these rates reflect *only incidents that occurred in the 12 months prior to completing the survey* and do not represent the entire time on active duty (Bastian et al., 1996).

Nearly two-thirds (64 percent) of the women surveyed reported experiencing one or more incidents of unwanted, uninvited sexual attention or behaviors at work (1988). In the 1995 study, the numbers decreased to 55 percent of the women. For men, 17 percent reported unwanted, uninvited sexual attention or behaviors in 1988, and 14 percent in 1995.

The list of "uninvited, unwanted sexual attention" on this survey included: actual or attempted rape; pressure for sexual favors; sexual touching; sexually suggestive looks or gestures; letters or materials of a sexual nature; sexual teasing or remarks of a sexual nature; and attempts at involvement with a sexually oriented activity (e.g., group sex or posing nude). (p. 48)

The reported rates of sexual harassment increase substantially when looking at the findings from those who completed Form B. This survey differed from Form A because it included an expanded list of potentially sexually harassing behaviors and specific examples of such. As stated earlier, Form A was a replication of the 1988 survey. Therefore, the extended list in 1995's Form B allowed for a more complete look at the problem.

The extended list of "unwanted sex-related attention" used on Form B included some of the items from Form A and others such as: display of pornography at the workplace; offensive, sexist remarks; bribes to engage in sex (or offered special favors); sex-related threats or coercion; attempts to kiss or fondle; and attempts to have sex against one's will (pp. 68-69).

When given specific examples of sexual harassment on an expanded list of items, the numbers of respondents reporting such behaviors increased. More than three-fourths (78 percent) of women reported experiencing a behavior consistent with a form of sexual harassment or sexual assault, and 38 percent of the men indicated that they also experienced at least one event in the preceding twelve months.

The rates of unwanted sexual experiences for men were similar across the services with 39 percent of Army men reporting, and 37 percent reporting from each of the other service branches. For women, the rates across the service branches varied significantly: 86 percent of female Marines experienced sexual harassment or sexual assault as compared to 82 percent of Army women; 77 percent in the Navy; 74 percent in the Air Force; and 75 percent in the Coast Guard.

Specific types of sexual harassment also were reported. The following are two key findings in these areas: Sexual coercion (e.g., implied job benefits for compliance with or penalties for refusing demands for sex) was reported by more than 10 percent of military women and 2 percent of men. Requests or demands for sexual favors were reported by 11 percent of the active-duty women.

The incidence of sexual harassment in the U.S. armed forces is still quite high, even though there was a decline reported from 1988 to 1995. In addition, the reported rates of rape or attempted rape were also significant. One in every twenty-five active-duty women (4 percent) and one in 100 military men (1 percent) were victims of rape or attempted rape in the twelve months prior to completing this survey. Specifically, 9 percent of women in the Marines, 8 percent of women in the Army, 6 percent of women in the Navy, and 4 percent of women in the Air Force and Coast Guard were victims of rape or attempted rape *in one year alone.*

Although the Department of Defense had confirmation of the magnitude of the problem some six years earlier, very little was done to effectively remedy a problem that was affecting nearly two-thirds of their female troops and a third of their male troops (Bastian et al., 1996). Other studies substantiated the problem as well. Most notably, the Army's Senior Review Panel on Sexual Harassment, the Federal Advisory Committee's Report on Gender Integrated Training and Related Issues, and the General Accounting Office have all assessed the problem.

With the exposure of the intolerable abuses of trainees at Army training installations (namely, but not only, Aberdeen Proving Ground, Fort Leonard Wood, and Fort Jackson) the issue was once again in the news. This time the headlines and the reports captured the attention of Congress. It seemed that everyone was now listening. Senators Olympia Snowe and Charles Robb were interviewed about their response to sexual harassment in the military. Senator Olympia Snowe made the following comments about this crisis:

> *The situation at Aberdeen is quite serious. It is pervasive... when you consider the fact that you have 50 percent of the drill instructors at Aberdeen under suspension, under question at this point, there may be more.* (Warner, 1997)

In agreement, Senator Robb recognized sexual harassment is a problem in society as well as in the military (Warner, 1997).

It did not take long for the Army to respond to the crisis, not wanting to repeat the mistakes the Navy officials made in their delayed and prolonged response to the Tailhook allegations. Secretary of the Army Togo West developed a senior review panel of retired, active-duty, and senior army officials to study the issue and to report back to him promptly with their findings.

The panel hit an early snag. One of its select members, Sergeant Major of the Army Gene McKinney, was charged with sexual misconduct allegations and released from the panel after the allegations were made public some months later. Despite this disruption, the panel made good on its mission to assess the problem of sexual misconduct and made the report public in the fall of 1997.

The group surveyed and interviewed 30,000 troops at visits to fifty-nine Army facilities worldwide. A surprising and disturbing finding surfaced: "84 percent of women reported they experienced unwanted sexual attention, coercion or assault, yet only 22 percent said they were sexually harassed" (Priest, 1997a, p. A1). This data suggests that there may be some confusion among the troops as to what exactly constitutes sexual harassment (Bastian et al., 1996). Or is it perhaps that military women have grown accustomed to unwanted sexual innuendoes or behaviors and therefore are not as likely to be offended by the remarks or gestures? Even the Army's review panel discovered:

> Sexual harassment is so commonplace that "soldiers seem to accept such behaviors as a normal part of Army life" (Schafer, 1997).

In the PBS interview, "War on Harassment—Sexual Harassment in the Military," Phil Ponce interviewed members of the Army's Senior Review Panel to address their recent assessment of the problem. Ponce summarized some of the panel's findings including that sexual harassment and sexual discrimination occur throughout the Army and affect both genders, all races, and all ranks. Moreover, Ponce reported that some soldiers do not trust the system, and sometimes they do not trust their leaders with this issue either (Ponce, 1997).

Others reported similar concerns about the panel's findings and the Army's response: In September of 1997 the Army issues a scathing critique of itself, saying that its mechanism for reporting sex harassment and discrimination charges is woefully inadequate and that Army leaders have allowed the problem to persist. (Healy, 1998)

In response to their findings, the panel created 128 recommendations to address the problems of sexual harassment and sexual abuse in the Army. It is unknown as to how many of those recommendations have actually been implemented to date. However, of significant note, the Army's own panel concluded that the service "lacks the institutional commitment" to treat women equally ("Army Investigation," 1997).

Despite the sharp criticisms and the carefully developed recommendations from his own senior review panel, Togo West still did not think sexual abuse was endemic in the Army (Healy, 1998). Once again, the opinions of leadership were not reflective of the concerns of the majority of female members of the Army nor of the general public.

In the extensive PBS series on sexual harassment in the military, Betty Ann Bowser interviewed female soldiers one month after the breaking news about the Aberdeen and Fort Leonard Wood abuses. First, Bowser summarized the magnitude of the issue facing women in the military. She noted that the Army hotline received over 5,000 calls in less than two months—of which 800 calls warranted further investigation. She recalled the

Pentagon's own survey just one year earlier when more than half of the military women indicated that they had been sexually harassed while on active duty. Then, she interviewed the group of female soldiers and listened to their perspectives to get a better understanding of the problem. In the process, Bowser discovered "when women were asked to participate in group sessions to talk about sexual harassment, officials said what they heard surprised them" (Bowser, 1996).

Despite the facts to the contrary, Army leaders repeatedly misinterpreted or openly denied the pervasiveness of the problem. According to an article in the *Congressional Quarterly Weekly Report,* "Army leadership seem to think that most women are happy in the Army despite a 1995 survey showing that less that 50 percent feel their abuse and sexual harassment charges would be taken seriously" (Gruenwald, 1997, p. 376).

Similar reports of minimizing the problem were noted when Army officials appeared to attribute the complaints of widespread abuse from Aberdeen as a "few bad apples." It was not until the reports escalated and the allegations included other training sites that Pentagon officials reevaluated their initial conclusions.

The problem of minimizing or dismissing the issue of sexual harassment and sexual assault against women occurred long before the news at Aberdeen. According to a 1997 article, "The Army failed to identify the warning signs of the problem's pervasiveness for over twenty years. In 1980, 150 of 300 women in the 3rd Infantry Division in Germany reported that they were subject to unwanted physical advances. In 1989 and 1996 a majority of women responding to polls conducted in all branches of the military reported that they had encountered some form of sexual harassment. Many of the women also reported that their complaints were met with ridicule and indifference at best and retaliation at worst." (Feminists News, February 10, 1997).

The survey findings from 1988 and 1995 are frequently cited since they represent the Department of Defense's best efforts at trying to understand the magnitude of the problem. Although the follow-up survey in 1995 did find that reports of sexual harassment had decreased somewhat, over half of the women in the military still faced sexually abusive behavior on active duty.

The high incidence of sexual victimization is substantiated in other research studies as well. For example, Maureen Murdoch and Kristin Nichol of the Minneapolis Veterans Affairs Medical Center surveyed women who were being treated at the medical center. Ninety percent of the women in the study, under the age of fifty, were victims of sexual harassment on active duty while 30 percent of the older respondents reported a history of sexual harassment while in the service (Murdoch and Nichol, 1995).

Murdoch and Nichol (1995) found that the incidence of violence against female veterans is much higher than in the general population. They concluded: "Both domestic violence and sexual harassment while in the military are common experiences for female veterans. Attempted and completed sexual assaults were reported at rates 20 times (higher than) those reported for other government workers" (p. 411).

The DoD released some very different statistics in their annual tracking of reported cases of sexual harassment. The Washington Times reported that sexual harassment allegations actually declined in all branches of service except the Navy in 1996. The annual figures revealed that the Navy's sexual harassment complaints increased from 184 to 197 in 1996; the Army's reported cases dropped from 424 to 355; the Marine Corps cases decreased from 96 to 82; and the Air Force also reported fewer cases from the previous year, from 329 to 279 in 1996 (Scarborough, 1998).

Ironically, only two years earlier, the Department of Veterans Affairs noted that the highest percentages of service women reporting sexual harassment or assault were Gulf War veterans (Johnston Haas, 1994). How is it that the DoD statistics of reported cases are lower than the VA for the same decade? Why is it that so many women (more than half) consistently admit on confidential surveys that they have been victims of sexual harassment or sexual abuse in the military, yet the Department of Defense's official statistics for 1996 show only a few hundred reported cases a year?

The confounding figures may be because the number of rape and sexual harassment victims far exceeds the number of reported cases. This is also true in the civilian sector at the municipal, county, and federal levels. More often than not, victims do not make official reports of sexual violence. The estimates on reporting rape range from 5 percent (Fisher et al., 2000) to 16 percent (National Victim Center, 1992) to 32 percent (Bureau of Justice Statistics, 1996).

Rape and domestic violence are the most under-reported of all violent crimes, regardless of the jurisdiction (Bureau of Justice Statistics, 1996). Some of the underlying reasons for the low reporting rates are probably similar for military and civilian victims: fear of the perpetrator, shame and embarrassment, mistrust of the criminal justice system, or a lack of information about the available resources. The military, however, has additional systemic barriers for victims who may want to report these crimes. These obstacles are addressed firsthand in Chapters 5 and 6 by service women and men who tried to report their sexual assault or harassment.

The barriers and problems of sexual abuse are not limited to service members. Some civilian employees working at military installations have also found themselves victims of abuse by military personnel. Consider the implications of the following example involving civilians at one military installation.

The New York Times reported that twenty-three civilian, female employees at Fort Bliss, Texas, had filed a class action lawsuit because they stated they were forced to "pose nude and perform sexual acts" while on the job (Lombardi, 1996). In one of the cases involving a Fort Bliss Army colonel, the Equal Employment Opportunity Commission recommended the Army pay $300,000 in damages plus medical and legal costs to the sexual harassment victim. The civilian employee alleged that her boss, a colonel in the U.S. Army, threatened her over a six-year period that she would lose her job if she did not submit to his sexual demands. After the Army investigated the allegations, they gave the colonel a letter of reprimand and ordered him to retire early.

In this case, as with many sexual harassment allegations, the Army claims that it is not liable for the colonel's illegal and abusive behavior. Army officials believe they are exempt from liability in part because the victim did not use the established internal procedures for filing her complaint. However, the Supreme Court has ruled that employers may be held liable for their employees' sexually harassing behavior. In such cases, the military is exempt from some of the laws to which other employers must adhere. Debates about jurisdiction, military oversight, and liability are the sources of contention in many sexual harassment and abuse cases ("EEOC Judge Recommends," 1997).

Reports of sexual misconduct by military personnel against civilian employees, civilians, and other service members are numerous. Many of these allegations spark debate and controversy over how the military is handling such matters. One of the most public investigations of sexual victimization in the military stemmed from the widespread abuse by drill instructors at the previously mentioned Aberdeen Proving Ground in Maryland. The public as well as advocacy groups, such as the NAACP (National Association for the Advancement of Colored People), kept a watchful eye on how the military was responding to the allegations.

Undoubtedly, this external oversight prompted a change in the way the military would respond to these issues. Within the first week of the public notification of the allegations, four drill instructors and a captain were suspended and charged, along with fifteen other service men. The Army's hotline was set up immediately to take calls and received nearly 2,000 calls in the first weeks. Army officials noted that over 150 of those initial calls appeared to be credible allegations requiring further investigation (Barrett, 1996).

Finally, by the end of the twentieth century, it seemed as though the public and the Pentagon had a better understanding of the extent of sexual misconduct in the military. This was in part due to the increased publicity regarding rape, abuse, and sexual harassment reports and due to the toll-free hotlines. In addition, allegations came from veterans, retirees, Department of Defense civilian employees, and other civilians—stateside and abroad. As more victims came forward, it seemed as though some of the reported abuses were more incredulous. The following are further examples of the types of harassment and violence committed by U.S. Service members found on public record.

- A female cadet at the Air Force Academy mock prisoner-of-war camp is urinated on, sexually humiliated and beaten unconscious.
- Four marines are charged in the rape of a female sailor in Iceland.
- A Naval petty officer from the U.S.S. Belleau Wood (a U.S. amphibious assault ship) reportedly molested a Japanese girl in Nagasaki, Japan.
- Several men threatened a female Coast Guard petty officer with a screwdriver demanding she perform oral sex on them.
- Two SEAL trainees are charged with the rape and murder of a Georgia college student.
- A fourteen-year-old American girl was allegedly raped at Kadena Air Force base, Okinawa, by a twenty-four-year-old U.S. Service member.
- At Annapolis, Maryland, one midshipman twice raped a high school girl and her sister.
- Male trainees are tortured by Marine Corps officers at Camp Lejeune and Camp Smith survival trainings. Their genitals were burned with cigarettes and Tabasco sauce.
- A twenty-four-year-old woman was beaten to death with a hammer by a U.S. Service member in Japan.

Violence by military personnel has no apparent boundaries. The victims inlued children as well as the elderly and frail; the abuse is sometimes sadistic or homicidal; the perpetrators show no regard for their victims. The uncontrolled violence reaches well beyond U.S. borders into peacekeeping missions and allied countries. The result is that far too many U.S. servicemen misbehave in ways that other countries will not tolerate. Yet our own country has indulged some of these offenders. Abuse by U.S. military personnel abroad made international headlines.

INTERNATIONAL CASES OF VIOLENCE

The soldier, be he friend or foe, is charged with the protection of the weak and unarmed. It is the very essence and reason of his being. When he violates this sacred trust, he not only profanes his entire cult but threatens the fabric of international society.

— GENERAL DOUGLAS MACARTHUR (MANCHESTER, 1978)

Rape and other forms of violence by U.S. military personnel have occurred all over the world (Mercier, 1997; Kelly, 1998; Frankel et al., 2000; Enloe, 2000). In fact, the issue is so problematic that it has drawn the attention and public disdain of military leadership abroad on several occasions. For example, in 1997 (following an investigation in Germany involving at least twenty-three possible victims) the United States Army Europe leadership issued a clear message to the troops condemning sexual victimization by military personnel:

> It is both the individual responsibility and command priority to ensure that dignity and respect are accorded to all. There is no room in today's Army for troopers or leaders who would take advantage of another soldier or family member. ("Combating Sexual Harassment" 1997, p. 2)

Similarly, in April of 1998, the commander of the U.S. Navy forces in the Pacific Fleet (some 215,000 active-duty sailors and Marines) sent a personal message of concern to all officers in charge, commanders, and flag officers. In the memo, Fleet Admiral Archie Clemins addressed the increasing numbers of rape, sexual assaults, and family violence by sailors and Marines in the Pacific Fleet. According to the Pacific Stars and Stripes, Navy spokesman Lieutenant Jeff Davis reported: "Navy figures recorded nearly seven rape reports and more than eight sexual assaults per month in the Pacific Fleet's regions as of December, 1997" (Kelly, 1998, p. 1).

Given these figures, the commander's concern is understandable. However, Lieutenant Davis also noted that the Pacific Fleet, including civilians and family members, includes nearly half a million people. Therefore, he reasoned that the numbers were not too alarming. "So really, 6.8 rapes reported each month, that's actually pretty good" (Kelly, 1998, p. 7). Apparently, Admiral Clemins did not agree that nearly seven rapes and eight other sexual assaults per month were of no concern since he personally warned his commanders to pay closer attention to this issue.

Admiral Clemins was correct in his assessment. Uncontrolled violence against women and children by U.S. military personnel abroad is both extensive and of great concern. The following point to a few examples of sexual misconduct allegations by male service members representing America in other countries:

Darmstadt, Germany, 1997: Eleven female soldiers accused three male instructors of sexual abuse and harassment at a military training facility. One of the instructors who was found guilty on several counts apologized after the court-martial to the females, to his unit, and to the Army "for tarnishing its image." He was convicted of raping a subordinate, three counts of forcible sodomy, kidnapping, indecent assault, cruelty and maltreatment, fraternization, and unlawful entry.

Izmir, Turkey, 1998: A major general of the Army was accused of forcing a colleague's wife into a four-month sexual relationship while assigned to Turkey as the deputy commanding general of NATO's allied land forces in southeastern Europe. He was later named deputy inspector general for the Army. Four months into the position, he asked and was allowed to retire honorably while still under investigation by the Pentagon's inspector general.

Kosovo, 1999: Army service members of an international peacekeeping force were sexually molesting women and girls during crowd control operations in what were supposed to be general searches. Both enlisted and officers were implicated in the improper touching and misconduct toward ethnic Kosovar Albanian citizens. Other acts of abuse, interrogations, and beatings also occurred at the hands of U.S. peacekeepers according to military investigators.

Okinawa, Japan, 2000: A marine entered a family's private residence off base and sexually assaulted their fourteen-year-old daughter. He was found guilty by a military court of unlawful entry, committing an indecent act, drunken driving, underage drinking, and disorderly conduct. He was sentenced to two years in prison. In an unprecedented move and show of remorse, Marine Corps Lieutenant General Earl Hailston promptly met with Japanese government officials to make a formal apology and a bow of contrition.

Chatan, Japan, 2001: An Air Force sergeant stationed at Kadena Air Base was turned over to Japanese authorities for raping a young woman in the parking lot outside of the American Village near the base. He was only the second American Service man ever to be turned over to Japanese authorities before being formally charged by the U.S. military. This diplomatic agreement was in response to the growing outrage regarding violence against Japanese citizens by American Service men.

Crete, Greece, 2002: A Naval officer of over twenty years and commander of a 300-member flight squadron faced charges of raping a junior enlisted sailor under his command. Hours prior to the military hearing stateside on the charges, the forty-three year-old commander called his defense attorney to say he would not be there. Sometime shortly thereafter, he committed suicide.

The effects of sexual assault by U.S. service members abroad are far-reaching and often tragic. The victims' lives are forever changed after the abuse; the offenders must find ways to face and cope with their actions; family members suffer; and the military suffers too. This issue is of great importance with significant implications to all concerned.

In some cases, these sexual crimes (and the military response) can severely strain relationships with our foreign allies. In the article, "Way Off Base—The Shameful History of

Military Rape in Okinawa," Rick Mercier describes the impact of the military presence and the subsequent extent of violence in Okinawa, Japan, after two marines and a sailor were found guilty of raping a local girl.

The connection between militarism and sexual violence could not have been articulated more clearly, and it is especially apt in light of the abduction and rape of a 12-year-old Okinawan schoolgirl by three U.S. Service men in September 1995. "That crime was no isolated incident" (Mercier, 1997). Mercier reported that U.S. military personnel in Okinawa have committed thirty-four murders since 1995, of which twenty-three were women and girls. Rape and violence against women and girls in allied countries, particularly Asian countries, have been problematic for some time (Enloe, 1983; Ahn, n.d.; Francke, 1997).

Several local and international advocacy groups have formed as a result of the pervasiveness of the problem and also due to concerns about the U.S. military's response to violence against women and children. One of the groups, the Asia Pacific Center for Justice and Peace, issued a press release in October 6, 1998, condemning the violence against women in Asia by U.S. servicemen. A press conference was also held with women from the Philippines, Korea, Japan, and the United States who expressed their concerns. The women also told about some of their personal experiences of abuse by U.S. military personnel.

In conjunction with the press release, the East Asia-U.S. Women's Network Against Militarism held a conference on this issue in Washington, DC, which included many of the groups who have been most vocal about these concerns. A member of the Okinawan Women Act Against Military Violence, Suzuyo Takazata, concluded in the press release that community women become the outlets for service members' aggression.

The East Asia-U.S. Women's Network Against U.S. Militarism is comprised of a group of women activists, policymakers, and scholars from Japan, South Korea, the Philippines, and the United States. They have been working collectively since 1997 due to concerns regarding the impact of the presence of the U.S. military on the lives of women and children in occupied countries. At their conference in 1998 in Washington, DC, they met with members of Congress and officials from the State and Justice Departments to advocate for the safety of women and children in countries where U.S. military personnel are stationed.

In addition to organized efforts by international and national advocacy groups such as the East Asia-U.S. Women's Network, there are also efforts behind the scenes to increase safety and to focus on prevention of sexual assaults by U.S. military personnel. The following exemplifies one attempt at a Marine base overseas following numerous allegations of sexual assaults and unlawful entries into the women's rooms. This account was carefully documented by a marine who, when stationed in Japan, experienced repeated sexual harassment and abuse by her fellow marines.

Apparently there were far too many incidents of men forcefully entering the women [marines'] bedrooms at night. It seems that many of these men enter the rooms uninvited and often through the windows while the women sleep. Upon breaking and entering into the private sleeping quarters of the service women, the male marines get on top of the women and then force sex upon them. These marines are raping their fellow female marines and threatening them not to tell anyone.

No one knows for certain how many female marines have been victimized or raped at that base. What we do know, however, is that some of the women decided to tell someone about the intrusions and at least one brave young marine reported her rape to the authorities.

Because there were several complaints about men going into the women's rooms at night through the windows, the leadership decided to cut down on these late night escapades. According to the marine who reported these allegations, the leadership issued metal bars to the women marines to use in their windows "to keep the rapists out." Yes, the United States Marine Corps issued metal bars (just like they issue boots, M-16 rifles, and helmets) one per room to the women in the barracks. Presumably, the metal bars were not intended to be used as weapons for self-defense, though we wonder how marine leaders would have responded to an unconscious male marine on a woman's bed with a bump on his head and his Skivvies around his ankles?

The most appalling aspect of the leadership response is not so much that someone thought the bars would be a good way to address the problem of rape, but it is what happened to the women when they tried to report these incidents. This marine veteran wanted others to know exactly what happened to her when she tried to report the sexual assault and subsequent harassment. She has also detailed how the Marines responded to her rape allegations in letters to her Congressmen.

The problems of violence against women by U.S. Service men abroad are not limited to Asia, however. This issue seems to be a dilemma wherever U.S. armed forces personnel are stationed. There are numerous reports of sexual assault and abuse by military personnel on foreign soil from Iceland to the Persian Gulf, during peacetime and during war (Francke, 1997; Mercier, 1997; Kelly, 1998; Enloe, 2000; Larimer, 2001).

For example, the murder and sexual abuse of an eleven-year-old ethnic Albanian girl resulted in the most serious charges ever faced by a peacekeeper from any other country since the NATO mission came to the Balkans. According to an Associated Press article, "The girl's death raised tensions between peacekeeping troops in Kosovo and ethnic Albanians who already had been critical of other alleged mistreatment, including inappropriate body searches of women" (Boehmer, 2000). Although this incident should not reflect poorly on the entire peacekeeping force or on other U.S. soldiers, it does affect our presence in other countries in peace and in war.

SEXUAL HARASSMENT AND ABUSE IN TIMES OF WAR

I was sexually harassed during the Gulf War. The Army pretty much ignored the case until CNN broadcast a story. I was investigated; the harasser officially denied everything in a letter to the commanding general; the general disregarded witness statements and threw out an investigating officer's report that substantiated it, and that was that.

—— A FEMALE SOLDIER FIGHTING SEXUAL HARASSMENT AS
SHE SERVED IN THE GULF WAR

In *Bearing Witness: Sexual Harassment and Beyond* (1994), Celia Morris recounts reports of victimization experienced by U.S. military women during the Persian Gulf War. News broke about the Persian Gulf War and the horrors of rape when two women soldiers were captured and raped by Iraqis. Soon thereafter, a twenty-nine-year-old Persian Gulf veteran testified to Congress about how she was "forcibly sodomized by her sergeant in broad daylight" (p. 177). As it turned out, 24 other U.S. servicewomen who came forward to tell about rape by their peers and superiors. Further reports came out indicating over one-third of military women experienced sexual harassment. More women testified to Congress about abuse and harassment in the military and the abuse by the military in the aftermath of the crime.

In response to the congressional testimony about one of the reported Persian Gulf rapes, Representative Pat Schroeder concluded, "the military affirmatively acted to harass the complainant and scuttle the complaint" (p. 177).

When it comes to war, military and civilian women are often the sexual and aggressive targets of the enemy (as well as victims of their fellow soldiers). Moreover, few, if any, boundaries protect women and children from the potential threat of sexual assault during war. Consequently, war and rape all too often go hand in hand. The armed forces endure rigorous and dangerous conditions, especially in war. They make sacrifices and risk their lives for their country. Service members who face the horrors of war deserve to be honored and highly regarded. However, when a member of the U.S. military commits rape, he denigrates the mission and stands apart from those who serve honorably and selflessly. War is not a justifiable excuse to commit sexual assault.

Yet it is particularly difficult for rape victims to come forward with such heinous charges against a service member. Allegations and charges of sexual violence should never be made lightly or falsely, especially when a country is at war. Yet this does not excuse those who sexually abuse civilians or other service members. Sexual violence should not be tolerated by the U.S. armed forces at any time or under any circumstance. Unfortunately, this does not make it easier for victims to report such an incident.

Military rape victims may be reluctant to come forward because they do not want to tarnish the reputation of their unit or of the armed forces when service members are losing their lives for their country. Moreover, they may not feel safe reporting sexual assault or harassment during war for fear of reprisal from their command or from the perpetrator. Likewise, civilian women and youths who are targets of sexual violence by U.S. military servicemen may also fear repercussions to themselves or to their families if they report the abuse. They may be concerned about the impact on their community, especially if the perpetrator was a member of a peacekeeping mission.

This was part of the problem in Kosovo when service members sexually abused civilians. The Army issued a 600-page report confirming that several members of the 3rd Battalion, 504th Parachute Infantry Regiment were involved in misconduct against Kosovar Albanian citizens, including groping female body parts "for cheap thrills" during crowd control operations (Burlas, 2000). Five enlisted members and four officers were disciplined for "behaving in a manner inconsistent with the command's rules of engagement, the Uniform Code of Military Justice and the Army's core values" (Burlas, 2000).

The peacekeeping force was assigned to Kosovo to provide humanitarian service. This did not afford them the privilege to do whatever they wanted. However, it would be incredibly difficult to accuse someone of rape knowing that the perpetrator was also responsible for protecting your family and your country. As the father of Merita Shabiu, an eleven-year-old Albanian girl who was sexually assaulted and murdered by a U.S. Army staff sergeant, said, "We could never believe that this could have been done by a soldier" (Frankel et al., 2000, p. 103).

Only months earlier, Merita was one of the Albanian children who welcomed the soldiers to Kosovo with cheers of "NATO." Merita's family and her community regarded the peacekeepers as helpful, not potentially hurtful. In fact, the majority of the 6,000 who served behaved very honorably during their mission, although some soldiers violated the boundaries.

For many women and girls in occupied countries, rape is a part of life in peace and in war (Mercier, 1997; Larimer, 2001; Ahn, n.d.). Moreover, some females are forced into a sex industry that does not protect them from rape or physical abuse. In peacetime, military men abroad may frequent brothels, clubs, or bars where women and girls are the commodity. Yet in war civilian females often become the collateral damage. Although much has been written about rape as a war crime, no one knows for certain how many lives have suffered because of those who have hidden behind the uniform to mask their rapes or other sexual crimes.

Author Linda Bird Francke (1997) gave examples of how women and their bodies are used as targets during war. During the Vietnam War, a woman was left naked with a company patch between her legs as if to designate property rights, or a calling card to denote "we were here." Other women had grenades, or other objects, forced into their vaginas. It seems there is no limit to the horrors of war and the consequences of collateral damage. Francke (1997) concluded that the reason rape was not declared a war crime until 1996 by the International Criminal Tribunal in The Hague was because, "Sexually assaulting women was...auniversally accepted by-product of military male behavior" (p. 160). A more likely reason is because so few victims report the atrocities done to them.

Female and male victims of abuse by U.S. military personnel have come forward—often not until years later, when they believed it was finally safe to do so. More and more victims have spoken out due to increased media attention and greater public awareness. The final decade of the twentieth century opened the doors for many service members, veterans, and civilians to acknowledge what happened to them—including those sexually abused during wartime.

In one such case in 1997, four nurses went public to talk about the abuses they endured while serving in Vietnam. In an interview with reporter Peter Van Sant for the ABC telecast *Public Eye,* these veterans talked about the sexual harassment and rape that occurred while they were on active duty. The following summarizes their experiences as reported in the broadcast:

Connie was a lieutenant colonel in the Army Reserves. She recalled that her life was changed forever after being raped while on duty. She spoke of the physical and emotional scars that stayed with her after she left Vietnam. Joan was a nurse in the Air Force who remembered that sexual harassment was everywhere. She gave the example of a party that she and some fellow officers were invited to attend. They were advised to dress in short shorts. When the women arrived at the party, they were stunned to find a replica of a huge penis on the table as a centerpiece. The climate of the party was offensive and degrading toward women, according to Joan, who was raped and sodomized by two officers at the event. She was too ashamed to report the abuse at the time. Jane was another nurse who was ordered to go to parties after work. She sensed that the women were being told it was their duty to be there for the men.

The nurses knew that going to the parties would likely entail some sexual harassment or other compromising situations, but they did not expect to be sexually assaulted by co-workers or colleagues. Another Vietnam-era veteran, Agnes, acknowledged that abuse was prevalent. Although the incidents were not reported at the time of the sexual assaults, she concurred with the other women: the problem was finally surfacing after all these years.

Van Sant referred to the women who served in Vietnam as patriots. He said that they were there to do their duty—not to be raped or sexually harassed. It was important for them to speak out even after so much time had passed. They did not want to discredit their fellow service members or to bring charges against them. They just needed to tell someone what really happened while they were serving their country during the war in Vietnam (Van Sant, 1997).

Whether during peacetime or war, telling someone about rape or sexual harassment is a significant decision. Yet these women and countless other victims were unable to report the abuse to their military leaders. In part, this is often due to a climate of harassment that is known and tolerated by the chain of command. This breakdown in leadership contributes to the problem. When service members see their leaders fall, their confidence weakens a bit further. During war, trust and confidence in military leaders are especially important. The U.S. armed forces cannot afford for their leaders to be the weakest link in the chain of command at any time.

CASES INVOLVING HIGH-RANKING MILITARY LEADERS

Each breakdown in personal conduct by a member of the uniformed services
is nothing less than an assault against organizational discipline,
the bedrock of any fighting force.

—— JOHN G. ROOS (1996)

Good leadership is critical to any organization. The power and authority that goes with these positions may have its privileges, but it does not exempt someone from the Uniform Code of Military Justice nor from the public's opinion. Over time, sexual allegations have implicated some notable and high-ranking figures. Following are some of the cases that involved leaders in the Department of Defense and Department of Veterans Affairs.

- A two-star admiral was relieved of his duties as commander of the Navy's supply system and oversight of 10,000 employees. The commander allegedly made repeated propositions to a subordinate and created a hostile working environment (Priest, 1997b).
- The inspector general investigated the Army's general counsel in 1997 for allegations of sexual harassment arising from a complaint made to the Army's hotline (Priest, 1997b). The Defense Department confirmed the investigation of the general counsel on the heels of sexual conduct allegations against other top military officials.
- A two-star general was given a written reprimand for sexually harassing a three-star general and for conduct unbecoming an officer, according to Army officials. This case, which gained public attention due to the high-ranking officers involved, is discussed in more detail in the conclusion of this chapter.
- The Army's deputy inspector general in the Pentagon faced an Article 32 investigation stemming from allegations of improper sexual relationships and obstructing an official investigation (Schafer, 1998c). Given that the deputy inspector general's job was entwined with the investigation of military misconduct, it was both ironic and characteristic of the problem that he also faced such allegations.
- Nine officials at the Department of Veterans Affairs were accused of sexually harassing employees from 1994 to 1997. After an investigation into the complaints, seven of the nine were allowed to retire and one received a $25,000 buyout (McAllister, 1997a,b). Current and former employees testified to a House subcommittee about intolerable levels of harassment and that their complaints were often disregarded or minimized. In at least one of the cases, the Equal Employment Opportunity Commission substantiated claims of sexual harassment against a VA director. In response to these allegations, the VA transferred the former director (expenses paid) to a new job that was reportedly created for him at a Florida VA hospital. Moreover, he was able to keep his $106,000 annual salary intact (McAllister, 1997a,b).

The most notable military leader charged with sexual misconduct thus far was the Army's highest-ranking enlisted man, former Sergeant Major (SGM) of the Army Gene C. McKinney. Due to the high-ranking personnel involved, this case brought a different perspective to the problems of sexual harassment in the military. Although McKinney faced a public court-martial, six accusers, and nineteen charges, he was eventually found guilty in 1998 on only one charge of obstruction of justice. Many still believe this case and the final verdict characterize the military's overall response to the issues of sexual harassment and sexual abuse: minimize the problem. Veterans and active-duty service members spoke out regarding McKinney's verdict and its implications. Their responses are highlighted in Chapter 4.

At the end of the court-martial, only one thing was certain: once again, national attention was drawn to the problems of sexual harassment and sexual abuse in the U.S. military. This time, however, the accused was the Army's top gun. He had an impeccable record of twenty-eight years in the service as a decorated and valued soldier. In his role as SGM of the Army, he was an advisor to the chief of staff and to the secretary of the Army. To put it simply, there was no one higher than McKinney in the enlisted ranks.

The first woman to publicly accuse McKinney was SGM Brenda Hoster. She was also very highly regarded in her twenty-two years of service with an outstanding military record and a Bronze Star. Hoster decided to retire early as a result of the harassment. In light of the problem, she felt she had no other options but to cut short her career. She retired at the rank of sergeant major (only one rank below sergeant major of the army). Ironically, this is the same rank that McKinney was forced to retire at—leaving both of them as equals in retirement.

In addition to the issues of rank and race (McKinney is black; his six accusers are white), this case also taught the public some lessons about the military criminal justice system and how the military responds to sexual harassment complaints. SGM Hoster reiterated during interviews with the press that she told McKinney his advances were offensive and she wanted the behaviors to stop. She also tried to report the alleged harassment to a superior a few weeks after it occurred. Hoster noted that her complaints were virtually ignored and her requests for transfers were denied.

When Hoster learned that McKinney was appointed as one of the select few to the secretary of the Army's senior review panel on sexual harassment, she felt it was imperative to report the allegations to the authorities. Despite her allegations against him months earlier, McKinney remained on the review panel until one day after the case was reported to the Criminal Investigation Division. The media quickly brought the issue to the public's attention and McKinney was soon relieved of his duties on the panel.

Hoster went public with her allegations and appeared in televised interviews, including one with Sam Donaldson on *Primetime Live* in February 1997. During the interview, Hoster talked about her response to McKinney and her concerns about reporting the allegations. She also summarized her account of what happened.

At first she let McKinney know the behaviors were offensive to her. She indicated the sexual innuendos were inappropriate because he was her boss. Hoster said she questioned herself and wondered why this was happening to her. Many women who experience sexual harassment wonder if they did something that may have given the alleged offender the wrong message. It is not uncommon for victims of sexual harassment to question their own behaviors, communications, or responses. The idea of being abused by someone they trust is incomprehensible. The women try to find an answer as to why it happened by blaming or questioning themselves.

For the same reason, many sexual harassment victims in this study did not report the abuse. Victims of sexual assault and harassment wonder who would believe that the offender could do such a thing. Hoster echoed similar concerns during the interview on *Primetime Live* in 1997. She said that she did not report it right away because she was scared and worried that no one would believe her. "I really just wanted to try and forget about it." Hoster testified at the court-martial, "I just couldn't believe it was happening" (Jones, 1998a). Since the allegations were her word versus his, she expected people would believe him because he was the sergeant major of the Army.

Hoster did try calling the Army hotline (to find out more about the process), but she did not leave her name because she did not trust the system. She believed her report would have been covered up because of McKinney's rank and role in the Army. Her concerns were confirmed when she finally did report the abuse to a superior in her chain of command, Colonel Gaylord, the deputy chief at the Army Office of Public Affairs. In the interview, Hoster stated that the colonel took no formal action on the allegations, to her knowledge.

Shortly thereafter, Hoster learned about McKinney's appointment to the Army's senior review panel on sexual harassment. It was not until then that she decided to go public with her complaints against McKinney. She hoped that her efforts in coming forward would help other women.

McKinney, himself, had a few things to say about sexual harassment. Ironically, some of his comments were made shortly before the allegations against him were made public—as he still held a key role in the Army's response to sexual harassment. The sergeant major of the Army was featured in a videotaped training program that was developed by the Army. In the training video for his subordinates, McKinney affirmed that sexual harassment does not belong in "America's Army."

Ironically, McKinney spoke to his troops about Army values and policies on sexual harassment just weeks before his own sexual harassment allegations became public: "They [NCOs] said to me, 'We realized we have a few bad apples.' Those people [who allegedly violated soldiers' trust] have not and did not espouse the values of America's Army. They do not represent the majority; they represent the few who are out there" (Gilmore, 1996).

McKinney was responding to the widespread allegations of sexual abuse at Aberdeen Proving Ground, following a visit to talk to the troops about the problem. Weeks later, six accusers came forward charging him with sexual harassment. In light of the numerous allegations against McKinney, how could the troops still respect his message?

In April 2000, the Pentagon investigated yet another allegation of sexual harassment by a high-ranking official. The allegation was reported by Lieutenant General Claudia J. Kennedy, the Army's highest-ranking female officer to date—the first woman to hold a three-star rank in the Army. At the time, Kennedy was the chief of intelligence.

Upon learning about the allegation, Secretary of Defense William Cohen acknowledged the investigation and restated that the U.S. military has a zero-tolerance policy against sexual harassment. Cohen was cautious in making further comments in such a high-profile case.

According to *The Washington Post* (Ricks, 2000) Lieutenant General Kennedy reportedly tried to deal with the situation quietly, but brought charges... after the man she had accused was promoted. According to one Army official, she made the formal allegation because she felt the Army hadn't kept its implicit promise to not further advance his career . . . (p. A6)

Soon after the allegation of sexual harassment become public, attacks on Kennedy and her professionalism surfaced. The criticisms flowed despite the fact that Kennedy was considered a strong candidate to head the Army's Training and Doctrine Command. The appointment would have likely included a promotion making Kennedy the first female four-star general in U.S. history. Her military record was impeccable. However, it was not until Kennedy made the sexual harassment charge that her character and leadership capabilities came under public attack. Kennedy reportedly opted for an early retirement. How many more military careers will be cut short because of the repercussions of sexual harassment or sexual assault?

As with many cases, the credibility and integrity of the alleged victim often comes into question. This pattern of "blaming the victim" and minimizing or denying sexual abuse occurs is rampant from top to bottom in the armed forces. No one—regardless of rank, longevity, or record can escape the barrage that comes with reporting sexual harassment or rape in the military.

The allegations of sexual harassment by Lieutenant General Claudia Kennedy and Sergeant Major Brenda Hoster gave this issue a different face. Sexual harassment was reaching beyond trainees and drill sergeants. The reports made by Kennedy and Hoster, two high-ranking, respected, military women, revealed to the public that sexual violations can and do cut across ranks and racial lines. Sexual harassment and rape can affect anyone, regardless of rank, race, gender, or background.

Sexual victimization of any kind should never be taken lightly, especially when it involves abuse of power. Nonetheless, some military leaders fell asleep on the job when it came to protecting their troops, implementing military policies, and upholding their trust in their authority. Their responses, or lack thereof, contribute to the problem of sexual victimization in the military.

ADMITTING THE PROBLEM EXISTS

All of us in the army are deeply troubled by the allegations of sexual misconduct and rape which occurred. That is unacceptable conduct for soldiers. It's unacceptable to the army.

—— GENERAL DENNIS REIMER CHIEF OF STAFF, U.S. ARMY (BOWSER, 1996)

Abuse, harassment, and uncontrolled violence by military personnel have longstanding roots in the history of the armed forces. It did not just start to be a problem with the integration of women into the services. Sexual harassment and violence by service members were well known within military circles long before the media exposed some of the top stories.

In 1979 and 1980, four congressional hearings were held by the 96th Congress to assess the status of women in the all-volunteer armed forces. On February 11, 1980, the focus of the hearings shifted to sexual harassment when female service members provided detailed testimonies and answered questions about sexual victimization in the military. The women told about their experiences with harassment, rape, and the military climate. They addressed the reasons that it was difficult, if not impossible, to report such abuses. They talked about how their careers in the military were changed as a result. Author Linda Bird Francke (1997) summarized the impact of their horrific testimonies: "By the end of the day . . . both Congress and the services knew everything they needed to know—and subsequently would ignore—about sexual harassment" (p. 169).

The information that came out of those hearings, albeit shocking and distressing, did not begin to address the problem. In fact, the U.S. armed forces still refused to admit that rape and sexual harassment warranted their immediate attention. Nearly two decades would pass before the military services were ready to admit a problem existed.

In the Navy, for example, although a statement on sexual harassment was developed in 1980, very little was done beyond writing the policy. Sexual victimization and harassment were indeed problems for women and men long before 1980. One male veteran in this study told of his experience during the Vietnam era of being raped and then ridiculed by fellow shipmates. Accusations of homosexuality were made against him because he was raped by a man. When he tried to report the rape to his command, he was accused of sodomy and threatened with a discharge. Although male-on-male sexual assault was occurring in the Navy and other branches, few came forward to report the abuse. The culture made it difficult, if not impossible, for victims to come forward. This is still true today, particularly for male victims whose masculinity and sexual identity may be called into question if they are sexually assaulted.

In fact, women opened the doors to addressing this problem in the Navy. The issue brought to the Navy's attention in an official capacity as early as 1980 when women started speaking out publicly regarding their concerns. One high-ranking Naval officer, Rear Admiral Fran McKee, provided testimony to the House Armed Services Committee that sexual harassment was occurring Navy-wide, and that women often did not officially report the abuse due to fear of repercussions, particularly to their jobs (Ebbert and Hall, 1999). (These same concerns were reported in this study two decades later.)

Despite the rear admiral's strong message, it was not until some seven years had passed that a 1987 Navy study, *The Progress of Women,* agreed: sexual harassment was indeed a pervasive problem. Moreover, upon review of numerous complaints of sexual harassment at a base in the Philippines, DACOWITS (the Defense Advisory Committee on Women in the Service) also found, "Navy and Marine leaders condoned overt and blatant sexual harassment of women in the services" (Ebbert and Hall, 1999, p. 207).

Ironically, it would be another four years before Tailhook blew the cover in 1991 and the Navy was faced with the public humiliation and pressure to address this "pervasive" problem. The following statement, made by the inspector general, was in his official report on the Tailhook investigations: "After 1985, it became routine practice for the President of Tailhook Association to write to squadron commanders ...to ensure that conduct in the hospitality suites comported with the standards of decency" (Department of Defense, Office of the Inspector General, 1992, p. 3).

In August of 1991, a similar letter was sent out warning against "late night gang mentality." Seven years of letters of concern seemed to fall on deaf ears of some aviators in the Tailhook Association.

Refusal to admit the problem or a lack of concern and commitment on the part of Navy leadership served only to contribute to the culture of uncontrolled violence. It was not until 1990 that sexual harassment was included as an offense in Navy regulations—ten years after Rear Admiral McKee reported that the problem was occurring at most, if not all, naval bases (Ebbert and Hall, 1999).

Not long after Tailhook, the Navy got on board and issued stronger messages to their personnel. In 1993, the Department of the Navy disbursed a revised policy on sexual harassment to all ships and stations. The policy included clear definitions and examples of sexually harassing behaviors, including rape. Moreover, the policy affirmed the Navy's enforcement through "punitive, disciplinary or administrative action, including the violation of a lawful order under Article 92 of the UCMJ" (Department of the Navy, 1993). The policy also emphasized punitive responses for anyone who reprises against a sexual harassment victim. Punitive responses include an administrative separation from the Navy or Marine Corps on the "first, substantiated incident of harassment" as determined by a court-martial or a commanding officer (Department of the Navy, 1993).

In 1995, the Commandant of the Marine Corps released the findings of the first equal opportunity and sexual harassment survey conducted in 1994. The survey was sent to 10,000 active-duty Marines to assess the climate and the occurrences of harassment. Responses were received by 48 percent of those who were mailed surveys. The report cited the following findings (Marine Corps Commandant, 1995):

- Almost half of all female PFCs and LCPLs (private first class and lance corporals) were harassed in the past year.
- Most harassment was unwanted sexual attention, not coercion.
- Few victims complain (report the abuse) when unable to handle the situation themselves, primarily because of repercussions.
- Satisfaction with the complaint process was low.
- Being sexually harassed had a negative impact on women's career plans.

One year after the revised Department of the Navy policy was disbursed, sexual harassment was still present within the Marine Corps, according to their own assessment. The policy and subsequent prevention programs seemed to have little, if any, effect on the occurrences of sexual harassment and the fear of reprisals. However, by this point, the Navy and Marines were getting closer to acknowledging and accepting that sexual harassment was a problem within their ranks.

As for the Air Force, admitting the problem and developing a swift response was a high priority at the start of the 1990s. Air Force policies were developed, disbursed, and incorporated into mandatory training programs for military and civilian personnel. In addition, in 1992, the Department of the Air Force sent a follow-up memorandum to all commanders reiterating the policy and the need for commanders to "take a closer look at the equal opportunity and sexual harassment programs in their command, to include reviewing policies, trends, education and training" (Department of the Air Force, 1992). In the memo, the Air Force chief of staff also stressed to commanders: "make sure that no person feels threatened if he/she reports discrimination/harassment."

The messages were clear: The sexual harassment policy is to be known by all, enforced by leadership, and dealt with appropriately and without reprisal to the victims. These themes were reinforced in the comprehensive Air Force sexual harassment education program and through handouts as well (Department of the Air Force, 1993).

Similarly, the Army also had numerous claims and sufficient evidence to suggest that sexual harassment and rape were problems for the majority of women in uniform and for some men as well. Some of the studies, policies, and the Army's responses are addressed in more detail in other sections of this book. Each of the service branches has gathered sufficient information over the past two decades to confirm that sexual harassment and rape have been long-standing and pervasive problems within their ranks for quite some time.

The General Accounting Office (GAO) has reviewed many of the armed forces' studies on sexual abuse and harassment in the military and at military academies. The GAO reviewed the recommendations of some earlier studies, and determined to what extent the Service branches followed the recommendations. In addition, the GAO scrutinized the Equal Employment Opportunity (EEO) process for filing sexual harassment complaints within each of the services to gain a better understanding of EEO policies in practice.

Upon completion of its evaluations, the GAO sent copies of the final reports to the secretaries of defense, the Air Force, the Army, and the Navy; to the superintendents of the three service academies; and to interested congressional committees. With the numerous studies and the GAO evaluations, it would seem that the Department of Defense and the service academies should have sufficient information to conclude that sexual assault and harassment were indeed significant problems in need of immediate, corrective attention.

However, the abusive behavior by U.S. military service members is not limited to sexual harassment and rape. The problems of uncontrolled violence and harassment by military personnel are far-reaching, to include attacks on civilian women, children, and homosexuals. The abuses include a scope of violence from murder to "daily psychological warfare" (one woman soldier's description of the perpetual harassment she endured on active duty). The violence by military personnel includes thousands of documented and undocumented cases of rape, battering, stalking, child abuse, kidnapping, torture, emotional abuse, harassment, and homicide.

Of all the types of abuse, the incidents of family violence in the military are particularly high. For example, a 1996 study by the Pentagon found that from 1991 to 1995, more than 50,000 active-duty service members had hit or physically hurt their spouses (Thompson, 1997). In 1986 alone there were 27,783 cases of reported family violence and that number nearly doubled only seven years later in 1993 when there were 46,287 reported cases (Thompson, 1994). Moreover, according to a *Time* magazine article by Mark Thompson, "A confidential—and unprecedented—Army survey obtained by *Time* suggests that spousal abuse is occurring in one of every three Army families each year—double the civilian rate. Each week someone dies at the hands of a relative in uniform" (Thompson, 1994, p. 48).

Researcher Peter Neidig and Behavioral Science Associates in New York compiled the information that Thompson mentioned in his article. However, similar studies have also reported increasingly alarming rates and concerns about the extent of domestic abuse in all service branches. Violence against women is indeed a growing problem everywhere, and the military is certainly not exempt.

The accounts of abuse by U.S. service members paint a very troubling picture. In fact, the problem of sexual violence in the military becomes more realized with each case that is reported in the news. In the *Newsweek* article, "A Question of Consent," Evan Thomas and Gregory Vistica point to the complexity of the problem facing the military: "When the Aberdeen story first broke last fall, there were troubling reports about a 'rape ring.' But after months of testimony and investigation, the scandal appears to be more complicated than originally thought" (Thomas and Vistica, 1997a, p. 41).

Civilians and military members echoed similar comments across the nation. In a 1996 National Public Radio interview on *All Things Considered* (Bradley, 1996), Susan Barnes, president of Women Active in Our Nation's Defense (a coalition of military and civilian women formed after the Tailhook scandal) noted that the sheer number of calls to the Army hotline indicated, if nothing else, that the problem was indeed extensive.

Even Togo West publicly affirmed his disdain of the widespread reports of abuse within the military family. He made the following comments in his address to the Senate Armed Services Committee on February 4, 1997: "Let me be clear: From the number and nature of the allegations, we in the Army have a problem of significant proportions" (West and Reimer, 1997). He went on to address the allegations of abuse reported at Army training facilities:

We took immediate action to ensure that the victims were properly cared for, that the rights of the accused were protected and that the specific incidents were addressed swift and appropriately.... What is alleged to have occurred at Aberdeen was particularly troublesome to us because it involved abuses of authority and it appeared that the incidents either had gone unreported or were not addressed. (West and Reimer, 1997)

In the aftermath of Aberdeen (and because of the increased awareness to the issues), the flow of news reports on sexual misconduct in the military continued at a steady pace. The problem was treated to a regular dose of military sexual mayhem, as the media reported stories of sexual indiscretions and affairs involving Pentagon officials, top-ranking brass, military pilots, and others.

The national and international attention to sexual harassment and sexual abuse finally penetrated the Pentagon and the Department of Defense. However, admitting there was a problem was a gradual process—one that is still met with resistance by many military leaders. Secretary of the Army Togo West issued many statements in the aftermath of Aberdeen, Fort Leonard Wood, and the appointment of McKinney to the senior review panel on sexual harassment. West was often cautious and politically guarded in his responses—reluctant to admit the problem was endemic. At one point, he even tried to assure parents that if their daughters enlisted in the Army, they would be safe. West also reminded the public that the accused are not assumed guilty until proven guilty, but drill instructors would be suspended for any infraction—as a matter of policy due to their role of overseeing trainees.

In one statement to the press, West admitted: "Sexual harassment is particularly repugnant when it involves abuse of authority" (Department of the Army, Public Affairs, 1996). However, he later indicated that abuses found at Aberdeen were an "aberration" (Schafer, 1997, p. A1). Many disagreed with West's conclusion that the multiple abuses and "rape ring" at Aberdeen were an aberration. Although it is uncertain as to which definition of aberration West was referring to (e.g., an abnormality, insanity, illusion, or an irregularity), his message that the abuses at Aberdeen were atypical contraindicated reports of similar problems at other U.S. military installations around the world. As noted in the article, "The Enemy Within...": "It's clear from recent events that despite the Tailhook scandal in 1991 . . . too many men in the military still consider such behavior [sexually victimizing women] their privilege" (Roos, 1996).

Despite the numerous reports of abuse, the hundreds of victims coming forward, and the media's attention to this issue, there was still reluctance on the part of Department of Defense officials and high-ranking military leaders to accept that sexual abuse was indeed a part of the military culture. To the point, the culture (and its members) acquiesced to the sexual victimization of military and civilian women. If the leadership would not openly acknowledge the problem and take a stand, then why should the troops be any different? Thus, the problem was more easily perpetuated and tolerated within the culture.

Admitting a problem exists is only the first step. Addressing the culture that tolerates the abuse is imperative to resolving this problem.

A Personal Account of Harassment in the Navy

Laura is a Navy veteran who was sexually harassed by her supervisor immediately after a training session on Navy rights and responsibilities. At the time, she was at a military base in Italy, still trying to come to terms with the impact of her supervisor's actions.

When the Tailhook abuses occurred some ten years prior, Laura was still in grade school. She may not have known the black marks left on the Navy from the Las Vegas conventions, but she knew very well that what her supervisor did to her was wrong. Her supervisor, however, was old enough to remember Tailhook, but he obviously did not learn the lesson. He was in a leadership position and should have known better.

Laura rebuffed the advances of her supervisor and later paid the price with a poor job evaluation and an early discharge. She did not report the incident while still on active duty. Yet, to this day, she wonders how things might be different if she had reported the abuse. Would she still have her career in the Navy? Would her abuser be out of the military?

In the following text, Laura describes how that one incident of abuse had such a lasting effect on her. She now sees herself as "on the outside looking in." (Note: Although Laura did identify herself, the military base where the abuse occurred is her husband's current duty station; names were deleted to protect her identity and his career.)

I was active 3 years back, as a corpsman in the Navy. My husband is also a corpsmen—that is how we met. I was stationed at . . . the Naval Hospital there and was working military sick call. I had a division officer who was a Navy nurse and he was in charge of us corpsman in sick call.

I went to a class on Navy Rights and Responsibilities one day during the week and we had gotten out early from this class. Instead of going back to work, I just went on home; I didn't bother reporting back to work like I should have. I just thought I could leave.

I was called back to work to report to my Division Officer (the Navy Nurse). I was called back to his office in sick call. It was around 4:30 p.m. and everyone was gone. No one was around. I thought at first that all he was going to do was yell at me and tell me not to go home without first being secured from him. I went into his office with him and he shut and locked the door and yelled at me. He started rambling on and on about stuff. I couldn't quite understand him. I was getting nervous because he was throwing things in the room off of his desk. That's when I decided to get the heck out of there. I unlocked the door and tried to leave. He pulled me back and then stood in front of it saying that if I left I was disobeying an officer. So I stayed till he was finished, then he started grabbing at me on my shirt and stuff. I just got scared and left——meaning I opened the door, got him out of the way and ran down the hall back to the barracks and never said anything to anyone about it.

The next day I was called into the Department Head's office with him and they gave me my evaluations, which I thought were terrible. I was so upset that I went down to the first floor in physical exams where my fiancé (now my husband) was at the time and I showed them to him. I never mentioned what had happened the previous day and never did till we were stationed in . . . Italy. I got out of the Navy early ...I think I would of never gotten out if I had told someone, but back in '93 I don't think they took sexual harassment like they do now . . .

Some years later I came to the conclusion that if I had slept with him or maybe let him do something which I didn't give him the chance to do, maybe my career wouldn't have went down the toilet.

I finally told my husband during a session with a psychologist here about what happened. I wish I would have done something about it, and not let it boil up inside and make me depressed about the events leading to getting out. I still wish I could of completed my tour, but being a female in the Navy is rough. I mean I am not saying this happens to everyone but ...I was naive to the situation. I was never one to put out. My husband was the first and I believe in marriage.

I don't mind flattery in the military but touching and making you get bad evals or not liked because of a turn down or trying to get away from the situation was not in my best interest. I do think that some woman do put out to these type of people for the sake of getting better evals or maybe better treatment.

I feel it's unfair but now all I can say is after having some counseling, I am still mad about it. That guy, the Navy Nurse, is in Spain still with a career and me being on the outside looking in. I wish I could of told the real reason I wanted out.

That is my story. It's not like having been raped but I was assaulted in some way, feeling uncomfortable and having the outcome being bad with the evals. I hope this helps.

I did get a letter in the mail from the military asking questions if I have ever had been assaulted etc....I never complied back at all. I let it go. I thought it was the best. Maybe it still is because who is gonna believe a E-3/HN over a LT, ya know?

My husband works in a clinic in processing recruits and sexual harassment still goes on with his subordinates and nothing gets done about it. I think it is sad.

3

THE TRUTH ABOUT SEXUAL HARASSMENT, RAPE, AND SEXUAL OFFENDERS

*We never talked about what was going on. It was an
unspoken truth most of us tried to deny.*

—— VICTIM OF SEXUAL ABUSE IN THE MILITARY

UNDERSTANDING SEXUAL HARASSMENT

*The best available estimates suggest that each year roughly a million working
women are pressured to have sex with their job supervisors.*

—— STEPHEN SCHULHOFTER (1998, P. 57)

*First you need to define harassment and assault. I had a couple of instances that I
remember right off hand that could have gone either way
[c. 1968 Lejeune and 1970 Pendleton] depending on how I reacted.*

—— FEMALE MARINE AND SEXUAL ASSAULT VICTIM

SEXUAL HARASSMENT IS not only a problem in the military, but in the public and private sectors as well (Bastian, Lancaster, and Reyst, 1996; Fitzgerald, 1993; U. S. Merit Systems

—— 43 ——

Protection Board, 1987; Gutek, 1985; Koss et al., 1994). Over three decades ago, Title VII of the Civil Rights Act of 1964 included gender as one of the areas of protection under federal law. However, it was not until 1977 that the Supreme Court ruled speech or conduct in itself may be considered a "hostile environment" and a violation of the Civil Rights Act. Prior to 1976, there was very little recognition of sexual harassment in the United States or abroad. It was not until the 1970s that the term was first recognized as the early definitions of sexual harassment were beginning to emerge in social contexts (MacKinnon, 1979).

Reminders of how far the nation has come in dealing with this issue were highlighted in a 1998 *Time* magazine article, "Just 25 years ago, sexual harassment was considered a radical-fringe by-product of feminist theory. Today it's embedded in multiple Supreme Court decisions. Since 1991, juries have returned well over 500 verdicts on sexual harassment. Such cases are still being filed at the rate of 15,500 a year—some 60 new cases every working day." (Cloud, 1998, p. 49).

Indeed, there have been many changes and challenges to society's understanding of what constitutes sexual harassment since it first emerged as a social issue in the 1970s. Even the Supreme Court continues to fine-tune its interpretations of this complex social problem.

Some researchers believe that there should be *legal* definitions of sexual harassment and *psychological* definitions (Fitzgerald, Swan, and Magley, 1997). They argue that the numerous, and sometimes conflicting, definitions of sexual harassment make it difficult for everyone. Researchers O'Donohue, Downs, and Yeater noted in their review of the literature on sexual harassment (1998) that most existing definitions seem to have only one point in common, "sexual harassment is improper behavior that has a sexual dimension" (p. 112).

The DoD definition adopted from the Equal Employment Opportunity Commission's federal definition (Eskenazi and Gallen, 1992) makes some other very important distinctions. In 1988, the secretary of defense directed all branches of the service to incorporate the following definition into their regulations. The DoD memorandum explicitly states:

Sexual harassment is a form of sex discrimination that involves unwelcome sexual advances, requests for sexual favors, and other verbal and physical conduct of a sexual nature when:

1. *submission to or rejection of such conduct is made either explicitly or implicitly a term or condition of a person's job, pay, or career, or*
2. *submission to or rejection of such conduct by a person is used as a basis for career employment decisions affecting that person, or*

3. *such conduct interferes with an individual's performance or creates an intimidating, hostile, or offensive environment.*

Any person in a supervisory or command position who uses or condones implicit or explicit sexual behavior to control, influence, or affect the career, pay, or job of a military member or civilian employee is engaging in sexual harassment.

Similarly, any military member or civilian employee who makes deliberate or repeated unwelcome verbal comments, gestures, or physical contact of a sexual nature is also engaging in sexual harassment. (General Accounting Office, 1995b)

Despite clear DoD policies restricting such behaviors and abuses, several indicators suggest that sexual harassment remains a big problem for women in the military. Nearly two-thirds (64 percent) of the women in the military in 1988 and over half (55 percent) in 1995 reported experiencing some type of sexual harassment or unwanted sexual behavior (Bastian et al., 1996).

Similar conclusions were reported a decade earlier in "An Examination of Sexual Harassment Complaints in the Air Force for FY 1987." Researcher Paula Popovich noted the following: "The Department of Defense (DoD) appointed a task force to study the current status of women in the military. It was the finding of this task force that sexual harassment remains a significant problem in all services." (Popovich, 1988, p. 1)

To their credit, the Air Force persisted in addressing this issue and in training their personnel. In 1993, after the Popovich study and the findings from the DoD task force were released, the Department of the Air Force developed a "Sexual Harassment Awareness Education Handout." The training handout demonstrates further attempts by the Air Force to speak out against sexual harassment and to communicate with their personnel about the issue.

Similarly, the other service branches have developed policies and issued memorandums of zero tolerance. For example, the Department of the Army's policy on sexual harassment is clearly documented: ". . . any military member or civilian employee who makes deliberate or repeated unwelcome verbal comments, gestures, or physical contact of a sexual nature is engaging in sexual harassment" (Department of the Army, 1998).

Nonetheless, policies and mandatory trainings are virtually worthless unless they are fully endorsed by leadership. The armed forces need their leaders to acknowledge and to confront the problem. Research has shown: "Units in which members report leadership takes a strong stand against sexual harassment, protects targets, and levies punitive sanctions against offenders have less sexual harassment as well as more satisfied and committed personnel, in general" (Fitzgerald et al., 1997, p. 22).

An example of strong leadership came from the commander of the 104th area support group in Hanau, Germany, Colonel Charles W. Glover. Glover zeroed in on the core of the problem in his commentary (1997) to the troops when he said, "It boils down to mutual respect." His observation about a general lack of respect among the troops has resonated with many service members. Glover stepped forward once again when he made these remarks in the aftermath of reported rapes by U.S. service members in Germany:

> *While military officials have strived to achieve an atmosphere of 'zero tolerance' in the military, the fact is, just like American society in general, the 'zero tolerance' message hasn't been completely assimilated into the hearts and minds of everyone* (Glover, 1997).

Colonel Glover's willingness to take a stand supporting zero tolerance of sexual harassment and abuse reflects the qualities of a military leader with integrity. He did not minimize the issue, but simply acknowledged there is a problem that needs to be dealt with accordingly.

In March 1997, USAREUR (United States Army Europe) News Service issued a stronger statement titled, "Combating Sexual Harassment." Although the author is unknown, the message is worthy of repeating as yet another example of strong leadership recognizing personal responsibility and respect.

Sexual harassment is not a "woman thing"; it is a "human thing." Everyone has a responsibility to promote a positive work environment. It is not just a right to confront or report misconduct, it is a responsibility. As more attention focuses on the issue of sexual harassment, it is clear that there is often confusion about this issue. People of different generations or from different backgrounds do not always agree on what behavior is appropriate. However, in order to combat sexual harassment, everyone must be able to recognize it for what it is at its core. ("Combating Sexual Harassment," p. 1)

Despite the strong public statements and the policy of "zero tolerance," the problem continues to be minimized by some members of the armed forces. Consider the following case that was reported in the *Navy Times* in December 1998. Government lawyers defended the Navy's actions in a lawsuit by a former summer intern who worked for the Navy and was subsequently the victim of sexual harassment. In the 1996 lawsuit, the victim sued the Navy, indicating that it was remiss in informing personnel about its zero-tolerance policy. The lawsuit was one of the first to challenge an employer's sexual harassment guidelines since the Supreme Court decision on the topic.

In the court case, the government lawyers supported the Navy by stating the service did sufficiently alert employees regarding the sexual harassment policy by placing a poster on a wall documenting the policy. However, the civilian panel of District Court judges was not convinced that putting up a solitary poster relieved the Navy of its responsibility to inform personnel about sexual harassment policies. The Navy's case did more to minimize the issue of sexual harassment than to help it. In the end, the Navy's message was very clear: this issue is not worthy of our time or resources beyond a poster (Adde, 1998).

Such a response from the Navy is surprising given the bad publicity resulting from the Tailhook scandal. Even though it was one of the first to attract public attention to the widespread problems of sexual abuse in the military, the problem did not start there. Those who were in the service long before the Tailhook exposé know that sexual harassment has been occurring at least as long as women have been associated with the military. The exposure of Tailhook just opened the door to the public about sexual harassment in the military.

Sexual violations of women and other gross misbehaviors occurred regularly over the years at the Navy's annual Tailhook conventions in Las Vegas (Department of Defense, 1992). One of the first women known to report the abuse was Lieutenant Paula Coughlin, an admiral's aide. Coughlin was just coming out of an elevator at the hotel when she was forced to go through a gauntlet of officers who were verbally, physically, and sexually abusive toward her as she tried to escape them.

One aviator summarized the climate of the convention and the culture of the group of male Navy aviators this way:

> It's like a frenzy. It's like when sharks frenzy to eat. Because it's a feast, and people forget about human frailty. And when you're frenzied like that, it's tenfold. . . . And they see everybody else doing it so they think it's all right (Zimmerman, 1995, p. 58).

After Paula Coughlin was sexually assaulted at the gauntlet during the convention, she told her superior, Admiral Jack Snyder, about the attack the next morning. He acknowledged the abusive behavior, but minimized it, indicating she should have known better than to be among the drunken aviators. Even though her superior dismissed the complaint, Coughlin did not stop there. She tried for five weeks to tell her boss about the abuse. He still did nothing, according to Coughlin. Admiral Snyder had exhibited classic power failure. Although he knew about the abuse early on, he did not take official action against it.

When the abuse was finally acknowledged, twenty-six victims came forward. Zimmerman notes in her book, *Tailspin: Women at War in the Wake of Tailhook,* the Navy investigation named only two suspects as a result of "270 field agents involved, 2,193 interviews, over 20,000 man-hours invested, and $400,000 spent. After the full weight of the government bureaucracy had leaned upon the events of September 5-7, 1991, on whose shoulders did the stern hand of blame land? Two dudes" (Zimmerman, 1995, p. 62). Zimmerman went on, "It was like those old Richard Pryor jokes which always started out, 'two dude, two dudes . . .' and you instantly knew that those two dudes were the lowest, unluckiest dudes in the world" (p. 62).

It was not until Coughlin went public with the allegations that the Navy really started to move. By this time, the public was also paying attention. Two days later, Secretary of the Navy H. Lawrence Garrett III resigned, taking "full responsibility." Within three days of Garrett's resignation, Acting Secretary of the Navy J. Daniel Howard broke the unspoken honor code of silence when he adamantly spoke out about Tailhook. He told an audience of 300 officers at the Pentagon that something did go wrong at Tailhook and something was wrong with the Navy as a whole for allowing it to happen. He was one of the few to speak out.

Howard was proactive and it was long overdue. He called for a five-point plan to revamp the Navy culture that supported the good ole' boy philosophy. He supported the following actions: an immediate, one-day stand-down; the development of a Standing Committee on Women in the Navy and Marine Corps; the introduction of sexual harassment as an offense under the Uniform Code of Military Justice; the demise of the Tailhook Association; and the call for all Navy and Marine pilots who had knowledge of the 1991 Tailhook abuses to come forward with "honesty and honor."

Although Howard was responding to the crisis in such a way that might have restored the public's faith in the Navy, his response and public admonishments of the Navy apparently were not well received in Washington nor at the Pentagon. His diligent efforts to break the code of silence with honor and honesty lasted only three weeks before he was very quickly removed from the post. Then-President George Bush replaced him with Sean O'Keefe.

Tailhook concluded, or so it seemed, in the same way the scandal started: dirty deeds with very little integrity among the group who started it all and among the leaders who turned their heads to it. In the final hours, two top Navy leaders fell and there were no judicial disciplines for any of the participants, although many did receive military intervention with letters in their files or limits on promotion.

In the end, after the inspector general's (IG) office stepped in, 117 officers were implicated for acts of sexual assault, sexual misconduct, and indecent exposure. Then the IG turned the blame on Navy leaders for allowing the abusive behavior to persist. Although many careers came to a halt, no one was ever successfully court-martialed for the sexual assaults.

The leaders who did not take action were acquiescing to the abuse as coconspirators. The power failure by Navy leadership was comparable to the violations against the women at the convention. Even the deputy inspector general (IG) of the Department of Defense was critical of how naval leadership responded or failed to respond to the reported harassment charges. The following statement was made by the deputy inspector general in the Report of the Investigation of Tail-hook '91, Part One (DoD, 1992):

The inadequacies in the investigations were due to the collaborative management failures and personal failures on the part of the Under Secretary, the Navy IG, the Navy JAG (Judge Advocate General), and the Commander of NIS (Navy Investigative System). In our view, the deficiencies in the investigations were the result of an attempt to limit the exposure of the Navy and senior Navy officials to criticism regarding Tailhook '91.

For the first time ever, sexual harassment allegations involving members of the U.S. armed forces resulted in widespread admonishment from the top down for failing to respond appropriately to the charges. It took the Department of Defense inspector general's office to do it, but the point was clear: In the end, the weakened leaders had no more integrity than the drunken participants who participated in the gauntlet.

Once again, power failure prevailed and the reputation of the Navy was scarred, but not for long. Less than eight years later, by the close of the decade, the Navy was once again considering resuming its connection to the Tailhook Association. Despite the debauchery of the investigation and the shame that fell upon the Navy after the scandal, it appears that all may be too quickly forgotten. The legacy of Tailhook (with no regard for the victims) could have been summarized by the words of columnist Linda Chavez (1996): "In its rush to protect its image, the Navy let guilty people go free and failed to protect the rights of those it accused." (p. 15A).

The incidents at the Tailhook convention and the subsequent leadership failures have probably been the most written about of all military abuse scandals to date. However, what happened with these Navy and Marine aviators in Las Vegas was just the tip of the iceberg. Continued reports of sexual assault and harassment publicized since that time have further validated the complexity and pervasiveness of this ongoing problem in the U.S. armed forces.

Despite the media's focus on this issue, countless incidents of harassment are not reported. One form of sexual harassment that is often kept out of the public's purview is linked to gender harassment and homophobia. Both are uncomfortable topics for the military but are nonetheless important to address when looking at sexual harassment.

SEXUAL HARASSMENT AND HOMOPHOBIA

The reality of women and homosexuals serving in the military has been so distressing to some service members and leaders that sexual harassment has actually been used as a tool to rid the ranks of women (gay or straight) and homosexual men (Cammermeyer and Fisher, 1994; Enloe, 1983; Francke, 1997; Morris, 1994; Shilts, 1993). Author Linda Bird Francke (1997) called it "sexual blackmail" (p. 177), whereas others have referred to this underground practice as "lesbian-baiting," "witch-hunts," or another by-product of the predominately white male military force. They cite that both groups (women and homosexuals) have faced the obstacles of not being wanted or fully accepted in the military by the dominant culture. Thus, they are targets of repeated harassment and victims of highly suspect military discharges from those who disagree with the changing social order within the ranks.

This type of sexual harassment has been going on for some time, but it undoubtedly escalated after 1981 for two reasons. First, increasing numbers of women enlisted in the all-volunteer force, thereby integrating more women into predominately male jobs. Second, the Department of Defense strengthened its policy against homosexuals, mandating that anyone who desires, intends to engage in, or does engage in any homosexual act would be discharged (GAO, 1992). This policy alone gave rise to allegations of homosexuality and subsequent discharges at a rate that was unprecedented (as noted later in this chapter). Consider the following remarks on this topic by author Celia Morris (1994):

Nowhere in American culture has sexual harassment been more blatant than in the armed services.... Men would hit on women . . . and as often as not, the women who turned them down were called "dykes." Since homosexuals were outlawed in the armed services, this accusation, if sustained, could mean that the women would be discharged. (p. 173)

Over the years, patterns of linking sexual harassment and homosexuality included women who declined the advances of male service members. In retaliation to the rejection, some men reported the women as lesbians. Many of these women were subsequently discharged or sexually harassed when they rebuffed the sexual advances of a male service member (Cammermeyer and Fisher, 1994). The implications of such allegations and sexual coercion are incredulous. As author Randy Shilts noted: "Some women have allowed themselves to be raped by male officers, afraid that the alternative would be a discharge of lesbianism" (Shilts, 1993, p. 5).

In addition, women considered or "rumored" to be lesbians were sometimes raped as a means of punishing them or in an effort to turn them "on" to men. How many times have we heard "all she needs is a good man" in reference to this misguided perception that lesbians will "return to heterosexuality" if only they had sex with a man?

Many service members, both men and women, have spoken out regarding the high incidence of sexual harassment associated with accusations of homosexuality (regardless of the validity of the rumors). Both heterosexual and homosexual women and men have been targets of sexual harassment, sexual assault, and improper disciplinary action or discharges due to allegations of homosexuality.

According to a General Accounting Office report (GAO, 1992), "women in all services were discharged for homosexuality at a rate consistently ranging from two to three times higher than their rate of representation." Moreover, in the past decade, women were separated [from the service] at three times the rate of men (Cammermeyer and Fisher, 1994, p. 293).

Administrative discharges due to homosexuality for women and men have been entwined with blatant and covert acts of sexual harassment for some time. Enloe reported that in 1979, U.S. Army records indicated: "Women were six times more likely than men to be discharged from the army on the grounds of homosexuality" (Enloe, 1983, p. 143). Nearly twenty years have passed, yet the problem persists. The Service Members Legal Defense Network and other advocacy groups have continued to express their concerns about this ongoing issue (Francke, 1997).

Unfortunately, the links between homophobia, the gender wars, and sexual harassment are rarely connected by military authorities, as noted in the 1999 death of PFC Winchell. The private was targeted as a homosexual and subsequently murdered by his fellow soldiers. A summary of Winchell's case is presented in Chapter 9. Sadly, Winchell's family and many others have discovered that allegations of homosexuality can be lethal in the U.S. military. The devastating implications of such allegations and harassment have been previously noted: "Short of driving women to suicide, charges of lesbianism proved to be the single most effective weapon in driving women out of the services" (Francke, 1997, p.180).

As long as members of the predominate military culture continue to harbor underlying sentiments against women and homosexuals in the armed forces, the sexual harassment, coercion, violence, and potentially lethal attacks will likely continue within the ranks.

RAPE

The only difference between a rape and a good time depends on whether the girl's parents were awake when she finally got home.

— ALFRED KINSEY (BROWNMILLER, 1975, P. 179)

The nation is yet to understand how prevalent rape is in our society.

— RON AARON (NOVEMBER, 1996)

Public misconceptions about rape are perpetuated in our society as well as within the military culture for years. It is hard to know what to believe. How common is rape in America? One in five, one in four, one in three? These questions are impossible to answer with certainty because many factors make it difficult to know exactly how prevalent rape is in our culture. Even the experts and federal reporting agencies seem to disagree.

For example, in a national study on the rate of sexual victimization, the Department of Justice found that a woman is raped every two minutes in the United States (BJS, 1994). However, the National Victim Center reported that there are 1.3 forcible rapes of adult women every minute in America (NVC, 1992). In addition, the Justice Department reported that there were 430,000 rapes/sexual assaults in one year (BJS, 1996), whereas the National Victim Center suggested there are almost double that number each year—over 683,000 (NVC, 1992).

There are many reasons for the differences. First, the reporting agencies and other independent surveys define differently what constitutes rape. Some studies may include other sexual offenses along with rape (such as attempted rape, sexual touching, etc.). Second, the studies use different sample groups and different methods for collecting their data. For example, the National Crime Victimization Survey (NCVS) generally does not include respondents who are not residing in a household residence. Therefore, women who are institutionalized, homeless, or incarcerated may not be included (Goodman et al., 1993). In addition, because the survey is conducted over the phone, other barriers may prohibit some people from being involved, such as language barriers, privacy concerns, and cultural issues. Koss also points to a list of concerns about the interview and the screening questions that "impede rapport, lack confidentiality of responses, and a survey context that activates stereotypes" (Koss, 1993, p. 1062). Furthermore, even the Department of Justice acknowledged differences in reporting data due to the redesign of their survey (BJS, 1997b). These are only a few of the criticisms about the national data collection efforts for rates of sexual assault.

Similar concerns relate to the military's servicewide studies on sexual harassment in 1988 and 1995 when 5 and 4 percent of the women, respectively, indicated they were victims of sexual assault or rape. First, the fact that rape was included as a form of sexual harassment could have minimized sexual assaults by categorizing them under sexual harassment. The cover page indicated that this survey was going to look at "how men and women work together" (Bastian et al., 1996, p. 43). Rape victims often have a difficult time defining what happened to them as rape (Warshaw, 1988) and therefore may be less likely to indicate as such on a survey that is looking at working relationships between men and women. Although confidentiality was assured in the study, military respondents may have been highly suspicious about reporting rape on a public survey with identifying data. This is a barrier for most research dealing with such sensitive topics.

It is also important to note that the majority of rape victims do not report their sexual assault to anyone, particularly to an official source, such as law enforcement (BJS, 1996; Greenfield, 1997; NVC, 1992). In fact, rape and sexual assaults are consistently the most under-reported of all violent crimes (BJS, 1996). Therefore, inhibitions regarding reporting, identifying oneself as a rape victim, and concerns about confidentiality can all contribute to the ambiguity about the prevalence of rape in society and in the military.

For those women who did identify themselves as victims of rape or sexual assault while on active duty, the rates of victimization vary from 4 percent in the DoD study (Bastian et. al, 1996) to 43 percent in a selected sample of women receiving treatment at a veterans' affairs program for stress disorders (Fontana and Rosencheck, 1998). Women who are in treatment, particularly for post-traumatic stress disorder, often have higher rates of reported sexual victimizations. The following represent several comparable studies of the female veteran population:

- Of 327 women treated at a VA facility for stress disorders, 63 percent reported physical sexual harassment and 43 percent reported rape or attempted rape (Fontana and Rosencheck, 1998).
- In a national telephone survey of 558 female vets who served since the Vietnam era, 30 percent experienced rape during their military service (Sadler et al., 2000).
- From a national sample of 3,632 women who received care at a VA outpatient facility, 23 percent reported "military-related sexual assaults" (Hankin et al., 1999).
- Of 429 women who received care at a veterans affairs medical center in Boston in the six months prior to the mailed survey, 30 percent reported "sexual abuse" ("pressure to do something sexual") and 28.7 percent reported rape ("forced into unwanted sexual intercourse") while on active duty (Coyle, Wolan, and Van Horn, 1996).

Of particular interest in the study by Coyle, Wolan, and Van Horn, the researchers also assessed victimization rates based on the year that the women entered active duty. Their study revealed:

- 45 percent of women who entered active duty before 1974 reported being a victim of sexual abuse or rape;

- 58 percent of women who entered the service from 1974 to 1981 reported being a victim of either rape or sexual abuse;
- 49 percent of women who entered active duty after 1981 reported being a victim of rape or sexual abuse while in the military.

Their findings also suggest that the incidence of sexual victimization has been steady through the years, with a slightly higher rate at the time that women were initially integrated into basic training and in other jobs with their male cohorts.

Attempts to understand why rape occurs in our culture have produced different theories and changing social attitudes over time. These differing perspectives (combined with the difficulty in knowing the magnitude of the problem) cause much debate and confusion. The current viewpoints on rape in our society may however help to further explain why sexual violence is such a problem for the military.

In "The Rape Culture," Dianne Herman points out a common theory on the links between socialized male aggression and sex: "Our society is a rape culture because it fosters and encourages rape by teaching males and females that it is natural and normal for sexual relations to involve aggressive behavior on the part of males" (Herman, 1984, p. 34).

In our culture, the connection between aggression and sex can lead to rape. However, that does not mean that all aggressive men will become rapists. Men in our society are often encouraged to be aggressive as well as sexually active. Consequently, some men do believe that masculinity and aggression go together. They may believe that sex should be rough, dominating, and aggressive. Unfortunately, these men do not always make the intuitive connection between aggression and sexual assault. Rape is, after all, the ultimate form of aggression against someone—short of homicide.

The link between aggression and rape in our culture is often missed. For example, consider the following portrayal in the media of a sex scene. A man and a woman are arguing until she slaps him in the face. Then he slaps her. Seconds later, they are in the throes of passion—kissing, groping, and tearing off each other's clothes. Then he forcefully pushes her up against the wall and bangs her against it repeatedly while they are still standing in the hallway. The scene depicts a common though mild example of how aggression and sex are played out in the media as normal, masculine, sexual behavior.

Most people would not think twice about that sex scene because we have become desensitized toward much of the violence in our lives. It is everywhere from the morning newspaper to the evening news to the entertainment we choose. These depictions of violence and sex serve only to perpetuate the confusion about sex in our culture. Even in subtle forms, they contribute to the problem of violence against women.

Although the majority of Americans might agree that rape is an act of violence, many still cannot grasp that rape is not an expression of sex. An example of rape as a means of control, degradation, and humiliation is found within the prison population. Men will frequently rape other men in prison to demonstrate their power, control, and ability to dominate. These prison rapists generally do not consider themselves homosexual despite the sexual violence toward someone of the same gender. Moreover, the rapists are engaging in the aggressive act to show domination and to subject the "weaker" men to the more passive, submissive, "female" role. Therefore, it is not uncommon to hear the male victims referred to as "women," thereby emasculating them into a less powerful role in the prison culture.

Similar examples of feminizing men are also found in the military. References are frequently made, especially in basic training, to a man's masculinity and ability to perform. Those who do not meet the standards are often referred to as a "wimp, pussy, or girl." Drill instructors have been known to call their troops "ladies" as a form of degradation and humiliation. The male persona is one that is strong, powerful, and in control, whereas the female stereotype is considered weaker, powerless, and physically unequal to their male counterparts. This particular aspect of military culture serves only to complicate the problems of integrating women as equal partners in the military. As Herman (1984) noted: "The U.S. military has generally eulogized the values of masculinity and emphasized aggressiveness; the Marines built their image on their ability to form "men" out of adolescent youths ...Cowardice in the face of the enemy is equated with femininity." (p. 26).

Some would argue that such attitudes about men and women contribute to the violent victimization of women in the military. Advocates who work with victims raped by military personnel agree that the public misconceptions make the situation worse. In the aftermath of reports about widespread sexual abuse of recruits at military training posts, the executive director of the Rape Crisis Center in San Antonio, Ron Aaron, wrote an editorial to *USA Today* to clarify some misconceptions. The Rape Crisis Center of San Antonio counsels numerous military rape victims due to their proximity to many Army and Air Force bases. Aaron wrote, "Rape is a crime of violence, but too many still believe it's a crime of sex. It's not. It is a violent crime of power, control, domination and anger" (Aaron, 1996).

However, sexual assault is not a normal part of all cultures. Anthropologist and sociologist Margaret Mead found cultures, such as the Arapesh, that do not understand the concept of rape. A reason sexual assault is not a part of their society is that men and women in that culture treat each other with respect and gentleness. Rape is neither instinctual nor natural. It is, in fact, a learned part of our culture (Herman, 1984).

SEXUAL OFFENDERS

I honestly believe he didn't think he did anything wrong. The worst part is, the Army vindicated him by not disciplining him. How many more women he will rape because they let him go? As far as I'm concerned, the Army is an accomplice to any other rapes he commits. ...I just know he will do it again.

— AN ARMY RAPE VICTIM WHO NEVER RECEIVED JUSTICE
AFTER REPORTING HER OFFENDER

We're in a country where allegations are not proven facts. Accused are not assumed guilty until proven guilty.

— TOGO WEST (1997B)

What distinguishes a person who rapes from someone who does not? The single characteristic most often linked to convicted rapists is a greater tendency to express rage and aggression through violence. Other personal attributes such as appearance, intelligence, sexual drive, and personality traits are usually comparable to the general population and are not atypical among sexual offenders.

Rapists may be good looking, intelligent, charismatic, well-respected men (or women) in our communities. A rapist may be an unkempt, unemployed middle-aged man who feels empty and alone. He or she may be the boy next door, an NFL football star, a popular college professor, the parent of a newborn baby, a retired grandfather with heart problems, a high school scholar from a well-to-do neighborhood, or the priest at your church. Likewise, a rapist can be a decorated U.S. service member who fought for his country in war but raped civilian women and children in the local villages. A rapist can also be a highly respected company commander who does an excellent job as a respected military leader by day and sexually abuses his daughter when he comes home at night. It is hard to imagine, but these are examples of sexual offenders living in our military and civilian communities.

Statistics show that most rapists are men. Beyond that, there are no distinguishing external characteristics to identify a rapist—other than the aggression and control expressed through the rape. Underneath their exterior disguise, there is likely an inferior shell just barely holding them together. There is no way to know if someone is a rapist by how they look or by what they say. In fact, the majority of these men and women will deny that they are sexual offenders—especially if they are caught.

Once convicted, rapists are more likely to talk about their crimes, but they will also hide behind excuses and justifications. Researchers Diane Scully and Joseph Marolla discovered what convicted rapists had to say about why they committed rape. Not surprisingly, their findings revealed that rapists denied that the rape occurred or they gave reasons to explain or to justify the rape. The researchers reported their findings in the 1984 *Journal of Social Problems.* The following highlights some of their discoveries.

Scully and Marolla summarized that the convicted rapists they interviewed were generally "deniers" or "admitters" regarding the sexual assault. Both groups attempted to justify or to make excuses for the rape. In justifying the rape, the deniers made the victim responsible. Five themes were common among their responses: (1) woman were the seductresses or aggressors; (2) women mean "yes" when they say "no"; (3) most women enjoy it; (4) nice girls do not get raped; and (5) the rapists minimally realized their guilt, if at all.

The deniers thought the victim got what she deserved. They also claimed their victims had wrongly accused them. Deniers attempted to discredit and blame the victim and to justify their actions. None of the deniers saw themselves as rapists.

In contrast, the admitters saw their behavior as morally wrong and beyond justification. According to the researchers, "The admitters tried to explain their crime in a way that allowed them to retain a semblance of moral integrity." Excuses also permitted them to view their behavior as idiosyncratic rather than typical and thus to believe they "were not 'really' rapists" (Scully and Marolla, 1984, p. 538). A minority of the admitters attempted to lessen the impact of their crime by claiming the victim enjoyed being raped. The three common themes among the admitters included: (1) alcohol or drug use; (2) emotional problems; and (3) a "nice guy image." The researchers concluded that justifications and excuses are buttressed by the cultural view of women as sexual commodities, dehumanized and devoid of autonomy and dignity. In this sense, the sexual objectification of women must be understood as an important factor contributing to an environment that trivializes, neutralizes, or perhaps facilitates rape. (Scully and Marolla, 1984, p. 542)

This sentiment is a point of contention for the military because the armed forces are sometimes accused of inhibiting gender equality and not promoting the value of women. Some speculate that the devaluation of females is the root cause of the military's problems of widespread violence against women. However, like any other social dilemma, many factors ultimately contribute to the problem of sexual assault in the military.

The criminal justice response can make the difference in the victims' attitudes about reporting the crime and ultimately prosecuting the sexual offender. For military rape victims, however, there are many obstacles to the successful court-martial (prosecution) of a fellow service member. The initial barriers are the military laws on sexual offenses. Although the Uniform Code of Military Justice (UCMJ) is very direct about what constitutes rape ("sexual intercourse by force and without consent"), there is a need to update military law as it pertains to this and other sexual offenses.

To understand the potential loopholes and obstacles for military sexual assault victims, consider what the UCMJ states regarding rape. First, notice that "carnal knowledge" is not specifically defined in the UCMJ. Most state laws distinguish sexual conduct (penetration of any kind by any part of the body or an object) from sexual contact (sexual touching with no penetration). The UCMJ does not define other types of sexual assault, except perhaps under "sodomy."

Moreover, until the recent changes to this section of the UCMJ in 1992 and 1996, the military still granted "marital privilege." It was not illegal to force your wife to have sexual intercourse. Also, prior to the updates in the 1990s, men were not considered as rape victims under military law (UCMJ, 2001). Although the changes significantly improved article 120 (Rape and Carnal Knowledge) of the UCMJ, the law, as it is currently written, is lacking in comparison to civilian statutes on sexual offenses. The following summarizes the offense of rape according to the Uniform Code of Military Justice in the U.S. Code.

UCMJ: 920. ART. 120. Rape and Carnal Knowledge:

(a). *Any person subject to this chapter who commits an act of sexual intercourse by force and without consent, is guilty of rape . . .*

(b). *Any person subject to this chapter who, under circumstances not amounting to rape, commits an act of sexual intercourse with a person who has not attained the age of sixteen years, is guilty of carnal knowledge . . .*

(c). *Penetration, however slight, is sufficient to complete . . . these offenses.*

The UCMJ is only one of the potential problems facing sexual assault victims seeking justice in a military court-martial. Rape victims in the military face every barrier that rape victims in the civilian community encounter, plus more. The repercussions and implications of reporting rape are incomprehensible, according to victims who have spoken out about their experiences. These women and men faced far too many barriers when they tried to report sexual assault or sexual harassment. Their comments speak for themselves. The following is one veteran's remarks about military justice:

> All I wanted was some justice for what he did to me, but all I got was another
> nightmare and another trauma to try to forget. If I had known I was going to be
> the one on trial, I would have never told anyone about the rape.... At least the rape
> was over in a few minutes. What happened afterward went on for months. I felt
> violated again and again and again.
>
> —— A SERVICE MEMBER WHO SOUGHT JUSTICE THROUGH COURT-MARTIAL

This veteran's experience is not atypical. Her comments are consistent with what many other service members have said about military justice when it comes to rape and sexual harassment. The following summarizes what one Air Force captain encountered in her long search for justice.

A PERSONAL ACCOUNT OF HARASSMENT IN THE AIR FORCE

Dorothy reported repeated sexual harassment by two fellow officers while on active duty at an Air Force base in Ohio. After she left the service, Dorothy filed a civil lawsuit in an effort to hold the government and her two harassers accountable for the abuse she encountered. The following is brief synopsis of Dorothy's case, reprinted with her permission from STAMP (Survivors Taking Action Against Abuse by Military Personnel).

Dorothy was a captain in the Air Force whose job was to enforce the military's own codes of conduct and justice toward its personnel. Her superior officers were the highest authorities on any sort of personnel complaints on the base. Of all people, they should have known better, but they were the ones who subjected Dorothy to nearly a full year of harassment, assault, and intimidation. "He was watching Tailhook on TV while he was busy molesting me," Dorothy recounted. Finally, a subordinate said, "Captain, you're a great commander and there are many who see what is happening to you, but if you do not leave this job those two men will kill you".

Despite her own flashbacks, depression, and post-traumatic stress, Dorothy has spent the past several years on a burning quest for justice—not just for herself but for other men, women, and children. After resigning her commission as an officer of the United States Air Force, Dorothy sought justice outside the military system by filing a civil lawsuit against her two harassers and then the government. However, this was no ordinary case. Of particular note was that her lawsuit questioned four longstanding statutes pertaining to military personnel.

First, a service member cannot receive a judgment against the military or the federal government for wrongful action. In other words, no one in the military can successfully sue the U.S. government for incidents that occur relative to service. This law (referred to as the Feres Doctrine) has been on the books for several decades now. According to the Feres Doctrine: "the Government is not liable under the Federal Tort Claims Act for injuries to servicemen where the injuries arise out of or are in the course of activity incident to service" (U.S. Supreme Court, 1950). Therefore, persons who are victims of rape, sexual harassment, and subsequent secondary trauma by military personnel have no legal recourse against the military. This was the first obstacle that Dorothy faced in making her perpetrators be held accountable for their abusive behavior.

Second, there is a legal question as to whether these men were acting in the capacity of their employment when the alleged abuse occurred. If the court determined these men were indeed acting in an official capacity on behalf of the U.S. Air Force, then the case becomes one against the U.S. Air Force (as the employer) and not against the individual servicemen. Hence, any such lawsuit with the U.S. government as the defendant would be thrown out due to the Feres Doctrine, effectively dismissing the government's liability. Dorothy's case was seeking to demonstrate that the men were acting on their own and not on behalf of the U.S. Air Force in the capacity of their employment.

Dorothy's lawsuit went through several levels of judicial review including the U.S. District Court and, finally, the United States Supreme Court on two occasions, in 1998 and in 2000. In the spring of 2001, Dorothy and her attorney Jo Anne Jocha-Ervin finally received some feedback on the case from the United States Supreme Court. On March 26, the following statement was issued on behalf of Dorothy's case: "The U.S. Supreme Court today denied military personnel the right to bring sexual harassment charges against the government or individual harassers when it let stand lower court rulings that sexual harassment was within the "scope of employment." (John Marshall Law School, 2001).

One of the other attorneys representing the case, Mark Wojcik, a professor at The John Marshall Law School, added these comments: "Federal law should not shield acts of sexual harassment in the military, especially when the military is trying to rid itself of sexual harassment. "(John Marshall Law School, 2001)

Despite the Supreme Court's decision on the case, Dorothy's struggle for justice persists. She has been a vocal advocate for victims of violence by military personnel and a leader of the organization STAMP. Dorothy is trying to make a difference so that other victims will not encounter these obstacles when seeking justice after rape, abuse, or sexual harassment. Her efforts may one day pave the way for other victims of abuse by military personnel who travel the same road seeking justice.

PART II

HOW THE MILITARY RESPONDS TO SEXUAL HARASSMENT AND RAPE

4

ASSESSING THE PROBLEM

Pentagon officials can tell you exactly how many tanks and Humvees the new C-17
"Globemaster III" can carry. They can tell you the height, weight and speed of
every airplane and ship . . . But ask them how many military women have been
attacked by servicemen and their statistical wizardry vanishes.

— PARDUE AND MONIZ (1996)

NUMBER OF CASES REPORTED

Bureaucracies hope things go away.

— LAWRENCE KORB (1996)

I didn't think anyone would believe me. So I didn't report it.

—FEMALE SERVICE MEMBER RAPED BY A SUPERIOR OFFICER

FROM THE PENTAGON to the president, no one really knows for sure the extent of sexual abuse in the military in part because so few victims come forward. It is nearly impossible to get an accurate glimpse of the magnitude of the problem. The Department of Veterans Affairs estimated that some 60,000 to 200,000 women veterans were victims of sexual assault while on active duty (Pardue and Moniz, 1996). In fact, even these numbers are only a best guess as to how many women and men are sexually assaulted in the service.

There are many reasons why the magnitude of this problem remains elusive to the DoD and to the nation. Underlying these reasons is the reality that rape and domestic violence are by far two of the most underreported crimes in our society today. Moreover, for women and men in the military, additional barriers add to the dilemma of reporting these offenses or seeking help. The following are some of the top concerns cited by military victims who participated in the research study I conducted from 1996 to 2000:

1. *Women and men who are sexually assaulted, harassed, or battered often feel afraid to, concerned about, or too intimidated to report the abuse or the abuser.* Far too many women and men never report the abuse because they fear further repercussions from the perpetrator, their commander or their unit. Furthermore, some victims do not trust their commander's ability to deal with the issue appropriately or in their best interest. Some of the service members are highly skeptical that their report would be handled in a serious, sensitive, or confidential manner. This concern alone was enough to deter numerous victims from reporting their sexual assault or harassment.

2. *Of those who do make an unofficial complaint to the commander or a criminal report to the military police, many of these allegations are "handled internally" and never recorded as a crime.* These types of cases are often cleared without charges, or the commanders address the complaint at their own discretion (never officially documenting the offense). Some women indicated they never reported the abuse because they honestly did not think it would do any good. Many victims believed that reporting the abuse would hurt them or their careers more than it would have helped them.

3. *When complaints are reported to the appropriate authorities and considered as offenses under the Uniform Code of Military Justice, there are often great inconsistencies in how these crimes are handled.* These disparities are frequently seen in the areas of offender sentencing and victim treatment. The military's track record in these two areas are reason enough for some crime victims not to report their complaints. Many of the participants in the research study echoed their distrust of the military justice system when it comes to sentencing offenders or upholding victims' rights in the process. They wondered if it would happen in their cases as well. Ultimately, some crime victims make a deliberate decision not to report the abuse because they would rather not participate in a process that they suspect will cause more harm or possibly do no good at all.

The reasons for not reporting sexual abuse and harassment (as cited by servicewomen and -men in this study) are consistent with other research findings on the topic. Moreover, the same rationale is restated in official documents used by the armed forces. For example, in the Sexual Harassment Awareness Education Handout the Air Force lists the following:

> *Reasons why sexual harassment is not reported: (1) unaware of Air Force policy and behaviors; (2) confusion; (3) socialization; and (4) fear of not being believed, being labeled as a trouble maker, humiliation, ostracism, retribution, damaging one's career, guilt, shame, embarrassment, and distrust in the "system* (Department of the Air Force, 1993, p. 10).

Ironically, when calls to the Air Force harassment hotline dropped by a significant 75 percent in just one year, military leaders credited the decline in reports as being "on the right track." It is possible but unrealistically hopeful to attribute this dramatic decrease in reported calls to fewer actual incidents of abuse in that year. However, the reasons that victims do not report sexual harassment and rape should not be forgotten, especially in light of such a dramatic and atypical decrease. The toll-free Air Force hotline consistently received over 400 calls every year the line was in operation until 1998, when only 110 calls were reported. According to the *Air Force Times,* there were 413 calls in 1997, 419 calls in 1996, and 478 calls in 1995, when the hotline was first established (Glenn, 1999). The decrease in reports in 1998 does not necessarily signify a decrease in abuse. However, it does pose some speculation as to what happened in 1998 in the Air Force.

The National Organization for Women (NOW) also voiced reservations about equating the decrease in hotline calls to a decrease in abuse. NOW official Karen Johnson, who is a retired Air Force lieutenant colonel and works on military issues for the women's rights organization, was quoted on the topic in the *Air Force Times* article, "Harassment Hotline Calls Are Dropping":

> *I think there is a lot of cynicism whether reporting sexual harassment does anything other than make more trouble for the individual. It doesn't seem that the complaints that come to me havesloweddown....Ido think visibility is a big issue. That has some impact with the number of calls.* (Glenn, 1999, p. 7)

Given these concerns, and the fact that sexual assault and sexual harassment are so rarely reported in the general population, it is understandable that the DoD does not really know how many people have been victims of violence at the hands of military personnel. For the same reasons, the number of calls to the harassment hotlines does not reflect the extent of abuse that is actually occurring.

The problem goes well beyond the victims' reservations about reporting, however. Another major reason for the low numbers is a systemic issue related to the command's ultimate authority in many of these cases. For example, commanders are given the discretion to resolve complaints internally. Command authority highly affects the disposition of a complaint (for example, if the case is officially reported as a sexual assault, referred for criminal investigation, or dropped with no further action). As a result, many reports of sexual assault or harassment do not go beyond the commander's office.

The matter is further muddied if the commander is a part of the problem or is known to be sympathetic toward sexual offenders. In some units, the commander may be the worst offender of all with regard to abusive behavior. If a victim tries to report an offense to an unsympathetic commander, he or she may end up withdrawing the complaint, requesting a transfer, or accepting a discharge to avoid further repercussions for making a sexual abuse allegation in a unit where the command condones the behavior.

In cases such as these, the reports will never be documented officially and no one will be the wiser. The complaint is not entered into the base statistics, and another abuser remains free to victimize again. Many incidents of sexual abuse perpetrated by military personnel will remain a "secret" between the victim, the offender, and often the commander.

Efforts to better understand the problem are sometimes met with serious resistance. Two reporters from *The State* tried in 1996 to obtain statistics from the Army, Navy, and Air Force of the number of rapes reported each year by military women (Pardue and Moniz, 1996). After three months of inquiry, the reporters were told the following: "The Air Force representative was unable to locate such information. The Air Force Automated Military Justice Analysis and Management System (AMJAMS) does not track any information by the victim" (Pardue and Moniz, p. A8).

The Navy did provide statistics to the reporters from 1991 to 1995. An average of 200 cases a year are reported and investigated by Naval Criminal Investigation Services (which includes marine complaints). These figures do not include sexual assaults that were reported to commanders but were never referred for an investigation.

The Army also provided statistics on the number of rape investigations (again, not the number of actual rape reports). These two sets of data (investigated rapes and reported rapes) can be quite different based on a number of factors addressed earlier. The Army indicated that an average of 460 rapes were investigated in the years 1990 to 1994. In addition, the Army was able to retrieve statistics from its crime database from

1972 to 1987. The number of reported rapes were an average of 111 a year for that time period.

Investigative reporters discovered that it was much more difficult to get information from individual military bases. In South Carolina, for example, they were able to obtain statistics only from two of the five installations in the state. In 1995, these two bases reported a total of only seven rapes. Their conclusion is that it is nearly impossible to make any comparisons between the service branches, given the inconsistent reporting and the different percentages of women within each service.

A similar warning was expressed to me when I inquired with the Pentagon for updated statistics for each service branch. Initially, my experience of trying to obtain data on rape in the armed forces was also somewhat of a formidable task. I started my inquiry with the Office of Public Affairs for each of the services. After several weeks passed (with no access to this public data) my search lead me to a very helpful representative from the Pentagon, specifically, the Office of the Undersecretary of Defense (Personnel and Readiness).

The person I consulted with was a Lieutenant Colonel and Deputy Director of Legal Policy. He spoke at length about the difficulties of obtaining accurate data from each of the services due to differing reporting standards, especially prior to 1996.

The data sent to me from the Pentagon was a six-year statistical analysis (1991-1996) based on data provided by the Department of the Army, the Air Force, and the Navy (the Marine Corps reports are included in the Navy data). As it turned out, this six-year summary was readily available since it was compiled in response to a specific request by Senator Snowe's office.

Of particular note, prior to Senator Snowe's request for the summary, this information was not routinely maintained according to my source at the Pentagon. No wonder it was so difficult to find out how many rapes were reported if statistics were not compiled. However, it is hard to believe that the DoD did not keep accurate, annual records of violent crimes perpetrated by military personnel, especially given the increased attention to this problem. Furthermore, considering the results of the DoD's own repeated studies in 1987 and 1995 indicating that over half of military women reported some type of sexual victimization or harassment, one would wonder why such data were not being closely tracked and monitored.

The six-year report appears to be the most recent compilation of this information that is readily available to the public. The data offer a wide range of varying information from each of the service branches including: reported rapes, cases tried, number convicted, percent reported versus tried, percent tried versus convicted, percent resulting in punitive discharges, and the average sentence.

CONVICTION RATES AND SENTENCING

The Office of the Undersecretary of Defense also provided a three-year summary of reported rape cases ending in conviction. There are several interesting points to make about this information. The most striking point of contention is the significant increase in reported cases for the Navy/Marines and a sharp decrease in the average sentencing for that same timeframe. The reported cases jumped from 292 in 1995 to 412 in 1996; whereas for the same years, the average sentence decreased dramatically from 20.86 years in 1995 to 8.9 years in 1996. Ironically, the average sentence was even lower in 1994 at 3.95 years for a rape conviction. Conviction rates for this period were between 6 and 15 per cent (varying by Service)

A significantly reduced sentencing of less than four years for a felony rape conviction preceded the Tailhook scandal. Did the negative national attention of Tailhook cause a backlash of sympathy among Navy peers resulting in reduced sentencing terms by the court-martial juries? We may never know the answer as to why sentencing rates dropped so low following Tailhook. However, in the civilian sector, sentencing for rape in many states is up to twenty-five years. A rape sentence could have resulted in the death penalty under the Uniform Code of Military Justice not long ago. The recent changes in the Navy's sentencing patterns for rapists raise many questions about their commitment to zero tolerance. What does a four-year sentence for a rape conviction say to rape victims or to sexual offenders?

Another interesting point comes from the Air Force's data and the percentage of cases court-martialed. From 1992 on, the Air Force consistently has tried a greater percentage of reported cases than any of the other services. One might conclude from these data that the Air Force is more likely to press charges and court-martial a case than the Army, Navy, or Marines. These data reflect highly on the commitment of the Air Force in responding to these types of cases. The Navy/Marines had the worst conviction rates for 1991 to 1996, with less than a third of the cases that were actually tried resulting in a conviction.

Of particular note, an important statistic that the summary did not include was the percentage of reported rape cases that resulted in a conviction. Fortunately, this information was easy enough to calculate using the number of reported cases and the number of convicted cases. Although this calculation does not account for any cases with multiple reports, it does offer an overview of how many reported cases actually resulted in convictions.

The information speaks volumes about how the military is responding to rape reports. The most striking is the Navy's record for rape convictions in 1992. During that year, sexual harassment awareness in the Navy was probably at an all-time high given the national media attention to the issue following Tailhook. However, Navy sentencing rates dropped significantly and conviction rates were also surprisingly low.

Another startling fact is that over 95 percent of the accused rapists in the Navy and Marines in 1992 were found *not guilty* of the alleged rapes and were not convicted of the crimes. Only 4.5 percent of the reported rapes in the Navy and the Marine Corps ended in a conviction. Moreover, of the 422 reported cases that year, 81 percent of the alleged rapists (341) never faced a court-martial.

Almost every reported rapist in the Navy or the Marine Corps in 1992 was found not guilty. They were free to go on with their lives (or to stay in the service) if they so desired.

How can so few cases warrant a conviction? More to the point, how can so many alleged sexual offenders go free? For comparison, consider the FBI's findings that 46.9 percent of rapes reported to civilian law enforcement agencies resulted in an arrest (FBI, 2000). The rates are vastly different for the military. The following data come from the respective service branches JAG or NCIS offices on rape cases reported, investigated, and courts-martialed in 1996 or 1997. Note that the data is not collected or reported in the same manner by each branch, so comparisons between the services will be skewed. Rape reports do not include other sexual offenses unless noted.

Air Force: 30 percent of rape cases were charged and 15 percent of reported rape were convicted. 110 rape reports: 34 sent to court-martial; 7 convicted (Air Force Judge Advocate, 1997).

Navy: 17 percent of sexual assault cases received disciplinary action and 3 percent of sexual assault reports were convicted, but 100 percent of courts-martial were convicted. 238 sexual assaults: 41 cases forwarded for disciplinary action, of which 7 were sent for court-martial; all 7 were convicted (Annual Sexual Assault Data, 1997).

Marine Corps: 57 percent of sexual assaults were investigated and 42 percent of cases were closed with no investigation; convictions were not reported. 141 sexual assaults were reported: 81 were investigated; 60 dropped at victims' request; no data on disposition or conviction rates (United States Marine Corps, 1997).

Army: 76 percent of sexual assault reports by female soldiers were substantiated and 56 percent of those arraigned were found guilty. 274 sexual assault reports by female soldier victims: 210 substantiated, 64 unsubstantiated or insufficient evidence; 78 arraigned, of which 44 were found guilty) (Office of the Judge Advocate General, 1997).

Although these numbers are surprising, the underlying problem of sexual assault is not found in the statistics. The core of the problem is what the institution *does* with this information. This point was summarized very effectively by an unlikely source:

> You've got to remember, if you acknowledge a problem,
> you've got to do something about it.

> — LAWRENCE KORB ASSISTANT SECRETARY OF DEFENSE FOR MANPOWER,
> PRESIDENT REAGAN'S ADMINISTRATION
> (KNIGHT-RIDDER/TRIBUNE NEWS SERVICE, 1996A).

Indeed, if the DoD does not believe a problem exists, then it has no problem to resolve. Six years' worth of data has accumulated, yet the average military conviction rate is still less than 10 percent of reported cases. Such figures do not reflect highly on the zero-tolerance policy. In fact, these data nullify the policy. In reality, 90 percent of reported military rapists are never court-martialed. In practice or in theory, this is not zero tolerance, no matter what kind of a spin is put on it. Many military victims would agree.

CASE EXAMPLES AND OUTCOMES

> The sexual objectification of women must be understood as an important factor
> contributing to an environment that trivializes, neutralizes,
> and, perhaps, facilitates rape.

> — SCULLY AND MAROLLA (1984, P. 542)

You can learn a great deal about an organization and its commitment to an issue by looking at the manner in which it responds to internal stressors and crises. The U.S. armed forces had it share of crises and negative publicity in 1996 and 1997 following the reported widespread sexual abuse of trainees at military installations and the court-martial of the sergeant major of the Army. The following section looks more closely at how each of the service branches actually responded to some of the individual cases of rape and sexual harassment during that timeframe. In addition to single case examples from each of the services, the

Army's organizational responses are offered as examples since the Army was under public scrutiny during those two years.

- In 1996, the Air Force disclosed that eight male instructors at Lackland Air Force Base faced disciplinary action due to sexual harassment. All were reassigned from their teaching positions. In addition, the guilty received varying degrees of disciplinary action ranging from one year in jail to a loss of rank ("Air Force Discloses," 1996).
- Similarly, the Army faced similar problems with training instructors from Aberdeen Proving Ground and Fort Leonard Wood. In one case, the Army disciplined Drill Sergeant Loren Taylor with five months' confinement and a bad conduct discharge for having sex with three female recruits and improper conduct with two others. Taylor faced a fourteen-year prison sentence. Instead, he was offered a discharge from the military.
- The Navy also investigated sexual abuse in its ranks when three sailors at the U.S. Naval Submarine Base were accused of gang raping a sixteen-year-old female at a Navy lodge. All three of the men were charged with sexual assault pending further investigation ("Three Sailors," 1996).
- One of the highest-ranking officers at a Florida Air Force base was facing a court-martial for sexual misconduct. Colonel David C. Raunhecker was accused of fondling and kissing a female captain against her will. He was also charged with "having an unprofessional relationship with his secretary, maltreatment of a subordinate, indecent assault, and conduct unbecoming an officer" ("Air Force Colonel Faces," 1997). He was removed from his command.
- Naval Rear Admiral R. M. Mitchell Jr. was relieved of his duties as commander of the Navy Supply Systems Command in Pennsylvania due to allegations of conduct unbecoming an officer stemming from sexual harassment allegations made by a member of his command.
- A U.S. sailor was arrested near Tokyo for allegedly beating and raping his twenty-one-year-old Japanese girlfriend. The woman was reportedly hospitalized with a broken collarbone and numerous abrasions and bruises on her body. The Japanese police had full jurisdiction over the case due to new legal arrangements that resulted from the 1995 rape by three U.S. service members of an Okinawan schoolgirl.
- In Darmstadt, Germany, a military court convicted U.S. Army Sergeant Paul Fuller of rape against a subordinate, indecent assault, three counts of forcible sodomy, three counts of cruelty and maltreatment, fraternization, kidnapping,

and a reduced charge of unlawful entry. An earlier rape charge against Fuller was reduced to indecent assault and another rape charge was dismissed due to technicalities. Throughout the ordeal, Fuller denied all charges, saying the sex was consensual. Despite the severity of the convictions, a military jury sentenced him to only five years in military prison. The jury could have given Fuller life in prison for the rape charge alone ("Military Court Convicts," 1997).

- The same military court in Darmstadt cleared another soldier, Sergeant Julius Davis, of six counts of rape. The jury did not fully "ignore" the charges, however, but opted to sentence Davis to only two years in military prison for multiple counts of indecent assault. Davis was ordered to be released from military service with a bad conduct discharge before returning to society ("Military Court Convicts," 1997).

- In Wisconsin, Air Force recruiter Technical Sergeant Robert Dean Hayden admitted that he made sexual advances and had sex with recruits in his office and at a party. His sentence was seven months in prison and a bad conduct discharge from the military.

- Amid the incoming reports of abuse by military personnel, the commander of Aberdeen Proving Ground, Major General John Longhouser, announced his early retirement when it was discovered that he had an affair with a civilian woman during a separation from his wife. Secretary of Defense William Cohen concluded that it could be a "compromising position" for the major general since it was up to him as the commander of Aberdeen Proving Ground to decide if others would face military trials for sex-related offenses. To avoid the conflict of interest, the general opted to retire early, at the lower rank of one-star general. Although there is no comparison between a sexual affair and sexual assault, the general did the right thing to take himself out of the leadership role of judging others for sexual misconduct at Aberdeen ("Army Men Retire," 1997).

The scandal at Aberdeen Proving Ground in 1996 was one of the most widely publicized military sexual abuse cases of the decade. It was also the impetus for the Army's sexual abuse hotline, resulting in hundreds of reports of sexual misconduct by enlisted men and officers in the Army. At the conclusion of the Aberdeen case, numerous charges were made against twelve soldiers (drill instructors and commanders) who were involved in the "sex abuse ring" as some referred to it. The outcomes of the cases varied greatly from no conviction to twenty-five years in prison. Some of the top cases and their dispositions are noted here as further clarification of the Army's response to rape and sexual harassment (Dishneau, 1997a, b, c).

A plea bargain was earned for the highest-ranking service member involved in the sex abuse scandal. Captain Derrick Robertson pled guilty to conduct unbecoming an officer, adultery, and consensual sodomy in exchange for dropping the charges of rape and forcible sodomy. He was given a four-month prison term and a discharge.

Staff Sergeant Vernell Robinson Jr. was sentenced to six months in prison, a dishonorable discharge, demotion to private, and forfeiture of pay and benefits for his role for participating in an ongoing contest in which he and other drill sergeants preyed on incoming trainees as potential sexual partners. The drill sergeants then told each other about their sexual conquests in their competition. Robinson's lighter sentence followed his emotional plea, acknowledgment of guilt, and a statement of remorse to the court and to the jury. He had asked to stay in the Army, describing it as his life for twelve years. Robinson, who reportedly referred to himself as a "gangster" (meaning that he was untouchable) was facing up to fifty-five and a half years in prison.

The most serious case at Aberdeen involved Staff Sergeant Delmar Simpson who was charged with more than fifty counts of sexual misconduct. He was found guilty of eighteen of nineteen rape counts and other charges of sexual misconduct. Simpson intimidated the trainees into having sex with him, either by implied threats of harm due to his size and rank, or explicit threats, including a threat to kill one woman if she told anyone. He admitted he had consensual sex with sixteen trainees in 1995 and 1996 during his tenure as a drill instructor and pled guilty to sixteen charges of a violation of a lawful order. He was reportedly involved in the sexual conquest game that another drill sergeant described in testimony in exchange for immunity. Simpson was sentenced to twenty-five years in prison— an average of 1.4 years for each rape count. He also received a demotion to private, loss of pay and benefits, and a dishonorable discharge. He could have received life in prison (Gilmore, 1997; Dishneau, 1997a).

Allegations of sexual misconduct were everywhere. It was impossible not to notice the multitude of news reports. By mid 1997, the problem had surfaced repeatedly, affecting numerous careers and ultimately leaving a negative mark on the armed forces. The secretary of defense had no choice but to acknowledge the problem, particularly at training facilities. In response, the Federal Advisory Committee on Gender-Integrated Training and Related Issues was established.

It was no coincidence that in June 1997, Cohen directed a committee to assess the training policies of the Army, Navy, Air Force, and Marine Corps. The Federal Advisory Committee on Gender-Integrated Training and Related Issues chaired by former senator Nancy Kassebaum Baker and included a team of eleven civilians, retired officers, and a retired senior noncommissioned officer. The committee issued a report of their findings on December 16, 1997, with thirty recommendations.

In addition, the Defense Advisory Committee on Women in the Services (DACOWITS) assessed the problem of gender issues in the military. DACOWITS has been in force since 1951 to advise secretaries of defense on the roles of women in the armed forces. DACOWITS, which consists of thirty to forty civilians, visits Army, Air Force, Navy, Marine Corps, and Coast Guard installations all over the world to gain an understanding of the issues facing women in the service. Its focus in 1997 was on training issues per the request of the secretary of defense. DACOWITS provided a summary report to Cohen, recommending continued appraisals of training installations as well as some specific suggestions on women and their role in the military.

In December 1997, the Federal Advisory Committee on Gender-Integrated Training and Related Issues submitted their final report to the secretary of defense. The report included numerous recommendations, including: increase the number of female recruiters; increase the number of female trainers; clarify trainers' authority; and improve values training in all initial entry training programs (Federal Advisory Committee, 1997). Some of the more specific recommendations based on their interviews with active-duty service members are as follows:

- Enforce policies to stop degrading references to gender.
- Screen cadre more effectively.
- Train cadre to curtail abuses of power.
- Ensure strict punishments for false accusations pertaining to harassment and abuse. (Federal Advisory Committee, 1997)

Another committee actively involved in visiting and interviewing the troops in 1997 was the secretary of the army's senior review panel on sexual harassment. The panel consisted of seven members—two retired general officers recalled to active duty, two active-duty general officers, a senior noncommissioned officer, and two DoD civilians. (As noted previously, former sergeant major of the army Gene McKinney was initially named to the panel until it was discovered that he was also the subject of several sexual harassment allegations.)

The senior review panel concluded its study and sent a report to the secretary of the Army in July 1997. When the report was finally released to the public in September 1997, it included forty recommendations including what some called a scathing critique of the military's response to the problem of sexual harassment. Some of the varied recommendations of the Army's panel on how to deal with sexual harassment included:

- Revamp the equal opportunity sexual harassment training program.
- Add another week to basic training to incorporate lessons on values and ethics.

- Place more chaplains at Army bases to advise soldiers.
- Modify and toughen the standards for drill sergeant selection.
- Add additional lieutenants to advanced training units to increase commanders' availability with their troops.

The panel was direct and bold with their appraisal of the extent and status of sexual harassment within the Army. They reviewed leadership and questioned the Army's commitment to resolving the problem (Schafer, 1997). The panel may have given the Army more than it bargained for when the secretary of the Army originally appointed the team to assess the problem following the scandals at Army training facilities.

It is now clear why West wanted more time before making this information available to the public. The facts about the abuses within the military were now out in the open for all to judge. The senior review panel's exposure of the problem would not be easily squelched.

In addition to the formal reports from military panels, victims' advocacy groups were speaking out in record numbers. Several advocacy organizations formed alliances of military victims of abuse. Groups such as STAMP, the Miles Foundation, and the East Asia-

U.S. Network Against Militarism have members from around the world advocating on behalf of victims of abuse by military personnel. These groups have a great deal in common. They want the truth to be known. More important, they want to see the uncontrolled violence by military personnel stopped. Their efforts have uncovered further evidence of abuse and a side of the story that is not always told in the military assessments of the problem.

A PERSONAL ACCOUNT OF ABUSE BY A COMMAND SERGEANT MAJOR

Tina is a retired senior Army noncommissioned officer stationed in Korea where she reportedly experienced recurrent sexual harassment from a command sergeant major (CSM) throughout most of her tour of duty. In her repeated efforts to report the abuse, she experienced a lack of response and inaction from her command as well as many others (including the Army's sexual harassment hotline). Ironically, Tina had evidence from the perpetrator to corroborate her reports of abuse, but no formal action was ever taken against the CSM.*

Sexual harassment is still alive and well within the secret walls of the military. I am angry with the results of my complaint that was filed while in Korea. I received nasty letters from a now retired CSM. I reported this...and the command did not speak to me until (one month later). At that time, I provided them with a vulgar, demeaning letter that this pervert had written me. Only then did they swing into action. . . . *They should have spoken to me within 72 hours, but... other "mission essential" tasks were more important.*

I went above and beyond to express my disinterest with this behavior. Initially, the CSM approached the situation as if it was genuine leadership concern. I have no problem with being friends, but when vibes and statements of deeper concern were noticed, I did in fact tell him that I was not interested. He took his position . . . and began to retaliate. He would punish me for not pursuing a relationship. [He] utilized his position to make changes to the Senior NCO living quarters, changes that put me in close proximity to his room. He then took advantage of the situation by constantly knocking on my door. He even obtained my room phone number and called constantly. He would let the phone ring twenty or thirty times. I told him to stop calling my room, but to no avail. I stopped answering my phone and told any other callers to utilize the code I established. [He] would turn off the hallway lights, and when I questioned this practice he would site "energy conservation." With the lights off in the hall, he could tell when I was inside my room without having to come down the hall. I was forced to rearrange my room, and put tape to the bottom of my door.

This is a family man, and if companionship is what he was searching for, for the sake of his career and mine, he should have taken no for no, and moved on. I can respect a person for honesty, but this was far beyond a simple compliment. I have a right to refuse a situation that I am not interested in. He acted as if I was an entitlement that came with the tour.

I honestly know that this situation would have played out different if the command itself was not corrupt. There have been numerous sexual harassment complaints against soldiers and even rape.... [The] CSM said that if my case was allowed to go forward, he would "expose a lot of stuff." When I told [him] that I would go public with his behavior, he informed me that he was not concerned because if he went down, a lot of other people would go down with him, and "they aren't below me." The corruption was rampant within the command, to include officers and warrant officers. This was the ace in the hole that CSM held.

After I told of my harassment, I was an instant outcast from the upper command. I even voiced my concerns to a major.... She acted as if she was concerned, but in the end, she didn't do a damn thing! She has her own skeletons in the closet! These are some of the things CSM threatened to expose!

While in Korea, I went to the IG, CID, Chaplain, 8th Army, to no prevail. It was one big cover up that stretches beyond the realm of the [battalion].

I attempted to get this wrong corrected once I returned home [from Korea]. I went to the Pentagon in January and spoke directly to SMA [sergeant major of the army]. He was well briefed with this case because I had taken him a copy of the investigation about a week prior to my visit. He actually sat there and told me that there was "nothing" he could do. I didn't expect a miracle, for I am aware that his position is just that of visibility. As the senior enlisted NCO in the Army, I did expect an honest reply.

He spoke to me as if I was insane or mentally ill. He even wanted me to go see a shrink, that same day, in the Pentagon. He also wanted me to go to the Department of the Army Inspector General [IG]. His assistant actually made a phone call to the office of the IG as I sat there. What alarmed me was that I had called the IG as soon as I returned home [from Korea] and they stated that there was nothing they could do. Now that his office was calling, they wanted to assist me. I even called the sexual harassment hotline, and they informed me that I needed to report to my next duty station to file a complaint.

Tina went on to talk about the ways in which the CSM harassed her and another service member.

He [the CSM] was forced to give a sexual harassment class because of his behavior in the club. He was seen dancing [sexually grinding] with a PFC [private first class]. This soldier who filed the complaint against him was treated bad from that point on.

[He] was negligent [abusive] in many other aspects—asking me for a pair of "worn underwear, since I refused to have sex with [him]."

Is this the type of leadership you want leading you into war? Would you be willing to risk your life for a leadership who just may turn their back when the rounds start flying? We deserve better. I should not have to worry about being harassed by the soldiers that I will be in the foxhole with. Now I ask— who are the real enemies?

I am so enraged because of the trauma that I experienced. I did not get closure while in Korea. I was forced to bring this luggage home, luggage that I did not carry over there. I opted for the early retirement. . .

*Tina provided her name as well as that of the unit and the CSM, The names and identities were deleted or changed to protect all parties involved since there were no convictions.

5

INSIDE THE MILITARY: REFLECTIONS FROM WOMEN WHO HAVE BEEN THERE

*I was sexually harassed and raped while in the Army a few years back. Even though
there were other women whom this sick man defiled, he was given the choice to
resign his commission at the article 32 hearing. I have tried many times to
have my voice heard. Nobody has listened. I certainly don't hate the Army,
but I believe that this problem is more widespread than anyone is willing
to talk about. ...I have also had contact in the past with other
military women who have had similar experiences.*

— ACTIVE-DUTY ARMY SERVICE MEMBER STATIONED IN GERMANY

WOMEN IN THE MILITARY

I loved the military. It was my life.

— DISABLED ARMY VETERAN RAPED ON ACTIVE DUTY BY HER FIRST SERGEANT

MOST WOMEN WHO have been in the military are more than willing to talk about their
experiences in the armed forces. No one knows better about what really happens
behind the scenes than those who have been there—in the formations and in the trenches.

As a Behavioral Sciences Specialist working at two prominent Army hospitals (5th General Hospital in Stuttgart, Germany, and William Beaumont Army Medical Center in El Paso, Texas), I listened to many women speak about their difficulties in the military. From these service members, I gained a better understanding of the very different experiences of women and men in the military.

The struggles of being a woman in the military can be daunting at times. It is, after all, a man's world in the service. The overwhelming ratio of males to females can make the situation uncomfortable for many women and for some men. Sexual tension can take its toll as the potential for sexual innuendo, flirtations, harassment, or abuse becomes a reality.

There are many other reasons why it is difficult for women in the military. Women struggle for acceptance and gender equality in the face of discrimination and harassment on the job. According to DoD's own studies, sexual harassment or rape are a reality for more than half of the women who join the military (Bastian et al., 1996). Despite the high incidence of sexual victimization, many women think very highly of their time in the service. They proudly call themselves veterans. This sentiment was often repeated by military women in my research—regardless of whether they experienced sexual abuse in the service. For many, serving in the military was a valuable and memorable experience at a very important time in their lives.

SERVING WITH PRIDE AND PATRIOTISM

> *They [women marines] don't have a nickname, and they don't need one. They get their basic training in a marine atmosphere, at a marine post. They inherit the traditions of the Marines. They are marines.*

— LIEUTENANT GENERAL THOMAS HOLCOMB

Being in the military is a challenging and honorable experience. All service members encounter physical and psychological demands that test their strength, their will, and their commitment. Yet women must also face the many gender barriers that are inherent in this profession. Despite these obstacles, or maybe because of them, women are often proud of their time in the armed forces. Serving in the U.S. military is indeed an accomplishment that is distinctly different from any other profession.

For some, military service is a family tradition—an obligation and an honor to carry on the line of patriotism from one generation to the next. It was not surprising that so many women expressed a sense of duty—a patriotic response that was both heartfelt and honorable.

I was proud to serve my country. It's something my dad and my brother did and I wanted to help out too. I wanted to carry on the family tradition, so I enlisted.

Other women referred to their service in the military as a learning and growth experience that occurred at an impressionable time in their lives. They spoke about their jobs, the training, the travel, the relationships, and much more.

I was praised often, perfect military evaluations . . . overall, it was a real fun, educational time of my life. . . .

Departing with Mixed Feelings

Not all women spoke favorably of their time on active duty. Some had mixed feelings. For example, there were women who experienced sexual harassment, but were able to separate the abuse from their other experiences in the military. In those situations in which the harassment was not as traumatic nor as abusive, many women were able to "take it in stride" as one woman stated. For some, sexual harassment was just another part of the job.

My NCOIC [noncommissioned officer in charge] harassed me on a daily basis with rude, crude comments. . . Through all of this I still loved my experience with the military and would do it again.

My experience has been good for the most part, but like many women, I have had my share of bad experiences being a woman in the military.

Not surprisingly, many women who were abused or raped by fellow service members had more negative reactions often conflicting with their pride in serving.

You better believe when I hear a young woman . . . talk about going into the military, I encourage her to do otherwise. I hope and pray that I do more to persuade her than any recruiter could do. The ironic part of it all: I still feel pride having been in the U.S. Army.

I joined the Navy hoping for a career and all I got was a lot of harassment and torture...I was raped... Rumors got around that I was selling myself and that I was easy....I hope the military can learn to deal with women in a better manner.

Some women spoke about their respect for the military, despite the adversity or the abuse they endured. Their respect often stemmed from their pride in serving, their patriotism, or their beliefs in a just world. These women who still revered the military wanted to speak about their concerns, but they meant no harm nor malice toward the armed forces. One woman summarized eloquently what many others tried to say.

I wish to bring no discredit to the military, only to strengthen our standards so that all of us who serve now and in the future can do so . . . honorably.

PERSPECTIVES ON SEXUAL HARASSMENT AND RAPE IN THE MILITARY

Rape is obviously not an exclusive preserve of military men, but it may be that there are aspects of the military institution and ideology which greatly increase the pressure to "perform" sexually. . . .

—— CYNTHIA ENLOE (1983, P. 35)

Countless lives were forever changed due to sexual harassment and rape. The following section highlights some of the different perspectives, experiences, and opinions on these issues.

SPEAKING OUT: PERSONAL EXPERIENCES WITH ABUSE

They are going to find out that it is happening a lot more than it is reported.

—— A VICTIM OF RAPE BY A FELLOW MARINE

Many active-duty service members and veterans from around the world recounted their ordeals and perspectives of sexual harassment or assault in this study. Although there were some common elements in their stories, each victim's account was unique, as each told a very personal story of trauma or crisis. These messages came from both women and men in each of the service branches. The victims' identities and the names of the sexual offenders were deleted to ensure no further trauma to the victim nor the accused. Their personal messages describe the extent and nature of sexual victimization in the U.S. military.

I was raped while on active duty by another active-duty member in 1991. Upon reporting the incident, the Coast Guard launched an investigation (very thorough). An article 32 hearing followed, resulting in a court-martial, and eventually a guilty verdict for my attacker. My kudos to the CGI team that investigated and interviewed. They left no stone unturned, and I felt their manner with me was respectful without patronizing. The government prosecutor was extremely helpful to me; he personally saw to it my command put me in for counseling. He never lied to me about what to expect in court. My biggest issues would probably be the sentence—this man was found guilty of rape, adultery, and indecent sexual assault, and was "awarded" only six months time (in addition to reduction to E-1, loss of pay, and an other than honorable discharge). I feel that the military still has some strides to make in recognizing the seriousness of this crime, even in a "date" setting. I hold no negative feelings toward the military in general though I am firmly convinced there are perpetrators everywhere in life, in every organization, and the military does not hold a license on sexual offenders. Most of the men I served with were respectful, honorable men, many of whom stood by me during the court-martial.

Both my story and the one that I witnessed were horrible. The one I witnessed is still happening. The victim was physically beaten and hospitalized; the perpetrator (after being dishonorably discharged) still harasses this soldier.

During technical training I had one of the worst experiences of my life...I passed out almost immediately ...woke up...and [he] was about one second away from having sex with my passed out body. ...He came over and raped me. I didn't know what to do....He told me to go back upstairs, and not to tell anyone what happened ...I laid on my bed in shock. ...I spent the next twelve hours having to tell senior drill sergeant, CID, and the emergency room what happened. I had decided that it was my responsibility as the leader of the female cadets to make sure none of them were put in the same situation.

I received letters from an E-8 during work hours propositioning me for a sexual relationship. Based on the outcome of [another] incident at [name deleted] I figured I had no recourse against this high-ranking enlisted member...I was not his only victim. Another woman reported him and nothing was done.

[I was] kidnapped by a civilian who had no official authorization to be on the active-duty base. ...I was driven to a remote location, beaten into a coma, and raped. I was a virgin; this was my introduction to sex.

I was in the Army '80-'83. I trained along side of men starting at Fort McClellan, Alabama. I am a survivor of kidnapping [by an MP {military policeman}] including rape, rape by a classmate, and other sexual harassment. I didn't want to date because I was trying to focus on my AIT [Advanced Individual Training] school. I was treated as a whore—like it was my duty to have sex or give sexual favors because I was a female in the army. If you were not branded a whore, you were branded a dyke. I couldn't win either way.

I came into the Army and did my training at [name deleted] when they first opened it to women. It was a bad situation, but it was worse in... That's where my real trauma started [at my next duty station].

Perspectives about sexual harassment and sexual assault in the military are as diverse as the service members themselves. Some spoke favorably about the military's response to these issues and others were angry and critical. The following section offers some additional perspectives and responses that women encountered.

TIMES HAVE CHANGED

In the '70s the advice would have been to keep your mouth shut and deal with it.
In the '80s, the advice was that it was not tolerated and to blow the whistle—you
owed it to yourself and [to] all women not to allow this type of behavior. Now it's
the nineties, and we seem to have come full circle.

—A FEMALE VETERAN SPEAKING ABOUT SEXUAL HARASSMENT IN THE MILITARY

The military and the public have witnessed numerous shifts in society's attitudes toward sexual harassment and rape. Ever since women have been members of the armed forces, there have been changes in attitudes regarding these issues. Not that long ago, the term *sexual harassment* was first conceived and much of the terminology and the legal definitions did not appear until two to three decades ago. In fact, acknowledging a rape was taboo during most of the 1940s and 1950s. We did not speak about it in public and there were no educational programs on rape awareness in the general population or in the military.

Service members reflected on the changing times and the changing military climate that went hand in hand with emerging social issues. Their comments help us to understand that the military's response to sexual harassment and rape was often consistent with that of the current social climate of an era. In other words, what was once acceptable behavior in the 1950s (for a superior to call his female employee "honey") later became a part of the zero-tolerance policies of the 1990s. The following comments discuss the changing times and the changing social responses to rape and sexual harassment.

I was in MCWR during WWII. We knew we were in so the men could go fight. We wanted them to come back safely, and didn't pay any attention to jibes or jokes—it was part of the boy/girl thing! At the present time, it is harder since it's a career and women should have equal opportunities.

I think basic [training] should be separated for the sexes. Can one really expect guys to be out learning to wield bayonets during the day, then expect them to be polite and open doors for gals, etc., in the evening? The guys jibe each other, and I expect the gals still do the same. Why must one be on the offensive when it's between the sexes?

When I served in the Army from 1981 to 1984, I actually felt like a piece of meat! It was so bad that a woman soldier could not walk anywhere by herself, even in daylight. Alot [of the harassers] were commissioned officers.

In the 1970s, a woman hardly spoke of the rampant sexual abuse and harassment that was everywhere. In the 1980s, everyone was worried about their career, not the victim. I didn't care anymore. Three years later when I was reactivated for Desert Storm, nothing had changed.

IT IS BETTER THAN IT USED TO BE

> *They [the services] are generally responding better (as of my 1994 retirement) compared to 1962 . . . [when] women who reported rape got a psych eval and an "offer" of an honorable discharge. So, anything better than that is an improvement.*

—RETIRED VETERAN, YEARS OF SERVICE 1962-1994

Perspective in terms of time, social trends, and legal changes are critical to understanding this issue. The nature and extent of the issues are different in the military now because the social context of sexual harassment and rape has changed over time. For example, it is now illegal to rape your wife in most states. It is also now unconstitutional to discriminate against someone in the workplace due to gender or sexual orientation. Furthermore, it is illegal to sexually harass an employee in the work setting.

The times have changed, the laws have changed, and, in some cases, the military has changed too. However, some of the civilian laws do not apply to the military since it has its own rules of governing. Some of the military laws in the Uniform Code of Military Justice (UCMJ) have not adapted to the social shifts. Despite the dated UCMJ, however, many firmly believe the military is getting better with its response to sexual harassment and sexual assault. The following is what some active-duty service members and veterans had to say about the improvements within the military on these issues.

I think things are getting better. It was a real problem back when women first started getting assigned to ships. The old salty chiefs didn't know how to handle a complaint.

The system works better now than it did, and it still has a lot of flaws. A big one is that as long as there is a prohibition against gays in the military, there will be harassment for women who will be told to put out or be labeled gay.

I have experienced my share of harassment. ...I will not defend the Army's EO policy except to say that it is 100 percent better than when I first joined and becoming better. . . .

It is getting better but it is still more protective than effective. As long as the ban on gays exists, women will be subjected to lesbian baiting as a form of harassment.

THE MILITARY STILL HAS A WAY TO GO

I was in the military long enough to see many changes for the better.
They are not there yet. Eyes need to be opened.

—— A FEMALE VETERAN ON THE MILITARY'S
RESPONSE TO SEXUAL HARASSMENT AND RAPE

Many of the women and men had mixed perceptions about the military's response to abuse. Some service members indicated they have seen some changes over time, but there still needs to be more attention and better response to the issues, particularly to the victims. The following are selections of some of the ambivalent perspectives.

The active-duty community is now responding—at least making the effort. The reserve and guard community are still in the old days of cover-up and closed ranks! Many guard officers/personnel are "old service" and do not have any concept about a modern atmosphere of equal, fair, and impartial treatment of gender and/or race. The guard is still very much a good ole' boys club!

The military says it is very hard on sexual harassment, and I think for the most part it is. But when it comes to rape and sexual assault that isn't "clear-cut"...My offender admitted that I said "NO" to him, but the lawyers still didn't think I could win my case. That is bad.

I think that the military is still going "onward through the fog." Don't get me wrong. I like being in the Army. I just think it needs lots of improvement.

It definitely needs improvement. . . . Attitudes haven't changed much in thirty years.

I think that the military has the message and is usually doing a good job. There will always be a need for alertness to violations.

ONGOING DILEMMAS

There has to be some kind of happy medium. You cannot take offense at
every joke told or language used. Females have some of the worst
vocabulary there is. Double standards don't work.

—— FEMALE VETERAN ON SEXUAL HARASSMENT

It's impossible to go through the military without being sexually harassed or raped.

—— ANOTHER FEMALE VETERAN SHARES HER OPINION ABOUT THE MILITARY

There are many extenuating factors that can adversely impact women who report sexual abuse of any kind. There are mixed opinions as to what constitutes sexual harassment or how to intervene with allegations. This can lead to negative feelings about women who report sexual assault or harassment. Some reactions are accusatory, blaming, or charging that the victim is making a false allegation. In some situations, a climate of disbelief may discredit the person who comes forward with an allegation of abuse. Some military members also claim that underlying racial discrimination is at the core of many rape complaints and investigations. These factors all contribute to a climate on no tolerance, not of the abuse but of the allegations of such abuse. In short, the accuser becomes the target for negative feedback.

This indifference and intolerance toward the victim creates a divisiveness and alienation among women. A female who reports abuse may find herself at odds with some of the other women in her unit. The sentiment may be that she could have or should have done more to prevent it, or maybe she did not want to prevent it. These criticisms serve only to further complicate the problems of sexual abuse in the military.

THE EXTENT OF THE PROBLEM

If you're a woman in the military, sexual harassment is a part of the job.

—— FEMALE ARMY VETERAN ON SEXUAL HARASSMENT AND ACTIVE DUTY SERVICE

How big is this problem for women in the military? There are indeed some conflicting opinions depending on who is asked. Clearly, not everyone believes that sexual harassment or abuse is a pervasive problem in the military. In fact, some of the women and men perceive it to be no worse than in the civilian sector. As two service members summarized:

Sexual harassment in the military exists just as it does outside of the military.
The military is a mirror reflection of society.

Comments such as these express a commonly held belief "what happens in society happens in the military as well." The presumption is that sexual harassment and rape in the armed forces are not any more or less of a problem just because they occur in the context of the military environment. As one senior officer noted, "There are good apples and bad apples wherever you go." Many service members agreed with this perspective, although more males than by females repeated this sentiment.

Another important point, made by a Vietnam-era veteran, questioned how sexual harassment is interpreted: *What one person interprets as offensive, another may consider a joke or a flirtation.*

Most service members and veterans in this study seemed to provide a balanced perspective based on their personal experiences. One woman, an active-duty sergeant in the USMC, provided the following insight based on her years in service.

I often think I am one of the few women in the military today who has never been sexually harassed. As a woman marine attached to a ground combat unit, I suppose I should be at high risk for harassment, but it has never been a problem. After eight years, I think there are fewer and fewer women in the military in my shoes. Harassment hasn't been an issue [for me], but discrimination has.

Women who were sexually exploited or raped were much less likely to share this sergeant's perspective. In fact, these women were more likely to view sexual victimization as pervasive and more problematic than those service members who never experienced any difficulties. Two service members said it this way:

The sexual harassment stuff was so real . . . the harassment was always there.
I've become "hardened" to it [the sexual harassment].

Another service member spoke more directly about the abusive overtones and the harassing climate in her predominately-male unit when she stated, *The fear was prevalent. I wasn't the only one [in the unit] that was afraid.*

The fear experienced by this service member and other women in her unit lend credibility to the magnitude of this problem. Moreover, the message "it's not just me" was repeated over and again. Sexual abuse by military personnel is not an isolated issue.

In addition, there were concerns about leadership involvement. Senior-ranking military officials have been identified and implicated as perpetrators of sexual victimization against their troops. Many women in this study included the names and ranks of their sexual offenders in their comments. It was evident from their responses that sexual abuse by military personnel has crossed all lines including rank, age, gender, race, and sexual orientation. This is not just a problem at the training sites or in the field units. Sexual harassment and rape occurs at all installations and in any occupation. One veteran summarized the extent of the problem as follows:

Don't tell me the problem exists only out in the field units. It starts at the top.

Concerns about the leadership's failure to respond appropriately and failure to recognize the problem were recurrent, underlying themes in this research. Moreover, some leaders complicated, exacerbated, and often perpetuated the sexual abuse and harassment.

MIXED REACTIONS TOWARD VICTIMS OF ABUSE

Some of the females are not the innocent victims the media has portrayed them to be.

— DRILL SGT. MARIANA SHORTER SPEAKING ABOUT THE ALLEGATIONS AGAINST DRILL SERGEANTS AT ABERDEEN TRAINING GROUND (WEST, 1996, P. 48)

It is not uncommon for victims of abuse to encounter negative remarks from others in the aftermath of sexual harassment or sexual assault. Some service members and civilians question the allegations and the victim's motives, suggesting that the issues were exaggerated. These misconceptions minimize the problem by blaming the victim or identifying with the perpetrator. This common and often blatant sentiment was evident in the following remark directed toward a service woman when she tried to report her abuse to a military authority:

I was told that "boys will be boys" and that they [the guys] were under a lot of stress.

AVOIDING FURTHER ABUSE

Some military women emphasized their own ability to deter the advances of harassment made by their male counterparts. Their comments were well intentioned, but their implicit message is that abuse can be avoided if you try hard enough. These women were able to handle the situations on their own without further incidence. Although this may be the preferred initial intervention, in some cases saying a forceful "No" may not be sufficient to intimidate or to stop an abuser. The following are examples of how some military women were able to curtail further abuse.

I have never had any more problems with him or any other men. I stood my ground and had an attitude of "don't bother me."

I am no hero, but I am a large woman [5' 8"—the size of some men] and in the first instance, an icy voice and hard eye-to-eye contact was enough to stop it. In the second instance, I actually sucker punched him and sat him down. I really don't know what I would have done had he gotten up, but he was so surprised that he didn't.

I never bothered to report the instances as they were over and neither person ever tried it again, though I worked for the second one for about four years after the occurrence.

Some service members in this study offered advice to women on how to best deal with sexual harassment situations. Some of these comments promoted more tolerance among women and men, and others had a lack of tolerance for women who give mixed messages and later complain or "whine" about the issue. Overall, the advice was generally directed toward women on what they should do to prevent sexual harassment.

Some understanding, tolerance, not being so quick to take offense, on both sides, might help us all get along better. I certainly don't approve of anyone pushing someone else around.

Women have to work harder and develop "thick skin" to earn respect...the military is no place for whiners. Military women have earned the respect of their peers by consistently exceeding performance standards (i.e., working longer hours)... some women make the rest of us look bad by whining and manipulating male supervisors . . .

Women... must be able to perceive the difference between whining and legitimate complaints. I've seen valid complaints, whining, and misuse of the complaint system.

BLAMING THE VICTIM

Some of the respondents questioned the legitimacy of sexual harassment or rape complaints and subsequently faulted the women who alleged sexual abuse. This is a familiar message in our culture— blaming the female victim for her part in the incident. How many times have we heard that she must have done something to provoke it or to lead him on, or maybe she gave him the wrong impression, and so on? As in any other crime, this crime occurs because the perpetrator makes it happen, not because of something the victim did or did not do. Blaming the victim does not make the criminal any less culpable.

I know women who have gotten themselves into a bad situation that they couldn't control when they shouldn't have been there in the first place.

Some . . . women manipulate the system.

Blaming the victim further confounds the real issue of the abusive behavior. It distracts from the perpetrators' actions and focuses on the victim, opening the door for skepticism and doubt. It places the responsibility of stopping the unwanted behavior on the victim, not the offender. Consider some of the following responses to service members who tried to report their sexual harassment or sexual abuse to a military authority.

I was asked what I was wearing that night, if I had sex before, who I was with...

I "did not act enough like a victim" according to the perpetrator's battalion commander.

My chief petty officer said "Don't wear your uniform shirts so snug across your breasts."

In most cases a female [that] makes an allegation is sent for a psychiatric evaluation.... Then they try to find a way to make her the cause of the crime since she is reporting [it].

There were an alarming number of women who indicated they were referred for a psychiatric evaluation (not counseling) or for a psychiatric discharge when they reported rape or sexual harassment to their commander. These tactics used by some military leaders are another example of denying or minimizing the real problem.

Far too many women also reported they were discharged (against their own desires) shortly after reporting sexual harassment or assault. These discharges often fell under categories of incompatibility with military service or, in some cases, the women were labeled with personality disorders. This issue was so significant that it raised concerns among some veterans affairs sexual-trauma counselors who noticed higher than usual numbers of females discharged due to a "personality disorder." In addition, the counselors noticed an unusually high frequency of incompatibility diagnoses on the discharge papers of women who reported rape or other sexual abuse. Overall, these women (some with several years in service) were reportedly functioning quite well prior to the abuse. It is difficult to know for certain if the abuse trauma had such an impact that it necessitated the discharge or, if given the appropriate treatment and intervention, their military careers could have been saved.

Far too many women are doubted, questioned, and blamed for their role in the abuse. The implications of such skepticism are substantial. Victims of rape and sexual harassment are often the target of accusations and disbelief from co-workers, commanders, and criminal investigators. The following comments, which were made by military leaders in the wake of the sexual abuse of trainees at Aberdeen Proving Ground, are evidence of such:

> *These privates (basic trainees) are not that innocent. Some have come here having slept with 20 or 30 men.* (Castaneda, 1996, p. 4A)
>
> *We had to tell some of the young ladies that you cannot walk around with no bra, or in skimpy shorts.* (West, 1996, p. 48)

These military leaders focused on blaming the women even though the real issue was that Army leaders abused their powers to sexually coerce trainees. This narrow point of view is a common response in many sexual assault or misconduct cases. The focus quickly shifts from the abuse and the abuser to the behaviors or integrity of the person who was victimized.

A blatant example of this shift of focus was repeatedly used in the high profile sexual misconduct case against Gene McKinney. During the investigation and the court-martial, there were numerous allegations against the six women who reported the alleged abuses. Both McKinney and his lawyers made negative comments about the accusers, suggesting that some of the women were out for revenge and all six of them were lying (Gearan,

1998a). There were also attacks on the women's personal and professional integrity (Jones, 1998b).

The verdict in this case indicates the military jury did not fully believe any of the six women or their charges. These cases often come down to her word against his. Many victim advocates point to this as yet another example of how victims of sexual harassment or rape are doubted and often not believed, especially in the armed forces.

FALSE ALLEGATIONS OR ACCUSATIONS OF FALSE ALLEGATIONS

False allegations... reflect impulsive and desperate efforts to cope with personal and social stress situations. (Kanin, 1994, p. 81)

Is she telling the truth or lying? Maybe she is just trying to advance her career. She just wants revenge because he turned her down.

Comments such as these are often thrown out as a diversion or a defense in the aftermath of sexual-assault allegations. The reality is that the truth of what actually happened may never really be told.

There is very little agreement when it comes to the issue of false allegations in rape cases. In fact, even the experts are unsure about how often this situation actually occurs. Estimates of false rape reports generally range from 2 percent (Haws, 1997) to 60 percent (Farrell, 1993). The following summarizes a wide range of findings from studies on selected populations.

In 1994, researcher Eugene Kanin indicated that 41 percent (forty-five rape reports) were "officially false." The study was done at a small, metropolitan, Midwestern police department over a nine-year period. In one year alone, Kanin found seven out of ten reports were false. He emphasized that a rape report was considered false only if the victim indicated as such and recanted the allegations. Moreover, in Kanin's study, a "serious offer" to polygraph both the accused and the accusers was made in all of the rape investigations (1994, p. 82). Kanin did not fully address the potential impact of introducing the polygraph on true victims of sexual assault. *In other words, would rape victims be more likely to recant and drop charges rather than proceed with what they might interpret to be a hostile or traumatizing investigation?* He does acknowledge that "secondary victimization" is often used to question the validity of the findings and that his study should not be used to generalize the findings to other populations (Kanin, 1994; Haws, 1997).

In an Air Force study involving the review of 556 alleged rape cases, researcher Charles P. McDowell reported that 27 percent of the women in those cases "eventually admitted they had lied" before taking or after failing a polygraph test (Farrell, 1993, p. 322). Once again, a lie detector test is used as a routine part of the investigation of a rape case—unlike any other crime. In addition, a team of independent investigators also reviewed some of the other cases that seemed suspect. McDowell concluded, "To my considerable chagrin, we found that at least 60 percent of all the [556] rape allegations were false" (Farrell, 1993, 322). More information about McDowell's findings and the development his rape allegation checklist for investigators is addressed in Chapter 7.

In Philadelphia in the 1990s "thousands of…sexual assault [cases] were dismissed, shelved, swept under the rug" because law enforcement either did not want to investigate the crimes or did not think they warranted investigation (McCoy, 2000, p. 31). In 1999, Police Commissioner John Timoney acted swiftly to correct the problem after it was brought to his attention. Cases that were once discarded as "unfounded—when the alleged victims, in other words, were not believed" (McCoy, 2000, p. 31) were being reviewed by teams of law enforcement and victim advocates. What happened in Philadelphia speaks to the widespread notion that sexual assault reports should be considered highly suspect, unless proven otherwise.

The armed forces are not exempt from presupposing that most rape allegations are suspect. For example, the following erroneous statement is documented as fact in the Department of the Army's Field Manual on Law Enforcement Investigations. The manual is the "how to" guide for military police charged with investigating all crimes on military installations. Chapter 18 (Sex Offenses, FM 19-20) includes this opening statement in the second paragraph: *False and exaggerated sex complaints are common. The motives behind such complaints may be hard to discern.* (Headquarters, Department of the Army, 1985)

It is understandable why so many rape victims would be suspected of lying if this is the message taught to military police officers and law enforcement investigators in the Army. Not surprisingly, the issue of false allegations surfaced in this study as well. Some of the respondents pointed to the infrequency of false reports. Most of the commentaries, however, berated persons who make false charges and the negative impact they have on true victims.

I think this problem has gotten too far out of hand and is far too easy for women to bring this up and falsely accuse men….as one who was falsely accused, I think it is wrong that the woman is believed before the facts.

I know there are women in the military that have really been sexually harassed or rape but I really believe that is a small percentage. . . . and if you're out getting drunk with the guy…. now come on! I've got a surefire way to stop sexual harassment . . . put on about 300 pounds and quit bathing.

It's incomprehensible that people don't take this issue seriously.

I was listening to a talk show on the radio. The man said his son was in the military and experienced nothing of what was being said in the media. They had someone representing the military saying a lot of what was being said was not true....it was more consensual sex, etc. I was so angry and hurt by what was being said.

False allegations of harassment as a means of retaliation are a danger that should not be tolerated in the military or civilian community.

When people use the complaint of harassment of any sort as a means of retaliation . . . this further detracts from the effort...to ensure and guarantee an environment free from discrimination, harassment, and equal opportunity for all.

False allegations take away from the credibility of these women who do suffer harassment.

In addition to attacks against the women who falsely accuse men of sexual abuse or rape, there were also strikes directed toward the military. These remarks suggest that the military's emphasis on false allegations results in a diversion from the actual cases. This creates further hardships or barriers for women who do try to report their perpetrators. Women are less likely to report abuses if they view the climate as hostile or indifferent.

Rape happens a hell of a lot more than it is ever reported (falsely or otherwise).

There is no way I would have reported what happened to me, not after I saw what happened to the other women who came forward. I wanted to support them, but I felt I had to keep quiet to protect myself. I will have to live with the fact that I knew they weren't lying, but I couldn't come forward. I just couldn't risk it.

THE LINK BETWEEN RACIAL DISCRIMINATION AND ABUSE

Women need to stand united against rape, not divided by race, sexual orientation, rank, class or any other such difference.

—— SEXUAL TRAUMA COUNSELOR AND VETERAN, 1997

The potential link between racial discrimination and sexual harassment is often the topic of many highly charged debates. In this study, most of the comments had two common viewpoints. First, the public perception is often that race is undeniably an issue, especially when the alleged perpetrator is a minority and the victim is a white woman. Many believe (and there is sufficient research to support the fact) that black men are convicted more often and sentenced more harshly than their white counterparts, especially for sex crimes.

As Robert Davis, a former Navy commander, stated, "In the Navy we're told not to complain about racism, but it's always there. ...If you're an African American and you're accused [of sexual harassment], it's over" (Thomas and Vistica, 1997b, p. 32).

This concern was echoed in some of the cases at Aberdeen Proving Ground in 1996 when black drill sergeants were accused (and later found guilty) of rape or sexual misconduct with white trainees. At the onset of the investigation, there were accusations that the sexual offenders were targets of racial discrimination. There were demands for an independent investigation of the case. This situation, as with many others, raised questions about the possible link between racial discrimination and sexual abuse investigations.

However, as one service member said:

Anyone who uses their ethnic background or gender to launch false allegations trivializes true offenses that do occur.

The following comment exemplifies a familiar sentiment. It was made by a woman responding to the research study on sexual abuse in the military. She was commenting on the Aberdeen abuse allegations.

I feel that race may have played a part in it...I have seen this before, white girls who want to save face in their community and not be seen as having had sex with a black man change their story to rape, as evidenced in the Aberdeen scandal. Even the twenty witnesses who came forward said that the women would slap each other high-fives and brag about scoring. . . . These girls were whores plain and simple. Last time I checked, being eighteen classifies you as an adult. This "vulnerability" talk does not apply if you had consensual sex as an adult.

Don't get me wrong. No one, regardless of race and sex, deserves to be raped. That black female homosexual who was sexually harassing other women and then would use race as an excuse should be punished. The bottom line is that race does play a part in sexual harassment.

Some believe strongly that race should not be a part of the equation when looking at sexual harassment. In fact, some respondents were indignant that racism is brought up as a factor in sexual harassment and assault cases as a "diversion from the real issue." The following are other comments on this topic.

What does race have to do with sexual harassment? . . . Stop trying to divide the issue upon racial lines.

I think the race of the victims or the attackers has no place in the discussion.

Racism is not the primary issue here.

Stop trying to pretend it's the fault of those who are most disadvantaged by discrimination.

Racial and ethnic minorities are more likely to be alert to the possibility of discrimination because whites generally do not experience racial discrimination in our culture. Someone who has not had the experience may be less likely to see the connections between racism and sexual harassment. This is an important point that should be given consideration when addressing the complexities of the impact of racism.

Not surprisingly, some respondents noted that sexual harassment and rape are, in their own right, complex issues that involve many other variables, including racism and discrimination. In addition, there were several comments suggesting that racism is used as a diversion from the real issue—the sexual victimization of women. Overall, there was very little agreement on the possible connection between sexual victimization of women and racism.

Inappropriate conduct is inappropriate conduct. A person's race or sex does not excuse or condemn him or her.

Sexual harassment is a gender issue, not a racial issue. Sexual harassment is wrong—regardless of the victim's race or sexual orientation or the race or sexual orientation of the abuser.

Men who sexually victimize women are the real problem, not the color of their skin.

WOMEN UNITED AND DIVIDED

> *It is the fault of many to allow such unstable women into the military and it is the fault of some of the women to allow themselves to get into the situation.*

> —VETERAN SPEAKING OUT ABOUT SEXUAL ABUSE IN THE MILITARY

In addition to the examples of racial division, there was also a division between and within genders on this topic. Women united and divided was a recurrent theme apparent in many of the commentaries. Even though some of the women did not state it as explicitly as others, there is clearly tension among women on this issue.

The dividing line frequently separates those who have experienced a traumatic or abusive situation and those who have not. It is important to note that some of the women who did experience sexual harassment did not view themselves as victims because they were not hurt by the abusive comments or behaviors.

The women who experienced abuse or harassment were generally more sensitive and empathic to the issue. Some of them were still very angry and hurt. Whereas, women who were not victimized did not have the same intensity of emotion in their responses. Although some of these women were sensitive, aware, or concerned about violence against women, they were not as outspoken as the women who were victimized. It was not unusual to find the following types of empathic comments directed toward victims of sexual abuse by military personnel, regardless of whether they experienced any abuse firsthand.

You ought to think about how many of those women were probably told that they would never advance their careers if they didn't provide sexual favors.

I've been lucky, I guess. I never had to face anything so bad. I don't know how some of the women put up with it every day.

I'm thankful for what the women before me did to open doors and to make my time in the service easier.

Although most women were sympathetic to the issues, some had less compassion toward their sisters in service. The most remarkable comments were those that were overflowing with hostility and indignation toward women who reported abuse or harassment. This sentiment often leads to dissociation from the women who were victimized—and an underlying belief that "it happened to you, but it could never happen to me." The following comments exemplify a lack of sympathy and insensitivity toward women who are raped or harassed.

Some women just want it both ways. There's no room for double standards, dykes, or whores in the military. They make it harder on the rest of us who are trying to make it.

If my daughter allowed herself to be sexually harassed, I would tell her that she had no business in any career field where she can't take care of herself.

There are some women who need to learn how to say no.

Insensitivity toward rape or abuse victims was echoed far too many times. In fact, this conviction was evident even as women offered advice on how sexual harassment could be avoided. Although most of the respondents did not intend to be malicious, their underlying message was that women can avoid these situations if they really try. There is still a very prevalent belief that women need to do more, say more, be stronger, have a "thicker skin" and "get over it" if they are faced with sexual harassment or rape. Clearly, for some women this approach works, but it does not work in every situation. Ample advice was offered on how women should avoid sexual harassment and what to do when saying no is not enough. Following are two suggestions that stood out among the many responses.

I found in most instances if there is no hesitation in your response, you have better luck in getting them to take "no" seriously—that applies to females [lesbians] as well. Also, being too "nice" and being afraid of hurting a person's feelings is completely useless in demanding respect for yourself.

In the military dating world, if you repeatedly turn down dates [by fellow male service members] you'll be labeled as a lesbian.

Women in the military face many of the same dilemmas that their civilian counterparts may experience when it comes to sexual harassment and rape. However, they also experience other obstacles that are unique to the military. These dilemmas can become very problematic when women are trying to maintain their career in the service. The following section addresses some of the barriers that women on active duty must confront in making their decision to report the abuse.

OBSTACLES FACING VICTIMS OF ABUSE

*Let's just say I found it difficult to say no. The pressure was there. He told me I
need to trade him a favor for it.... maybe we should have been awarded medals for
how much harassment we tolerated.*

—— FEMALE SERVICE MEMBER WHO ENCOUNTERED
REPEATED SEXUAL HARASSMENT

Despite the affirming comments regarding the military's progress on this issue, an overwhelming number of critical responses cited the barriers for victims of sexual abuse in the service. Not surprising, other military studies and reports noted similar concerns from victims about the many obstacles and reasons for not reporting rape and sexual harassment. For example, the Air Force listed the following fears as reasons sexual harassment is not reported: not being believed; being labeled as a troublemaker; humiliation; ostracism; retribution; damaging one's career, and feelings of guilt, shame, embarrassment, and distrust of the system (Department of the Air Force, 1993).

In the DoD service wide study, the most frequently cited reason for not reporting sexual harassment on active duty was that the victims took care of the harassment themselves. Other top reasons cited were as follows: the harassment was not viewed as important enough to report; it would make work unpleasant; thought nothing would be done; thought I would be labeled as a troublemaker; and too embarrassed (Bastian et al., 1996). Interestingly, in the DoD study, another reason given for not reporting was that the victim did not want to hurt the harasser.

These barriers hinder reporting, investigating, prosecuting, and, most importantly, they hinder the victim's healing and recovery. It is imperative that these obstacles are addressed if progress on this issue is to continue in the military.

Most of the concerns in this study came from women who were sexually assaulted on active duty, but there were also statements from men who were victimized, as well as from the parents and spouses of family members who were sexually assaulted in the service. Although their individual comments were quite diverse, this group collectively shared a common concern about how the military responds to this issue.

Concerns Regarding Reporting

Reporting the rape was never an option for me or for many of the other women who were also abused by men in our unit. How could we tell anyone? It wouldn't have made a difference. Everyone in that unit from the commander down knew what was going on, but they never did anything to stop the abuse. Even though I felt scared, ashamed, and alone, I knew that reporting the rape would only make it worse. I feared for my life.

—— A veteran and victim of rape in the military in the 1970s

There are numerous concerns about how the military responds to sexual victimization, but the most alarming problem relates to fear of repercussions of reporting sexual harassment and assault. Many women do not feel safe due to external social pressure. Very few of the respondents in this research study made an official police report. If they did, it was often due to extenuating circumstances, such as needing medical treatment. One victim recounted her reasons for deciding to make a police report after initially not wanting to do so.

I knew that I had to find the strength to tell, because I was now beginning to fear for my safety. I felt as if I was being stalked. I wondered what extreme he would go to.

Guilt and Shame

I was called in and questioned by AFOSI [Air Force Office of Special Investigations]. At the time I minimized the assault. I did not want to see this man go to jail. I believed I did something to provoke the assault.

—— Air Force rape victim

—— 101 ——

One of the reasons that victims of sexual harassment or rape are reluctant to come forward to report the victimization is their struggle with conflicting feelings of guilt or shame about the abuse. These feelings may stem from social pressures and misperceptions about rape or sexual harassment.

Many victims will experience self-blame. It is often their way of trying to make some sense of this unexpected, horrific event. If they blame themselves or their own behaviors, they can try to find some reason why this happened to them. The self-blame then becomes a coping strategy as a protection from future abuse. For example, a woman who was raped when out jogging alone might believe that if she had not been jogging alone, she would not have been raped. Therefore, if she accepts that the rape occurred because she was jogging alone, she feels some responsibility for what happened. Ironically, this type of psychological defense can both help and hurt the victim's recovery. It is very common reaction among victims of sexual assault.

The following are examples of some comments from women who experienced abuse by military personnel and then blamed themselves or felt blamed for the abuse.

I decided not to report the rape because I felt responsible. . . .

I blame myself for being in an environment where I trusted my co-workers! I blame myself for drinking alcohol that night.

I screwed up big time. I drank. But I did not asked to be raped.

If I reported it, I would have been humiliated in front of my unit.

Who would believe me?

You have to have witnesses or no one will believe you.

Women are often considered guilty if they report a sexual assault—or that they are "crying rape."

Over the years I have learned that women in the military who report harassment or sexual assault become the guilty party. Most women don't report such crimes because they fear no one will believe them or it will ruin their career. Women who make reports are considered troublemakers, in most cases. Some women give up on the military as their career [after reporting sexual harassment or sexual assault].

A LACK OF RESPONSE

> *The Marine Corps and the senior enlisted and officers "dismissed" it and allowed these "marines" to carry on as if nothing happened.*

—— FEMALE MARINE WHOSE REPORT WAS DISREGARDED
WITH NO CHARGES OR DISCIPLINARY ACTION

In addition to the mixed feelings about reporting, women have many concerns about how the military and military personnel respond when a report is made. Many victims of abuse remain silent about their own victimization because of what they witnessed happening (or not happening) to victims who did come forward. The following comments are reflective of cases in which the reported allegations and the abuse were ignored without further action. As one woman retorted in response to what happened in the aftermath of her report of sexual abuse, *The Air Force did nothing, absolutely nothing.* Others shared similar experiences:

> *They ignore it or blame the female [the victim].*
> *Other males witnessed these assaults and they neither said nor did anything.*
> *I would never come forward again [to report a rape in the military]. Why should I give up my career just because some jerk harassed me?*
> *All I can say is that the Air Force creates an environment where it is unsafe to report assaults. They are going to find out that it is happening a lot more than it is reported.*

SECONDARY VICTIMIZATION

> *If I had it all to do over again, I probably wouldn't tell. The punishment, shame, and humiliation I felt in the months afterward were worse than the rape itself.*

> —— VICTIM OF RAPE WHO REGRETTED MAKING A REPORT
> (MADIGAN AND GAMBLE 1989, P. 59)

One of the most frequently cited concerns about reporting an abusive situation in the military is the additional victimization or harassment from the command, the investigators, or co-workers. Numerous women spoke about the further harassment or insensitive treatment that occurred as a result of reporting their abuse. Women and men in the service indicated a fear that this type of negative response would occur. Furthermore, this was cited most often as one of the primary reasons for not making a report and for not telling anyone. Sexual harassment and rape victims feared the response by command or by the investigators would be adverse and possibly more harmful.

In some cases, the trepidations about reporting were based on witnessing command's response to similar allegations. Again, the climate of the unit as set by the commander has a tremendous impact on how the troops respond. If victims sense hostility or insensitivity to these issues in the unit, they are much less likely to report the crime. In fact, based on the feedback from service members who were in such units, victims rarely take the risk to report sexual abuse in these commands. The decision to remain silent is often made to protect oneself from further harassment, humiliation, shame, or degradation.

Far too many service members who reported rape or sexual harassment in the military were further abused by the very system that was supposed to help them. In fact, some rape victims described what happened to them in the process of reporting as more traumatic than the sexual assault because people who were supposed to help made it worse. This type of response is referred to as *secondary victimization* because it often occurs in the context of someone seeking help or reporting an initial victimization. The following is what some of the women said about the secondary victimization they endured when they tried to make a report or to get help.

The military largely covers up the sexual abuse unless it serves its own purpose to prosecute. More often than not, the military re-victimizes the woman who has been assaulted.

[I was] violently raped in the first week... encountered repeated sexual harassment and discrimination . . . called a whore.

The retaliation she suffered in that section was unbelievable.

Because of the rank of everyone involved, no one would help or even talk to me.

I have no idea what kind of punishment he got. All I know is that I was harassed by everyone—even my commander!

The whole command treated me like it was my fault.

I was admitted [to the hospital], evidence was collected, and I was treated and released. . . . Upon arriving at [the] AFB, I was presented with an article 15 for being AWOL—a t no point did the Air Force offer any assistance to me...the Air Force betrayed and persecuted me.

I was required to write an appeal. ...re-victimized while the rapist was being protected.

After what happened to another woman in our unit, I knew I could never tell anyone in my command about it. I just kept quiet and did my time until I was finally transferred. It was easier that way—to just put up with it. I knew nothing good would come from me reporting him.

In short, the barriers to reporting may be due to either internal (interpersonal) or external (environmental) factors. Negative command response, secondary victimization, or known repercussions can also significantly inhibit reporting. Above all, repercussions for reporting rape or sexual harassment are by far the most insidious obstacles that military victims experience.

REPERCUSSIONS AFTER REPORTING

The raping of my career by the Air Force I loved was far worse than the rape of my body.

—A VICTIM OF RAPE AND REPERCUSSIONS IN THE US AIR FORCE

Intimidating rape victims with repercussions happens all too often in the armed forces. It was the most frequently cited complaint and concern for military victims. Examples include: verbal harassment, physical threats, career or job interference, disciplinary action, psychiatric referrals, job transfers, or discharges from the service. Men and women reported these malicious and intentional acts. Their responses were categorized to summarize the types of backlash experienced by victims in the military.

HARASSMENT AND RE-VICTIMIZATION

> *I couldn't escape the gossip and the crude remarks about me after I reported a supervisor for rape and sexual harassment. I was stationed in Japan, away from my family and friends. I had to live and work with these guys [including the man who raped me] twenty-four hours a day, every day. No one seemed to believe me. They all supported him, including the commander. The good ole' boy network was alive and well. It was just too much to bear. It finally drove me out of the Marines—the Marines I loved so dearly before all this happened.*

—— MARINE VETERAN WHO LEFT THE SERVICE EARLY DUE TO REPERCUSSIONS AND
HARASSMENT IN HER UNIT AFTER REPORTING A FELLOW MARINE

Many of the respondents endured further harassment by military personnel after their abuse was disclosed or became public knowledge. In some cases, if a victim made a report to command, other members of the unit found out about the allegation directly from the command. The unwarranted release of this confidential information often led to gossip or further harassment in the unit, especially if the alleged offender was in the same company. In some units when this happens, the group quickly divides in support of the accused or in support of the victim. It is not uncommon for unit gossip to escalate to the point that it becomes unbearable for the victim to remain in the service.

This type of unit harassment (often preceded by a breach of confidentiality of the report) is extremely traumatic and troubling to many victims. They are dealing not only with the aftermath of the abuse by the sexual offender, but they are also subjected to gossip among their colleagues at work or in the barracks. This ongoing secondary victimization in the work or living environment can significantly complicate recovery and job performance. The following are some examples of repercussions involving further harassment or re-victimization in the aftermath of the abuse disclosure.

The men gave me even more harassment after I complained.

I was harassed, followed home, threatened, [received] flat tires....

I was hesitant about doing anything because of the demonstrated lack of follow-up by Marine Corps police. After awhile, I got used to the remarks.

As soon as the word was out about what happened, I couldn't bear to be in that unit anymore. So I left the Army instead of facing the rumors every day. Now I don't care what they say about me.

JOB OR CAREER INTERFERENCE

> *This rape caused me to lose out on promotions. [I was fourteen years in grade of E-5 before being promoted to E-6.] Also I could not after many tries get a top-secret clearance. I could not "be all I could be."*

—ARMY VET SPEAKING OUT ON CAREER REPERCUSSIONS AFTER RAPE

Repercussions toward an individual's career are commonplace and may be experienced in many ways. For example, some women find that their careers are unexpectedly cut short. They are denied promotion, demoted, put on probation, transferred, given a new job, forced to leave the military against their will, or feel compelled to leave the service. Women and men who reported rape or sexual harassment in the armed forces have experienced these types of job or career repercussions in the aftermath of a report. Career interference was a significant problem encountered by active duty military.

In general, there are three underlying reasons behind career interference. First, the offender may be the supervisor or in the chain of command with direct control over jobs, promotions, transfers, and work assignments. Second, the command's intervention may be considered suspect if the commander is a friend to the harasser. The friendship would make it difficult for the commander to fairly appraise the situation or to believe the victim. The third reason is due to the psychological impact of the abuse or the abusive work setting. The effect may be so detrimental that it causes the service member to leave the military on her or his own accord. However, the individual might not have left the service if the abuse had not occurred or if she or he was supported in reporting the perpetrator.

Career interference due to sexual harassment or sexual assault is also manifested in many different ways. Some women find they are treated differently by their supervisors or by their commanders after they make sexual abuse allegations against another service member. Women find that they are denied promotion for the first time in their career, or they are denied the opportunities to advance.

Some women face other obstacles. One Navy vet described the change as though she was now on one side and "the good ole' boys" were on the other side, protecting each other. She felt as though she did not have a chance to overcome the unity of their camaraderie. She eventually left the service, cutting short a promising career and ending her plans to retire from the military. Other women expressed similar dismay, frustration, and sadness about the loss of their military career.

I gave the Marines my all and this is what I got in return—a disability and an early out.

I was a good soldier really. I didn't tell anyone that I was gay because I planned to stay in the Army and retire. I guess Sergeant [her rapist's name was deleted] suspected I was gay because he kept telling me all I needed was a good man. I just couldn't stay it after the rape. They kept Sergeant [the rapist's name] in the same unit with me. How was I supposed to keep working there after he raped me and he knew I turned him in? They gave him an article 15 and recommended me for a chapter five discharge. I really didn't have a choice in the matter. I wanted to stay in the service but I just couldn't work alongside him every day like nothing happened. I really liked being in the Army before this happened. I blame him for this, for ending my career. I haven't been able to keep a good job since.

After I turned [him] in, I was denied recommendation for a promotion.

After the incident happened, I was discharged from the Army on a chapter five that stated I refused to respect a fellow NCO!

I was forced out early on a medical retirement, which stemmed from problems associated with the harassment.

Disciplinary Action Against the Victim

> *They tried to court-martial me on false charges, but failed. They did force me*
> *to appear before an officers' board of inquiry, which found me innocent of any*
> *charges. My legal bills have come to about $30,000.*

> —— Navy physician who reported sexual harassment
> and faced disciplinary charges as a result

A surprising finding was the frequency in which victims are subject to an investigation or disciplinary action after reporting sexual harassment or rape. Numerous women came forward only to find the tables turned on them. This response was especially difficult since it occurred at a time when the service member most needed help and support from his or her command. Women and men who received disciplinary action after making a sexual assault report were subsequently found guilty of an assortment of violations under

UCMJ resulting in letters in their personnel files, article 15s, or unfavorable military discharges.

According to the victims, the disciplinary actions against them were unwarranted retributions for making an abuse report. Some saw the disciplinary action or threats as an effort by the command to have the abuse allegations withdrawn. Often this type of derogatory intervention succeeded in discouraging victims from pursuing the criminal or EO (equal opportunity) charges. The following comments are further evidence of some of the disciplinary actions that victims faced.

I was subjected to investigation, loss of security clearance, psychiatric evaluation, and even when charges were substantiated, there was no action [against him].

I received an article 15 for making sexual advances on him! I was discharged—he is still assigned to the same unit.

In a [rape] case that I witnessed, she [the victim] was given article 15 for adultery.

The military command contacted NCIS [Navy Criminal Investigation Services] to have me investigated. They denied me gynecology surgery within one week of reporting the assault, forcing

my military doctor to cancel the surgery. They said that they were bringing charges against me. They did not want me to tell anyone.

TRANSFERRED, MOVED, OR ISOLATED

They separated me from the others—told me I deserved it.

—— SEXUAL ABUSE SURVIVOR WHO REPORTED THE ABUSE IN HER SECTION

Isolation and transfer are two other repercussions military women may face for their roles as victims of sexual harassment or assault. The implicit message "you do not belong here anymore" is one that was experienced by many rape victims. As one woman summarized, it felt as if the Air Force did not want her anymore after she reported that a supervisor sexually harassed and groped her after they had just attended a class together on sexual harassment. She wanted charges to be filed but the commander did not believe her and he refused to address it. Soon thereafter, she received overseas orders. Although the timing may have been purely coincidental, she attributed her transfer orders to the abuse report. Nothing ever happened with the case. Others had similar experiences.

They sent me away to Portsmouth [Virginia] and forgot about me for three months. I had no family or friends close by.

I was transferred to another watch section.

Maybe a month later I was transferred to another boat.
I was transferred to a new section and blame was placed on me.

PSYCHIATRIC REFERRALS AND DISCHARGES

They made me feel like I was crazy. All I needed was a little support. Instead, they
locked me up in psych with some really, really sick people, drugged me to where I
could barely walk, and never, not once, got me in to see a counselor.
They said I had a personality disorder and then they discharged me.
The counselor I see now is really good, but she doesn't think I have a
personality disorder. I think they screwed me 'til the end.

—— ARMY VETERAN WITH POSTTRAUMATIC STRESS DISABILITY

Of all the repercussions experienced by victims of sexual abuse in the military, the most incred-ulous are the command-ordered psychiatric referrals. A commander's order for psychiatric care in these cases is not always a helpful gesture for traumatized service members. Rather, the psy-chiatric order is sometimes an attempt to label the woman either "crazy, lying, or incompatible with military service" as numerous service women discovered firsthand. Many of the women who were "ordered" to undergo psychiatric evaluation indicated their commanders or first ser-geants did not believe them and thought they were malingering or they had an ulterior motive to "cry rape," such as revenge for a date gone wrong. The psychiatric referral that followed soon thereafter was never intended to be helpful, according to many veterans who had this experi-ence. Quite the contrary, they believed the commander's intent was malicious and destructive.

One woman testified before the House Armed Services Committee in 1994 and regarding what happened to her after she reported her sexual victimization to her com-mand. Despite the fact that she had proof of her allegations, she was referred for a psychiat-ric evaluation (Palmer, 1994). The woman further testified to members of congress about the pain and suffering that followed after she reported the sexual abuse.

Sexual assault victims who encountered this response were treated with the utmost of disrespect for human suffering and trauma. Some were called liars and others were told they were crazy. Some were ordered to sign statements denying the allegations.

In one example, a service woman became withdrawn after her commander called her a liar when she reported a gang rape. The woman isolated herself in her room the day after and tried to commit suicide. The commander then sent her to the hospital with a recommendation for a discharge since she could not adapt to military life. Given her suicide attempt, the psychiatric referral was appropriate; however, the recommendation for her military discharge was premature. With the proper treatment, this woman may have returned to duty. Prior to the rape, she was a model soldier. As the command dictated, she never did return as a part of that unit because she was discharged soon thereafter. Her psychological wounds have yet to heal.

She reported that it still causes her pain today that her commander called her a liar.

The following are additional comments from victims of rape or sexual harassment that were given psychiatric referrals or psychiatric discharges after reporting the incidents.

[The command] tried to order a psychiatric evaluation. I refused!

In twenty-two years [of military service], there were numerous incidents; the first one I reported and I was sent to psychiatrist; I never reported the others.

My command sent me to a psychiatrist . . . saying that I had tried to commit suicide.

The first incident I didn't report; the second incident I was blamed; the third incident, I was referred to counseling where I was put on drugs and hung out to dry.

BARRIERS TO GETTING COUNSELING OR OTHER ASSISTANCE

> *I keep wondering if I would still be dealing with this today [almost twenty years later] if my commander would have helped me to get the help and counseling I needed after the rape. There was no place in the Army where I could get help that I knew of or trusted. So I never told anyone else in the Army after that.*

—— FORTY-ONE-YEAR-OLD VETERAN WHO WAS NOT REFERRED FOR COUNSELING
AFTER SHE TOLD HER COMMANDER SHE WAS RAPED

Victims of sexual harassment or assault frequently do not get the help they need. One of the most significant reasons many victims never tell anyone is because there are far too many systemic barriers that make it difficult to get help. The very systems that are in place to be a resource sometimes become the obstacle. The following are some other examples from veterans about the barriers they encountered when trying to get help from the military or veterans' systems.

I went to therapy at a vet center after my military service was over. I was told I was narcissistic and hated all men. I was belittled by a male counselor. I went home in tears.

I tried to get a copy of my military records for five years. When they finally came, that timeframe [from the rape] was missing from my records.

The VA diagnosed me bipolar and never looked at my sexual abuse issues. The programs I encountered through the VA for women and their issues were "storefront." I feel there is alot of politics going on there. Reminds me what the Vietnam vets went through. Hope it doesn't take twenty years for us to get what is due.

Part of my issues are with the way they [the VA] treated me and ignored the [sexual assault] issue. I was hospitalized twice and they chose to ignore it. I do not trust them.

If the commander does not help, then who can a victim of sexual abuse turn to within the military system? This question gets at the very core of the problem. Women have seen and experienced time and again that their military leaders have let them down when it comes to sexual harassment and rape. When high-ranking officials abuse their power, they make the situation much worse for all service men and women and the military community as a whole.

The comments from service members, veterans, and retirees in this chapter provide important insight into this problem. These women pointed out the many dilemmas and obstacles that victims encounter when trying to report abuse or trying to get help. Their feedback shows that the underlying problem has its roots in power failure. Military leaders and their individual responses to rape and sexual harassment can make all the difference.

6

POSITIVE AND NEGATIVE RESPONSES TO ABUSE

*The military largely covers up the sexual abuse unless it serves their
own purpose to prosecute. More often than not, the military
re-victimizes the woman who has been assaulted.*

—— FEMALE SERVICE MEMBER RAPED ON ACTIVE DUTY
WITH NO CHARGES FILED AGAINST RAPIST

PERSONAL PERSPECTIVES

NO ONE CAN offer a closer look at sexual harassment and rape in the military than those who were victims. Personal experiences and perspectives provide an incredible insight to the issue. With that in mind, female and male victims were asked to provide feedback on how the military intervened in the aftermath of their abuse. Although there were a wide range of experiences, remarks easily fell into two distinct categories: positive or favorable responses, and negative or unfavorable responses.

At first glance, the outcome was very slanted. There were very few positive statements about how the military responded to victims after an incident was reported or disclosed. Notably, even some of the favorable comments could be considered more neutral than positive.

It is important to note that persons who respond to such studies may be more likely to generate negative feedback. Persons with a positive or more neutral experience may not feel as compelled to speak out or to participate in such research. Nonetheless, the experiences and the feedback of any of the victims of abuse who provided input for the study should not be arbitrarily discounted. Caution must be taken to not make generalizations about the entire population of military sexual harassment or rape victims, sexual offenders, or military leaders based solely on the input from a self-selected sample population. With that in mind, the overwhelming numbers of negative experiences that follow do not suggest that all victims of abuse in the military had an unfavorable reaction by military leadership. However, their comments offer great insight to the challenges that victims in the military may face.

Both the favorable and unfavorable assertions from the victims of sexual abuse provide numerous, detailed accounts of reactions (or inactions) by commanders, investigators, co-workers, military medical or mental health professionals, EEO or social actions staff, and other military leaders.

POSITIVE AND FAVORABLE RESPONSES

The responses by military personnel that are cited as most helpful by victims of sexual abuse are those that demonstrate some sensitivity and compassion toward the victim as well as an awareness of the topic. In particular, it is important for victims to feel believed and supported by the person with whom they disclose the abuse. It is also helpful to be in a supportive environment where leaders, co-workers and friends are not blaming the victim. In addition, many military victims of abuse just wanted to know that there was someone that would listen—whether a professional counselor or a trusted friend. Numerous women cited counseling referrals as a priority in helping sexual abuse victims. The following are some of the specific comments from victims of abuse about helpful responses by military personnel.

COUNSELING OPTIONS

Social actions got involved (and helped) after the hospital told my supervisor there was a six-month waiting list for counseling.

—— AIR FORCE RAPE VICTIM HELPED BY SOCIAL ACTIONS

Several abuse victims mentioned counseling as one of the most helpful responses in the aftermath of abuse. Although some of the service members started therapy as active-duty personnel, many of the women noted that their healing did not begin until after they left the service.

There were many favorable comments about the Vet Centers and the VA Sexual Trauma Counseling Programs that have been operating in select locations in the United States since 1993. This specialized program offers confidential counseling to female and male veterans who were sexually assaulted in the military. The counselors have extensive training in the treatment of sexual trauma, and some of them also have a military background. Most of the sexual trauma counseling programs operate as a part of the community vet centers, but there are also women's programs at some of the veteran's medical centers across the United States. The following comments from female veterans validate the importance of having specialized sexual trauma counselors within the military and within the Department of Veterans Affairs.

The VA sexual trauma counselor really helped me to get through this.

My counselor from the vet center listened and arranged for me to go to the woman's PTSD inpatient program in Palo Alto, California.

At the vet center, I found a good counselor. I had to wait until I retired though. There was no support in the Air Force. The Air Force created an environment where I couldn't report it.

I have been in treatment for PTSD at the VA several years now. . . . The VA has been marvelous (in San Francisco).

In addition to women who sought counseling at VA programs, the following are some comments from women who received help while still on active duty.

Military mental health helped to convince my command to let me "go home awaiting orders" to get me away from my workplace.

Family Advocacy in Japan was very helpful listening to what happened to me.

A month after the incident, I finally "cracked" and went to see a chaplain. He was the first person to suggest I get help and that I needed to report the rape.

SUPPORTIVE LEADERS

My senior chief (when he got my phone call at his home) listened to me.

——NAVY SERVICEWOMAN DESCRIBING WHAT HELPED HER MOST AFTER THE ABUSE)

Some military leaders had a positive impact on the lives of sexual-trauma victims. Both women and men commented about the helpfulness of a supportive authority figure such as a commander, a drill sergeant, or a supervisor. These superiors had the power to make a difference in the recovery and in the lives of their fellow service members. In some cases, the leaders also had a favorable impact on the job retention of the service members who experienced sexual harassment or rape. In short, the victims found that the power inherent in the positions of leadership in the military could make or break the future of a service member dealing with this type of trauma.

The *NCOIC [noncommissioned officer in charge] of the section stood behind me. She was the only one to follow up with me and tell me what was happening with the charges and so forth. She is the only one who made me go to counseling after noticing problems with (my) work and finances.*

My primary drill sergeant was female. She was very supportive of me.

Staff Sergeant [name deleted], a former training instructor, insisted that something be done.

Female CDR [commander, first lieutenant] listened to me and tried to have the offender disciplined. She was not successful.

My CO [commanding officer] gave me a pep talk to go to school and to graduate so as to put it behind me.

The shop chief apologized [to me] and counseled the entire shop regarding proper behavior.

For the most part, I was treated fairly and with empathy by all parties.

I had very supportive superiors. The situation was never repeated. My job was not affected.

SUPPORTIVE CO-WORKERS AND FRIENDS

> *[The most helpful response was people] listening to me and not giving me mounds of advice or telling me how I should be or how I should feel.*
>
> —— RAPE VICTIM DESCRIBING WHAT HELPED HER THE MOST

Another helpful response frequently mentioned was the support of friends, co-workers, and colleagues in creating a safe, nonjudgmental work environment. Numerous service members addressed how their colleagues helped them to cope with the abuse by showing concern and offering reassurance. The most helpful responses were acceptance and compassion.

My female co-workers stood by me . . . constantly assuring me. They understood why I kept quiet at first, but I did the right thing to finally speak up.

A co-worker told me if I ever needed to talk, she would be there, night or day.

My eyewitness to the assault and my squad leader, Sergeant [name deleted] took me to see the post chaplain.

Accompaniment to hospital, arms to hug me, ears to listen (that's what was helpful).

A safe, trusted friend held me as I cried and cried and cried.

OPTION FOR TRANSFER

My first sergeant asked if I wanted to be transferred to a new unit, if it would help.
Just knowing he cared enough to ask made me feel safer. I decided to stay because I
knew there were people there who cared about me.

— ACTIVE-DUTY ARMY SPECIALIST

Only a few victims of abuse responded that the option to transfer to a new unit or a different duty station was one of the most helpful responses they encountered by military leadership. These women seemed to appreciate that the transfer was an option to consider and not an order to comply. Some felt the transfer was very useful in helping them to get on with their lives away from the sexual offender. One victim noted that she requested a transfer but it was denied and she had to continue working with the perpetrator. Shortly thereafter, she resigned her commission and left the service. Others chose not to move, but thought their abuser should be made to transfer. The following are a sample of the more favorable experiences.

This was a long investigation. [Since] it was so traumatizing to me, they moved me to another base. I was transferred to a different department per my request.

I decided to request a transfer and was granted that. The perpetrator was so unstable that my life was in danger.

NEGATIVE AND UNFAVORABLE RESPONSES

If I knew then what I know now, I would have never told anyone.
What happened after I told about the sexual harassment made life hell
for me in the Marines. Never again. Semper fi.

— MARINE VETERAN WHO REGRETS REPORTING SEXUAL HARASSMENT

Sadly, many military women and men shared the common experience of being further victimized or harassed when their abuse was reported. Several respondents specifically cited examples of further re-victimization as the least-helpful reaction to them. Many respondents also reported repercussions or further harassment by leadership, co-workers, investigative authorities, and, sometimes, repercussions by the abuser.

The respondents who indicated that the military's response to them was negative or unfavorable offered numerous, diverse examples to substantiate their claims. Overall, these responses were reflective of both unprofessional behavior and an insensitivity or lack of concern about sexual harassment or rape. The following are some examples of the unhelpful or hurtful responses.

COMMAND OR OTHER MILITARY LEADERS

> *My commander harassed me about everything. He belittled me and threatened to kick me out of the military "because I was a liar."*

—SERVICE MEMBER WHO WAS HARASSED BY HER COMMANDER

An overwhelming majority of the respondents expressed concern, dismay, or frustration with the manner in which military leadership responded to sexual harassment or assault. Their responses further document the pervasiveness of a breakdown in leadership (or power failure) in the military when it comes to the issues of sexual harassment or rape.

I will never forget what my commander said to me. I'll always wonder if it was my fault for going to that man's house and drinking that night. He [the commander] was right; I should have known better.

My commander and the IG [inspector general] made comments that made me feel as if the incident was my fault.

[My command] blamed me for being in an all-male unit. The commander stood in front of unit and announced that a woman in the unit said she was raped by another Marine. I was the only female in the unit.

They [the command] didn't report it any further.

My command authority did nothing!

[The command] had me file a report and said, "they will take it from there." That is exactly what happened. I never heard about it again.

I was told it would be fixed. It wasn't. I was afraid of ruining my good name so I kept silent. Now that it's too late I know I was wrong. I'll regret this forever! A selection board failed to select me for promotion because [they] thought I am gay.

I do believe that my service record was coded when the platoon leader found out what happened. (This comment was from a male service member who was a victim of sexual assault and harassment by other men.)

The section chief blamed me... promoted the bastard who attempted to rape me.

My first sergeant called me into his office, told me he knew I was lying, and told me that the fact I would have to work with my offender again was my problem.

My commanding officer filed false charges against me to punish me for filing a sexual harassment complaint and a reprisal complaint.

CO-WORKERS OR COLLEAGUES

I was called a queer by most of the men who found out about what happened.

—MALE SERVICE MEMBER RAPED BY ANOTHER U.S. SERVICEMAN

Negative responses by co-workers or colleagues also had a lasting impact on the victims. Some experienced derogatory remarks or rumors after the abuse allegation was discovered. Others felt alienated by their peers who supported the offender. For other victims, the secondary abuse by their peers was so bad that they decided to leave the military rather than deal with the further isolation and verbal put-downs from their fellow soldiers or co-workers. The following describes what some women and men experienced in the aftermath of a sexual assault or harassment.

Many of my co-workers gave no response or very little empathy. None suggested that I report the crime. Some even tried to talk me out of it.

A co-worker knew the names of these men [the perpetrators]. She refused to give our commander their names at first. She did later when coerced.

Someone asked me [after they found out], "Was his cock big?"

There was name-calling, teasing.

They ruined my reputation with their gossip. Nothing was ever quite the same after that.

As an MP [military police woman], I resented that my male peers considered the female MPs their property. . . .

SUPERVISORS

The first and only person I told, my supervisor, didn't care, acted irritated, and made excuses for the guy's behavior. I didn't pursue it any further.

— FEMALE ACTIVE-DUTY SERVICE MEMBER WHOSE
COMPLAINT WAS DISREGARDED

As with the commanders, supervisors have significant power in setting the example and the climate for subordinates. In cases where supervisors were insensitive, judgmental, or abusive, co-workers often followed suit. The leader sets the tolerance level for sexual harassment and abuse—whether it is a supervisor, a first sergeant, or a commander. In the following examples, service members tell about the negative responses they encountered with their military supervisors.

The general threw out the investigation and disregarded statements that substantiated it.

I was expelled from my AIT [advanced individual training] when I didn't meet the standards expected of me. My senior drill sergeant told me he could pull some strings for me if I had sex with him. This was two to three months after the rape, and I felt desperate and at a loss for what avenues I had [to stay in school].

They tried to ruin my reputation, take away my medical [upon] retirement, and give me an "other than honorable discharge."

My career was brought to an early end.

OTHER MILITARY AUTHORITIES

The whole command's attitude was "females were nothing but trouble."

—— FEMALE SERVICE MEMBER WHO EXPERIENCED HOSTILE WORK ENVIRONMENT
INFLUENCED BY MILITARY LEADERSHIP

Military protocol dictates that service members seek assistance through the chain of command starting with the immediate supervisor and moving up from there. However, if the climate within the unit is hostile or tolerates sexual harassment, a victim may need to get help outside of the chain of command. This in and of itself can be a risky move for many service members; it may be viewed as a betrayal to the unit or as an effort to supersede the command's authority.

Despite the potential for internal repercussions, several other military authorities are available to assist victims in the aftermath of sexual harassment or rape. They include counselors, chaplains, medical professionals, social actions or EO officers, military police, the Judge Advocate General (JAG), or Inspector General's Office. Some victims found that seeking assistance outside of the chain of command was not helpful for them. Following are some of their examples.

I couldn't speak for six months after it happened. I had someone [a hospital staff] tell me I was manipulative in using what happened to me to get sympathy.

I was told to forget about it by a Catholic priest with twenty years' active-duty experience.

A psychiatrist at [an] army hospital told me I had "an immature attitude toward sex." [This was his response to my expression of fear that this man would make another attempt to assault me sexually].

The least helpful response I encountered was that they did not listen to me and did not care about what happened to me psychologically from the incident.

I was interrogated and told, "What did you expect in this man's Army?"

I saw a lawyer (retired Army JAG [judge advocate general]). I was emotional. I probably seemed half nuts when I told him and it must have triggered some perverted spark and he grabbed my vagina and breasts.... This set me back tremendously. I had already gone almost a year without counseling for this and when this lawyer did this I wanted to kill myself over and over and over to just stop the hurt and humiliation.

I experienced a breach of confidentiality.

It hurt having to work with the same men after they were reprimanded.

They made me work with the four soldiers [the offenders].

They kept me in the same battalion motor pool where he worked so I had to still look at him every day. He ate in my mess [hall] and then I couldn't eat.

DISBELIEF OR BLAME FOR THE ABUSE

> *When I reported the sexual assault to Colonel [name deleted], she looked at me over her glasses and told me sodomy was against the law. You had to see her expression and tone. She was accusatory and disgusted. I feared she would report [that] I engaged in sodomy.*
>
> —— RAPE VICTIM ACCUSED OF LYING AND THEN
> THREATENED WITH DISCIPLINARY ACTION

Far too many victims of sexual harassment and rape in the military felt blamed when they tried to make a report or when the abuse was otherwise disclosed and made public. Many victims who tried to seek guidance were met with comments of disbelief or disapproval. Some women were told outright that they were lying, whereas others were told they provoked the sexual abuse because of their behavior or what they were wearing and so on.

These types of verbal put-downs and disparaging, blaming remarks resulted in further trauma for many women and men. For others, it provided the impetus to drop the charges or, in some cases, to deny that the abuse ever occurred. In some situations, women acknowledged the blame and felt guilty. Numerous women continued to live with the condemnations and blame for what happened to them.

The following is what respondents had to say about being blamed when they tried to report the abuse.

When I reported incidents I was labeled "troublemaker" by my commanding officer.

I was told it was my fault because I was female. I was put on day shift so they could "keep an eye on me."

I was ordered to the medical clinic and interrogated. They were sure I asked for it.

When I tried to report it, I felt blamed for what happened.

There was total disbelief—no reaction, no response.

Lieutenant Colonel [name deleted] called me a liar and gave me an article 15.

I wasn't believed. I became the target for investigation and temporarily lost my [security] clearance. They told me it was my fault.

I worked for a commanding general. His aide-de-camp called me at home and asked if I was gay. He heard at drill that I was making sexual advances toward enlisted women and [he said] I was a dyke because I reported an attempted sexual assault by the command sergeant major.

COERCED, THREATENED, OR INTIMIDATED

> *I was told (by command) this would hurt the whole unit, so I dropped it to avoid further problems. The threat was real and I believed it. No one crosses that line and survives.*
>
> —— SERVICE MEMBER WHO WITHDREW HER SEXUAL ASSAULT REPORT AFTER THREATS FROM HER COMMAND NOT TO PURSUE THE ALLEGATIONS

Coercion, threats, or intimidation by military leadership are unexpected, unprofessional and unethical. Nonetheless, it does indeed happen. Victims of sexual harassment and rape recounted horrendous acts of leadership abuse that they endured when they tried to report abuse to their commanders. Their experiences with military leaders were, at the very least, indicative of conduct unbecoming officers—a punishable charge under the UCMJ. Some of their experiences, however, are endemic of a more complex problem within the military culture.

In order for the perpetrator to be charged, I needed to sign a statement. I had been threatened by this person before and feared for my life. I would not sign and, therefore, no charges were brought to bear.

My commander discouraged me from making an official report. He said that things would get "difficult" if I reported the incident to EO. I took that as a threat not to report, so I didn't.

When I reported that I was raped by a higher-ranking man in my unit, I was told that it was my word against his and no one would believe me over an E-7. Command ordered me to "drop it and never accuse anyone of rape again or I would live to regret it." Life was hell for me in that unit after that. I couldn't take it anymore and got out of the service.

NO HELPFUL RESPONSE

Sadly, in answer to the question, "What was the most helpful response or action from anyone who knew about the incident?" a number of respondents stated specifically that there were no helpful responses. Some answered "Nothing" or "Absolutely nothing." One victim responded:

I never received any helpful responses—worked mostly with men during most of the time of the worst harassment on the ferry and on more boats.

These comments remind us that there are many Service members who do not get the help nor the response that they needed and deserved. In fact, many of these examples reflect the continuing need for military leadership to improve their responses to victims of sexual harassment and rape.

A Personal Account of Rape That Resulted in Pregnancy

Mary was on active duty in the Army when she was raped by two different Servicemen—one of whom was a higher-ranking man in her unit. Shortly thereafter, she discovered she was pregnant. Although Mary faced severe depression and a suicide attempt, she has survived today, in part, because of the hope that her son has given her. The following is Mary's story of how she coped.

I was raped twice on active duty in the Army. I told of the first rape and was not believed. I was alone, scared, confused, humiliated, embarrassed, suicidal, and what did my company do? They sent me to the field for more punishment where I was raped again—this time by an NCO [a noncommissioned officer and authority figure in her unit].

I never told of the second rape. Then I found out that I was pregnant. I kept the pregnancy a secret, did my job, and never complained about anything. The Army was my life and what I had lived for...I joined because of my father being a career military man. I wanted so much to walk in his footsteps—for him to be proud of me, for me to be proud of myself.

Instead, I was embarrassed, alone, humiliated, and a failure for all that happened. I still believe to this day that if I had succeeded in committing suicide, the Army would have had no choice but to believe that those men raped me. I wanted to forget the whole thing and pretend that it did not happen. [I wanted] to continue on in my career. I was not going to let these men ruin my career. The military meant everything to me. . . .

The only thing that kept me alive was the child that came from this ugly situation. He has been the only thing that has kept me alive for many years.

Fortunately, Mary has been able to turn the trauma of her sexual assaults into a positive energy toward her son. She is indeed a survivor in every way.

PART III

THE AFTEREFFECTS OF RAPE, SEXUAL HARASSMENT, AND ABUSE OF POWER

7

POWER FAILURE: THE BREAKDOWN OF AUTHORITY

Any member of the armed forces who believes himself wronged by his commanding officer [CO] and who, upon due application to that CO is refused redress, may complain to any superior CO, who shall forward the complaint to the office exercising court-martial jurisdiction over the officer against whom the complaint is made. The officer exercising general court-martial jurisdiction shall examine into the complaint.

— Uniform Code of Military Justice Subchapter XI,
Section 938, Article 138

LEADERSHIP AND COMMAND RESPONSE

After the rape, my commander let me down in the worst way possible. When I needed him to support and protect me, he turned his back—as though I was the enemy. Everyone in the unit followed his lead on this—because they didn't want to cross him. I felt like I had just been abandoned in a battle zone and no one cared if I lived or died. Now tell me, how could anyone trust this man in a war if he treats his soldiers this way? The sad part is, I would have trusted him with my life, until I saw him for what he really was—a shell of a man and definitely not a leader.

— Rape victim speaking about her commander's reaction

IN THE ARMED forces, the commander is unquestionably the leader and the authority on all issues. As a result, the tone set by the CO can make all the difference as to whether a service member will report sexual harassment or rape. A commander who proves that abuse will not be tolerated and demonstrates that victims will be treated with respect will foster trust and encourage reporting. On the other hand, a commander who has a known history of treating victims with disbelief and letting the alleged sexual offenders "off the hook" will reap the intended results by keeping the issue behind closed doors.

Even military regulations recognize the potential implications if their leaders do not "sustain a healthy command climate." As with the other branches, the Army has clearly defined the responsibilities of commanders when it comes to sexual harassment issues. The following comes from the Army's own policy on sexual harassment, Section 6-5, Chain of Command Responsibilities (Department of the Army, 1998):

The chain of command, whether military or civilian, is the primary channel for development and sustainment of a healthy command climate. This responsibility entails, but is not limited to:

- Promoting positive programs that enhance cohesion, esprit, and morale
- Communicating matters with EO significance to unit personnel and higher headquarters
- Correcting discriminatory practices by conducting rapid, objective, and impartial inquiries to resolve complaints of discrimination
- Encouraging the surfacing of problems
- Preventing reprisal for those who complain
- Enforcing administrative/legal sanctions for offenders guilty of some form of discrimination/sexual harassment.

In spite of such policies, commanders and their first sergeants still set the standards for their units by defining the limits of zero tolerance. They do so by covertly or overtly modeling their beliefs and opinions on issues such as sexual harassment, women, and gays in the military. It does not take long for the members of the unit to figure out what their commanders expect. This point was well made in the following statement:

The attitudes of commanding officers strongly influence how their subordinates act or react toward sexual harassment. Progressive, uncompromising views toward sexual harassment improve the likelihood it will be reported, which then has a chilling effect on further harassment. The opposite is true of lax or ambiguous leadership. (Seppa, 1997, p. 41).

Researchers and service members alike agree that poor leadership promotes or exacerbates sexual harassment. Leora Rosen, PhD, social anthropologist and analyst in the department of military psychiatry at Walter Reed Army Institute of Research, and co-researcher Lee Martin found there was less sexual harassment in Army units where there was high confidence in the leader as compared to units where there was ambiguity by the leaders about inappropriate behaviors (Rosen and Martin, 1997).

Researcher John Pryor and colleagues reported similar findings when they analyzed data from the Defense Manpower Data Center's 1988 survey (Pryor, LaVite, and Stoller, 1993). The researchers analyzed the Service members' perceptions of their COs' responses to sexual harassment. Not surprisingly, data showed that sexual harassment was more likely to occur when the CO encouraged (or tolerated) sexual harassment within the unit. If the commanders were indifferent or neutral, about two-thirds of the respondents still experienced sexual harassment. Under the leadership of commanders who discouraged sexual harassment, the incidence was indeed lower, but not significantly so at 58 percent. Likewise, the service members' perceptions of a hostile environment decreased when the CO discouraged sexual harassment in the unit. Pryor concluded, "Some men tend to behave in a sexually harassing way when local norms seem to suggest that they can get away with it" (Seppa, 1997, p. 41).

Moreover, Pryor and colleagues also looked at how the social norms of an organization may actually "permit sexual harassment" (Pryor, Giedd, and Williams, 1995, p. 69). They suggest that some persons have proclivities to commit sexually abusive behaviors and, when put in a setting where the abuse may be tolerated, they are more likely to commit offenses. An example of this is seen in some group dynamics when individuals go along with the group and do something that they might not otherwise do if they were on their own. Instances of gang rape often follow this pattern where one or two may initiate the idea and others will join in or encourage the rape on the sidelines. Pryor and colleagues acknowledged "...women are found more likely to experience sexual harassment in workplaces where men perceive the social norm as permitting such behavior" (p. 69). According to the respondents in this study, this is especially true in military units where the commander acquiesces or turns his or her head to the ongoing abusive behaviors, gestures, and derogatory language.

The remarks from victims of sexual harassment and victims of sexual assault overwhelmingly support these points. A majority of victims had unfavorable comments about their command's response to sexual harassment or assault. Their perspectives were reflective of a leadership that failed its members. Furthermore, in some cases the commander's actions had a significantly detrimental impact on the investigation and on the victim.

Fortunately, there are service members whose superior officers demonstrated strong leadership with a positive regard and an awareness of the zero-tolerance policy. These commanders exemplified the military code of honor, and the other military leaders desecrated the honor by perpetrating the abuse.

EFFECTIVE, SUPPORTIVE, PROFESSIONAL

I survived because of their professionalism [my platoon sergeants].
I graduated from [basic training] camp and six months later the
drill sergeant finally plea-bargained.

—— A SOLDIER SEXUALLY ABUSED IN BASIC TRAINING BY HER DRILL SERGEANT

Good leaders are the bedrock of the armed forces. Without them, the military would surely falter. The Department of Defense demands highly dependable leaders. That is why it puts a great deal of effort and resources into training top brass and top enlisted members. The military simply cannot afford to have a weak link in the chain of command.

In order to become a CO or high-ranking enlisted service member, candidates must participate in selective military leadership training programs. The armed forces make every effort to train their members how to be effective leaders. These training academies cover a wide range of topics, including classes on the UCMJ and on professional ethics. With regard to most topics, including sexual harassment, there are very clear and specific guidelines that have been set forth. The armed forces leave very little room for uncertainty. Consider, for example, this information on "leadership responsibilities" that comes directly from an Air Force handout on sexual harassment:

Air Force leaders are expected to adhere to the following responsibilities when dealing with sexual harassment: Be a good listener; be consistent; be informed; adopt a "no-nonsense" mind-set; be tuned in; use careful judgment and discretion; be nonjudgmental; investigate all complaints of sexual harassment; be willing to ask for help; be proactive—don't wait for a crisis; take prompt and swift action; provide feedback to complainants; and prevent retribution. (Department of the Air Force, 1993, pp. 10-11)

Once the candidates have passed the training classes, been promoted and assigned, they are given much authority and discretion to supervise their troops. Often, the commanders independently ascertain whether policies or regulations were violated. Moreover, they also get to determine the appropriate disposition or course of action (e.g., letter of reprimand in personnel file, referral for criminal investigation and possible court-martial, or a dismissal of the charges). An effective leader will impartially consider both sides and will seek additional support if need be. Power and authority is not used indiscriminately nor will it be influenced by personal bias.

The following commentaries are examples of effective leadership responses. The professionalism made all the difference to the sexual harassment or rape victim and possibly to the investigation. It is unfortunate, however, that there were so few positive comments about leadership's response in comparison to the number of unfavorable remarks. The difference between the two is strikingly apparent.

My drill sergeant was wonderfully sympathetic. I don't think I could have made it through without his genuine concern and support.

Some colonel decided it would be best to send me home, or at least switch companies. [The Service member indicated this was a helpful response in assisting her to cope with the abuse.]

The first sergeant made us write formal statements and meet with him individually. The issue was dealt with in the chain of command.

I knew that I could count on my supervisor to support me.

I honestly don't know how I would have gotten through this ordeal if my CO didn't believe me. He knew just what to say to help me through this. I haven't been able to thank him enough for his support during one of the most difficult times of my life. He was truly a godsend.

I hope that nothing like this ever happens under my command, but if it does, I know I will handle it in the best interest of the victim.

INEFFECTIVE, UNPROFESSIONAL, OR DETRIMENTAL

Overwhelmingly, victims of sexual harassment or assault indicated that their superiors' responses to sexual-abuse allegations were more often negative or harmful than helpful. The majority of their commanders' reactions were, at a minimum, insensitive to the issue and to the victims. Many of the commanders' responses were unprofessional and were certainly not in keeping with the expectations of the zero-tolerance policy against abuse or harassment of military personnel. Of particular concern was that in some situations, the commanders' responses were threatening, harassing, or abusive toward the victim. In fact, a number of service women and men described experiences with military leaders that were quite disconcerting and shocking.

Although the commanders' actions (or inactions) were sometimes incredulous or punishable under the UCMJ, their leadership prevailed. The following examples demonstrate a continued pattern of power failure from as early as the 1960s and as recent as 2000. To have a better understanding of the range of negative responses, the service members' personal experiences with military leaders have been grouped into the following categories: no response, insensitive responses, adversarial responses, and abusive or illegal responses.

NO RESPONSE

The officers and superiors—how could they not know what was going on?
They did nothing. I felt like I didn't belong but I was determined not
to drop out. I felt isolated—like a prisoner.

—— A SERVICE WOMAN WHOSE SUPERIORS IGNORED
THE SEXUAL ASSAULT IN HER UNIT

Most of the complaints and concerns about how commanders responded to sexual abuse were attributed to a lack of action on the part of the military leader. The superior officers simply did nothing when they were told about the sexual harassment or rape. A commander's lack of action was a slap in the face to many victims of sexual harassment and rape. Such disregard or minimization of the crime and the trauma generally suggested one of three things to victims of abuse: the commander did not take the issue seriously; the commander did not believe the victim; or the commander simply did not care.

This type of response by military leadership can have profound, rippling effects for the victim as well as for the unit. The commanders lead the unit. As the leaders, they are granted the appropriate authority and entrusted with the lives of their troops. The military system depends on leaders who will take care of their subordinates by making sound decisions in the best interests of the Armed Forces. More to the point, the military system can and will break down if the leadership is weak or wavering.

Military researcher John Pryor discovered: *If a woman feels that she cannot count on the organization to consider complaints seriously, then one avenue of coping with the harassment is cut off.* (Seppa, 1997, p. 41) If reporting the offense seems useless or ineffective to victims of abuse, eventually their view of the military will also change, according to Pryor's research. Similarly, other research has found that supportive leadership and unit cohesion are also associated with more favorable outcomes by service members who were sexually assaulted (Martin et al., 2000). In short, in units where the climate is supportive, victims of sexual trauma will do better and experience fewer mental health problems.

The service members know which military leaders truly practice zero tolerance and which exhibit power failure. A leader who does not take a strong stand by upholding the zero-tolerance policy ultimately becomes a part of the problem.

> *Our policy on sexual harassment is crystal clear. We believe that sexual harassment is wrong, ethically and morally. We believe it is wrong from the point of view of military discipline. And we believe it is wrong from the point of view of maintaining proper respect in the chain of command. And for all of these reasons therefore, we have a zero tolerance for sexual harassment* (Perry, 1996, p. 55).

Sexual trauma victims are also very aware of which superior officers uphold the zero-tolerance policy. They know who will support them and who will not. This is often the determining factor as to whether they decide to report the abuse. Just knowing how their commander would respond was enough to make some victims decide not to tell anyone. Once again, service members are hurt by power failure. Likewise, unit cohesion and morale takes another step back. We could reasonably conclude that in the absence of power failure the reporting rates would be higher since more victims would feel safer telling their commanders. Moreover, the incidence of abuse might also decrease if zero tolerance was truly enforced by military leadership (Pryor, Giedd, and Williams, 1995).

So, what happens when a commander ignores or minimizes a report of sexual abuse? Although it has a tremendous impact on the victim, apparently nothing much happens to military leaders who disregard sexual harassment or rape under their command. However, if more commanders were charged with failure to report a crime or dereliction of duty, it might encourage other leaders to respond more appropriately when confronted with a report of rape or sexual harassment.

The following comments are evidence of the lack of response by some military leaders. They also demonstrate what some victims of sexual abuse experienced when they went to their commanders for help.

I was kidnapped by two military men and raped at gunpoint. I reported it to my command. There was no support. No follow-up. No referrals for counseling.

The commander shook his head in disbelief when I told him what happened. Nothing happened after that.

Command refused to pursue the complaint I made.

The commander [said] it was ultimately my word against his and there wasn't anything he could do but warn the guy that . . . nothing happened to the guy.

Finally, I convinced my company commander to intervene. It took a few complaints and lots of convincing that I had not led him on. . . .

They never publicized the rape to alert others or to find the perpetrator.

A woman commander told me to drop the charges.

The investigation recommended action for conduct unbecoming an officer. The ARCOM general disregarded the investigator's report and accepted the denial the officer claimed.

The inspector general did not respond.

Our CSM would not let him go because he was so close to retirement. What a trade-off. Punish a man by allowing him to victimize the women under your command .

The commander chose not to prosecute because the perpetrator was already being kicked out of the service for other reasons.

My chain of command told me to "keep it under wraps."

INSENSITIVE RESPONSES

> *The chief had said for them to watch what they say to me because "I was being a*
> *bitch. [He said] they were just playing and I was being too sensitive."*

> —— A FEMALE EXPERIENCE WITH REPORTING SEXUAL HARASSMENT IN THE NAVY

Although it is difficult to measure sensitivity or sincerity, it is very obvious when someone is maliciously cruel. Some commanders were undeniably unprofessional and exhibited conduct unbecoming an officer.

My command section was standing there laughing at his behavior. I demanded that they help me, only to be told it was their night off. . . . [They] laughed and shooed me away.

I felt like they [command] were saying, "no one will believe you."

My commander wanted me to cooperate. However, I felt very responsible and was already receiving harassment from other airmen since everyone had heard—so I refused to cooperate. Then he accused me of lying and of "wanting it."

ADVERSARIAL RESPONSES

> *As the court trial progressed, my commander and NCO [noncommissioned*
> *officer] in charge increased work pressure on me. Every attempt*
> *on my part to obtain counseling ...was thwarted.*

> —— A FEMALE VETERAN SPEAKS ABOUT PASSIVE-AGGRESSIVE
> ACTIONS BY HER COMMAND

Some of the negative or unhelpful responses by military leaders were not as obvious to out-siders. These types of differential or adversarial treatment were delivered more covertly in a passive-aggressive attack. For example, one service woman indicated that her work schedule changed for the worse after she reported sexual harassment. Another found that it was difficult for her to get time off from work to go to counseling. In other cases, the questionable or adversarial actions by command were quite direct, as in the following situations.

The commander overturned the investigation ruling and the case was dismissed.

The first sergeant initiated an investigation into the harassment and personally concluded my claims were merely a result of the allegations made against me—an attempt to take the attention away from my own misconduct. . . . The first sergeant found the evidence inconclusive (it was his word against mine).

I was made to work alongside him even after I reported the rape to my section chief. It was as though they were punishing me for "telling on him."

ABUSIVE OR ILLEGAL RESPONSES

The man who raped me was an officer. He ordered me to go
with him on a duty assignment. Then he raped me.

— ARMY ACTIVE-DUTY SOLDIER RAPED BY A SUPERIOR OFFICER IN GERMANY

Some military leaders blatantly crossed the line into illegal and unethical behavior. In response to sexual assault or harassment reports, some commanders have been known to threaten or harass the victim into not making an official criminal report or dropping the charges. They have lied to victims and investigators, obstructed justice, forged the victims' signatures, falsified reports, lied under oath, or colluded with the offender to dismiss the case or to thwart a court-martial. Even more disturbing are cases in which the commanders are the sexual offenders.

The following messages are from respondents who experienced or witnessed leadership abuse firsthand.

The commander asked me if I wanted to become a member of the mile-high club.

I wanted to report it [the rape] to CID. The commander said he would press charges of adultery against me [if I reported it].

The command threatened us both, stating, "Things would get icy for us". The commander reported publicly that the findings were without merit. . . . [he] tried to have me placed in a

psychiatric ward... said I was crazy... said I had [attempted] suicide . . . [he] falsely reported to DOD he had given me a copy of the findings[and he] had his administrative troop forging my signature on documents.

ADDITIONAL COMMENTARIES ABOUT COMMAND RESPONSES

> *I think people in the military are more rapidly losing their confidence in commanders.* [The military has] *turned their heads to how complaints have been handled.*

—— A SERVICE MEMBER SPEAKS TO THE LOST CONFIDENCE IN MILITARY LEADERS

We will probably never know if most commanders do what is right and honorable when confronted with this problem in their unit. However, many service women indicated they could not count on their command to be there for them when they needed help. Unfortunately, their messages imply that many military leaders do not do what is right and honorable when it comes to dealing with sexual abuse or harassment in their units.

I was raped! The command did nothing! In my case the bottom line was—the USMC would rather save the career of six males than one female!

Don't count on senior leadership to stand behind you when a complaint is brought forth.

You can't interfere with command decisions.

Commanders, IGs [Inspector Generals]*, and all the way up to the top have handled complaints. They have now created an environment in the military departments where anyone can be accused of any crime without any evidence.*

[By reporting] you are ending your career, not his.

LAW ENFORCEMENT AND INVESTIGATIVE PRACTICES

> *Even consensual sex can be deemed rape if the recruit can show that she was afraid to say no to her superior.* (Thomas and Vistica, 1997a, p. 41)

The panel concludes that, because sex crimes are different from other crimes, they demand organizational and operational arrangements that recognize their unique characteristics. The Department [of Defense] needs a well-trained cadre of experienced agents organized to investigate serious sex crimes (Panel of the National Academy of Public Administration, 1999, in *Adapting Military Sex Crime Investigations to Changing Times,* report to the U.S. Congress and the Department of Defense).

When it comes to reporting rape and sexual harassment, far too many victims experience negative or inappropriate responses by military criminal investigators. According to the respondents in this study, military law enforcement and investigators treated an overwhelming number of women and men adversely. In fact, only a few respondents had favorable comments about the investigative process. However, the military is not alone when it comes to the disparaging treatment of rape victims. The civilian sector also has a long-standing history of secondary victimization of sexual assault victims in the criminal justice process (Madigan and Gamble, 1989).

In order to understand the negative feedback by military victims, it is important to recognize the common issues that are problematic to both civilian and military communities when it comes to reporting and investigating sexual offenses. First and most important, the majority of sexual assault and harassment incidents are never reported to law enforcement. Therefore, only a small percentage of rapes are actually investigated. As a result, it is nearly impossible to ascertain the incidence of sexual offenses or to estimate the percentage of cases that are reported. The low reporting rate further complicates the issue of accurate data collection and statistics on sexual assaults in the military.

For example, according to a study by the National Academy of Public Administration, there were over 2,600 adult sex crime investigations initiated by military criminal investigative organizations in 1997 (NAPA, 1999). Yet for that same year, statistics reported from each of the service branches to the Office of Undersecretary of Defense indicated that there were less than 1,000 adult rapes reported. Although there may be some discrepancies due to the differences in coding and reporting these crimes, this does not account for the significant differences in the data for that year from two reputable sources. In fact, we really do not know exactly how many sexual assaults are reported to military investigative or law enforcement authorities.

In the civilian sector, the National Victim Center and the U.S. Department of Justice estimate that 16 to 32 percent of sexual assaults are reported to law enforcement for investigation (National Victim Center, 1992; Greenfeld, 1997). In the military, however, the commanders have considerable authority and discretion over whether cases are referred to a military criminal investigative organization. It is quite likely, therefore, that the reporting rates are comparably lower for military communities since some cases are handled internally. These cases will very likely never be listed in any official report about sex crimes in the military because the investigative authorities are never notified.

However, there will be some changes in how the military keeps statistics on reported sex offenses in the twenty-first century. According to a 1996 Department of Defense directive (DoD, 1996, Directive 7730.47) all military branches are mandated to comply with the Defense Incident Based Reporting System (DIBRS) with regard to reporting criminal offenses, including hate crimes and sexual harassment when they constitute a criminal offense. Although the directive was distributed in 1996, military departments were unable to comply promptly with the mandate for many reasons, including a reported lack of resources to implement the new system. However, when the DIBRS system is fully operational and all commands are participating, there will be remarkable changes in the manner in which these statistics are reported: commanders will be required to report all sexual assault allegations when there are reasonable grounds to believe an offense was committed.

Furthermore, DIBRS may have a positive impact on enhancing the military's response to these crimes since the commanders and the investigative, judicial, and corrections authorities will also be required to report the disposition and outcome of cases. The following citation mandates command response to criminal offenses in compliance with DIBRS.

The commander may refer the case to staff agencies, dispose of the case pursuant to administrative or non-judicial authority; or refer the case to court-martial or to an appropriate convening authority for ultimate disposition. Once the action is complete, the commander taking final action with the case will report the final disposition action. . . .

In some cases, commanders will be required to initiate DIBRS reporting when a military law enforcement activity is not involved. Commanders must ensure there are reasonable grounds to believe an offense has been committed, and the person to be identified as the offender committed it. Preferral of charges, imposition of non-judicial punishment, approval of separation from the service, and conviction by a civilian court are all examples of reasonable grounds. Commanders shall ensure that reporting responsibilities and requirements as prescribed in this Manual are met in these cases. (DoD, 1998, Section 1, p. 9)

In other words, not only will we know how many cases are being reported, we will also be able to ascertain the disposition of the case and whether there was a conviction, disciplinary action, or an unfounded dismissal. If enacted properly and monitored for compliance, DIBRS can have long-range favorable implications for the military's response to rape and sexual harassment as well as other violent crimes, such as hate crimes, domestic violence, and child abuse. DIBRS will open the books on how each service branch is responding to these crimes.

Standardized protocols on reporting and responding to rape allegations will make a significant difference in how victims are treated by commanders, law enforcement, and investigators. However, there may be another factor contributing to the overwhelmingly negative responses to military investigative practices. In short, persons who were displeased, hurt, or angry by the investigation may be more likely to respond or speak out in a research study than those who had favorable experiences with the investigation process.

Sufficient documentation from military victims of sexual harassment or assault points to some very serious problems with the investigative process. Recall the previously mentioned case in which a female victim's allegations were taken seriously only after the national media became involved and reported her case, demonstrating the lack of response or interest by some military leaders toward this issue.

Other problems with investigative practices include the underlying theme of disrespectful treatment. There were concerns that cases were abruptly closed or dismissed because "her word against his word" meant the victim would not be believed. Several victims indicated the investigators were insensitive, unprofessional, or that they demonstrated a lack of awareness of how to deal with these kinds of cases effectively. Other victims were angered by the outcomes that resulted in minimal sentences for the accused or no disciplinary action at all.

One rape victim endured several months of "mental anguish" during the investigation only to find out that her rapist got off with little more than a discharge. As she said, "Now he's back into the civilian side, but he's still a free rapist." Her dismay and frustration with the investigation and the outcome of the case was not atypical. Another woman concluded her feelings about the investigation in one word: "demeaning."

Following are further examples of what some women encountered with military justice and the investigative process.

I thought I was entering the halls of justice to receive a fair and impartial hearing. Instead, I found myself at the mercy of a Navy legal system guided by strong-arm legal tactics of questionable ethics. I have appealed for assistance up through the chain of my command. . . .

I was raped by another Air Force [military police officer]. I had worked in investigations and witnessed the interrogation. I did not want to go through with that.

The military police were ineffective in their investigation as well as demeaning and insulting.

The MP (military police) were summoned and I was taken to the Army Hospital . . . went to CID for questioning. They kept asking me when I last had sex and how many boyfriends . . .

They [CID] asked me how many boyfriends I had and how many times I had sex.

I filed a complaint three years ago that is currently still being investigated.

I dropped the charges . . . the investigators told me it would be hard to protect us. These men had weapons and used them to kidnap us.

They [the investigators] *made me feel guilty for pursuing charges.*

Several Service members also expressed concerns about the investigation resulting in the dismissal of charges. There was a lack of understanding among the victims as to why the charges were dropped. In some instances, their cases were dismissed due to insufficient evidence; in other cases, the investigations were closed.

The end result [after two months of an article 32 hearing] *was not enough evidence to carry on with the investigation.*

Others witnessed it, but they [the military police] still did nothing. The case was dropped.

The report was missing information and evidence was destroyed.

In the CID investigative report entire pages are missing and all forensic evidence was destroyed months after I was raped.

I seemed to have made too many waves after reporting the rape. Once charges were dropped due to lack of "physical evidence", I was expected to go about my business as usual. Impossible!

I reported the rape, but nothing ever happened. Absolutely nothing. As far as I know, the rapist is still in the Army and still getting promoted.

To this day I still don't know what happened with the case. I was discharged and I haven't heard a thing since. I guess the case against him was dropped since they never called me back to testify.

Women repeatedly expressed concern about their cases being dropped and the offender being free to rape again. They felt powerless to do anything else since the investigation was out of their hands. In some instances, the victims sensed that very little attention was given to the case after the complaint was filed. It was not unusual for the complainant to be unaware of the outcome of the case. Many concluded that the charges were probably dropped since they were never called back to identify the perpetrator or testify against him. For those who encountered such indifference to their sexual abuse reports, the message could not have been clearer. They were left to believe that these cases are not a priority for investigation or prosecution in the military.

Data from the Department of Defense seem to validate these presumptions. The DoD statistics for 1996 (the most recent year that this analysis was available from the office of the undersecretary of defense) for reported rape cases that were tried in a court-martial are actually quite low. The Army reported 13 percent of their reported rape cases were tried; the Navy reported 19 percent for that same year; and the Air Force reported the highest ratio, with 20 percent of reported rapes going to trial (court-martial). These figures include persons who may not have been subject to the UCMJ.

Nonetheless, more than 80 percent of reported rape cases in the military never go to trial, according to DoD data. Therefore, only two of every ten rape victims who report the crime will ever see the case go to a court-martial and less than half of them will ever see their rapist convicted. With these odds, it is understandable that rape victims would conclude their cases are not a priority for military authorities. This may be another reason why victims have so many unfavorable remarks about the investigative process.

Other concerns about sex crime investigations came to the forefront when Congress called for an independent study of military criminal investigative organizations (MCIO) in 1997 under the Defense Authorization Act. This assessment was initiated in 1998 by the National Academy of Public Administration (NAPA) and concluded in 1999 with the report "Adapting Military Sex Crime Investigations to Changing Times."

The NAPA panel completed a thorough review of military criminal investigative organizations and made several important recommendations in their final report. The report addressed several areas pertaining to the investigation of sex offenses. For example, the panel suggested that investigators should be taught the necessary competency skills to respond appropriately to sexual abuse victims, rather than just learning these skills on the job. This training recommendation is highly necessary given that most investigators receive minimal sex crimes training. The complaints of inappropriate treatment by investigators corroborated the need for additional specialized training for investigative units.

Another important recommendation in the NAPA report was previously directed by the DoD in 1996 but had not been fully implemented. This recommendation pertains to the mandatory reporting of sex crime statistics by all military service branches. NAPA calls for the MCIOs to be in compliance with the national reporting requirements for all sex crimes, "Though it is required by law, and to be implemented by the DIBRS (Defense Incident Based Reporting System) the MCIO's are not reporting many crime incidents to the FBI's National Incidence Based Reporting System" (NAPA, 1999, p. 20). Compliance with the national reporting system requirements will enhance our understanding of the military's disposition of these crimes. However, according to a source at the Pentagon, as of 2001—five years after the mandate—the DIBRS was still not fully operational to include the mandatory reporting of sex crimes.

Another important concern raised in the NAPA study related to command interference with sex crime investigations. Command authority should not interfere with military criminal investigations. In response to this problematic issue, the NAPA study recommended "the Secretary of Defense strengthen and vigorously enforce guidance against command interference in MCIO investigations" (NAPA, 1999, p. 8). Such interference only adds to the problems for rape and sexual harassment victims. The cooperation among investigative authorities and command will certainly improve the military's response to sexual assault and harassment. In addition, it will serve to define more clearly the authority of the military criminal investigation organization in these cases.

The NAPA report offers a very good overview of the investigative process with some excellent recommendations for enhancing the military's investigation of sex crimes and their response to rape victims. Their assessment of the problem is consistent with the messages of many of the service members who participated in this study when it comes to the investigation of sex crimes. This report should serve as a guide for military criminal investigation units and for the DoD in enforcing existing policies and mandates.

REACTIONS OF HELPING PROFESSIONALS

Even though I went to the hospital for a rape exam, they never got a rape crisis counselor to talk to me. I could've used someone on my side. It felt like everyone else was so busy doing their job that they didn't have time to find out how I was.

— VICTIM OF RAPE IN THE AIR FORCE

In addition to criminal investigators, helping professionals (such as physicians, nurses, chaplains, and counselors) all have important roles in responding to sexual trauma victims. However, in this study there were very few comments about these professionals from the participants. Of those who did offer feedback, their viewpoints were quite diverse. Some of the service members encountered medical personnel who were unprofessional and insensitive, and others found them to be very caring, providing appropriate treatment.

A good example of the differences in experiences came from a woman who wrote about the treatment she received at two VA hospitals on opposite coasts. On the East Coast, she complimented the staff: "They were wonderful and helped a great deal." However, after a move to the West Coast, she found the approach to be very different: "they were willing to medicate me, but not willing to give me individual therapy..." She felt that her mental health treatment was restricted only to medication, thereby ignoring her concerns and needs for counseling for the sexual assault. Counseling and sensitive intervention is an important part of recovery for victims of sexual trauma (Foa and Rothbaum 1998; Koss et al., 1994; Madigan and Gamble, 1991). Although there is some debate as to what type of treatment model is most effective—(particularly immediately after the crisis) counseling should be offered to rape victims by helping professionals and other first responders (e.g., law enforcement).

Extensive research indicates that rape victims are likely to experience significant distress immediately after the trauma and some could experience prolonged or recurrent psychological effects years after the sexual assault (Angell, 1994; Coyle, Wolan, and Van Horn, 1996; Foa and Rothbaum, 1998; Koss et al., 1994.) However, most rape victims do not seek counseling or get medical treatment, nor do they tell many others about the assault (NVC, 1992; Center for Women Veterans, 2001). According to the Department of Veteran Affairs, Center for Women Veterans:

> *Many veterans who experienced an incident of sexual or personal trauma as a result of assault or harassment ...on active duty have had no professional counseling and have never discussed it with anyone.* (Center for Women Veterans, 2001)

Despite their reluctance to receive professional care, men and women who have been sexually assaulted can experience a wide range of physical and psychological effects. Therefore, when they do present for treatment, it may be due to medical concerns, often precipitated by posttraumatic stress.

For example, in one study, women with a history of sexual assault on active duty who were later treated at a VA medical facility reported a higher incidence of physical symptoms or medical disorders than women who did not have a sexual assault history (Frayne et al., 1999). These women had higher levels of hypertension, diabetes, and heart attacks compared to their cohorts. Other studies have reported similar findings suggesting that women with sexual trauma histories will have a higher incidence of physical complaints, psychiatric diagnoses, or alcohol abuse (Fontana and Rosencheck, 1998; Hankin et al., 1999; Koss, 1993; Sadler et al., 2000). The effects of sexual trauma are addressed in further detail in Chapter 8.

Given the higher incidence of physical and mental health concerns among rape victims (and that they rarely seek treatment specifically for their sexual victimization), it is especially important for helping professionals to respond appropriately when service members do seek assistance. The following are some of the comments and feedback from sexual assault patients about their experiences with helping professionals in the military.

The hospital staff were very caring, compassionate, and professional—even the male doctor. I was scared to death, but he was very kind.

I was given Valium [by the medical doctor on duty] *and sent home to the barracks.*

I was told that it would be six months before they could get me into counseling.

He [the doctor] *told me that my command had asked him to kick me out [of the service] anyway he could.*

The doctor yelled at me and held my legs down [during the rape exam].

When social actions got involved, the military hospital got me in to see a doctor—[a male doctor] and my husband had to be present. You can imagine how much talking I didn't do. . . .

I don't think I would have made it without my counselor. She was a Godsend.

The mixed comments about helping professionals' responses to victims are indicative of the diversity of expertise and experiences within the field. This may also be reflective of the need for a standardized rape protocol (or coordinated community response) for all military installations (as some states now have for civilian jurisdictions).

The feedback strongly suggests there is significant room for improvement in responding to victims of rape and sexual harassment. Specialized training should be given to commanders, law enforcement, investigators, and helping professionals who respond to rape or sexual harassment allegations. Improvements should be directed toward helping the victims as well as more appropriate responses to sexual offenders.

THE MILITARY'S RESPONSE TO SEXUAL OFFENDERS

There is no room in today's Army for troopers or leaders who would take advantage of another soldier or family member (Combating Sexual Harassment, 1997, p. 2).

Women and men who were sexually assaulted or harassed by military personnel often felt betrayed by the inadequate responses to sexual offenders. Their feelings toward the military often stem from the lack of disciplinary action taken against their perpetrators. Overall, the victims' perceptions were predominately unfavorable and filled with a great deal of anger, bitterness, and frustration. In fact, there were only a few positive comments.

One of the respondents with favorable feedback found that her supervisor's response to the sexual harassment report was both effective and professional. The servicewoman stated that although there was no official complaint, "the supervisor stopped the remarks, removed the pictures, and counseled the offender."

The commander's intervention in this case was a reasonable response to end the harassment. Furthermore, he ensured that the abuser was put on notice regarding his offensive behaviors. This positive example is a good model for effective leadership intervention.

Unfortunately, other examples given by military women and men were not as favorable. The military's disciplinary response to perpetrators of sexual abuse generally involves one of the following outcomes: an article 15, a transfer, a discharge offer, early retirement, or minimal or no action taken. Very rarely are these cases referred for court-martial hearing. Of those cases that do make it to the military justice system, the victims frequently found the cases resulted in minimal sentencing for high crimes such as rape or kidnapping.

To the contrary, the average sentence for a rape conviction in the armed forces appears to be on par with the civilian criminal justice system. However, this does not justify the lower sentencing rates for military sexual offenders. DoD data, procured from a Pentagon source, indicate the average sentence for a rape conviction among all service branches in 1996 was 9.6 years. These data may also include other charges in addition to the rape, such as sodomy or kidnapping.

Of particular note is the significant variance in rape sentencing rates within the service branches. For example, the average sentence for the Navy in 1994 was 3.95 years for a convicted rape as compared to the following year when the Navy's average jumped higher than any of the other Service to 20.28 years. Why was there such a huge change in sentencing? We may never know why the average rape sentence in the Navy increased fivefold in one year. However, we do know there seems to be no standard when it comes to disciplining a convicted rapist in the military. As some rapists serve hard time, other rapists remain free to keep their jobs and to collect their paychecks. This factor alone points to a disparaging problem and diversity in the military's response to sex crimes. The following section provides numerous examples of the military's wide range of response to sexual offenders as witnessed by the victims in their own cases.

TRANSFERS AND PROMOTIONS

> *My assailant was promoted from E-3 to E-4. My commanding officer* [who did nothing to help] *was promoted to admiral.*

> —— NAVY VICTIM OF SEXUAL HARASSMENT WHOSE OFFENDERS WERE PROMOTED

When sexual assault or harassment allegations arise, some commanders use their authority to deal with the situation by transferring the offender out of their jurisdiction. Sometimes this means a transfer to a new duty station with a fresh start for the sexual offender or a transfer with a promotion. Transferring the alleged perpetrator is certainly the easiest way for commanders to address the problem, although it is hardly the most ethical response.

A transfer lessens the potential for any uncomfortable or embarrassing public leaks about the sexual offense. Plus, the commander and the offender get to carry on with their lives without a lengthy investigation or court-martial. Transfers also "save" the accused from losing his rank or possibly his career if the allegations are proven true. Transferring the sexual offender was apparently considered a good solution by some commanders. The following comments bring attention to the other side of such decisions.

Although he was transferred to a new job, he was as supervisor (NCOIC) of a clinic and a few months later he was given another female to supervise.

He was given the opportunity for accelerated promotion [and took it].

There were two incidents: first incident: [command] *talked to him; second incident:* [command] *talked to him and there was an immediate transfer.*

In my case, he was transferred and lost rank. This was his punishment for raping me.

DISCHARGES OR RETIREMENT

> *He was allowed to retire early with only the loss of one filthy stripe,*
> *thereby maintaining his retirement pay of chief.*

—— A VETERAN'S COMMENTS ON THE MILITARY'S
RESPONSE TO HER SEXUAL OFFENDER

Another response to sexual offenders is the option to leave the service through early retirement or discharge. Commanders use these options often in lieu of a court-martial or other punishment. Similar to the transfer, these options also serve the commanders and the perpetrators very well. The commanders do not have to deal with the reality nor the problems of having a sexual offender in their unit and the perpetrators escape any discipline or criminal repercussions.

Most rape victims thought that allowing the perpetrators to leave the service with no disciplinary action was a slap in the face. This response is viewed as indifference to the problem and as another example of not holding rapists or harassers accountable for their behaviors. In addition, giving sexual offenders the option to leave the service sharply contradicts the zero-tolerance policy. The implied message is clear: zero tolerance has some loopholes. The following are specific examples of what happened to some rapists and sexual offenders in the military.

A command sergeant major of my battalion was federally convicted of mistreatment of his soldiers and forced to retire.

The lawyers recommended dishonorable discharge for him.

The unit commander rewarded the E-7 for his behavior by allowing him to retire quietly with no recourse for his actions.

The rapist was discharged from the Army.

Sure, they discharged him, but now he's a civilian free to rape other women. No one will know about his history in the Army. I'm sure his discharge papers are not stamped RAPIST, but they should be.

MINIMAL INTERVENTION

I found out that the Army judge who awarded punishment decided on a letter of reprimand. When I spoke with a counselor familiar with military "justice" she was not at all surprised that a letter of reprimand "was it." She said she hears it over again and again from women of all services. This created even more trauma for me. Can anyone explain the thought process behind punishing rape with a letter of reprimand?

— ARMY RAPE VICTIM

In the category of minimal intervention, there were a variety of outcomes ranging from an article 15 for rape to a letter of reprimand for repeated sexual harassment and extortion. Many of the respondents expressed indignation at the minimal disciplinary action for these serious offenses—many of which are considered felony crimes in the civilian sector. One woman captured the overriding sentiment with her three-word response, "Hands were slapped." Indeed, "hands were slapped" in many cases—adding insult to injury for these service members who had experienced sexual victimization by their fellow soldiers and a second "rape" by the military system of justice.

I was told...he got an article 15. Slap on the wrist! He retired with full benefits in less than a year. Nice retirement pay!

My rapist also harassed four girls and had two affairs and he lost one stripe. He was happy.

Disciplinary action? [He was] counseled by peers for five minutes.

I believe [he] got an article 15 for attempted rape and assault.... but he's still in the Air Force.

I am faced with him every day and recently was deployed with him where he nearly became my supervisor again. I had to confront my superiors and rehash the experience [again]. He did not become my supervisor after that. [The offenders] were verbally reprimanded but stayed on the job with me. . . .

[The offenders received] little or no punishment and the commander retired.

No Disciplinary Action

We finally went to court-martial and he was acquitted on the grounds of "hearsay."

— A VICTIM WHO FELT BETRAYED BY MILITARY INJUSTICE

It is far worse for victims of sexual assault and harassment if their sexual offender receives no disciplinary action whatsoever. When the military authorities disregard a report and take no action following an abuse allegation, the victims felt betrayed by their leaders and isolated from their military family. In these situations, victims may suffer far more from the command's lack of response than from their offender's abuse. The commander's unwillingness to pursue any disciplinary action toward the perpetrator is akin to telling the victim she was not believed or she was not as important to the unit as the alleged offender.

For some service members, this blatant disregard by their command led to their eventual discharge from the service. It changed the way they thought about the military when their leaders failed them. They could no longer trust their commander to do what was right and honorable. Simply put, they lost faith in the organization.

Nothing happened to him, but my life hasn't been the same ever since. I left the Army shortly thereafter. How could I stay in after that?

The rapist was questioned. He wasn't even relieved of duty by my commander....they felt that the "situation" was consensual....

No action taken on charges. I did not "act enough like a victim."

The supervisor laughed it off and pretended not to be able to find the offender.

Nothing happened ...He was on his way to warrant officer school the next month.

He continued on with his career as a captain.

The perpetrator wasn't punished and confidentiality wasn't maintained.

I was raped by an active-duty Army warrant officer who was not held accountable and no action was taken against him by the U.S. Army.

They protected him and his career by doing nothing.

My charges were not enough. [Now] he is a repeat offender.

There are many options for military commanders as well as for the court-martial judges and juries concerning disciplinary action against a sexual offender. The options can include confinement, loss of rank, loss of pay, dishonorable or honorable discharge, early retirement, transfer, mandatory counseling, psychiatric evaluation, an article 15, a fine, a warning in the offender's personnel file, a one-on-one talk, a nod and a wink—or not taking any actions at all. It used to be that rape was punishable by death under the UCMJ. No longer does the offense carry such a high penalty.

THE CASE AGAINST SERGEANT MAJOR MCKINNEY

*I think it was a sad day for the military and women when the verdict
was read. I believe it set the military back a lot of years. Women should
and will be afraid to come forward with complaints of their own.
I don't blame any women for not coming forward. Who would want
to open themselves up to such a horrendous ordeal? Their whole life
scrutinized, their character assassinated, and reputation destroyed?
That is what sexual harassment has come down to. Sad but true. Women must
now shut up and put up or else become victims of another heinous system.*

—— ONE OF THE WOMEN WHO ACCUSED SGM OF
THE ARMY MCKINNEY OF SEXUAL MISCONDUCT

*After seventeen years of active duty, I can honestly say that I
have never seen the system work as it should on this issue. Sorry.*

—— ACTIVE-DUTY SERVICE MEMBER'S RESPONSE TO
THE OUTCOME OF THE MCKINNEY COURT-MARTIAL

If there was one case that exemplified the military's response to this issue, it would be
the case against the former sergeant major of the Army Gene McKinney and his accusers.
The opposing sides in the debate about sexual misconduct in the military grew ever wider
during the court-martial. Indeed, the dividing lines were clearly drawn—those who were
on the former sergeant major's side and those who believed the six women who accused
him. The differing perspectives fueled the angst as the verdict (not guilty on all but one
count of obstruction) was announced.

As with any other highly charged and controversial sexual allegation involving a public
figure, the particulars of the case were presented for all to hear. The details of the accusations came from the radio, the television, newspapers, and, in some cases, even in Internet
chat rooms. Whatever or whomever was the source of the information, men and women
followed this case from coast to coast.

Military members and civilians alike offered their perspectives on the outcome of this
highly publicized case. Many of them also took the opportunity to voice their opinions
about sexual harassment in the military. The following section summarizes what some of
the military members and the public had to say when posed with these two specific questions as a part of this research study:

1. What do you think the impact of this verdict (in the McKinney court-martial) will be?
2. What do you think about the military's response to sexual harassment and sexual assault allegations?

Their responses and comments speak for themselves. The following is what Americans had to say about this high-profile case and the implications for the future.

You want to know how I feel about the McKinney verdict? I think it sends a terrible message to our sisters who are serving today. Based on the treatment and subsequent career-ending repercussions for those brave women who stood by Sergeant Major Hoster, it would appear that anyone who wants to go the distance had better keep their mouths closed. Pitiful!

My response to the McKinney verdict is, one more message of "put up and shut up." Once a woman makes a statement and is unwilling to compromise herself in this way, she becomes a target for ridicule and disrespect. There is no way to correct the system with one voice. Until senior officials find that there is truly something wrong with women being treated as garbage, we will continue to face this problem.

First of all, let me begin by explaining I was one of the victims of McKinney....I was appalled at the verdict, yet not surprised. I figured out early on that he would probably beat the charges, despite the fact all of us victims were telling the truth. The court-martial itself was a sham. I truly believe the jurors were protecting the institution by voting the way they did. It was a compromise verdict. They found him guilty of obstructing justice, but not guilty of sexual misconduct. Go figure. What was he obstructing?

The jurors protected the Army as a whole, but in doing that, they sacrificed us, the victims. Fact is, he is now a convicted felon, he is no longer the SMA [sergeant major of the army] and he is demoted to MSG [master sergeant]. For me, that is okay. I am satisfied at the sentence [not the verdict].

It's outrageous—hard to believe. It sends a bad message that generally, they'll back [support] their senior level officers/enlisted on these issues. If six victims aren't believed, no one person stands a chance alone.

My reaction to the Sergeant Major getting off for his misconduct is baloney. I don't think he would've gotten off if had it been a lower-ranking person. I also feel that because he hindered the investigation, he had something to hide. I think that it was wrong of them to not convict; but in the same token, the prosecutor didn't build a good case in order to do so.

It is a shame that these women are being treated as the bad guys instead of the victims. I remember when the girl in the room next to mine was raped. Every man in our unit accused her of being a slut and a liar, and she became the object of scrutiny instead of the man who hurt her. It made it so bad that the following weekend, when it happened to me, I didn't report it for fear that I would suffer the same fate as her. My father feels that these women were forced to be within his command and rather than accuse him and lose their jobs, they would wait for transfer to another command. It's very hard if you are not a strong person to stand up to the truth and all its harsh realities. When a person is treated as a criminal instead of a victim, then we [the victims] are the ones to blame. But, we also have to remember that we are guilty these days until proven innocent. The press crucifies its suspects so that no one gets an impartial day in court. We live in sad times and those who suffer are the ones to pay the piper.

McKinney's verdict was announced recently and I am saddened by the sheer disregard of these women's stories. They were re-victimized when attacked by the defense.

I am surprised at the level of audacity of this decision. I'm amazed the jury found him guilty of the obstruction of justice, but cleared him of

original misconduct. Isn't obstructing justice awfully strong circumstantial evidence of the original misconduct? Was there explicitly agreed corruption, or was the mistaken verdict a result of the military/dominant culture paradigm? By military/dominate culture paradigm, I mean all the underlying assumptions:

Good people don't commit these acts

The military advances good people

McKinney is senior (has been advanced many times)

McKinney must be a good person, which means he couldn't have committed these offenses.

In recruiting, I found the paradigms would bring people into the tent of corruption. They would unknowingly go along with corruption, because they believe the people leading them down the path were good people. Then they would realize that they were in the tent and had been for the last three or four decisions.

What an abominable travesty of justice. The idea that six women who never met, were never stationed together, and never knew of separate incidents, could be completely ignored by a jury is unconscionable but so typically military. A classic "cover your career" move; another example of the "brotherhood of the sword" protecting its embedded boys club; and yet another example of the degradation of women by the U.S. military. Where is House Bill 1072 that was attempting to correct this? Where is the Whistle-Blowers Protection Act in this scenario? If Congress isn't besieged by irate women and women's organizations over this abomination, then women in both the military and the civilian sector can just take off their shoes, fall ten steps behind men, bind their feet, put on a veil, and stay pregnant and indentured till the next millennium is over. Or shall we just sit around and wait for the McKinney movie, tell-all book, and miniseries?

I feel that the verdict sends a terrible message to women in the military——one man was believed over six women! Women accuse the president and they are mollycoddled, protected, and guarded. Women accuse a military man and they are scourged, attacked, slandered, and browbeaten. McKinney was found guilty of obstructing everything he was found innocent of doing——go figure on that one! And the Army says the military justice system worked——yeah, right. In the future if you have a complaint all you'll need is a third-party witness, videotapes, and a psychiatrist behind a one-way window to substantiate your complaint.

As a former sergeant in the Canadian Armed Forces (Army) who started as a field engineer and remustered to administration, I'm not at all surprised by the verdict, given my in-depth knowledge of the military justice system. I think it will cause some members of the military to alter some of their behavior for the better. It will encourage some victims of sexual harassment to come forward. And it will silence probably an equal number who would have come forward before.

The sad truth is that most formal claims of sexual harassment (and I speak from experience, as I handled an entire region's personnel and legal files) will never reach formal charges and will be buried. It's been that way for a long time and will most likely continue.

The sole determining factor in whether or not charges are taken seriously is the commanding officer's attitude regarding such cases. Units with commanders who demand they be taken seriously will have formal charges and less sexual harassment and units with commanders who want them ignored will have them ignored. This is my personal opinion, but is based upon extensive knowledge of individual cases and unit track records. Strong orders and attention from on high will always have more effect than any media coverage on the civilian side.

I believe that it is quite classic of the military. This is another prime example of the "good ole' boy's network" and the "officer's secret handshake." In my case, [they said] no one could have done those awful things to you and four other female staff noncommissioned officers because "he is a war decorated colonel"; or "he is a GS-14 who has never served in the military, doesn't have to live up to the military moral or ethic standards that you do, and will go to the Labor Union if we accuse him of any misconduct."

My response to the verdict is once again, the military system has protected its senior members. The question remains, why would someone who was innocent obstruct justice? Why would someone innocent feel a need to influence what a witness would say? Or to threaten a witness so intensely that they are placed into a witness protection program? Or to threaten to expose others guilty of sexual misconduct in an attempt to discourage their own prosecution? The message is very clear: that if you are senior enough, you can behave anyway you wish.

Women are ill advised to join the military. It does not improve the combat effectiveness of the military; it is purely a social experiment and pushed by the "politically correct." Drill sergeants and drill instructors are in positions of power, both physical and psychological. If any of them are sexually maladjusted (and it seems about 30 percent or better of the population is) then they will use that power via sex.

The Army clearing McKinney will no doubt require that all misdeeds of such nature be swept under the rug. From now on, all women in the Army need to carry concealed tape recorders or learn to knee men in the balls. Damn shame! Semper Fi.

My first reaction to this verdict is a simple word: "typical." From my own personal experiences with the Department of Defense, the "typical" response to any charges of sexual misconduct is that it is somehow the woman's fault. During one series of questioning by the Air Force investigators, they repeatedly asked me, "Were you wearing panties? Were you wearing a bra?" I felt as if I would have been the criminal had I not been wearing either of these undergarments! And what difference would it have made if I hadn't been wearing any bra or panties? For God's sake, I was in my own room in VOQ! I had on a T-shirt and jeans! However, it was the installation commander . . . who had propositioned me, with an understanding of how I could be promoted! He was quietly asked to retire—that's all. And that is just one of many incidents.

The military has a way of protecting its men. It also has a way of getting rid of women. The only thing that surprised me about the McKinney verdict was that they found him guilty on one charge. In the end, I would expect this verdict to be overturned, too. I know of

several incidents where male employees, civilians and military officers and enlisted, have been found guilty of sexual misconduct and have then had these charges removed from their record after filing appeals or other complaints about the system.

And what does the McKinney verdict imply about the military's response to sexual harassment and sexual assault? To me that is simple, too. The system has not changed. It remains as misleading, as nonexistent, and as controversial as ever. If you don't play by the military "rules" then you are not a part of the team. And as to the impact of this verdict, there have been many well-publicized accounts of sexual misconduct in the military in the past, and little has changed. Why would anyone expect the verdict in the McKinney case to have any long-lasting, positive impact? I believe that this case will fade to the background.

The Constitution clearly states "Congress shall have power to make rules for the government and regulation of the land and naval forces." Yet the U.S. military continues to run its own show, and what a burlesque it has become. The unmitigated gall of placing senior male military officers and NCOs above reproach has got to end soon. The blatant ignoring of the harassment of military women, on the part of the nation's leaders, is execrable.

The concept of allowing the " foxes in uniform to guard the hen houses" is ludicrous and subsequently permitting the military to mete its own punishment, without civilian scrutiny, is akin to letting the criminals run the judicial system! Write, mail, call, or fax your legislators now! Ask them to dig deeper.

During the trial of McKinney, the military took this issue very seriously. After that trial, they have become very laid back about this issue.

The comments from both inside and outside the armed forces were predominantly critical of the military's response to sexual harassment. The opinions were filled with many feelings including frustration, anger, lost hope, and cynicism. Some of the comments were from women and men who experienced firsthand the military's response to sexual harassment in their own cases. Other comments were from those who witnessed the abuse and the systemic responses to the problem.

Of particular note, no respondents voiced comments in agreement with the verdict or in approval of the military's response to sexual harassment. Unfortunately, since there were no responses submitted that represented or supported the other side of this highly charged issue; we are left with only speculation about their silence.

THE "RAPE ALLEGATION CHECKLIST"

Many service men and women indicated that their experiences of reporting the sexual assault were worse than the actual rape. This was especially true if the victims had to demonstrate they were telling the truth about the rape allegation.

Rather than assuming the crime did occur, some law enforcement and criminal justice authorities want the victim to prove it. If there is any suspicion or indication that the person reporting the rape may not be a credible witness, the "alleged victim" will be under high scrutiny. This scrutiny and outward disbelief by law enforcement, criminal justice, or medical authorities is one of the most psychologically damaging responses to rape victims. This type of treatment is referred to as "the second rape" for good reason (Madigan and Gamble, 1991).

For some military victims, being subjected to a "rape checklist" during the criminal investigation was a second rape. The checklist is an investigative tool used to "weed out" false rape allegations. However, it is rife with misconceptions about rape victims, including questions about their economic status, past sexual history, and if they reported any physical injuries. The rape checklist has reportedly been used against victims and circulated through the armed forces and civilian communities since the early 1990s ("The Checklist," 1992; Schulte, 1992).

The "rape allegation checklist" was developed by Charles P. McDowell, a retired Air Force Lieutenant Colonel with an extensive and impressive career in crime analysis and criminal justice. McDowell was a civilian supervisory special agent and senior investigative consultant for the Air Force Office of Special Investigations (AFOSI). He provided training on his rape checklist to military and civilian law enforcement and prosecutors. At the time, he was considered a leading expert on rape for the Air Force despite the controversy and protests surrounding his checklist.

The fifty-seven-item checklist proposes to assess the likelihood of whether the victim is making a false report. A higher score on the test is indicative of a false report. This could result in a quick disposal of the case by the investigator as unfounded. Even worse, with a high score there is the potential for charges brought against the victim for making a false report.

The sad irony is that the checklist cannot predict a false allegation any more successfully than a detective's hunch. In fact, according to well-known and respected researcher on rape, Dean Kilpatrick, "From a scientific perspective, there is absolutely no documentation of the validity of these test items [on the rape checklist]" (Brinkley, 1992, p. 2). Nonetheless, the rape allegation checklist was used. Moreover, it was given to military investigators who were personally trained by McDowell.

Training on the checklist was generally highly guarded and restricted only to specific audiences. For example, only certified police officers or district attorneys were allowed to register at one training session, which was cosponsored by the AFOSI. Even psychologists, psychotherapists, victim advocates, and rape crisis counselors were not authorized or allowed to attend at this training session. This factor alone raises suspicions about this checklist.

One of the two civilian prosecutors who was permitted to attend McDowell's class on "Indirect Assessment of Real and False Claims of Sexual Assault" reported about the training session and the rape allegation checklist. This prosecutor (who later became a judge) provided written documentation to prove that she attended the training session. She referred to McDowell's materials as well as her own notes from the class to provide this summary.

The training class I attended was held in 1992 cosponsored by the Air Force Office of Special Investigations (OSI). The presenter, Charles P. McDowell, said he was a special investigator for the OSI. The focus of the training class was on assessing the validity of rape allegations from alleged victims based on a rape assessment/checklist that was developed by the presenter. He began by saying that those of us working in the field should know that 60 percent of all allegations of rape are false. He then described sexual assault as "courtship behavior gone awry."

The presenter indicated that his thesis was based upon his personal observation ("research?") with three police departments. He refused to name those departments or to give us any indication of what exactly his data was based upon.

He went on to state very firmly the feminist theory that rape is a power crime was unequivocally wrong. Under his theory, the business of being a victim is a very powerful narcotic for immature, inadequate people (women). Because under his theory, the number of men and children that cry rape is "infinitesimally small."

The term that he coined to describe women that make rape reports is "false allegator." These were some of the examples he used in the training class to substantiate his theory that 60 percent of reported rapes are actually false allegations.

- *False allegators derive much pleasure from the recounting of their physical injuries.*
- *If we don't realize how many false allegators are out there, we run the risk of locking up (innocent) people and ruining their lives.*
- *Most of the falsely accused are "horny devils at the peak of their sexuality."*

These are some of his recommendations on interviewing the alleged rape victim:

- *Never allow a third party in the room when interviewing (i.e., support system, advocate, family . . .).*
- *Have the victim write a statement—she can write it in the form of a letter to the police (This was a bit disturbing for those of us who are prosecutors).*
- *Always maintain control of the interview.*
- *Watch for "pseudological fantastica" (the term he used for victim sexual fantasies leading to the allegation).*

He then went on to describe his theories of three personality types and their patterns of lying. He referred to them as: "N people, S people and I people—narcissists, sociopaths, and immature, impulsive, inadequate types." I presume he gave us this information to better assess "false or real claims" of rape.

Please note [when you look at the rape allegation checklist] there is absolutely no way a victim of sexual assault can score anything other than an "equivocal" on this list. For example, if she reports that a gun was utilized in the assault she gets 3 points—if she has financial problems, she gets 1 point—if she reports both anal and forced oral sex, she gets 1.5 points—sharp weapon lacerations are another 3 points—if the assailant wore a mask .5—if she has "shallow" scratches to face, neck, breasts, thighs, or stomach that is a 5 pointer and if she "demands" (in italics on the checklist) to be treated by a female physician or female officer, she gets another point. That score (which is from an actual sexual assault that I prosecuted where the rapist got sixty years) [according to Dr. McDowell's rape allegation checklist] would mean the "allegation is probably false."

To say the least, the presentation was disturbing and frightening. Most significant was the fact that he was absolutely unable to account for any basis for his theories.

The fifty-seven yes-or-no questions selected for the checklist call into question how these items were chosen and rated for the assessment. For example, the following items on the checklist all count as points against the "alleged" victim. However, each of these issues can indeed be a reality in sexual assault or other crimes. They do not suggest that the crime did not occur, nor should they be used against rape victim to assess the validity of the crime report.

- Does the victim report being abducted?
- Does the victim report being intoxicated at the time of the assault?
- Does the victim have difficulty in describing sexual details of the assault?
- Does the victim have a history of mental or emotional problems?
- Does the victim have a significant medical history?

After each of the fifty-seven items are answered yes or no, the assigned point value for each question is tallied to reveal the potential of a false allegation. With regard to scoring, McDowell's scale at the end of the questionnaire has made it easy for anyone to judge the validity of a rape allegation:

- 0-15 Equivocal [evasive, ambiguous, uncertain outcome, of doubtful nature]
- 16-35 Allegation probably false
- 36-75 False allegation
- 76+ up Overkill

Based on the scoring, if a victim answered no to fifty-six items, but yes to only one (she had difficulty in describing details of the assault, for example) her tally would fall in the category of "equivocal (evasive, ambiguous . . .)." Can we really expect a rape victim not to have difficulty describing the details of the rape? According to the checklist, this should raise suspicion.

How many rape victims were accused of lying or how many rapists were never charged because of the "rape allegation checklist"? Moreover, why did the military allow their investigators to receive training on assessing false allegations when the FBI indicated that the overwhelming majority of rape reports to law enforcement are true reports?

Continued efforts by the armed forces, particularly by investigative authorities, to disprove or discredit victims of sexual assault and harassment serve only to divert valuable time and resources away from the real problem. Checklists such as the "rape allegation checklist" hurt efforts to effectively address sexual assault and sexual harassment in the military. We can only hope that the DoD has banned the use of such assessments and will focus its efforts on more effective intervention strategies to assist the victims and prosecute the offenders.

8

THE HIGH PRICE OF SEXUAL
HARASSMENT AND RAPE

In the 1990s, sexual harassment is receiving increased attention. The costs to resolve incidents of sexual harassment are significant. Even more harmful and costly, however, are the negative effects sexual harassment has on productivity and readiness. These include costs associated with increased absenteeism, greater personnel turnover, lower morale, decreased effectiveness, and a loss of personal, organizational, and public trust. While not easily quantified, these costs are just as real and seriously affect the Department of the Navy's ability to meet the needs of our Nation.

—— DEPARTMENT OF THE NAVY, 1993

FINANCIAL COSTS

Sexual harassment in the U.S. Army alone costs about $250 million a year in lost productivity, personnel replacement costs, transfers and absenteeism (Seppa, 1997, p. 41).

THE FINANCIAL COSTS of sexual harassment are staggering. Yet it is difficult to ascertain exactly how much this problem costs the Department of Defense (hence, the taxpayers). According to Dr. Robert Faley, associate professor of management at Kent State University, the overall price tag is probably quite high due to the many hidden costs, such as absenteeism and lost productivity.

One of the best estimates of the potential cost of sexual harassment came from an extensive study by the U.S. Merit System Protection Board. They estimated that in 1981 alone over $100 million was lost due to sexual harassment of civilian employees within the federal government (U.S. MSPB, 1981). These cost projections were based on a number of factors that coincided with sexual harassment in the workplace. They considered the costs of absenteeism, lost work productivity, job turnover, training new employees, increases in health benefits, and lost time due to stress and emotional distress.

However, the financial loss for employers is minimal compared to the impact of sexual assault and harassment on the victims. According to the National Victim Center, many women who are raped suffer from mental health concerns in the aftermath of their victimization. Approximately one-third (31 percent) of women who experience a sexual assault will develop post-traumatic stress disorder. Others may develop depression, sometimes resulting in a severe, chronic depression. Rape victims are also thirteen times more likely to attempt suicide than women who have not been victims of crime (NVC, 1992). For some of the women and men who were sexually assaulted by military personnel, the price of rape becomes their life or their livelihood.

Serious mental health issues come at a high price for the military as well. The cost of long-term (sometimes lifelong) mental health and psychiatric care adds up when paying for victims' treatment. This expense affects the Department of Defense when the service member is on active duty and the Department of Veterans Affairs after military discharge or retirement. Providing treatment (including counseling, medical care, medications, and hospitalizations) for military victims of sexual trauma is undoubtedly very costly.

In response to this growing problem and the need to care for sexual trauma victims, the Department of Veterans Affairs developed a multi-million dollar sexual trauma counseling program operating at local vet centers across the nation. In 1995, during one of the first full years of the program operation, more than 5,000 women reportedly sought counseling for sexual trauma on active duty. These programs have been a valuable resource to military victims of sexual trauma as well as to the Department of Veterans Affairs.

In addition, in 1993 and 1994 the Department of Veterans Affairs funded the opening and operation of eight Women Veterans Comprehensive Health Centers at selected VA medical centers in the United States. The centers coordinate medical, surgical, and psychological care for female veterans. Most of the VA's 136 medical centers also have a Women Veterans' Coordinator to assist with the coordination of care for the women patients. By 1995, 51 percent of the medical centers also had a multidisciplinary sexual trauma team (Suris et al., 1998).

Another program funded in 1993 was the National Center for Post-Traumatic Stress Disorders, located at the Boston VA Medical Center. This was the first of such centers in the nation to study PTSD and trauma in women veterans. The center has been an asset to the Department of Veterans Affairs as well as to the military and civilian communities. Unfortunately, the need and the growing costs for these specialized programs will persist indefinitely given the extent of sexual victimization in the military and the nature of post-traumatic stress disorder.

There are also substantial expenses for evaluating and treating military sexual per-petrators. Recent federal legislation supports the need to carefully assess convicted sex offenders in terms of their proclivities and risks to repeat such crimes. Federal legislation, such as Meagan's Law, requires the courts to determine if the convicted individual is a *sexual predator* (someone who is likely to continue sexually assaulting others). Although the sexual predator laws (such as sex offender registration) have been contested, the military must comply with the existing federal laws until such time that they are appealed. The sexual predator and notification laws will entail costly psychiatric evaluations of all convicted sexual offenders in the military as well as additional manpower to oversee the notification and tracking of convicted perpetrators.

In addition to the multiple problems and costs brought on by military sexual offenders (including court-martials and confinements), the Department of Defense also is encum-bered with the costs of preventing sexual harassment and assault. Rape prevention and intervention programs come with a huge price tag. First and foremost, every new enlistee and officer must receive an indoctrination training on the topic. Then there are the manda-tory one-to two-hour "refresher" classes for all service members, often repeated throughout their military career. For example, according to the *Air Force Times,* during a twenty-year career, an enlisted member receives an average of thirteen hours of equal opportunity training and officers average twenty-five hours (Glenn, 1999).

In addition to the costs of the training programs, there are the costs of developing and redeveloping the model curriculums and training materials used in these programs. These costs include expenses for consultants to develop the programs, for production to develop the materials, and for personnel to implement the programs.

Other significant costs associated with sexual assault and harassment in the military includes the numerous studies and review panels. Many have concluded the same informa-tion over the past two decades. How many more panels of experts need to be compen-sated for expenses and flown to military bases all over the world before the Department of Defense accepts the existing findings? It is time to maximize our limited resources and focus on addressing the problem.

The combined direct and indirect financial costs of sexual harassment and rape in the military are enormous. However, the military pays a far greater price than a financial one for this invasive burden. How does an organization compensate for lost personnel, depressed morale, and a tarnished reputation? There may be no way to recover these losses except to learn from the past mistakes in order to avoid repeating them.

LOSS OF PERSONNEL

All charges of rape or sexual abuse are serious. The charges of rape, for example, can result in lifetime confinement (West, 1996, p. 48).

Retention is an issue for any organization. Universities, large corporations, and small family owned businesses know all too well about the cost of losing good people. The Department of Defense faces similar issues as an employer. Sexual harassment can have significant and consequential implications on retention (Fitzgerald, 1993). For the military, keeping the ranks full with good people is of particular concern especially if recruitment numbers are suffering. The Armed Forces *need* women to fill the ranks. Moreover, they need to keep the women who are currently on active duty in uniform. This is no small task given the numbers of women who have been raped or sexually harassed while in the military.

Conservative estimates from the Department of Veterans Affairs suggest that up to 200,000 of the nation's 1.2 million women veterans experienced sexual assault as an active-duty service member (Center for Women Veterans, 2001). Based on the incidence of sexual harassment in the latest DoD study, over a half a million women veterans experienced sexual harassment (Bastian et al., 1996).

It is unknown how many women or men the military has lost due to sexual assault or harassment. Personnel who are discharged or retire early because of sexual victimization can get lost in the shuffle. Service members are not usually asked if they are leaving the military because of sexual assault. Perhaps this should be a question asked and recorded anonymously for each and every discharge physical.

Consider the potential numbers of service members who were lost or let go because of a rape or sexual harassment:

How many enlisted members decided not to reenlist or officers chose not to sign on for more years even though they wanted a career in the military?

How many were discharged against their will because the commander determined they were no longer fit for service after they reported a rape or sexual harassment?

How many women or men lost opportunities for promotions after making a sexual harassment allegation only to find they could not advance any further in their career?

How many opted for an early retirement or a voluntarily discharge because of the abuse?

How many victims were ordered to have psychiatric evaluations and then involuntarily discharged as a result of being diagnosed falsely with personality disorders in the aftermath of a rape?

How many women or men left the military because of a true physical or mental health disability they incurred as a result of rape or sexual harassment or lack of appropriate medical treatment?

A good start to increase retention and attract new female recruits would be to demonstrate an earnest effort toward zero tolerance for any type of violence against women in the military. Until then, this issue will remain a costly retention problem for all branches of the service. The armed forces cannot afford to lose personnel to rape or sexual harassment. Given the numbers involved, one would think the DoD would be doing everything possible to alleviate this pervasive problem to its rank and file.

THE LASTING EMOTIONAL EFFECTS FOR VICTIMS AND THEIR FAMILIES

I cannot forgive the institution that took so much from me and
still today continues to look the other way!

—— RAPE VICTIM WHO LEFT THE MILITARY EARLIER THAN EXPECTED

I've been in the hospital twice now at the psychiatric unit for severe depression and
suicidal thoughts. I'm forty years old. Who would have thought that this would
still be a problem for me some twenty years later? I've been in counseling
for some time now and sometimes I actually feel like I'm going to be okay.
But I still have my bad days too.

—— AN ARMY VETERAN RAPED IN THE 1970S

How do you put a price on human suffering? How do we measure the personal cost of sexual harassment or rape—the loss of dignity, the loss of safety, the loss of trust in human-kind? The implications and the lasting effects can be overwhelming for the women and men who have experienced sexual assault. The consequences of sexual assault during military service can have a detrimental impact in other areas of a veteran's life as well. For example, more than ten years after victimization, some veterans still experience a decrease in quality of life, limits on educational and financial goals, and problems with work or interpersonal relationships in comparison to women who did not experience sexual trauma (Sadler et al., 2000). For these veterans, the trauma had a lasting impact. Far too many veterans will endure the impact of the abuse for the rest of their lives with medical disabilities or with chronic mental health effects.

It is important to note that not everyone who experiences sexual harassment or assault has lifelong effects. For some, their responses to the abuse may be acute and resolved soon after the incident. For others, there may be extenuating circumstances that complicate or extend the trauma. For example, if a woman reports a rape to her commander but she is not believed, she may experience a secondary victimization from the commander's actions. Her response to cope with the trauma may be very different from that of a woman who is believed, supported, and offered counseling after a rape. Therefore, the aftermath and the potential lasting effects will be different for different situations.

Some women and men who were victims of sexual trauma in the military discovered that the aftereffects of the trauma persisted well beyond their discharge from the service. They realized that just because the abuse stopped or because they left the military, their painful memories of the abuse did not necessarily go away. In fact, many victims experienced lingering or long-lasting symptoms in the aftermath of their abuse. This type of response is not uncommon for someone who has experienced a traumatic or life-threatening event—whether in the military or in civilian life.

Sexual harassment and assault can affect many areas of a person's life, including changes in self-esteem, relationships, job, career, socialization, sexual relations, body image, spirituality, and mental and physical health. Numerous research studies substantiate the wide range of effects of sexual trauma on women veterans (Butterfield et al., 1998; Fontana and Rosencheck, 1998; Hankin et al., 1999; Rosen and Martin, 1998; Wolfe, 1996). The following comments from abuse survivors point to some of the personal and professional implications of sexual victimization in the military as well as the long-term effects of such abuse.

It changed my life forever... alcoholism, agoraphobia . . . other problems too numerous to mention .

I couldn't hold jobs...I suffered panic disorder, depression, PTSD, alcoholism, self-destruction, patterns of sexual dysfunction . . . lack of trust in people . . .

I was in the Navy for four years. It was a living hell for me. I was treated so badly I nearly had a mental breakdown...I'm not surprised to see so many bad experiences.

POST-TRAUMATIC STRESS DISORDER

It is hard to fight an enemy who has outposts in your head.

— AUTHOR UNKNOWN

Many victims of a trauma experience symptoms of an anxiety condition called post-traumatic stress disorder (PTSD). Post-traumatic stress disorder is one of the most common mental health diagnoses for persons who have experienced a life-threatening trauma. Prevalence rates for persons at risk (e.g., combat veterans and rape victims) range from 3 to 58 percent (American Psychiatric Association, 1994). Military victims of sexual trauma are four times more likely to experience PTSD than persons with duty-related stress. This finding made the researchers conclude that sexual trauma on active duty is "particularly toxic for the development of PTSD" (Fontana and Rosencheck, 1998, p. 662).

PTSD is characterized by a re-experiencing of the traumatic event. The person may re-experience the trauma in a number of ways, including recurrent, intrusive thoughts, dreams, flashbacks, or intense distress when exposed to reminders of the trauma. For example, if a rape victim smells the aftershave that her rapist was wearing, she may have a flashback to the rape because the smell reminds her of the rapist and the trauma, even years later. Not everyone who has PTSD will have flashbacks, however.

Persons with PTSD experience three types of responses, according to the diagnostic criteria in the *Diagnostic and Statistical Manual of Mental Disorders* (DSM-IV) (American Psychiatric Association, 1994). These responses are avoidance, numbing, and increased arousal. In avoidance and numbing, the person tries to avoid re-experiencing or remembering the trauma by trying not to think about it. He or she may feel numb or detached, or try to avoid anything that might be a reminder of the trauma. For example, victims may avoid places, activities, and situations that they associate with the trauma. With increased arousal, however, victims experience some physical symptoms such as difficulty with sleep, poor concentration, anger outbursts, or hyper-vigilance (persistent watchfulness or guardedness).

The following are two examples from military victims of abuse revealing the unrelenting grip PTSD can have on trauma victims.

To this day, I struggle. I hate the evenings. They scare me. I hate my husband to touch me and I watch my children like a hawk. So much has changed in me that I'd really rather just die than deal with the struggle of trying to work out all of these feelings, emotions, and nightmares.

When I'm in public and I hear someone use the same first name that my rapist has, it hits me instantly. I can't even hear his first name without my heart racing and the fear overcoming me. Thankfully it's not a common name, but I hate that name because I will always think about what he did to me whenever I hear it.

Another rape victim described her symptoms that were characteristic of PTSD. She often finds herself "on guard" and hyper-vigilant in crowds—never quite fully relaxing as she remains keenly aware of everyone who is around her. She described what happens when she sees someone who resembles the man who raped her:

Every time I see a man that is his size and build in an Army uniform or an Army jacket, I freeze and my heart seems to skip a few beats. It stops me cold for fear that I may run into him again. I have to immediately go home just to feel safe again. Sometimes I have to talk myself into believing that it wasn't him. I don't know what I would do if I ever did really see him.

In this case, the woman's anxiety interferes with her daily functioning. Her fear becomes so great at times she would rather stay at home than to take the chance of seeing her rapist. She avoids treatment at VA facilities for fear that she may encounter her rapist. Although the rape occurred over a decade ago and hundreds of miles from her home, her anxiety is still very real to her.

These fears are a result of the rape she experienced in the military. They are also due to the secondary victimization she endured by her commander when she reported the sexual assault by her supervisor. The commander did not believe her and dismissed the charges. She was not referred for counseling after the rape, but was given a discharge soon thereafter for "failure to adapt to military life." She has been struggling with the effects of the rape and her subsequent removal from the service ever since. Her anxiety, fear, and post-traumatic stress disorder have now become a disability that interferes with her ability to work, to socialize, to have an intimate sexual relationship, and to be mentally and physically healthy. As with countless other veterans, this young woman has developed chronic PTSD attributed to the abuse she experienced in the military by her rapist and by her commander. Research on secondary victimization supports the claim that women may experience greater implications and mental health effects if they report the abuse to an unsympathetic command climate (Larsen, 1998; Rosen and Martin, 1998).

DEPRESSION

Some days, it feels like the sadness will never leave me. He has left
his mark on my life forever. I fear I may never be free from this dark
cloud that hovers over me, just like he did.

—— A VICTIM OF RAPE WHILE ON ACTIVE DUTY

In addition to PTSD and other anxiety disorders, many trauma victims experience depression, sometimes with suicidal thoughts. Some veterans will have repeated episodes of depression throughout their lives, whereas others may experience only a mild depression for a short period after the traumatic event. Depression among military sexual trauma survivors is well-documented (Angell, 1994; Butterfield et al., 1998; Center for Women Veterans, 2001; Hankin et al., 1999). In one study, depression was found to be three times higher for women who experienced sexual trauma on active duty than those who did not report a sexual trauma history (Hankin, et al., 1999). In combination with depression, some sexual trauma veterans also have higher rates of alcohol or other drug abuse (Butterfield et al., 1998). Women veterans who experienced a sexual assault during military service were twice as likely to have problems with alcohol as compared to women veterans who did not report being sexually assaulted (Hankin et al., 1999).

Depression or other mental health diagnoses can significantly affect the lives of women and men who were sexually assaulted on active duty. Of all the commentaries from victims of sexual trauma, the following were the most telling of the potentially devastating impact of abuse in the military.

[It was a] *barrier in my mind. . . . safely put away for now,. except for the sadness in my heart that I always carry with me.*

I was brutally and profoundly sexually abused repeatedly by a drill sergeant while in basic training. I developed severe depression, PTSD, and attempted suicide twice.

I tried to kill myself afterward, which resulted in hospitalization.

I buried it deep inside of me. It has now been two years and I am still not over what happened.

I wanted to die because the pain was so great. So, I tried to end my pain by ending my life.

SEXUAL RELATIONS

*I fear I will never be able to truly experience making love again because of the rape
that happened to me while I was in the Army.*

— VICTIM STILL HAUNTED TWENTY-THREE YEARS AFTER BEING RAPED

Although depression and post-traumatic stress disorder seem to be the two most common mental health diagnoses for sexual trauma survivors, many women and men experience difficulties in other areas of their lives as well. For example, some victims reported changes in their relationships involving trust, safety, and intimacy. Some found that there are certain aspects of sexual intimacy that have been difficult in the aftermath of the trauma. Some sexual abuse victims detach, withdraw, or lose interest in sex whereas others may feel emotionally numb and may become excessively sexually active or driven to a sexual addiction. The following comments are reflective of the diverse range of effects that sexual trauma can have on sexual intimacy and relationships.

I can barely stand for my husband to touch me in a sexual way. Hell, we've been together almost ten years. Every once in awhile we might try, but usually I get real tense and sometimes my heart starts to beat real fast. Then we have to stop. I try my best, but usually I just can't be intimate with him. I love him, but I'm afraid I'm going to lose him to this, so I keep trying. Sometimes

I just do it [for him] even though I'm dying inside. Thankfully, he's understanding and doesn't want sex too often.

It has never been the same for me. I just don't have any interest in sex since the rape.

My partner and I have been trying to get back some sexual intimacy. At first, I didn't want her to touch me at all. Then I went to counseling and we learned how to deal with some of the leftover issues that kept popping up in my head. It's getting better, but still there are times when I just shut down if she touches me the wrong way or does something that reminds me of Sergeant [name deleted]—the man who raped me. Just thinking about him makes me feel sick. It's been nearly twenty years now. I don't think I'll ever be completely over it.

After the rape, I felt used and worthless, so it didn't matter anymore how many men I had sex with because it was all meaningless now. It meant nothing. When my co-workers started to gossip about me, it just reinforced how I was already feeling— like a slut. I know it's terrible to say, but it's true. That's what the rapist did to me. He took away my ability to have a meaningful, loving, sexual relationship. He took away my dignity.

JOB AND CAREER

> *How could I stay in the service? After I reported the sexual harassment, things*
> *only got worse. I couldn't continue to work with him every day. It was as*
> *though he knew he could keep on doing it and they couldn't touch him.*
> *So, I decided to leave the military and abandon my career. As far as*
> *I know, he's still there and probably harassing someone else.*

—— FORMER AIR FORCE CAPTAIN HARASSED BY HIGHER-RANKING OFFICER

The effects of sexual harassment or assault on employment and career are another complex issue, especially for persons in the military. One of the reasons is that, by definition, sexual harassment usually occurs in the context of the work or supervisory setting. For military personnel, this could be applied twenty-four hours a day since some service members, especially trainees, reside where they work and are on duty at all times. The lines between personal and work time can become blurred.

In one case, an Air Force officer requested the assistance from her boss on her résumé. He offered to give her the advice after work at a nightclub. Then he proceeded to sexually harass her. In this case, as with many others, the supervisor's sexual harassment made it increasingly difficult for the woman to do her job. It became unbearable to the point that she left the service. The outcome was that her military career was forced short because of the sexual harassment.

The problems with sexual harassment in the military are further complicated due to the complex nature of the chain of command. Virtually any senior member has the right to give a junior service member orders. In essence, the superior ranking individual can be considered in the chain of command (or line of supervision) even if the supervisor is only one rank ahead. This creates a power imbalance (the breeding ground for sexual harassment) thereby confounding the issue for military personnel.

There are other effects on employment as well. Long-lasting attributes can affect the service member's career choice, ability to stay in the service, or ability to keep a job after experiencing an abusive situation with a supervisor.

Respondents in the DoD study indicated similar problems after reporting sexual harassment, such as hostility from supervisors or coworkers (Bastian et al., 1996). Sexual harassment in the military has far-reaching implications and can affect the person's job, duty assignment, and, potentially, career advancement. As one woman summarized, sexual harassment experienced in the military is especially difficult because "the women does not have the option to leave the job." Therefore, victims of sexual harassment in the military may find that the harassment is a part of their job and that they must learn to deal with it in order to stay in the service.

In addition, reporting sexual harassment or assault may also have a negative impact on a spouse's career. One woman indicated that her husband's career was threatened when she reported being raped by a fellow officer. Her husband's commander tried to discourage the rape report. The victim felt that her husband's career was compromised because she made the report. The commander implied that it would hurt her husband's career if the rape report was not dropped. Soon thereafter, her husband received orders for an overseas transfer.

The effects on the job and career are far-reaching in the military and may carry on long after the person leaves the service. The following are a few examples of how sexual trauma in the military affected some women.

Since I left the army, I have suffered from PTSD. It has gotten so bad for me, I haven't worked since October 1990. I even tried working on my college education on three different occasions in the past eight years.

I've been depressed since my discharge. I have not been able to hold jobs. . . . my relationships are hard, at best.

My career in the military was cut short because of the sexual assault. I planned to retire from the service, but I just couldn't work with him every day. I feel lost since my discharge and I still haven't found my way. It's been one menial job after another ever since.

HEALTH AND ILLNESS

> *I am infertile and have numerous other gynecological problems. I am losing the sight in my right eye; I have a brain tumor from the beating to my head and face; my nose and the right side of my face is noticeably different than my left....*
> [And I need] *ongoing psychiatric treatment for the mental impact of the attack.*
>
> —— VICTIM OF EXTENSIVE ABUSE BY A FELLOW MILITARY SERVICE MEMBER

The impact of sexual trauma on health and physical wellness can also be chronic, severe, and sometimes lifelong. Numerous women reported how their health has declined since the sexual abuse occurred. Specifically, some of the women identified the correlation between their emotional stress and the subsequent effects on their health. As one veteran stated, "My body is very sick due to being on the extreme alert mode for many years."

The links between exposure to stress and health are well documented. Moreover, the mind and body connections (as with depression and lower resistance to illness) have also been substantiated in the medical and mental health fields. It should be no surprise that so many victims of sexual abuse reported a negative impact on their health.

Some of the more common health problems associated with sexual abuse are sexual desire disorder, painful intercourse, or sexually transmitted diseases (STDs). However, women may also develop other complications (such as pelvic inflammatory disease) resulting from inadequate health care or lack of treatment. For some rape survivors, it can be particularly stressful to undergo a gynecological examination, so they may avoid getting treatment due to their heightened anxiety. Failure to seek treatment when symptoms first appear or abstaining from routine care can lead to potential complications and chronic medical conditions.

One Army veteran who raped on active duty by a supervisor reported how it took years for her to make an appointment with a gynecologist after the sexual assault. She did not want to go through the invasive examination nor to have "a stranger" that close to her. When she did finally have an appointment with a female gynecologist, her endometriosis (misdiagnosed by a military physician) had progressed to the point that she could no longer endure the pain. Her avoidance in seeking care (which stemmed from the anxiety associated with the rape) ultimately resulted in a total hysterectomy. Although this veteran receives disability compensation for the loss of her reproductive organs, she still grieves the reality that she will never have children—a lifelong loss that she attributes to the rape and its consequences.

Many women in this study expressed various concerns about pregnancy and childbearing. Some veterans indicated they could not have children as a result of physical or psychological harm from the abuse. Others who contracted a sexually transmitted disease from the sexual assault were concerned about the dangers when delivering a baby. In addition, some women became pregnant from the rape. As one service member noted in Chapter 6, the child she delivered after the sexual assault is a source of strength and a reminder of the beauty in life. Other women undoubtedly have faced an unexpected pregnancy from a sexual assault with a heavy heart and possibly a difficult decision. A pregnancy or an abortion resulting from rape could have a lifelong impact for anyone who faces this dilemma.

Some women also endure chronic medical conditions imposed by their rapist. Consequently, their medical diagnoses can complicate their mental health recovery. For example, a woman with genital warts (a lifelong STD with implications on childbearing) is reminded of her rapist every time she has an outbreak of the illness. This hampers her recovery and it fuels her depression and anger about the rape and about the inadequate medical care she received by a military gynecologist.

Aside from gynecological diagnoses, victims of sexual assault and harassment also experienced myriad other illnesses and physical complaints including chronic pain, headaches, weight gain or loss, gastrointestinal disorders, irritable bowel syndrome, ulcers, and eating disorders (Angell, 1994; Frayne et al., 1999; Sadler et al., 2000). Of particular significance were the numerous examples of women who experienced multiple conditions or illnesses. The women who reported chronic physical effects usually associated more than one illness or complaint with the rape or harassment. Very few women who addressed physical illnesses noted only one medical diagnosis. Consider the following feedback on how these medical conditions have changed their lives:

Half of my life gone to depression, migraine headaches, and PTSD. . .

The year spent in Korea was truly the most difficult time of my life. I am now a changed woman. Physically, I lost most of my hair and twenty pounds from my frame. Emotionally, I am depressed because I did what I felt I "must" do, and my chain of command neglected to act accordingly.

After I was raped, it took me almost ten years before I could go to a gynecologist, even though I was having some serious pain and other problems. My counselor worked with me for a long time to help me to even be able to go for an appointment to meet with a female doctor. I asked her to give me some Xanax [anxiety medicine] just so I could finally go to see the gynecologist. I was real lucky to find such a good, caring, female doctor. She diagnosed me with endometriosis. It had gotten so bad that I needed surgery. I still blame the man who raped me for all of this. I wouldn't be dealing with all these medical and mental problems now if he hadn't done that to me then. And the Army let him stay in after all that! He's probably enjoying his retirement pay by now while I have to deal with depression, surgery, PTSD, and lots of pain that will never fully go away.

RELATIONSHIPS

> *I have to screen what I watch on TV, not to mention the toll this has taken on my family. My first husband divorced me. My second husband has been through hell and back.*
>
> —— A SEXUAL ASSAULT VICTIM DEALING WITH THE
> NEGATIVE IMPACT ON HER RELATIONSHIPS

The effects of sexual abuse on relationships can be devastating and far-reaching according to some of the comments submitted. Many of the respondents indicated that both work and personal relationships were stressed, tested, and strained in the aftermath of sexual harassment or sexual assault. Being believed seemed to be one of the major factors in how or to what extent their relationships were affected. Persons who doubted the victim often increased the strain in the relationship due to their disbelief or indifference. In some situations, if the victim did not feel supported or believed by her partner, the relationship suffered to the point of demise.

However, some relationships were affirmed or strengthened by spouses, friends, or co-workers who supported and believed the victim. Often times an alliance formed in the aftermath of the crisis in which both parties united against the abuser or an abusive work situation. The relationship became stronger because of the support. As one victim said, "I knew I could count on my best friend whenever I needed to talk to someone about the rape. She was always there for me."

The strength in the relationship stems from the knowledge that the other person believes and supports them unconditionally. Nonetheless, even the relationships that were supportive may have experienced some of the detrimental effects of the sexual harassment or the rape. The following is what victims said about how their lives and their relationships have changed since the abuse.

The last ten years of my life have been hell. . . . lost hope of ever gaining recovery... panic attacks... clinical depression . . . inability to even date, let alone establish an intimate relationship.

I find it so difficult to trust anyone since all of this happened. The person who sexually harassed me was my direct supervisor. He was the first person to let me down. I never expected he would do that to me. Then my unit let me down by not standing behind me. No one wanted to get involved. Sometimes I feel so alone because I can't trust anyone.

I surrounded my world with women. I don't trust men [ever since being gang-raped on a military base].

I don't think I would have gotten through this without my husband. He has been a tremendous support—very loving, patient, and never doubted me. Having him in my life when I was dealing with the rape has made all the difference.

OTHER EMOTIONAL WOUNDS

It took me a long time to respond because sexual harassment . . . so often came up during my career and then in an odd twist ended it. I have sad memories of how it ended that will haunt me forever. All I can say is I did what good I could for my country, but in the end I was treated so hurtfully. I wish I had someone to talk with about what happened to me. I'm tormented.

—— FORMER MARINE STRUGGLING TO COPE WITH THE AFTERMATH OF RAPE

Sexual abuse in the military has left long-lasting emotional scars on some victims. Some victims are filled with an immense amount of rage and anger at the military for what has happened to them. A significant number feel let down or hurt by the military for what happened (or what did not happen) in the aftermath of the abuse. They often blame the military for how the service responds to sexual harassment or rape, for not doing a better job to protect or to defend them, or for causing more harm to them and for deserting them. These service members were left alone to deal with their hurt and their rage after the trauma.

One Navy veteran wrote extensively about her repeated harassment by a female supervisor when she was assigned to Puerto Rico during the Grenada invasion. In addition to the sexual harassment, she also encountered gender discrimination from her supervisor. This Service member was subjected to demeaning comments and job repercussions throughout the duration of her assignment. After months of repeated abuse on active duty, she has since retired with a medical disability. The following is what she had to say about the impact of the harassment on her life:

I was in the Navy from 1981 to 1987. It was really a rough time for me. And now I have been diagnosed with PTSD from the years of harassment that I endured. I was stationed in Puerto Rico where I experienced continual daily harassment, ridicule, belittling, and I even had my promotions withheld. This inhumane treatment all came from a female officer who truly enjoyed tormenting me. This "lieutenant from Hell" made my life a living nightmare with no way of escape.

Well, needless to say this has all had a tremendous impact on my life. I've had numerous breakdowns. I've been on all types of medicine for depression, anxiety, high blood pressure, high cholesterol, migraines, and weight problems. I will never go through another pregnancy again for fear of past experiences. I even have nightmares and flashbacks about that wicked woman I worked for.

Personally, I've taken various psychiatric meds and received inpatient and outpatient therapy for PTSD. Three of the inpatient hospitalizations were outside the VA system. Only a small portion of treatment was actually covered by the VA, despite my being service connected. . . . All of this has been so stressful for me; many times I've been suicidal. I've also been trying to finish my college education for the past ten years through voc rehab. but the PTSD seems to get the best of me . . .

Anyway, as far as the VA and their paperwork process...it took me eight years to get my compensation adjusted. I submitted at least four regional disagreements and finally appealed my case to Washington, DC, with help from the Paralyzed Veterans organization.

I personally feel that no human deserves to go through the degrading and dehumanizing treatment that I endured while I served in the Navy. Currently, I'm involved with a VA women's group for other female vets also suffering from PTSD. I hear so many stories from every female veteran I meet and there's many of us out there.

A number of victims of sexual harassment and sexual assault voiced powerful emotions. For some, their anger was so predominate it seemed to overshadow any peace or resolution. The following are some of the comments from victims who felt let down or hurt by the military after their abuse. For many, their despair continues years later.

It makes me incredibly sad to see [and] know that so many women have suffered this kind of abuse. The worst thing I experienced wasn't the assault. It was how I was treated by my command after the investigation was dropped.

The military does not care.

When I needed the support from the Air Force the most, they failed me.

Similarly, feelings of anger (of rage) were the focus of several commentaries.

I am so angry and frustrated. I have nowhere to direct my feelings, because they [the military] don't have anyone I can direct them toward!

I was raped on January 6, 1993. To this day, the USAF will not take responsibility for the injustice they imposed upon me. They still state that I only reported the rape on April 8, 1993 (three months later).... after I was informed I was being discharged. (This woman included a copy of her medical records documentation from the rape exam to prove that she did report the rape to military authorities in January, as she stated. Despite this evidence from a military physician's report, no charges were filed in the case and the victim was indeed discharged soon thereafter.)

How many names on the [women in military service] memorial registry were victims of rape? Why honor us when you do nothing to protect us?

My success in the Army was overshadowed and haunted by the real system, the one set up to silence victims and keep the military's image sparkling clean.

I was very bitter early on because of how they [command] treated me. I wondered why they weren't protecting me.

Two veterans offered some hope amidst the anger and sadness:

I am taking my rage and turning it around to make it work for myself and other women by confronting the truth.

I have fought hard to try to stop some of the harassment that occurs in the military and have tried to open doors for women that will follow me.

These comments from veterans and active-duty service members speak volumes about the impact of rape and sexual harassment. They have taught us that the effects of sexual trauma are as different as the women and men who experience them.

RAPE AND HARASSMENT AT THE MILITARY ACADEMIES

Military academies and colleges are the foundational support for grooming and fine-tuning many of the armed forces' prospective top officers. There are nine of these prestigious schools in the nation. Two are state supported; two are private; two are state-supported civilian schools with strong military programs; and three of the schools are financed by the Pentagon: the Air Force Academy, the Naval Academy, and West Point (Schmitt, 1997).

They all share a rich and deep history of discipline, structure, and adherence to military values and a military way of life. They are the training grounds for the military leaders of the future. In fact, numerous outstanding leaders received their start at a military college. These schools want only the best and demand the best from their cadets and midshipmen.

Despite hand selection from an elite group of outstanding high school graduates, the prestigious military academies still find sexual offenders among their students. Reports of rape and sexual harassment at the Naval, Army, and Air Force academies and other military institutes persist with troubling repercussions to the victims.

The GAO has repeatedly studied the extent and problem of sexual harassment at the three Department of Defense service academies due to the growing concerns about incidents of abuse. Their findings are a harsh critique of what really happens in the closed environment of the military academies. The GAO reported in 1995 that more than 70 percent of the women at the three federally financed military academies indicated they experienced sexual harassment on a monthly basis; 11 percent of the men reported the same. Over one-third of the women also reported that they were victims of "physical behavior that interfered with their performance or created a hostile environment" (GAO, 1995a). In addition, one to two women out of every ten had received sexual advances that linked to their job or educational endeavors at the academy.

The number of women reporting sexual harassment at two of the academies in the 1993-1994 study actually increased from a previous study in 1990-1991. It was only a few short years after the Tailhook exposé, but the students at the Naval and Air Force academies still did not seem to learn the lesson, as sexual harassment incidents continued to increase.

Given the chilly and often abusive climate against women at these academies, it is understandable that most victims would not want to report, much less talk about, the abuse. Reporting such an allegation against another cadet or midshipman within the tight brotherhood would likely cut short the woman's term at the academy or her prospective career in the military. Case after case that was released to the public through the media has shown exactly how difficult it is for women who do try to report rape or sexual harassment within the confines of these institutions. The following case chronology exemplifies what can happen to a criminal report of rape when it involves a military academy student.

June 2000

A female Naval Academy student reported that she was sexually assaulted by fellow Academy members at a party hosted by one of her classmates. She received a forensic evidence collection examination by a medical professional and an extensive interview by the police.

July 2000

Two Naval Academy midshipmen (and members of the football team) were charged with a second-degree rape and a second-degree sexual offense. They were suspended from the football team, but remained at the Academy.

November 2000

Another Academy student and football player (who was going to testify against his two teammates) was implicated with DNA evidence and also charged in the crimes. He was also suspended from the team but remained at the Academy.

The woman and the three accused sexual offenders remained at the academy in their junior year during the investigation. They were all under court order to have no contact with each other.

During the investigation, the men admitted to having sex with the woman but said it was consensual. One of the accused acknowledged to the police that the woman had "passed out" and slipped "in and out of consciousness" as they were having sex with her (as reported by Roig-Franza, 2001, in *The Washington Post*). It is a felony in most states to have sexual conduct with someone who is substantially impaired due to alcohol intoxication or mental capacity. Even the UCMJ calls it rape when "the victim is unable to resist because of the lack of mental or physical facilities." According to Dr. (Lieutenant Colonel) E. Cameron Ritchie, Office of the Assistant Secretary of Defense for Health Affairs, this could include someone who is intoxicated or drunk (Rhem, 2001).

March 2001

The defense team requested information about the woman's sexual activity for the six months prior to the alleged sexual assaults. Even though most state laws prohibit using a victim's past sexual history in trial, there are exceptions. The defense team wanted the jury to know that the woman told the hospital nurse that she had had consensual sex two nights earlier. Their premise was that the consensual sex two days before could have accounted for the vaginal tearing found by the medical examiners during the forensic evidence collection exam.

The attorneys for the accused asked for a psychiatric evaluation of the woman. The defendants also requested the right to review the woman's Naval academy disciplinary file for information that could be used to attack her credibility in trial.

The lead defense lawyer on the case, T. Joseph Touhey, responded to their requests for the victim's sexual history, academy files, and a psychiatric evaluation: "We're hopeful that these motions would give her pause in coming out to say the things that we think she's going to say at trial.... Certainly, if it leads to [her dropping charges], we're happy if it has that effect" (Roig-Franza, 2001).

March 15, 2001

To avoid a potentially difficult trial, all parties concerned agreed to a plea-bargain agreement. As a part of the deal, the men agreed to resign from the Naval Academy. The former midshipmen will not have to repay their tuitions to the academy due to a Pentagon rule that exempts persons who are charged before their junior year. The men were charged the summer before their junior year. Military academy tuition is paid from tax dollars at a cost of up to $210,000 to $282,000 per four-year graduate (Schmitt, 1997).

The men must get advance permission to be on campus at the Naval Academy and must avoid any contact with the alleged victim. They will be eligible to have their records expunged of the charges in three years but they will never be eligible for military service.

Almost nine months after the incident occurred, the woman could finally continue her classes at the academy without fear of running into any of these men on campus. The men are free to go on with their lives as well.

This case exemplifies what sexual assault victims may encounter and endure when reporting a sexual assault. It takes a great deal of courage to report rape or harassment. When victims do come forward to report a sexual offense, they deserve the same consideration and respect as any other crime victim. It is particularly repugnant to attempt to destroy the credibility of a military cadet, midshipman, or service member who was victimized on active duty in service to our country. It is time to stop blaming the victim— even if it makes a good defense.

PART IV

CONFRONTING THE PROBLEM

9

SUGGESTIONS FOR VICTIMS AND FOR THE MILITARY FROM SURVIVORS OF MILITARY SEXUAL TRAUMA

No matter what happens, don't ever give up.

—— A SURVIVOR OF RAPE AND SEXUAL HARASSMENT IN THE MILITARY

Even though there may be times when you feel like you are alone in this, remember that you are not alone. Even though there may be times when others call you a liar, remember that you are not a liar. Even though there may be times when you wonder if you will ever move beyond this, remember that you will survive and thrive and go on with your life.

—— FROM A VETERAN AND A SURVIVOR

THE VICTIMS WHO participated in this study willingly shared their insights and the lessons learned from their experiences. Many of them wanted to give advice on what should be done to make things better. Some of them needed to talk about the trauma they endured in hopes that it would not be repeated with anyone else. Most of them, however, wanted to pass along some words of wisdom to others who might face this issue in the service. The majority of these comments were heartfelt with a keen awareness of the difficulties ahead. Although their advice was directed toward other victims, anyone who works with service members who have been raped or harassed, especially military leaders can gain important insight from their perspectives.

REPORT THE ABUSE

If your chain of command isn't working for you, go outside of your command to make the report to MPs, IG, JAG, EEO, civilian authorities—go wherever you have to go until someone takes the charges seriously.

Many victims of sexual harassment and rape encouraged others to report the abuse to an authority. This advice was surprising since the majority of victims do not make an official report—as was the case with most of the participants in this study. It was almost as though the respondents were saying, "In retrospect, I wish I would have reported it." They passed along their wisdom and regrets to others facing the same decision.

If you are harassed, report it .

Go to the military police to file an official police report.

Go to the MPs, file a complaint for every possible charge in the UCMJ that applies.

Take it to your chain of command.

File assault charges with your local and military police immediately. The only way to stop it is to file outside military channels.

TAKE ACTION ON YOUR OWN BEHALF

Things don't change unless you take an active part and change them.

Contrary to the advice to report the abuse, many veterans suggested that women should take action on their own behalf and not wait for a commander or anyone else to do it for them. The underlying message to victims was that no one will advocate for you to the extent that you can do for yourself. Some Service members even suggested that these cases should be taken out of military jurisdiction. To that end, there is a growing movement by some veterans to take legal action through civil lawsuits. As mentioned previously, there is also an effort on the part of some veterans to get a reversal on the Feres Doctrine. The following is a selection of the comments that encouraged taking action outside the usual military channels if necessary.

Don't count on senior leadership to stand behind you.

Go public and start filing class action lawsuits against the military.

No one will stand up for you better than you can do for yourself.

REACH OUT FOR HELP

Help is available. You may have to keep looking, but there are good people out there who want to help you through this. Trust your instincts.

In addition to making a report and taking some type of action, victims were also encouraged to reach out for help. These messages were compassionate and supportive, offering a listening ear and a friend in the battle against sexual abuse in the military. The veterans' messages also attempted to decrease the isolation by reminding other victims that they are not alone.

For those of you who believe in seeking justice, just hang in there, help is on the way! It is not over, and justice will prevail!

Analyze the situation. Can you handle it alone or do you need help?

Reach out to other victims for support. You're not alone. We're here if you need someone who understands and cares.

BE RESPONSIVE TO VICTIMS

What should the military do to help victims of sexual harassment and rape and how can it best address this problem? Those were the two questions posed to Service members sexually assaulted or harassed in the military. The answers and suggestions they shared are based on their personal experiences on active duty.

Their feedback and recommendations encompassed several areas of concern: leadership response to the victims' sexual abuse and harassment, leadership response to the sexual offenders, disciplinary issues, the investigative and reporting process, victim sensitivity, counseling options, education, prevention, and systemic changes. Each of these areas is addressed in the following section with the specific suggestions as to how the military can do better in responding to this problem.

Of significant concern is how the military is actually responding to victims of sexual abuse. Many service members believe that the military needs to be more responsive to victims' needs, especially at the time of disclosure or when the report is made. In fact, numerous suggestions were given on the importance of offering the victim options and providing immediate access to counseling. In addition, the need for confidentiality was frequently cited. The following are some of the general suggestions offered by respondents.

Look at each case individually. Don't assume all women are lying.

They should take it seriously. They say that it is a serious issue, however, in reality, that's not the case.

Respond with more compassion!! Don't expect the victim to return to "normal" soon after an incident of this nature.

Support the victim—refer to civilian health professionals for support.

They should not prejudge anyone who has come forward with an allegation.

The victims should be protected at all costs. We go into the military to protect our country. We should be protected against rape and assault also.

I don't know how they should deal with it, but I do know how they should not deal with it. They didn't ask me what I wanted.

This perspective was shared by several other women. Many victims were detached from the investigative process and did not know what to expect. They wanted to be more informed of the investigation, the command's decision, and the outcome of their report. These women indicated they felt isolated from the case after making the report. They sensed that their opinion was neither wanted nor important. In fact, some women felt chastised in the reporting process. As one woman stated:

Don't punish victims (or witnesses) for reporting it.

SEPARATE THE VICTIM AND THE OFFENDER
Separate the victim and the offender into different units (the offender should go, not the victim).

A frequent suggestion on how to best assist victims of sexual abuse was to separate the victim and the offender, particularly if they worked at the same job site. Of the service members who made this remark, the majority of them favored giving the option of a transfer to the victim. Therefore, if the victim wants or needs to leave the duty station, that option should be given to him or her. If the victim does not want to leave, some stated that the offender should be transferred to avoid future contact and further trauma to the victim.

The recommendations to transfer sexual offenders bring up two very important questions. First, would the transfer be a part of the disciplinary action (and therefore could be implemented only in cases in which the alleged offender was indeed found guilty)? If so, does this option infringe upon the rights of the accused? Imposing discipline before the accused is found guilty is often dangerous territory (at least it is in civilian venues). Many opponents would suggest this option would be abused by those who wanted to have someone moved to another duty station. Those persons who believe that false accusations are common would likely insinuate that rape and harassment reports would become more suspect to false allegations. This would serve only to complicate the issue and possibly hurt more people in the long run.

Although transferring the offender could serve to decrease the victim's distress, this option could potentially become a substitute for adequately confronting and disciplining sexual offenders. In other words, some commanders might use this as a way of not dealing with the charges by ridding their units of sexual offenders. Then the sexual offenders become someone else's problem and, potentially, someone else's target. Many victims expressed concerns about the inadequacies of military disciplinary action and the potential loopholes for the offenders. Transferring sexual perpetrators to new units or discharging them into society does not effectively deal with the criminals nor does it stop their abusive behaviors. It simply "dumps" the problem onto another community.

Despite these two important considerations, the distressing comments of abuse victims who were further traumatized by the continued presence of their abuser at their job site should not be overlooked. It is indeed an issue that needs further consideration. The following is what some victims had to say about transfer or reassignment.

They should move [transfer] the people who did the crime or if the victim wants to transfer, they should move the victim.

If a victim has been assaulted by someone in the command, it would be helpful if there was an option to be reassigned or to have the offender reassigned.

Move victim to a new unit to avoid humiliation.

OFFER CONFIDENTIAL COUNSELING

The Pentagon would not dare consider a mission without ensuring the safety and well-being of their male soldiers. Is it really too much to ask for confidential rape counseling programs to ensure the safety and well-being of their female troops?

By far, the number one suggestion by respondents was the need for confidential counseling. Overwhelmingly, the majority of respondents cited counseling as the best way for the military to help victims of sexual abuse to respond to the issue. There was also a consensus as to how and when counseling should be made available to victims.

First and foremost, counseling should be offered immediately as an option to all victims of sexual assault (though it should not be mandatory). Second, counseling for victims should be provided by someone with specialized training in sexual trauma issues and experience working with victims. If no rape crisis counselors are available on base, the counseling referrals should include civilian counselors who are not associated with the military. Finally, but most important, the counseling should be strictly confidential between the therapist and the victim. The following are some of the recommendations affirming the need for counseling for sexual assault and sexual harassment victims, particularly in these identified priority areas.

MAKE PROMPT REFERRALS FOR COUNSELING

According to many survivors, the fact that counseling is available on base is not sufficient. They need to know as soon as possible that such support is readily available to them. "First responders" (such as the commanders, hospital staff, and military police) all need to be apprised of how to make prompt and appropriate referrals for counseling.

The timing of a counseling referral is crucial according to some women. It is very important for victims of sexual trauma to have the option of counseling at the time of disclosure. This is often a time of crisis, confusion, and severe distress for the victim. Therefore, the sooner the support is made available, the better it will be for the victim and her overall recovery. Written referral information, such as a handout or brochure, is helpful so that the victims may refer to it at a later time. Numerous women echoed this priority.

Get them help immediately! There should be a woman in every company battalion who is trained to help a woman victim of sexual assault. I felt so alone and scared—awfully scared!

Have the victims start counseling immediately upon reporting the incident.

Victims should receive support and counseling ASAP.

Counseling should be offered right away—including counseling to dependents on all military bases.

UTILIZE COUNSELORS WITH RAPE CRISIS EXPERTISE

The need for "good counselors," as many women noted, is imperative. Far too many rape and harassment victims had a negative or unfavorable experience with military or VA counselors who did not have adequate training or expertise with sexual trauma issues. This is not to suggest that the therapists were unethical (though some examples of unethical behavior were cited). More to the point, some of the counselors did not have the proper knowledge or expertise to treat sexual abuse (according to some of the victims who sought treatment).

Counselors who are uninformed about rape and sexual harassment may not be as effective with clients who are dealing with these issues. The therapist's lack of knowledge or minimal training on sexual trauma could also have a detrimental impact on the counseling. For example, one woman indicated that her counselor said it was important to go over every detail of the rape "to get over it." The client was very uncomfortable with this, but did so because the counselor said it was important. To the contrary, repeating the details of the rape may have been more traumatic for the woman at that time. It is neither necessary nor important for the victim to "purge" the trauma in such a way unless the victim feels a need to do so. The end result for rape victims is that their experiences with untrained counselors can be more harmful than helpful.

Receiving help from a counselor who has specialized experience with rape trauma or harassment issues can make a great difference in the victim's recovery. Many women said their positive experiences in therapy were a turning point in their lives. Some of the women specifically mentioned VA sexual trauma counseling programs or local rape crisis centers as their most helpful support after the abuse. These programs can serve as a model to the military for developing this important resource. Based on the feedback from service members, there is a critical need for highly qualified counselors trained in sexual trauma recovery. The following are some of the comments supporting the availability of trained rape crisis counselors at all military bases, both stateside and abroad.

My experiences with abuse in the military along with my experience in therapy have made me realize how much need there is for "good" counselors and therapists in this world. It has given me an insight and empathy that I feel a lot of counselors don't have. . . .

Have sexual assault counselors who specialize in this area.

[Rape] counseling for PTSD should be available at all veterans' hospitals.

Assign a trained advocate to all victims.

Have rape therapy groups.

Keep the VA sexual trauma counseling programs—expand the services, open more offices, help as many victims as you can.

SUPPORT CONFIDENTIALITY BETWEEN THERAPIST AND CLIENT

Confidentiality in counseling is a complicated issue on military installations. Members of the military (and their dependents) have not been afforded the right to confidentiality in counseling when seeking assistance on military bases. Although privileged communication exists between licensed psychotherapists and patients in the civilian sector, the same is not always true for military service members and their spouses or their children (GAO, 2000).

The DoD has been granted exception to the privacy of medical and mental health communications and records, in part because such absolute confidentiality is viewed as a threat to military readiness. The commanders' "need to know" about their troops apparently supersedes the patients' right to address personal issues in confidence with their therapist or doctor. Even the medical records do not belong to the patient.

Groups such as the American Psychiatric Association and the Defense Task Force on Domestic Violence have voiced strong opposition to the lack of patient confidentiality and privilege in the armed forces (GAO, 2000). This issue has also been studied extensively by the GAO and was the focus of a report to congressional committees in April of 2000. The GAO (1995b) noted:

According to DoD, the Privacy Act of 1974 is the foundation for confidentiality and privacy programs for DoD and military services. In general, the privacy act recognizes the legitimate needs of the federal government for information. One of the exceptions [to confidentiality] applicable to DoD is the disclosure of information to officers and employees who have a need to determine an individual's suitability for military duty. (p. 6)

Therefore, since commanders are responsible for the safety of their troops and their family members, counselors for the military must inform commanders when there may be a potential threat to the service member, family member, the unit, or the armed forces, in general. This includes cases in which the service member's mental health may hinder his or her "suitability" to do a job, as addressed later in this section.

However, there has been some progress in recognizing the need for confidentiality with civilians (military dependents) in counseling. Both the Supreme Court and federal legislation have recognized the importance of confidentiality in counseling. In the Supreme Court decision *Jaffee v. Redmond,* the court upheld confidentiality between a licensed counselor and patient—even if the patient is a federal employee. In the Violence Against Women Act of 1994, victims of violence were also afforded privileged communication—though this too has been challenged, particularly in cases involving unlicensed advocates at domestic violence shelters and rape crisis programs.

Nonetheless, the Judge Advocate General Corps of the U.S. armed forces and others in DoD continue to object to absolute confidentiality for military members and their dependents. They cite military necessities and personnel readiness as reasons that it is not practical for the armed forces to comply with federal legislation (including the prominent Supreme Court ruling upholding privileged communications as noted in *Jaffee v. Redmond*).

Confidentiality concerns are certain obstacles to getting treatment for many military service members and family members. It is especially important for abuse victims to know that they can talk freely to a professional who is not involved with the case. Consequently, there may be serious implications for persons who want or need therapy but are reluctant to seek help due to confidentiality concerns. Some Service members believe that victims of abuse should seek counseling off base with a civilian provider to ensure their privacy and safety.

Offer good counseling, with someone that the victim feels comfortable with—even if it means going downtown away from the military system.

Refer members to vet center or civilian health care—not to a military mental health clinic.

The need for confidential counseling (in a civilian setting, if necessary) raises questions regarding access to information and related concerns from many service members. For example, commanders have the authority to access mental health information of service members in their unit to ascertain the "mental fitness" of the individual. Military necessity or the commander's right to know to ensure safety of personnel and operations, supersedes the confidentiality of an individual service member. According to some of the women in this study, this information can be and has been used against rape victims in discharges, disciplinary hearings, and other military actions (such as a loss of security clearance).

The right of commanders to access confidential counseling records brings up numerous issues. Confidentiality is very important in a therapeutic relationship for trust to develop between the therapist and the client. It can also be critical in abuse cases where the information, if leaked, may become a threat to the victim's safety and wellbeing. Opponents of the confidentiality limitations argue that service members may be inhibited or less likely to seek counseling if their commander has access to the information. Indeed, this is probably true and very problematic for many service members. Those who do not want to risk their commander finding out may try to deal with their mental health problems on their own and sometimes unsuccessfully—potentially leading to an explosive situation including homicide or suicide. This is an underlying risk that the DoD is taking by limiting confidentiality.

However, a member of the American Psychiatric Association's Confidentiality Committee, Dr. Jay Weiss, and a former Army Colonel publicly recognized the issue of informing commanders of the mental status of their troops. Weiss had been a staunch supporter of complete confidentiality for military family members. In fact, he and colleague Mary Graves (a clinical social worker and former major in the U.S. Army) both opted to leave their military careers on grounds that confidentiality should be applied fully to family members who are receiving counseling at military installations (Jowers, 1997). Although Weiss appreciates the value of confidentiality in counseling, he also realizes the need for "military necessity" when it comes to active duty personnel. Perhaps the greater issue is: to what extent do commanders have a need to know about the personal counseling sessions of their troops? Consider what some service members had to say about this issue.

Refer them for sexual trauma counseling to a provider who can maintain confidentiality.

Keep the rape confidential.

Protect confidentiality of victim.

Make it easier to report in confidence and to seek help confidentially. Military commanders don't need to know if you get counseling. If someone who works at a nuclear power plant gets raped and seeks counseling, does the supervisor need to know? What about a pilot who is sexually harassed? Does the employer have a right to know about her therapy sessions ? Where does it end? Divorce? Abortion? Miscarriage? Infidelity? Isn't anything personal and deserving of privacy?

FURTHER SUGGESTIONS FOR THE MILITARY ON REPAIRING THE DAMAGE

In addition to suggestions on how to better serve victims of rape and sexual harassment, there were numerous comments about what the military should do to be more responsive to this issue overall. The areas of leadership response, criminal investigation, offender discipline, and military policies (such as zero tolerance) were all targets marked for improvement.

Military women and men offered a wealth of advice on how to repair the damage of sexual abuse in the military. Their recommendations are listed in order of the most often cited by the service members.

COMMAND AND LEADERSHIP RESPONSES

> *The supreme quality for a leader is unquestionably integrity. Without it,*
> *no real success is possible, no matter whether it is on a section gang,*
> *on a football field, in an army, or in an office. The first great need,*
> *therefore, is integrity and high purpose.*
>
> —— GENERAL DWIGHT D. EISENHOWER

There was a variety of suggestions as to how military leadership and command should respond to victims of sexual harassment or rape, especially at the time of disclosure of the allegations. The responses ranged from protecting the victim to offering information and support. Their emphasis was on treating victims of sexual harassment and rape with respect and dignity. The most frequently cited examples of how to demonstrate respect and dignity were believing the victim and not judging or blaming the victim for the abuse. The following suggestions from respondents offer advice on how military leaders can respond more effectively to victims of sexual abuse.

The chain of command should be concerned instead of acting like they don't believe you.

Listen. Believe. Keep them safe. Provide as much stability and safety for the victim as possible.

Protect victims from assailants even if there is no proof of the assault.

Prevention! Create an atmosphere in which such behavior is unacceptable.

Be patient, caring, and understanding.

Don't blame the victim!

Do not re-victimize the victims by treating them as criminals.

Refrain from making opinionated comments to the victim.

Tell victims of their rights and options.

Notify victims at discharge about their right to get counseling at VA sexual trauma programs.

They [commanders] should be more willing to talk about the incident and offer any kind of help.

Follow up with the victim—especially first sergeants and commanders. . . . Not just a "How are you doing" hallway greeting. Sit down in your office, make them feel like you care about their well-being and that they are being supported.

THE REPORTING PROCESS

Follow through (investigate) all reports.

—— A VICTIM OF SEXUAL ASSAULT WHOSE COMPLAINT WAS IGNORED BY COMMAND

With regard to reporting sexual harassment or rape, victims were adamant about two points. First, there needs to be an independent, impartial person (outside of the immediate chain of command) who will receive the reports and initiate the complaint process. This person, according to victims of sexual trauma, should have some specialized training in responding to these types of allegations and preferably be female. The role of this independent party would be primarily as an advocate or ombudsman to provide information to the victim and to act as the liaison between the victim, the commander, and the appropriate investigating authority (such as: EO officer, social actions office, military police). However, the advocate should have some authority and jurisdiction to refer cases outside of the command for follow-up investigation or to respond to any complaints of further harassment or intimidation of the victim.

Many respondents noted that it is extremely difficult (and possibly a conflict of interest) for the commander to oversee these complaints. The commander has the unit's best interest in mind. Therefore, the commander may be likely to determine that the allegations are unwarranted based on personal biases or operational needs within the command.

For example, if the first sergeant was accused of sexual harassment, it would very likely become a hardship for the commander to "lose" the first sergeant or to discipline him. Disciplinary action could also lead to the first sergeant's loss of respect in the unit. This could diminish the first sergeant's authority, thereby hampering the unit's effectiveness. Ultimately, commanders may prefer to deal with the allegations internally and quietly, which can and does result in a biased investigation and outcome. Far too many victims have witnessed this type of power failure. According to some military women, this is common in the "good ole' boy" network in which the men support each other, even if it means alienating a fellow female soldier.

An independent source, such as an advocate or ombudsman, would not have the same conflict of interest, as do most commanders. Thus, many victims have called for these cases to be reported and investigated outside of the chain of command and preferably by a higher-ranking female as the designated liaison. The following are some specific recommendations they provided on how to deal with this issue.

We need immediate access to a female superior who will be able to influence a positive course of action, to offer advice and counsel you once you report a man [for sexual harassment or rape].

Every command needs a female in the EEO position. I found that every male I spoke to [about the rape] fell on deaf ears.

Have more women involved in the reporting process of harassment. Enlisted are at the mercy of officers even in this case.

Appoint an investigating officer from outside the command.

Formalize procedures for reporting that are independent of the victim's chain of command.

I was responsible for the USMC's policy on how sexual harassment is handled. The processing of complaints must be removed from the chain of command. The CO only cares about keeping problems quiet. The IG needs to get actively involved as an inspector and women representatives should be set up as ombudsmen for [all those with] complaints.

Another suggestion on the reporting process that was echoed by numerous respondents was that of outside accountability beyond the chain of command. In testimony to the House Armed Services Committee, women urged the Pentagon to make the complaint process separate from the chain of command (Palmer, 1994). Carl Nyberg, a former Navy officer and Navy recruiting whistle-blower, prepared one of the lengthier yet more persuasive responses. In his own words, this veteran and advocate for military victims passionately addresses the need for accountability outside of the military. The following are his remarks from February 1999, used with permission, on demanding military accountability from outside of the armed forces:

The current system of military justice and investigation has no outside accountability except the rare case the media examines...And even in the rare instance when the media does cover a story about abuse of power in the military; outside accountability is limited to moral persuasion.

The military lacks outside accountability, because all prosecutorial discretion rests with the chain of command. The inspector general system assigns officers from the chain of command to investigate allegations of misconduct. The chain of command decides whether to call in civilian investigative agencies, like the Army's Criminal Investigation Division (CID) or the Navy Criminal Investigative Service (NCIS). The chain of command decides whether a warning or administrative action is appropriate. The chain of command decides if punishment will be handled through article 15 (nonjudicial punishment or office hours) or at courts-martial. If the case is handled at courts-martial the chain of command decides which level of courts-martial—there are three—determining the amount of punishment the accused will be exposed to. . . .

The lack of outside accountability makes it possible for the chain of command to hide misconduct. The evaluation and promotion system is the incentive to hide misconduct. This is especially true of sexual misconduct or incidents of racism. Incidents of sexual misconduct and racism raise the question of whether there was a sexist or racist command climate. A finding that the command has a climate of sexism or racism will damage, probably irreparably, the careers of the officers in the chain of command. Therefore, supervisors desire investigations, especially of sexual misconduct and incidents with racial overtones to be handled "in house," where the results of an investigation can be controlled. Telling investigators to rewrite investigations until the right conclusions are reached is one of the more heavy-handed methods of command influence. The chain of command, up to the secretary of defense, also benefits when local commanders minimize adverse publicity.

The military can be quite strict about theft, a legitimate threat to good order and discipline on a ship or in another military unit. However, supervisors may be willing to tolerate a subordinate who beats his wife, because it does not have any potential impact on the military mission in the eyes of the supervisors. Unfortunately, sexual abuse of service members still is not seen as a threat to good order and discipline in many cases.

If we, the United States, want our military to be the best it can be, we should demand a military with independent, outside accountability for misconduct by service members. . . . When the chain of command avoids dealing with problems, good order and discipline eventually suffer.

The need for outside accountability seems obvious, especially when looking at the existing patterns of responses to harassment and abuse within the military, including rape, sexual harassment, racial harassment, and harassment of gays in the military. An outside review with civilian experts could have positive results in helping the armed forces to address these complex problems. Many service members reiterated this viewpoint across the ranks, including retired Air Force lieutenant colonel Karen Johnson in a statement to the Air Force Times: An independent civilian agency, rather than the military, should investigate complaints. It's the only thing to do to be fair to all parties, both the accuser and the accused. ...How do you investigate yourself? (Glenn, 1999, p. 7)

Along the lines of accountability, another frequent request is for these allegations and reports to be taken seriously and followed up with an appropriate investigative response. This is a simple request from the service members. In fact, one of the reasons so many cases never make it beyond the initial report is that the victims are dissuaded from pursuing charges through the appropriate legal channels. Their allegations are discounted, minimized, and in some cases, laughed at. As many service members said, do not make rape or sexual harassment allegations into a joke. Take them seriously. Believe the victim when reports are made. These requests are not so unreasonable. In fact, it is appalling that so many reports of rape and sexual harassment have been disregarded or belittled.

Many respondents indicated that this was one of the primary deterrents for not reporting their abuse. They did not think they would be believed if they reported it. This is a significant deterrent and a problem in the military. It is not surprising that a common suggestion from victims to the military is, *"always* take it seriously."

INVESTIGATING RAPE AND SEXUAL HARASSMENT

> *The panel strongly believes that sexual misconduct incidents deserve special attention not only during the investigative phase, but also in the support services integral to proper treatment of victims. Improvements, it finds, are needed from the unit to the departmental level.*
>
> — R. S. FOSLER, PRESIDENT, ACADEMY OF PUBLIC ADMINISTRATION
> (NAPA, 1999, P. I)

The recommendations from Service members about investigating sexual harassment and sexual assault complaints were similar to the suggestions on reporting. The top two requests from victims of abuse were: (1) the investigation should be conducted by someone outside of the chain of command, and (2) all reports should be investigated. These requests were echoed repeatedly.

There were other suggestions of significant importance, but they were not cited as often. These included references to the investigative process, the response time, and the response to the victim. The following are a sample of some of the recommendations from service members on the investigation of sexual abuse in the military.

Quit concentrating 90 percent of the investigation on the victim's validity and 10 percent on the perpetrator.

Give credence to multiple complaints about the same assailant.

The investigation should be done by someone outside the unit.

Perform a quick and thorough investigation. This would increase the chances of people speaking out. All investigating should be done in writing so those involved cannot as easily change their story.

The investigations should be conducted rapidly, discreetly, and definitively to ensure fairness and secrecy until proceedings are done.

Investigate with care. If someone is guilty, there should be punishment beyond a hand slap.

OTHER MILITARY JUSTICE ISSUES

> *Justice will only be achieved when those who are not injured by crime feel as indignant as those who are.*
>
> — SOLOMON (635-577 B.C.)

Military justice was a concern for sexual abuse victims, many of whom felt betrayed by a justice system that failed them. Although individual experiences and feedback were quite diverse, the recurrent theme among them was that of justice and fairness. The following are some of their opinions and straightforward suggestions about military justice when it comes to sexual assault and harassment cases.

Prosecute these crimes.

Follow the law. Follow present regulations.

Appoint a legal representative for the victim.

Make available copies of written transcripts of any hearings to the victim.

Stop filing charges against the victim!

There should be public reporting of the incident.

Harassment should be dealt with as a crime and a violation of UCMJ—not as an EEO problem.

RESPONSES TO SEXUAL OFFENDERS

> *You ask, "How should the military respond to sexual offenders?"*
> *My response, "What happened to zero tolerance?"*

—— A MARINE WHO EXPERIENCED REPEATED SEXUAL HARASSMENT IN HIS UNIT

The most frequent recommendation from respondents as to how the military should respond to sexual offenders can be summed up in two words: zero tolerance. Although these two words have been used quite a bit in the past few years, according to male and female service members, the policy is generally not practiced. One needs only to look at the publicized cases since the Aberdeen sex abuse scandal to see that there is opposition to zero tolerance. Sure, it sounds good; but in reality it has not been successfully implemented.

The zero-tolerance policy has been a failure partly because there are still too many service members who are not on board with the policy. They simply do not subscribe to the tenets of zero tolerance. In addition, there are still too many high-ranking officers and enlisted who are themselves sexual predators. How can the military's upper echelon police itself when there are sexual offenders (albeit decorated leaders and war heroes) among them? Several active-duty and veteran service members voiced their concerns about the zero-tolerance policy.

"Zero tolerance," means that there is "nothing" in place. There is no set punishment for sexual harassers, unlike DUI. With DUI, you know up front what the penalty is. Tell me, what is the penalty for a proven harasser? Is retirement the answer?

Practice zero tolerance and nail the hell out of the offender.

If implemented properly, zero tolerance and offender discipline should go hand in hand. However, this is generally not the case when sexual offenders are let go with early retirements, quiet discharges, or verbal warnings behind closed doors. Such responses exemplify neither zero tolerance nor military justice, especially to someone who has been sexually assaulted by a fellow soldier.

As one might guess, there was very little sympathy from victims of sexual assault as to how the military should respond to sexual offenders. However, their suggestions were quite diverse, ranging from publishing the offender's name in the military newspaper to the age-old battle cry of "castrate the bastards." There was, however, consensus among the respondents that the military should always respond "vigorously, unequivocally, and very firmly" to sexual perpetrators. That specific sentiment was echoed repeatedly as noted in the following remarks.

The military should respond strictly. It happens all too often from high-ranking officials, not just low-ranking personnel.

Persons in positions of power and/or authority need to be properly investigated by a committee that is in no way connected to the military with survivors who are on the committee.

Any person who takes advantage of another person sexually [or in any other way that violates UCMJ] should be prosecuted.

If there is no proof or witnesses, keep the alleged assailant away from any contact with the victim, and observe him and his habits. If there is physical evidence or witnesses, prosecute the assailant. Don't hide the facts, or he will return to society and no one will know he is a perpetrator.

One recommendation focused on mandatory educational programs for less serious perpetrators who might be staying in the military community.

Send those [who assault or harass] to intensive eight-to ten-week courses. Take them off the job and make them sit for eight-hour classes. . . . Teach ethics courses, diversity training, moral conduct, behavior modification, whatever it takes.

DISCIPLINARY ACTION FOR SEXUAL OFFENDERS

The military suffers with disciplinary problems not because of what society and nature hand it——although that presents a major challenge——but because it tries to alter human nature. It does not search for the absolute best, and its application of justice and punishment are out of balance.

— MAJOR KEITH HUTCHESON, USAF, 1996

The questions about how the military should specifically discipline and respond to sexual offenders attracted numerous responses. It seemed that nearly every respondent had an opinion as to how perpetrators of sexual harassment or rape should be disciplined. Although their recommendations on disciplinary options varied greatly, the majority of respondents shared a common message: treat the offense seriously and with appropriate punishment to fit the crime. Overall, five different themes emerged from feedback about disciplining military sexual offenders: general discipline considerations, career implications, court-martial, military discharges, and confinements.

General Discipline Considerations

The broader category of general considerations in discipline included a range of comments from military victims of sexual abuse. They offered specific suggestions, such as calling for mandatory treatment for sexual offenders or a court-martial for all reported rapists. Others offered less specific recommendations with a wide range implications. For example, some of the respondents called for taking the commander out of the disciplinary line. They indicated there is too much room for a conflict of interest as well as a wide range of potential outcomes based on the commander's personal bias about rape and sexual harassment or about the accused or the victim. Several victims felt strongly that commanders have too much authority and discretion in these cases. For example, given the same case, two different commanders may chose extremely different disciplinary outcomes as a result of their sole discretion. This was a point of contention for several victims of abuse in the military. The following comments are a sample of the general discipline suggestions that were offered by respondents.

All offenders, regardless of their rank, should be reported and disciplined.

In my opinion, I think that the military should let someone outside of the accused's command decide what the punishment should be, instead of the accused's command deciding the outcome.

Discipline those who lesbian-bait as a result of reported harassment.

Mandatory counseling for minor infractions. Harsh penalties and bad discharges for major infractions. Plus mandatory volunteer work.

Punishment for the offender needs to be much harsher. Treat rape like government property cases. Someone can tamper with a computer and get a lot more reprimand than if they raped someone.

Career Implications

The recommendations regarding career implications were also quite diverse. Although most of the respondents indicated that some career impact was important, one military woman thought that such punishment was "too harsh" given that the military's rules and understanding regarding sexual harassment have been changing over time. Other participants in the study made suggestions about the fate of the sexual offender's military career. The following are some of their recommendations.

If they are allowed to stay in the military, this information should be recorded in their personnel file and should be taken into consideration when they are up for promotions, job advancement, or other career opportunities. There should be a red flag on their record—and a black mark on their career. Maybe this would prevent some of the sexual harassment if the senior leaders knew it would affect their careers too.

Immediately withdraw security clearance of the suspect pending investigation.

NJP (nonjudicial punishment) or discharge if found guilty. Try to prove it without ruining everyone's reputation.

Ending a career is usually too harsh as, for the most part, the rules changed while they were swimming, not before they jumped into the water.

Do you really want a rapist working alongside you at your job site or in your foxhole? I think not. They have no place in the military nor in the civilian sector, other than in prison with the other criminals.

Court–Martial

The opinions about prosecution or court-martial of sexual offenses had a common link—these service members thought that all sexual offenders should face court-martial or criminal prosecution. Victims of sexual abuse in this study were united in this opinion with very few exceptions. They noted that a court-martial or criminal prosecution provides the opportunity for an impartial review of the case and an independent decision about the disciplinary outcome (without the commander's influence). Victims of sexual assault stated very clearly "Military rapists should have their day in court."

Sexual assault and harassment must be stopped and predators need to be prosecuted.

The military should court-martial and dishonorably discharge any rapists.

All rape cases should be court-martialed—with no exception.

Military Discharges

Another disciplinary action for sexual offenders in the military is discharge from the service. Victims of abuse were adamant, for the most part, that any offender discharged due to sexual assault or harassment should be given a dishonorable or bad conduct discharge. As one victim eloquently stated, "There is no honor in raping your fellow soldier." Their contention is that such a dishonorable act is not deserving of an honorable discharge. In the process of committing sexual assault or harassment in uniform, they have dishonored the military service. Therefore, sexual offenders should not be entitled to an honorable discharge according to some of the respondents.

Another important point was made regarding using a discharge as the sole means of disciplinary action. As stated earlier, although the discharge option does serve the purpose of ridding sexual offenders from the military, it also "dumps" them into society—free to rape again. This taps into concerns about commanders who use discharges as a means of taking care of the problem in the short term but creating more problems for society in the long term. In such cases, the commanders are not acting honorably either, according to many service members.

Should the military be allowed to release known sexual offenders into society with no further repercussions, discipline, or treatment for the offender? This becomes a moral and an ethical question as well as a question of appropriate military discipline. Although federal laws now require the registration of convicted sexual predators, many of the military's known (or accused) sexual offenders are discharged in lieu of further action and therefore fall through the cracks of the mandatory reporting requirements for sexual predators. This issue is indeed a complicated one that may require further congressional input. In the meantime, victims of abuse are advocating for dishonorable or bad conduct discharges for all military sexual offenders, regardless of rank, time in service, military awards, or career history. They believe that military members who commit sexual offenses bring discredit to the armed services and therefore do not deserve to leave the military under honorable conditions. The following is a sample of their comments.

Every time the Army allows a rapist to leave with an honorable discharge, they devalue the discharges of every other veteran who did serve with honor.

Discharge them with dishonorable reasons.

Give them a dishonorable discharge without any benefits.

Label them as a sexual offender on their discharge papers.

Confinements

The last of the five recommendations on disciplining military sexual offenders is in favor of confinements or imprisonments in some form. Many victims compared the criminal justice system in the civilian sector where the outcome of a rape conviction usually results in a prison sentence. They wondered why so many military rapists can "get off" without imprisonment.

Indeed, it is true that not all sexual offenders who are found guilty in a military court-martial serve time. In fact, there are many options in sentencing military sexual offenders, ranging from a loss of rank to a loss of pay, discharge, or confinement. Although some sexual offenders face numerous sanctions in addition to confinement, statistics from the military service branches indicate that most courts-martial will not result in imprisonment for the sexual offender.

In fact, according to the Pentagon's Office of the Undersecretary of Defense, only about half of courts-martial result in a conviction. In 1996, for example, the percent of cases that were tried and convicted was 60 percent for the Army, 59 percent for the Air Force, and only 40 percent for the Navy/Marines. The statistics were worse in 1995 when only 29 percent of the rape cases tried by the Navy resulted in convictions.

Furthermore, as stated earlier, not all convictions result in imprisonment. These varied outcomes give rise to speculation, trepidation, and mistrust by victims of abuse. The response to sexual offenders by the authorities is of grave concern to many rape victims as well as other members of the military and civilian communities. The following is what a few had to say on the topic of confinement of sexual perpetrators in the armed forces.

It is a crime, a horrible sick crime and they should be locked up in Leavenworth.

For sexual assaults, there should be time in jail and automatic discharge regardless of your rank and past performances. You [sexual offenders] shouldn't get any benefits either. You should lose them all!

All convicted rapists should serve time. It is a crime, isn't it?

THE NEED FOR SYSTEMIC CHANGES

We must have and practice a no-tolerance policy on sexual harassment—not because it fits the mood of the moment in our corporate world, but because sexual harassment is morally wrong.

— MAJOR GENERAL JERRY E. WHITE, USAFR (1996, P. 34)

Victims of rape and sexual harassment endured a multitude of problems and barriers in the aftermath of their abuse. Service members offered some very insightful suggestions as to what systemic and organizational changes should be made to decrease these kinds of problems and to improve the military's response to sexual trauma. For example, consider the comments from two women regarding the underlying gender issues in the military culture. One linked the problem to contemptuous attitudes about women and the other questioned the lack of honorable behaviors among men.

As long as there is an attitude of contempt for women, we're not going to stop it [rape and sexual harassment].

Reinstitute honor? Chivalry? Codes of behavior? Whatever it takes.

The majority of the recommendations for system wide changes pertained to policies: enforcing existing policies, developing new polices, and establishing programmatic changes within the military. Others offered more idealistic ideas on how to change the system. Overall, the top five suggestions from respondents in this study were:

1. Increase leadership roles for females.
2. Decrease command's power and authority over these cases.
3. Enforce the zero-tolerance policy without exception by holding all Service members accountable.
4. Update the UCMJ relative to sexual offenses.
5. Create specialized services for victims of sexual assault. The following section highlights some specific suggestions as to what systemic changes should be made within the military to address sexual harassment and rape more effectively.

Increase Leadership Roles for Females

There are insufficient numbers of women in leadership roles in the military (Federal Advisory Committee, 1997). This problem is not new to the military system as they have previously faced shortages of minorities in all service branches in leadership positions.

For example, the numbers of African-American men who have been promoted to higher-ranking roles in the past decade increased significantly when this problem was brought to the attention of the DoD. Similarly, women are a minority group in the military, yet they still hold very few higher-ranking positions overall. Leadership roles, such as company commanders, drill sergeants, and base commanders should also reflect a higher percentage of women in these positions of authority. Similar recommendations were also made by the Federal Advisory Committee on Gender Integrated Training and by the Army's Senior Review Panel on Sexual Harassment.

The respondents suggested that more women in leadership roles serve a dual purpose. First, it will give more credence and respect to women in the service. If women's roles in the military are valued, there will be enhanced unit cohesion and increased military effectiveness overall. This would be beneficial for both men and women as well as for all of the armed services. Secondly, promoting women to leadership positions will offer more female role models and additional support for younger military women as they contemplate military careers. Furthermore, support by a female leader is important when a woman is seeking assistance in the aftermath of a rape or sexual harassment.

By increasing the numbers of women in leadership roles and higher-ranking positions, it will further gender integration as well as the acceptance and respect of women in the military services. A survey on "The Trends in Attitudes Toward Women in the Army" found that gender integration would have either a positive impact or no difference on group cohesion or work atmosphere. Less than one-third of the Service men surveyed thought that gender integration could have a negative impact on their work environment (U.S. Army Research Institute, 1999). This systemic change can have positive, long-range implications for decreasing the victimization of women in the military services, just as a similar change had on the acceptance of racial minorities into the military. The following are a sample of the comments from military women on this issue.

There need to be more female members of the military at senior levels to go to for support. The chain of command is usually an all-male obstacle course.

First of all, more women need to work in OSI, Social Actions.

It would really help to have a female advocate to turn to when dealing with sexual assault or sexual harassment.

How can women ever be fully accepted by men in the military if there are so few women in charge? One way to change how men treat women in the service is to promote more women to critical positions in the military and let us earn their respect. If nothing else, the men will have to show respect to the rank.

Decrease Command's Power and Authority Over These Cases

There are some very real concerns about the extent of command's authority and jurisdiction on rape and sexual harassment complaints as addressed previously. Many comments were made about this current practice in all service branches. Hence, a very significant change in the military system would be to revisit the issue of command authority in such cases. The following are some important questions to consider regarding command authority:

- Should protocol dictate that commanders report any and all allegations of sexual misconduct to a higher authority?
- Should all such cases be referred automatically for investigation by military police, the criminal investigation organization, or to the appropriate EEO office?
- Should there be oversight or case review of the outcome of cases involving commanders?

Many military victims of abuse thought there should be restrictions or oversight of command authority in rape and sexual harassment issues. Since command authority is rarely questioned, there were numerous comments from service members and veterans as to how to address this dilemma.

One solution is to implement a task force of military and civilian experts in the field to address some of these problems. The task force could implement a case review process or make recommendations to the DoD as to how to respond more effectively to violence against women in the military. A similar multidisciplinary task force was mandated by Congress to study domestic violence in the military. The Domestic Violence Task Force could serve as a model for a comparable Sexual Assault and Harassment Task Force.

Retired Lieutenant Colonel Karen Johnson, Vice President of the National Organization for Women, further exemplified the importance of command oversight in 1999 when she summarized concerns from women service members for the American News Service:

> *More than half of women in the military don't trust their commander to act responsibly if they report sexual harassment. That is the reality. I talk to women every month who are in the military and have tried to go through the chain of command to report sexual harassment. They get penalized.* (Zoll, 1999)

The following are some of the other significant concerns and comments from military victims about command's discretion and authority in sexual abuse cases.

What happens when the commander is also a sexual harasser? How many women do you think will report sexual harassment or rape in that unit? You can bet most women would keep their mouths shut and just deal with it. That's what I did.

Commanders shouldn't be responsible for handling these cases.

In my opinion, commanders have too much authority when it comes to sexual assault and sexual harassment. They can be the investigator, the judge, and the jury all within a matter of minutes of hearing the complaint. They have way too much power.

If your commander is a member of the good ole' boys network, you're out of luck.

Enforce the Zero-Tolerance Policy Without Exception

Every commander is accountable for zero tolerance. Every officer, enlisted member, and civilian is responsible for refusing to tolerate sexual harassment and for reporting it when it does happen. When incidents do occur, swift, fair action is the rule. (Johnmeyer, 1997, p. 3)

Service members still think that zero tolerance is a good policy that can make a difference—if it is truly enforced. In order for the zero-tolerance policy to be effective, service members say that the policy should be applied to all service members, regardless of rank, gender, race, or any other factors. No one would ever be given special consideration, slip through the cracks, or be "overlooked" if zero tolerance is truly put into practice. General Dennis J. Reimer, Army Chief of Staff, reiterated this point:

Sexual harassment has no place in today's—or tomorrow's— Army. Consideration for other soldiers is a fundamental principle upon which our Army is built. Our leaders must be wholly committed to this principle, and that commitment must be understood by all. (Army Investigates, 1996).

The overwhelming message about zero tolerance was that everyone from the top down should be held accountable to the same standards for responding to sexual assault allegations. Respondents all echoed their concerns and suggestions about zero tolerance of sexual assault and harassment in the military.

Command should not tolerate it. If they do nothing, it's as though they approve of the abuse.

The military should set an atmosphere of real trust, so when needed, a soldier is more likely to report it. When it is a "good ole' boys" setting, a soldier learns quickly [not to report it].

Hold all ranks accountable.

Zero means none, without exception. Put that in front of sexual harassment and what do you get? That's what the Army, Marines, Navy, and Air Force should be practicing instead of just preaching.

Update the UCMJ

Another important change to improve the military's response to sexual assault would involve updating the UCMJ. There were several comments from service members and veterans who indicated the UCMJ is "antiquated" or "behind the times." Consequently, there are concerns that the military's regulations are not reflective of today's social culture.

The UCMJ has undergone some changes over the past few decades. Most notably, the crime of rape is no longer punishable by death. One would wonder if the shift in the punishment for rape is indicative of a shift in thinking about the crime. Granted, the death penalty is not used in rape cases in the civilian criminal justice system either. However, did the downgrading of the penalty in the UCMJ make the crime less serious or less heinous in the eyes of military justice or was it just a sign of the times or the cultural shifts about rape? We may never know for sure.

What we do know is that the UCMJ represents the rules and regulations of the armed forces. Laws, regulations, and policies must keep pace with the changing world. It was not that long ago that the UCMJ did not recognize marital rape or rape against men. The UCMJ should be regularly updated to reflect the emerging issues of society, including all forms of violence against women and men.

The UCMJ does not do justice for many, especially women who experience violence at the hands of military personnel. I think the UCMJ needs to be updated to be consistent with what's real in our society today.

Revise the UCMJ, but have some women JAGs and other women attorneys involved in the process from start to finish.

Create Specialized Services for Victims of Sexual Assault

The last of the five systemic changes suggested by the respondents is for each military branch to offer specialized services for victims of sexual assault and harassment. It is apparent that sexual assault is a problem in each of the services. Therefore, adequate attention and resources should be applied to address this problem.

Far too many victims in the military reported a lack of services and a lack of support to help them in the aftermath of the rape or harassment. In fact, some Service members indicated personnel who did not know how to respond appropriately actually subjected them to further victimization.

The lack of rape crisis services at most military installations both stateside and abroad causes subsequent problems for the victim and for the military. These problems could be averted or decreased if accessible, appropriate care was available for rape and sexual harassment victims.

The health and well-being of all service members is important to the military and to the mission. Yet without specialized rape crisis services accessible to all victims, the health and well-being of these service members is compromised. It was no surprise that many victims called for sexual assault protocols, crisis-response programs, or designated advocates to be available at all military installations. Services similar to the VA's sexual trauma counseling programs and civilian rape crisis programs would be excellent models for the military branches to follow. Here is what some rape victims had to say on this issue.

They need to implement a system for responding to victims. All they do now is put a victim into a mental health inpatient unit with depressed patients and substance abuse patients.

Employ trained sexual abuse counselors.

Get survivors involved who are willing to speak out and to help develop new programs. Listen to what the survivors are saying.

There should be a rape crisis program at every military base or at least at every military hospital. Women and men who have been raped need someone who has been specially trained to help them. This would cut down on a lot of problems.

Provide More Education to All Service Members of All Ranks

Service members feel a need for more education on the topic despite the fact that each of the branches offer regular trainings on sexual harassment as well as educational programs on rape awareness in basic training. The problem, they say, is not so much the frequency of the training since there are reportedly annual, mandatory sexual harassment classes in some units. Rather, there is more of a need for higher quality, up-to-date programs with consistent messages for both women and men about the regulations, the implications, the options (for reporting and getting help), and the potential threat to military careers.

Whatever training model or materials are used, we know that the zero-tolerance message is not effective nor accepted. The philosophy of zero tolerance has great potential. Yet in practice, it appears to have failed miserably in the military according to the respondents in this study. Service members simply do not trust or believe in zero tolerance based on the military's track record. Consider what a retired senior Army noncommissioned officer and a reservist had to say about zero-tolerance policies and the military's sexual harassment training:

As for battalion policy letters, we had numerous classes on fraternization and sexual harassment, but this was a damn joke. Even the commander conducting the class laughed and joked throughout the class. They had policies because it was mandatory, but it was not mandatory that they enforce them! It would have been impossible to enforce what they, the policy enforcers, were doing themselves!

I was activated in 1992 and sent to Biloxi, Mississippi, for two days for sexual assault and harassment training. The films were ridiculous and there was a mass devaluing of the issue. What a waste of time and money. The message from the military was clear: "We have to do this training, but you don't have to take it seriously.

Although the sexual harassment trainings are offered regularly and the zero-tolerance policies are in place, they have not earned the respect of the service members who are required to attend the programs nor have they earned the respect of the leaders who are obligated to conduct the trainings. The military culture has denigrated the topic to such an extent that the trainings are generally viewed as "a meaningless waste of time." The value and subsequent impact of the educational programs, therefore, is virtually nonexistent.

Nonetheless, training on this topic is imperative, but it must be delivered effectively. There were several excellent suggestions made by military women and men for improving sexual harassment and rape awareness education in the services. The following are some of the comments and recommendations on educating military personnel that might shed some light on this dilemma.

First of all, educate all persons. Then, teach supervisors and department heads how to take a report and to listen to a subordinate who comes to them for help. And keep it quieter and more discreet.

Use specific examples of service members who have been found guilty and what their punishment was for the sexual harassment or sexual assault. This may bring the zero-tolerance policy home for some people.

Educate people by using outside rape crisis counselors who know the topic.

Orientation should be provided in basic training by contracted, nonmilitary personnel. Each soldier should be given a packet with contacts, resource phone numbers, and definitions of types of abuse. During orientation, soldiers should be introduced to the dangers and factors contributing to victimization.

There are many stereotypes of how women are to blame for sexual harassment. Education of all service men and women about these stereotypes will help the victims to feel less blame and shame.

Educate men and women about sexual assault, the rules and regulations, and where to go for help.

Be more proactive [more than just giving an annual program on sexual harassment].

There should be thorough education of all commanders down to squad leaders as to the effects of sexual assault on personnel.

ADDITIONAL WAYS TO IMPROVE THE RESPONSE TO THE ISSUE

The best advice I can pass on to my successor is the same advice that was given to me: Take care of the troops, and they will take care of our national security.

— SECRETARY OF DEFENSE WILLIAM J. PERRY (1997, p. 55)

For every victim of rape or sexual harassment whose comments were included in this study, there were several suggestions as to how the military can improve its response to this issue. Many of their perspectives are included throughout this book. However, numerous comments and recommendations were not included due to space limitations or due to some replications of ideas with similar sentiments. Several of the respondents spoke in terms of the future. A wide selection of their suggestions for the future was reserved for this chapter in answer to the remaining question, "What should the military do to improve its response to sexual harassment and rape?"

Although a vast array of perspectives and personal experiences reflects the complexity and extent of this problem, there is not one single answer, not one extraordinary solution, nor one quick fix to this crisis. One thing is certain: this dilemma will not resolve itself.

Rape and sexual harassment in the U.S. military date back to the origins of the Armed Forces—long before women were officially allowed to serve. However, the problem has grown increasingly with the integration of women on active duty. Despite the passage of time and growing concern about sexual assault and harassment, this issue still has yet to be effectively addressed. In fact, based on the reports in the 1990s (from Tailhook to the Aberdeen Proving Ground crises) the problem has gotten worse. Something must be done to stop the abuse that far too many women, men, and children endure at the hands of military personnel.

If there is one basic element in our Constitution, it is civilian control of the military.

— PRESIDENT HARRY TRUMAN

The U.S. military needs civilian support to meet its mission—including the support of veterans and retirees, DoD employees, members of Congress, and the general public. They all have an impact on the military mission. When it comes to addressing the widespread problems of sexual assault and harassment, the military also needs assistance from Service members who were abused on active duty. The Armed Forces need these men and women in order to effectively solve this pervasive problem in the military family.

No one knows this problem better than those on the inside of the US Military. These Service members have an important insight to this problem. Their perspectives and comments can help the Armed Forces to assess more accurately the existing problems and the future challenges of rape and sexual harassment. The following are some of the key suggestions and inside perspectives worthy of consideration.

I hope the military will instruct their senior officers and senior enlisted men to have respect, and understand that no person in a position of direct authority should try to instigate a sexual relationship with a person of lower status.

This is an organizational problem that needs to be attacked from the leadership on down. Make examples of the higher-ranking officials who are not addressing the issue. . . .

Hold commands accountable for their actions or lack thereof.

If the military continues to attack the problem from the bottom, victims will continue to get **** on.

Victims deserve to be treated fairly and respectfully.

Each offender should be treated the same. If the military is going to say "zero tolerance," they should mean it. Take the stripes and the pay or put them out of the military altogether. Don't just slap their hands and promote them to a new job and then make the victim face them every day as if nothing happened.

Prosecute all offenders to the fullest under UCMJ.

Congress needs to implement changes in military justice.

Sexual harassment can be controlled with comprehensive education and strict enforcement of the zero-tolerance policy.

I feel the military still has a double standard—different for female versus male; officer versus enlisted. The rules need to be applied to all no matter what your rank, gender, race, or age. Sexual assault and harassment is wrong. It needs to be stopped now!

I believe they need to enforce their policies. In the past twelve years I've seen it go from not being talked about to at least being acknowledged. I believe we have yearly training on the subject. But it still seems to be one of those sensitive subjects.

Educate. Educate. Educate! And punish. Realize just because an offender has a great family, goes to church, and has a good PIF [personnel file] doesn't mean he is innocent.

I think that we should take another look at how we mix the sexes when away from home and in battlefield conditions. We should create a situation of separation where good people are not exposed to too much temptation.

I think more disclosure should be fully encouraged by any victims without undue harassment or being labeled psycho or neurotic [for reporting abuse].

Most individuals who are sexually assaulting and harassing are very sick. There should be a way to catch these people upon psychological screening when processing in the military in the first place.

[Congress should] override the Feres Doctrine to enable women to file lawsuits against the military in these cases.

Basic training for females should have all female drill sergeants.

If women are going to continue to be assigned to ships there has to be plenty of training on work issues, how to handle professional versus private relationships and manners.

Treat each service member fairly and investigate fully with as little exposure as possible until a decision is made. This leaves reputations intact until after [disciplinary] action.

Unless there is a civil service position for this problem, nothing will change.

Bring in civilian experts to help out. Military women are less likely to trust other military on this issue. There's no confidentiality.

There needs to be a rape crisis counselor or advocate stationed at every military base—stateside and overseas—bar none.

Previously accepted behavior can no longer be tolerated or excused.

Something has to change. Sexual harassment is everywhere. It's a common factor of being in the military and it shouldn't be that way.

Listen to what the survivors are saying.

This last message is what this book is all about. We need to listen very carefully to the women and men who have been the victims of sexual abuse in the military. In doing so, we are forced to give this issue a more serious look.

MOVING FORWARD, LEST HISTORY REPEATS ITSELF

We cannot let this control our lives, nor can we sit back in silence. We need to find
a way to make some good of this experience—to make it better for those
who will follow in the years to come. We need to help the military to
move forward to stop this abuse from happening.

— VICTIM OF REPEATED SEXUAL HARASSMENT ON ACTIVE DUTY

Moving forward after a crisis is no easy task no matter who you are. It is not easy for a rape victim who is trying to make sense of her life after the trauma nor is it easy for the U.S. military when facing the ever-present and ever-growing reports of rape and sexual harassment among the ranks. One thing is certain: whether you are a rape victim or an organization such as the DoD, you cannot remain in a state of crisis indefinitely. Eventually, you must move on.

Unfortunately, not everyone moves forward after a crisis. Some will slip backward and find themselves forever changed from the trauma. They may feel destined to repeat the past and accept it as a cycle they cannot escape. Many will lose hope that things will ever be better.

For those who are able to move forward, there is hope. They have a sense of progress, of meeting goals, and of moving beyond the crisis. This progression can lead the person or the organization out of the crisis.

Ideally, all victims of sexual assault and the armed forces will find a way to move beyond the crisis and into the future with some resolution. The following section offers some reflections on how those involved with the problems of sexual abuse in the military can move in a positive direction so as not to continue repeating the mistakes of the past.

FOR THE VICTIMS OF RAPE AND SEXUAL HARASSMENT IN THE MILITARY

Sexual assault or repeated sexual harassment can have significant implications. Most sexual trauma victims will find themselves on one of two paths in their own personal journey of recovery. Some believe that they will recover; others will have continued despair that things may not get better. The victims of sexual abuse who demonstrated the best indicators of moving forward and healing were those who had hope rather than despair. The women and men in this study who shared these reflections seemed more at peace than those who were still fighting the battle, often internally. The following are examples from two veterans who have been moving forward since their abuse.

I'm strong because I've got a wonderfully supportive husband and I've been in counseling for the past five-and-a-half years. My therapist is a wonderful person who has helped lead me down the path of knowledge so that I learned what I needed to know and not just be told that this is the way it is.

What's done is done. I can't change what happened to me, but I can try to help other women to get through it. Over the years, I have learned that there is no greater satisfaction than seeing someone heal from this and get their life back. I got through it with the help of some good people and I feel blessed to not be tormented by the rape like so many women are. There is hope.

These two veterans noted the importance of supportive people in their lives. For these women and for many other rape and harassment victims, reclaiming their lives is their resolution to the abuse. Having emotionally and physically healthy and productive lives are their indicators for healing and moving on from the abuse.

Not everyone thinks of moving forward in the same way, however. Consider the words from one veteran when she reflected on healing and moving forward.

Most of my healing will come when I see the men and some women change their attitudes about women having the same opportunities—also, when the crime of sexual assault and harassment of any kind can be accounted for appropriately.

For many victims of sexual assault or harassment in the military, their healing is enmeshed with the organization's recovery. As long as the Army, Navy, Marines, and Air Force are still struggling with ongoing abuse and victimization of women, some of their victims will also continue to struggle. Reminders of this ongoing problem when cases are reported in the media serve to validate some victims that the battle (and their personal suffering) continues.

These victims may identify the military as a second perpetrator that betrayed them in the aftermath of the abuse. The military leaders failed them when they needed help; the military turned away from them; and in some instances, the organization further contributed to their trauma. These women and men are waiting for their apology or corrective action—an indication that the military is acknowledging the problem and taking appropriate steps to rectify the issue.

Until this happens, these victims will not likely realize a resolution. They are holding onto their despair and anger about what happened to them and it is getting in the way of their healing. In all likelihood, they may continue to struggle with the victimization since their recovery is enmeshed with the organization.

Ironically, some of these veterans are more likely to be strong advocates for change in the military system. Many of them will learn to channel their anger and despair toward their battle against the system—whether it will be the VA for disability benefits, the DoD for stricter penalties, or the Supreme Court for the right to sue the military.

These veterans cannot possibly extinguish the fire that fuels their rage because they want to effect a change in the system that wronged them. Their energy to fight the battle stems from the pain and betrayal they endured during and after the abuse. It is a sad irony that they do not believe they can move forward from the abuse until they have won this war with the military.

For some victims of military abuse, the battles they fight are internalized instead of externalized in the public forum. These victims are often suffering from debilitating, chronic depression or posttraumatic stress resulting from the abuse. Their lives have been forever changed by the trauma. It could result in a lifelong struggle of disability for some victims of military abuse. Likewise, they may never see the remorse nor get the apology that they are so desperately needing to allow them to move forward. Sadly, these are the veterans who are destined to repeat the trauma again and again in their own minds. For some, this grip can be tormenting and life threatening.

The road to recovery has many turns for victims of sexual assault. Some will move forward in their lives and never look back. Others will carry the torch and fight the public battles in hopes of effecting change. Others will become prisoners of war to the past, continuing to fight the enemy in their heads. Whatever their path, each one of them have been forever changed by their experiences in the military. For better or for worse, their lives will never be the same.

FOR THE MILITARY SERVICES

The Services can take several paths to move forward from this crisis. The military's prompt and deliberate response to this issue is critical, as it can hurt or help the situation. The following section highlights a priority list of recommendations based on feedback from military victims. These suggestions can serve as a framework of how the DoD and military leaders should proceed in moving forward, lest they repeat the mistakes of the past.

Ten Actions the Military Services and Its Leaders Should NOT Repeat When Dealing with Sexual Assault or Harassment

1. Do *not* ignore the problem—it will not go away.
2. Do *not* minimize or deny the problem or its impact on the mission and the troops (i.e., "This is just the result of a few bad apples").

3. Do *not* tolerate, condone, excuse, absolve, vindicate, or promote leaders who engage in rape, sexual abuse, or sexual harassment of any kind.

4. Do *not* tolerate, condone, excuse, absolve, vindicate, or promote leaders who do not enforce the zero-tolerance policy or those who "look the other way" when they are aware of sexual assault or harassment in their unit.

5. Do *not* tolerate, condone, excuse, absolve, vindicate, or promote leaders who do not comply with the Defense Initiated Based Reporting System (DIBRS) requirements for reporting sexual assault, domestic violence, child abuse, or other sex crimes.

6. Do *not* tolerate, condone, excuse, absolve, vindicate, or promote *any* service member who is court-martialed for rape or sexual harassment.

7. Do *not* have low conviction rates and low sentencing terms for sexual offenders who are court-martialed.

8. Do *not* disregard allegations of sexual harassment or assault and protective orders in domestic violence and stalking cases.

9. Do *not* tell rape or sexual harassment victims that they are lying, crazy, or only trying to get revenge.

10. Do *not* perpetuate or contribute to a culture that tolerates or promotes any kind of violence against women or children.

Ten Recommendations the Military Services and Its Leaders Should USE to Improve the Response to Sexual Assault and Harassment

1. Openly acknowledge that rape and sexual harassment are problems in the military and demonstrate your awareness and concern through swift, corrective actions to make these issues a priority.

2. Enforce the zero-tolerance policy from the top down, effective immediately with no reservation, no hesitation, and no special circumstances. Practice zero tolerance system wide with no exceptions.

3. Discipline leaders who do not enforce zero tolerance or DIBRS reporting requirements with no exceptions and red flag their personnel file regarding the disciplinary action.

4. Court-martial all sexual offenders and their accomplices (including military leaders who acquiesce to the abuse). Enforce appropriate disciplinary action, including registry to a national sex offender database for convicted military sex offenders. Comply with federal laws on sex-offender classifications and notifications upon the

sex offender's discharge from the military service. Refer cases to civilian jurisdiction and oversight as appropriate.

5. Allow victims to report rape or sexual harassment to someone other than their command. Appoint a victim's advocate or ombudsman with specialized training in responding to victims of rape, sexual harassment, and domestic violence to each military installation as the liaison on such cases. The advocate should be a higher-ranking female with the authority to ensure these cases are handled effectively by command and investigated by the appropriate authorities.

6. Ensure that *confidential* counseling is available and offered to all victims of rape and sexual harassment who report such abuse. Specialized services, such as rape crisis counseling, should also be available at minimum at each military hospital.

7. Each victim of crime should be given a copy of a victims' rights brochure immediately upon reporting any sexual abuse, domestic violence, or stalking. Copies of this brochure should also be readily available at public locations at all installations, such as the hospitals, clinics, and at the units.

8. Each of the service branches needs to address potential systemic changes in the following areas to reflect a more effective response to rape and sexual harassment: leadership response; military criminal investigations; the zero-tolerance policy and the UCMJ; military protocols for responding to sexual abuse allegations; medical protocols for the rape evidence collection examination; DIBRS reporting mandates; mandatory and recurrent training in the areas of response and prevention for all service members; increasing females in leadership roles system-wide; and enhancing the perception of the services' commitment to the issue.

9. Treat every victim of sexual assault and harassment with respect and dignity, as you would want to be treated if it happened to you or to a loved one. Do not tolerate anything less from any military leader, subordinate, co-worker, or fellow service member. Take personal responsibility to act honorably.

10. Do whatever you can to promote a culture or a climate that does not accept, condone, or tolerate violence against women in any way. Lead with integrity.

Ten steps toward a more effective, more sensitive, and more appropriate response to rape and sexual harassment is all it would take to move forward. Certainly, some of the steps are mighty tasks, but not without their reward. Imagine a U.S. military in which all leaders do their job with integrity and in which zero tolerance is a reality.

There will be no forward movement unless the DoD and the armed forces make this issue a priority concern. Until then, the Army, Navy, Marines, and Air Force will be destined to repeat the mistakes of the past and the sexual abuse will continue to be perpetuated among the ranks. The time is now to move forward. There should never be another person who becomes a victim at the hands of indifference and power failure in the military.

POWER FAILURE EXEMPLIFIED: THE DEATH OF A SOLDIER

Power Failure: (1) When leaders disregard their professional values or code of conduct and use their authority to abuse or to harass others; or (2) when leaders openly or discreetly ignore, minimize, acquiesce, or tolerate the abuse or harassment of others. Note: Both types of power failure can result in irreparable harm to the recipient, to the mission, and to the organization. Furthermore, both types of power failure are underlying, contributing factors to the widespread problem of rape, sexual harassment, and other abuses in the U.S. military.

> *Due to the "hate crime" of a homo in the Army, we now have to take extra steps to ensure the safety of the queer who has "told" [not kept his part of the DOD "don't ask, don't tell" policy]. Commanders now bear responsibility if someone decides to assault the young backside ranger.*

—— LIEUTENANT COLONEL EDWARD L. MELTON

These are the words of a high-ranking Marine officer. Only a few months earlier, this military leader was interviewed for a cover story in the *Marine Times* on mentoring junior marines. Seven months after spouting the importance of personal responsibility, Melton reportedly sent this message in an e-mail to his subordinates about the Pentagon's "Don't ask, don't tell, don't pursue" policy. As the article stated, "[Melton] failed the most basic tenet of leadership—setting a good example" (p. 44).

Melton's e-mail message, and apparent disregard for homosexual soldiers, did more to hamper the military's progress than we may ever know. The role of a military leader is critical to training new recruits and to developing unit cohesion. In some cases, the leadership role is critical to survival. Army Private First Class Barry Winchell lost his life in 1999 because of a failure in leadership and the resulting abuse by his peers. Winchell was repeatedly harassed and ultimately murdered because military leaders failed to act when fellow soldiers at Fort Campbell, Kentucky, suspected he was gay.

Apparently, these soldiers never got the message that such harassment was unacceptable in the Army. Where were the military leaders when the harassment was occurring? Who were the leaders that overlooked the abuse or acquiesced to the recurring taunts? Why was Barry Winchell not protected by the military leaders that he was willing to risk his life for? Winchell and countless others who are harassed or abused in the military deserve better from their leaders.

The *Air Force Times* article on Melton summed it up best: "protecting subordinates—every last one, regardless of ethnicity, gender, religion or sexual orientation—is every leader's responsibility. It's not optional... maybe the problem with 'don't ask, don't tell' isn't gays in the military. Maybe it's really just a failure of leadership" (p. 44). If military leaders do not tolerate or condone sexual abuse or harassment, who will?

The problems of rape, abuse, and harassment by military personnel must stop with leadership. Military leaders hold the power to prevent further abuse and to prevent lost lives, such as Barry Winchell. From the top down, sexual assault and harassment should never be tolerated by anyone, any gender, or any rank—never.

10

IN CONCLUSION

As a values-based institution, soldiers must have absolute trust and confidence in their leaders. Soldiers must trust that their leaders are selfless, objective, knowledgeable and dedicated to doing what is best for them, their unit and the Army. They must be confident that their leaders' decisions always support these same core values. In short, they must have confidence in the chain of command, and that confidence must be earned.

— GENERAL DENNIS J. REIMER ARMY CHIEF OF STAFF
(WEST AND REIMER, 1997)

A MODEL OF LEADERSHIP

LEADERSHIP CAN MAKE or break a mission or an organization. Whether good or bad, leaders have significant impact. Throughout history, we have witnessed numerous examples of the enormous, inherent power of leadership. Consider well-known leaders such as Gandhi, Roosevelt, Hitler, Mother Teresa, and Mussolini. Despite the diversity of their leadership, each of these individuals was effective at practicing their beliefs with many faithful supporters. Each one of them had an enormous influence on their mission and among their followers. Most leaders have considerable potential to influence the mission, the organization, and individuals. Military leaders are no exception. Their decisions, right or wrong, can be life changing for many people.

Although there are many different models of leadership, the U.S. military adheres to a hierarchical approach. In order for this model to work effectively, the armed forces must demand, at minimum, the following of its members:

1. Knowledge of the ranking system and the rules supporting the hierarchical model
2. Willingness to accept the rules and the leaders' authority without question
3. Adherence to a belief system that leadership is essential to the mission, hence the leaders deserve and require respect

Any display of antagonism or opposition to these basic tenets may hinder the authority of the leaders and possibly hurt the mission. Therefore, all three of these premises are integral to a successful military mission. However, these basic tenets can also be enmeshed with sexual harassment and abuse by military personnel. Therein lies the problem. In order to effectively address sexual trauma in the military, it is imperative to understand the connections and implications of this conflict.

All service members must have a complete understanding of the ranking system and the rules supporting the leadership model.

All service members are required to learn the military ranking system in their first few days of service to begin the process of assimilation into the culture. The trainees are immediately taught the hierarchy of who is in charge and how to demonstrate respect to the leaders. As soon as the recruits step off the bus at the training station, they are greeted with the authoritative jabs of the drill sergeants that aim to strip the trainees of any power whatsoever. From day one, the recruits quickly learn the absolute power of leadership. If the drill sergeant tells a recruit to drop and do fifty push-ups, the enlistee will do it without hesitation and without question because he or she has already incorporated the reality that rank equals power.

The military's hierarchical model of leadership is based on the premise that those with seniority (by virtue of rank) are granted authority over any subordinate. This follows all levels in the hierarchy, such that a private with two stripes has authority over a private with one stripe—even though they may have the same amount of time in service. Therefore, the ranking system distinctly identifies who is in charge in any given situation.

This model also demands power over others as opposed to shared power or shared leadership. This requires strict adherence to the rules in order to support the leader's authority. The leader's power is reinforced by the norms and by rules of the organization as delineated in the UCMJ.

There are many good reasons why the military utilizes the hierarchical and authoritative leadership model. It is an appropriate model for the armed forces and for their missions. Hence, the UCMJ that supports the hierarchical model is the ultimate authority on appropriate military behavior. The following are some clear examples from the UCMJ demonstrating the absolute power and authority that is granted to military leaders by virtue of rank.

Section 809. ART. 90. ASSAULTING OR WILLFULLY DISOBEYING SUPERIOR COMMISSIONED OFFICER: "Any person subject to this chapter who...(2) willfully disobeys a lawful command of his superior commissioned officer shall be punished. . . ."

Section 892. ART. 92. FAILURE TO OBEY ORDER OR REGULATION: "Any person subject to this chapter who (1) violates or fails to obey any lawful general order or regulation; (2) having knowledge of any other lawful order issued by any member of the armed forces, which it is his duty to obey, fails to obey the order; or (3) is derelict in the performance of his duties; shall be punished as a court-martial may direct."

Section 891. ART. 91. INSUBORDINATE CONDUCT TOWARD WARRANT OFFICER, NONCOMMISSIONED OFFICER, OR PETTY OFFICER: "Any warrant officer or enlisted member who . . . (2) willfully disobeys the lawful order of a warrant officer, noncommissioned officer, or petty officer; or (3) treats with contempt or is disrespectful in language or deportment toward a warrant officer, noncommissioned officer, or petty officer while that officer is in the execution of his office; shall be punished as a court-martial may direct."

All Service members are very aware of the laws in the UCMJ governing military lifestyle and supporting the power structure. In fact, learning about the ranking system (the lines of authority) and the laws that validate the power structure are the first of the three tenets that recruits are taught about the military culture. The second lesson is compliance with the laws and the power structure.

All service members shall accept the rules and the authority of military leaders without question.

Strict adherence to the UCMJ and the military hierarchy is absolutely necessary to support the mission in times of war and life or death situations. The military cannot tolerate questioners or antagonists—especially during a crisis. Particularly in times of war, someone must be in charge to make the difficult decisions pertaining to survival or sacrifice for the good of the mission. Therefore, the critical message of supporting the leader without question is ingrained into all recruits from day one. Full support is imperative to the military mission. This message was reiterated by the army chief of staff in his remarks to the Senate Armed Services Committee in 1997.

Military leaders potentially have to make life and death decisions that affect their soldiers through the orders they issue. At the critical time when orders need to be followed without question, doubt and lack of confidence in the chain of command will cause casualties . . . The circumstances that foster trust and confidence must prevail. Leader-subordinate relationships defined by these tenets are absolute and essential to mission accomplishment.

—— GENERAL DENNIS J. REIMER (WEST AND REIMER, 1997)

Any service member who does not obey an order is in violation of UCMJ regulations and is therefore subject to disciplinary action by court-martial, discharge, or by order of a superior officer. This directive gives immeasurable power to all commanding officers. Commanders are authorized to use their discretion in disciplining troops for any number of violations under the UCMJ. Since all service members must follow the UCMJ, their unconditional compliance to leadership authority is also mandated by military law.

This can create tremendous problems if a service member has legitimate questions or concerns about a leader's directive. Addressing the issue could potentially be viewed as violating or failing to obey an order. This unconditional authority given to military leaders can foster a false belief that leaders will always be considered right. This can become problematic in some situations, such as cases in which the superior officer condones sexual harassment or may be a sexual offender as well.

Some victims of rape and sexual harassment reported that their commanding officer actually ordered them to do something that eventually led to the sexual assault. One victim in this study recounted how her commander ordered her to drive him out to the field (presumably for duty). She complied with the order, yet all the while his only intent was to use the remote location as an opportunity to rape her. Although she did not feel comfortable driving the commander to the isolated location, she did not believe she had the right to refuse the order.

Rarely are service members entitled to go outside of their chain of command to resolve or address an issue. In fact, subverting the chain of command is highly discouraged. Service members are specifically taught to "go through your chain of command to solve a problem." This in itself is problematic if the conflict or concern is about someone in the chain of command. For some, it is comparable to reporting someone in their family to the legal authorities. Most people would have a hard time "turning in" a family member due to their sense of loyalty or due to a fear of repercussions by others in the family. The military unit is very similar with the superior officer often viewed as a parent figure. Since seeking assistance outside of the chain of command is generally discouraged, any attempt to do so could be considered a violation of UCMJ or, at the very least, an attack on the unit's reputation and cohesion.

The rules about authority and power in the military are not without their murkiness. Nonetheless, acceptance of the military laws and acceptance of the leadership's authority to enforce the laws is imperative for the military to work successfully toward its mission.

Military leaders deserve and require respect.

The third message about the military model of leadership is that leadership is essential to the mission; therefore, all leaders deserve and require respect. Positions of authority come with unconditional and unquestionable respect. This unconditional respect is often based on rank alone, not on the personal qualities or integrity of the leader.

The presumption is that leaders will earn their place in the hierarchy based on their capabilities. This is only part true, however. Not all rank is earned based on leadership qualities. Some will advance due to their time in service, their high aptitude test scores, or because someone put in a good word or a letter of recommendation for opportunities leading to advancement. Clearly, the military system is prone to flaws just as any other organization.

The reality is, some people make it to positions of authority when they have no business being there. Yet based on the military model of leadership, these "leaders" are still due the respect that goes with the rank. It does not matter if professional ethics or morals are lacking. This is irrelevant when it comes to respecting the rank.

Thus, the most significant message ingrained into every service member is that all leaders deserve and require respect by virtue of their rank alone. If someone is higher in the ranking system (whether officer or enlisted), respect for his or her authority is mandated in accordance with UCMJ as noted:

Any warrant officer or enlisted member who . . . treats with contempt or is disrespectful in language or deportment toward a warrant officer, noncommissioned officer, or petty officer while that officer is in the execution of his office; shall be punished as a court-martial may direct. (Uniform Code of Military Justice, Section 891, ART. 91)

This unconditional respect for rank can falter with leaders who are inadequate, corrupt, or abusive. Are leaders truly still deserving of the respect that comes with their role—even if their motives are suspect or their ethics are lacking? There have been numerous public cases in the last decade of highly regarded leaders who have stumbled or lost sight of their professional ethics. Do we simply turn our heads to their misdeeds or illegal behaviors our of respect for the rank or position? Obviously the U.S. armed forces continue to struggle with this dilemma, particularly if it involves higher-ranking officials—or leaders who have abused their rank and power.

DEFINING TRAITS OF EFFECTIVE MILITARY LEADERS

In order to be a leader, a man must have followers. And to have followers,
a man must have their confidence. Hence, the supreme
quality for a leader is unquestionably integrity.

— GENERAL DWIGHT EISENHOWER (WHITE, 1996)

As with any other organization, the military has some good male and female leaders as well as some who are simply unethical. Numerous examples have been cited by the respondents for this book of leaders who should have never been given the rank or the positions of authority. Clearly, the armed forces are not immune to putting persons in positions of power who are inadequate, corrupt, or abusive. However, due to the military power structure, service members who earn the grade find themselves in leadership positions. Yet just because someone wears the rank does not mean he or she is a good leader.

So what makes someone an effective leader in the military? Each of the Service branches has its own way of defining what makes a good leader, as noted in the following:

The leadership traits for U.S. Marines are: develop a sense of responsibility
among your subordinates; set the example; make sound and timely
decisions; know your Marines and look out for their welfare.

— U.S. MARINE CORPS, 1998

Commanders set the standards for professional conduct, create the climate of
mutual respect, evaluate their people and make recommendations for promotion.

— SHEILA WIDNALL, SECRETARY OF THE AIR FORCE
(WIDNALL AND DORN, 1995)

Navy commanders and supervisors are responsible for leading the men
and women under their control. . . . They must set the example in
treating all people with mutual respect and dignity.

— SECRETARY OF THE NAVY, SEXUAL HARASSMENT POLICY, 1993

The philosophy I use with commanders and soldiers has served me well.... First,
do what's right, legally and morally, every day. Second, create an
environment that permits everyone to be all they can be. Finally,
follow the "golden rule," treat others as you would have them treat you.

— GENERAL DENNIS J. REIMER (WEST AND REIMER, 1997)

The messages are similar when it comes to good leadership—leaders should set the example with ethical conduct, respect for others, and concerns for the welfare of their troops. Military leaders should be role models for their troops. In fact, most of them probably are good models of military demeanor and professionalism.

These basic principles are taught in military leadership classes. The classes are designed to prepare their senior enlisted and officers for the challenges that come with the power and authority inherent in the rank. In one such class, the focus and required readings address ethics and the characteristics of a good military leader. In the article, "Personal Ethics versus Professional Ethics," the author points out: "Integrity, honesty and moral conduct are essential elements in a good leader.... Since becoming a general officer, I have heard senior leaders say at various times to closed-door gatherings of general officers, "If you are sleeping around with someone other than your spouse, stop it! You will be discovered. If you insist on such conduct, have the integrity to resign and take off your uniform." (White, 1996, p. 30)

Major General White's article addresses the issues of professional and personal ethics as the underpinnings of a good leader. The two go together, according to White. As an example, consider the following regulation in the UCMJ governing the unbecoming conduct of an officer and a gentleman. This regulation attempts to regulate both personal and professional ethical behavior for officers.

Section 1 933. ART. 133. CONDUCT UNBECOMING AN OFFICER AND A GENTLEMAN: *Any commissioned officer, cadet, or midshipman who is convicted of conduct unbecoming an officer and a gentleman shall be punished as a court-martial may direct.*

The problems with this regulation, however, are twofold. First, it does not clearly define what is considered "conduct unbecoming." Without any clear guidelines, the interpretation of what behaviors are "unbecoming" can vary from commander to commander (largely based on each individual's own personal ethics).

The second problem with this regulation is that it only references "officers" and "gentlemen." Women and enlisted are not included in this particular UCMJ article. This gives the false impression that enlisted members and women are not subject to the same ethical standards of behavior. This regulation by itself supports a class system that delineates the male officer as superior to women and to any enlisted service member. This again reinforces the hierarchy—authority and power over others can be attained by rank alone—giving male officers more power than females and enlisted, regardless of time in service.

In short, this UCMJ regulation indicates that an officer (a role model and leader) should have ethical or "gentlemanly" type behavior. This antiquated regulation has had no place in the service of the past fifty years. It is, however, a good example of how military culture has continued to perpetuate some of the beliefs and practices of an outdated society. It is time to reevaluate what makes a good leader in today's armed forces and to define more clearly, what makes an unfavorable leader.

Effective leaders are role models who behave with integrity and teach others how to do the same. A program implemented by the U.S. Marines utilizes this very premise. Jackson Katz, a former college football player who has moved into the national front to promote men's efforts toward ending violence against women, developed the program model. The message of his training is simple but direct: take personal responsibility and speak up when a wrong has been done. For example, Katz tells men not to sit back in silence when they witness or are personally aware of acts of violence against women. To do nothing, for men and women, is a part of the problem. Part of the solution is to act with integrity and as a role model to others. The premise of this model is a good start at decreasing violence toward women, especially in male-dominated cultures, such as the military. However, showing respect, taking responsibility, and being a good role model should apply to both genders, not just men.

A LEADERSHIP DILEMMA: THE DRILL SERGEANT

We want those individuals out in front of our soldiers in formation or in front of them in a classroom to be leaders, not lechers.

— MAJOR GENERAL ROBERT SHADLEY (NOVEMBER 8, 1996)

Ideally, drill sergeants are mentors, strict disciplinarians, big brothers or sisters, guidance counselors and amateur psychologists. (Schmitt, 1996, p. 37)

Drill sergeants have tough jobs. They have to transform civilians into soldiers in less than two months time. To accomplish this task, they have absolute authority and control over their recruits. This can be a vulnerable time for both the drill sergeant and the recruit. Consequently, some drill instructors may find themselves at the other end of harassment allegations. However, not all drill sergeants deserve a bad reputation. In fact, many men and women undoubtedly seek out the role because of their pride in the service and their commitment to make it better.

The following comments demonstrate a wide range of opinions about drill instructors from military service members. These statements were reported in news articles in 1996 after the allegations of widespread sexual abuse of trainees at military installations (Castaneda, 1996):

My drill sergeant is like my father. I love who he is.

—— A PRIVATE AND BASIC TRAINEE

A drill sergeant is a scary person. They can make you
do things you normally wouldn't do.

—— AN ARMY SERGEANT

If he [my drill sergeant] said "Jump off that wall,"
I would have jumped off that wall.

—— FEMALE DRILL INSTRUCTOR

People looked on him [one of the drill sergeants involved in
the sexual abuse at Aberdeen] like a demigod.

—— TESTIMONY FROM ONE OF THE RAPE VICTIMS AT ABERDEEN

Society used to look at drill sergeants as God. ...now society is looking
at us and asking if we're fit to train their children.

—— DRILL SERGEANT-IN-TRAINING AT FORT JACKSON,
SOUTH CAROLINA (SCHMITT, 1996B)

The reactions toward drill sergeants are as varied as the experiences of the recruits. There does seem to be a consensus that drill instructors as well as trainees can misunderstand the power inherent in the role. The Federal Advisory Committee on Gender Integrated Training and Related Issues came to some similar conclusions in their study of basic training and gender integration in 1997. The following is a brief excerpt of their findings as it pertains to drill sergeants:

> *The role played by the Army's drill sergeants, the Marine's drill instructors,*
> *the Navy's recruit division commanders, and the Air Force's military training*
> *instructors is unique in terms of its influence and control. . . . Their behavior and*
> *attitudes greatly influence the behavior and attitudes of the recruits.*
> *The committee found that the quality of leadership provided by the training*
> *cadre varies widely both within and among the services. The committee*
> *also found, mainly as a result of the incidents at Aberdeen, that many*
> *of the Army's drill sergeants are demoralized. In the Army the majority*
> *of drill sergeants are not volunteers, and the committee observed,*
> *for the most part, a demoralized training cadre that does not believe it has*
> *the support of the chain of command, believes it is often considered "guilty until*
> *proven guilty" and believes a tour as a drill sergeant is not career-enhancing.*

> ——FEDERAL ADVISORY COMMITTEE ON GENDER INTEGRATED
> TRAINING AND RELATED ISSUES, 1997

In recognition of the difficult job a drill instructor, Secretary of the Army Togo West made the following statement to the Senate Armed Services Committee in the months following the negative publicity about Aberdeen Proving Ground and Fort Leonard Wood. "Our drill sergeants and cadre of instructors are responsible for teaching and mentoring the next generation of American soldiers. The great body of Army leaders, including the vast majority of drill sergeants and instructors, have given nothing but exceptional service during their military careers. They have earned and deserve our unwavering trust." (West and Reimer, 1997)

Nonetheless, the difficulties that are inherent in the role of a drill instructor do not excuse abusive behavior. In fact, some would argue that sexual abuse by drill sergeants in basic training is unconscionable given that they have been entrusted with the care of new recruits. Trainees are vulnerable when they enter the service. They are more easily manipulated by the power of leadership, and have no choice but to trust their leader. When leaders use their positions of trust to take advantage of someone's vulnerability, it demonstrates the epitome of power failure.

The issue of sexual abuse of recruits understandably raised great concern among military leaders, the general public, prospective recruits, and their parents. In the aftermath of the news reports in 1996 and 1997, many military leaders and civilians spoke out about the issue. However, their perspectives on the problem differed significantly. The following is what a few noted spokespersons had to say in the months after the disclosure of abuses at military training installations.

We had a leadership failure...I want to reemphasize my great respect and admiration for those great drill sergeants, the vast majority of them out there, who do such a great job. At the same time we had some leaders that let the military down. And we have to deal with that.

— GENERAL DENNIS REIMER, ARMY CHIEF OF STAFF (PONCE, 1997)

The particular incidents ...have to do with the question of whether people in positions of authority abuse that authority by violating clear rules of leadership, of conduct, and of law.

— ARMY SECRETARY TOGO WEST (BRADLEY, 1996)

There are Lieutenant Colonels who were protecting sergeants who were protecting the drill sergeants who are perpetrating the acts and there's something in the culture which permits that to go on.

— SUSAN BARNES, PRESIDENT OF WOMEN ACTIVE IN OUR NATION'S DEFENSE (BRADLEY, 1996)

I don't believe that there was a leadership void. I acknowledge that there were some leaders and some units that were not doing all that they were supposed to be doing. We did have some problems at training centers...I don't know if these drill sergeants were lacking in values. They knew right from wrong. They just chose not to do the right thing... They were lacking in the ability to follow the rules, regulations, military traditions and the law.

— SERGEANT MAJOR OF THE ARMY ROBERT E. HALL (DICKEY, 1998, P. 1)

The implications of sexual abuse and harassment by military leaders, especially drill instructors, can have rippling effects in the military organization and culture. Brigadier General Evelyn Foote, the first female Brigadier General at the Department of the Army's Inspector General's Office, recognized the potential impact of abuse by military leaders. When the leadership demeans women—badmouths them in front of subordinates—they create an environment that says sexual harassment is okay. (Morris, 1994, p. 179)

Based on the experiences and perspectives of service members and veterans, it seems that the environment and the culture did tolerate sexual harassment and sexual abuse, particularly in basic training. However, in light of the military's response to some recent cases, there does appear to be a shift toward intolerance of sexually abusive behaviors, especially among the leaders and drill instructors. Although there have been some positive steps forward, they are nowhere near zero tolerance yet.

CONFRONTING THE ENEMY WITHIN

Anyone still wasting time disparaging women, fighting their integration or subjecting them to sexual harassment is a dragging anchor for the entire Navy and Marine Corps. Anyone who still believes in the image of a drunken, skirt-chasing warrior back from the sea is about half a century out of date. If that is you, we don't need you.

— J. DANIEL HOWARD, ACTING SECRETARY OF THE NAVY
(ZIMMERMAN, 1995, P. 97)

It's a readiness issue. It's a medical issue. It's an issue for all of us.

— DOCTOR (LIEUTENANT COLONEL) E. CAMERON RITCHIE, OFFICE OF THE
ASSISTANT SECRETARY OF DEFENSE FOR HEALTH AFFAIRS (RHEM, 2001)

Rape and sexual harassment in the armed services go far beyond the two months of basic training and the purview of the drill sergeant. In fact, these problems have invaded military organizations from the top down for some time now based on repeated studies of the problem. For example, during the same time that the Federal Advisory Committee on Gender Integrated Training and Related Issues was conducting its study, the secretary of the army appointed a senior review panel on sexual harassment to look at similar issues within the ranks of the Army. Not surprisingly, these two important studies came to similar conclusions: the problems of leadership abuse are system wide and not solely a factor of the basic-training environment.

The Army's senior review panel was very open and direct in their final report even though some of the findings were highly critical of leadership response. The panel concluded that the widespread sexual abuse in the Army was indeed detrimental to the mission. They also came to this significant conclusion in their study of sexual harassment in the Army: "Passive leadership has allowed sexual harassment to persist" (Army Investigation, 1997).

These two points speak volumes about the military's recurrent problem with rape and sexual harassment within the ranks. Poor leadership has contributed to the problem either directly as the perpetrators of the sexual abuse or indirectly as the silent partners to the abuse. Even some of the "good" leaders, when put to the test, have failed to act when confronted with this issue. They have turned their heads and let the abusive behavior go on. They are the silent conspirators who allow the sexual abuse to continue in the military. And so it goes on. It has been over a decade since the Tailhook exposé, and what lessons were learned?

The secretary of the Navy issued a firm policy on sexual harassment in 1993 on the heels of Tailhook. The policy specifically points to the issues of leadership, role models, neglect, failure to report, and responsibility. The following are some of the highlights of the Department of the Navy's policy on sexual harassment:

Leadership is the key to eliminating all forms of unlawful discrimination. Sound leadership must be the cornerstone of the effort to eliminate sexual harassment. . . .(Secretary of the Navy, 1993, Section 7).

Commanders and supervisors are responsible for leading the men and women under their control. . . . They must set the example in treating all people with mutual respect and dignity, fostering a climate free of all forms of discrimination, and eliminating sexual harassment. Such a climate is essential to maintain high morale, discipline, and readiness.

Commanders and supervisors are responsible for and must be committed to preventing sexual harassment in their commands and work environments. They must not ignore or condone sexual harassment in any form, and they must take whatever action is required to ensure that a recipient of sexual harassment is not subsequently also the victim of reprisal or retaliation.

These responsibilities regarding sexual harassment are part of the broader responsibility of commanders and supervisors to foster a positive climate and take appropriate corrective action when conduct is disruptive, provoking, discriminatory, or otherwise unprofessional (Secretary of the Navy, 1993, Section 9a).

The policy looks good in writing, but it is totally meaningless unless it is enforced and implemented across the ranks. Leaders who continue to set a standard of corruption, abuse, and indifference should be demoted. There should be no place in leadership for someone who cannot follow the organization's policies. Such leadership breeds mistrust, disrespect, and a breakdown in the organization. Many military members, highly respected leaders, and civilians share this sentiment.

The service members uniformly do not have trust and confidence in their leaders [with regard to the issue of sexual harassment]. This is in part due to the fact that many commanders have ignored the complaints and the problem of sexual harassment for years. (Schafer, 1997, p. A1)

> *Drill sergeants and training cadres are the stewards of a special trust and responsibility. We must ensure they do not abuse their power.*

—— ARMY MAJOR GENERAL ROBERT D. SHADLEY (BARRETT, 1996)

A FINAL NOTE

When trust has been stripped away, it is a long road to rebuilding. Based on the inside perspectives from military leaders and victims of sexual abuse, the U.S. military still has a long way to go to confront the enemy within and to achieve zero tolerance. To do so, each and every Service member should be valued. They need to know that if someone harasses or violates them or a fellow service member, the military will be there to support them. No incident of abuse or harassment against another person should ever be blamed on the victim, go unnoticed, or be minimized. When abuse is disregarded or minimized, it diminishes and devalues the worth of the person who was the target. It sends a message loud and clear that they are not important to the organization. They are not worthy of support.

The women and men in the U.S. armed forces deserve better for all that they do and sacrifice in service to their country. They work long, demanding schedules—sometimes on call for twenty-four-hour periods. Their pay is often much lower than that of their civilian counterparts. They endure rigorous physical training, field duty, and extended absences (sometimes up to two years) away from their loved ones. They have to be ready to go at a moment's notice with no certainty that they will return. They risk their lives for us, for liberty, and for love of country.

Dedicated and honorable service members and military leaders have worked hard to uphold the laws, values, and esprit de corps that are integral to the military. They understand that rape and sexual harassment in the U.S. armed forces is not consistent with the military values of honor, integrity, and duty to service and country. Among the men and women who sacrifice so much to serve their country, there should be no tolerance of such abuse.

There is much to be done to truly reach zero tolerance, but the first step has been taken. It is time to confront rape and sexual harassment in the military if for no other reason than because it is the right thing to do. From at least one veteran, hope for change does exist.

I swore to never be silent whenever and wherever human beings endure suffering and humiliation. We must always take sides. Neutrality helps the oppressor, never the victim. Silence encourages the tormentor, never the tormented. Sometimes we must interfere.

— ELIE WIESEL (ABRAMS, 1995, P. 105)

Addendums (2015)

For Service Members and Their Loved Ones
For Military Leaders and
Other Professionals
Resources For the Good of All Concerned

Addendum I

For Victims and Their Loved Ones
Coping with Military Sexual Trauma

My whole life I have wanted to be in the military. I was proud to
serve my country. I wanted to carry on the family tradition, so I enlisted.
I loved the military. It was my life.

— From a Victim of Military Sexual Trauma who
Left the Military Soon After She was Raped.

T HE FOLLOWING SECTION developed by Sugati Publications specifically for Service members and veterans who experienced a sexual assault. However, it also offers important
information for others affected by military sexual trauma, including friends and family of
victims and professionals who work with military victims.

This resource addresses some concerns about sexual assault, the recovery process and
the unique reporting options and challenges for victims of assault in the military. It is not
a substitute for medical, psychological or legal advice. Individuals should seek professional
consultation for specific medical, psychological or legal concerns and questions.

The original booklet in the series was developed as a national resource with the
assistance and expertise of many individuals and organizations across the United States
with a grant from the Violence Against Women Office, Office of Justice Programs, U.S.
Department of Justice. Points of view included do not necessarily represent the position of
the U.S. Department of Justice or the Department of Defense (DoD) except where specific
laws or DoD policies or directives have been cited. All references and existing policies

cited were current based on availability at the time of publication but are subject to change and regular updates. For more information and updates about the DoD Sexual Assault Prevention and Response (SAPR) policies, go to website at: www.sapr.mil.

This section is also available as a pamphlet via Sugati Publications for individual or bulk copies at www.SugatiPublications.com. An additional resource for active duty Service members on the current SAPR policies, resources, and reporting options for victims is also available.

Some important things you should know

Chances are, you are reading this because you or someone you care about was the victim of a sexual assault or sexual harassment while serving in the military. This information was developed specifically for women and men who were victims of any type of sexual trauma on active duty. This is also a good resource for family members, friends and helping professionals to learn more about military sexual trauma and supporting you through this difficult time. Also included is an overview of the Department of Defense policies on Sexual Assault Prevention and Response (DoD SAPR) as well as other valuable information on victims' concerns, reporting barriers, medical issues, family impact and the recovery process. To begin, her are a few important facts you should know about sexual assault and harassment.

- *Many people are affected by sexual assault/harassment.* Sexual assault or harassment can happen to anyone—no matter what his or her background, rank, gender or situation. Persons in new situations or trainees can be at a greater risk for sexual assault due to the power differences and the greater potential for abuse of power and authority.
- *Sexual assaults occur in different types of situations.* Whatever the circumstances leading up to the assault, it is never the victim's fault. For example, you may have decided to leave your window open on a summer night, go for a walk alone, get drunk at a party, go home with someone you just met, or said no to your date or your spouse about sex. None of these actions or decisions gives anyone the right to take advantage of you. The offender is fully responsible for what happened. You did not cause this to happen by anything you did or said.
- *Everyone deserves support.* Many resources and people are available to be of assistance. It is important to find the resource that is best for you. However, since military and veteran services and state laws can be different, you might want to contact the SAPR Program, the VA Medical Center, your nearest Vet Center or a local, civilian rape crisis program if you need specific information for your community. Remember, there are many people available to support you.

- *Survivors of sexual assault and harassment deserve respect when trying to get help.* Be informed about your choices in medical care, the military and civilian justice systems, your legal rights, and counseling options. With this information, you will be able to make the decisions that are best for you. Remember, victims of crime are also entitled to specific rights under federal law (as addressed in a later section). Remember, you do not have to deal with this alone.

What is military sexual trauma (MST)?

The Department of Veteran Affairs and other professionals use the term "military sexual trauma" to refer to any type of sexual assault or sexual harassment towards a Service member. Military sexual trauma includes any type of sexual assault or sexual harassment that happens on active duty. It can occur during peacetime, wartime and training exercises. In fact, some research has found that the occurrence of sexual assault and sexual harassment is higher during wartime, possibly in part due to the increased stress associated with war while deployed.

Who is affected by MST?

Military sexual trauma can have a negative effect on the victim, the unit and the mission. Anyone serving in the military can be a victim of military sexual trauma. This includes women and men, officers and enlisted and persons from all races, backgrounds, religions and any sexual orientation. The offender could be someone of the opposite or the same gender as the victim. However, when someone sexually assaults another person of the same gender (such as when a man rapes another man) it does not mean this was a homosexual act. In fact, both the victim and the offender might be heterosexual. Sexual assault is an act of power and control. It is not a method of expressing sexual desire or intimacy. Similarly, sexual harassment is also about degrading, humiliating and controlling the victim—regardless of the victim's gender or sexual orientation. If a sexual assault or sexual harassment occurs against specifically because of his or her sexual orientation, race or religion, it is a hate crime and is punishable by federal law.

Understanding sexual assault and sexual harassment

In the military, there can be overlap between sexual assault and sexual harassment. This is primarily because both can occur between persons in a chain-of-command (such as a supervisor who commits an offense against someone under their rank or authority). The following section highlights the key differences and provides the current DoD definitions as applied service-wide.

What are the differences?

- Sexual assault always involves some type of unwanted, physical, sexual contact.
- Sexual harassment can include a variety of unwelcome behaviors of a sexual nature, including verbal remarks, gestures, pictures and pressure for sex.
- Sexual harassment is sexual assault when it includes unwanted physical contact of a sexual nature (touching, kissing or any sexual contact).
- Sexual assault can occur in any location--and not necessarily related to work or work relationships.
- Sexual harassment generally pertains to persons with a working relationship or in the context of a work or school setting--often involving a person in a supervisory role.

Key points about sexual harassment

- Sexual harassment is never the victim's fault.
- The harasser's conduct is unwelcome and uninvited by the victim.
- If possible, the victim should inform the harasser that the conduct is unwelcome and the behaviors must stop (unless it is dangerous to confront the harasser).
- The distinction between welcome and unwelcome behavior is essential because sexual conduct becomes unlawful when it is unwanted.
- If possible, victims should use the chain of command, EEO or MEO (Military Equal Opportunity).

DoD Definitions of sexual assault and sexual harassment

Sexual assault is intentional sexual contact using force, physical threat or abuse of authority or if the victim does not or cannot consent. Sexual assault includes rape, nonconsensual sodomy (oral or anal sex), indecent assault (unwanted, inappropriate sexual contact or fondling), and any attempts to commit these acts. Sexual assault can occur regardless of gender of the victim or offender, spousal relationship between the victim and offender, or age of victim. However, if the victim is a minor, it would likely be considered child sexual abuse.

The definition of sexual assault also addresses the very important distinctions about consent and lack of consent. Consent does not mean the victim did not offer physical resistance. Examples of a lack of consent include force, threat of force, coercion or if the victim is asleep, incapacitated, or unconscious.

Some examples of sexual assault

When most of us hear the words sexual assault, we think of rape. However, many different kinds of unwanted sexual contact are sexual assault, but not rape. In general, if any type of unwanted penetration occurs, however slight and with any body part (mouth, vagina, and anus) it is most likely rape. The following are some examples of different types of sexual assault including rape:

- Grabbing or touching a person's breast, vagina, penis or buttocks without their permission
- Making someone give (or receive) oral sex by forcing, coercing or pressuring them
- Threatening or coercing someone to have sex
- Using an object to touch a person's breasts, vagina, penis or anus (on the inside or outside of their body) against their wishes or without their consent
- Having sex with someone who is unable to give or to deny consent due to being mentally incapable, drugged or severely intoxicated with alcohol

Alcohol and other drugs in sexual assault

Many sexual assaults involve alcohol or other drugs. You did not deserve to be sexually assaulted even if you were intoxicated or under the influence of other drugs. You are not to blame for what happened. No one has the right to sexually violate you or take advantage of you in that way at any time.

Alcohol and other drugs can increase your vulnerability. The can put anyone at greater risk for sexual assault leading to impairment, blacking out or passing out. Sexual offenders look for this opportunity to victimize someone and to take advantage of the situation and the person's vulnerable state. Some sexual offenders also try to control their victims' ability to resist by putting drugs in their intended victim's drink or by giving them more alcohol. In fact, alcohol is the number one drug used by sexual offenders to commit rape.

Common concerns for victims of military sexual assault

Reporting barriers and concerns

Victims of sexual assault may have concerns about telling someone about what happened or reporting the crime to law enforcement. What happened to you was a personal violation. If you know the person who did this to you, it may also feel like a betrayal of trust. In addition, if you work with the person (or if he/she is in your chain of command) it can pose other problems or challenges. The following are some concerns about reporting for military victims:

- Feel ashamed, guilty or blame themselves for what happened

- Fear further repercussions or harm by the offender
- Fear repercussions on the job or by a superior
- Concerns about not being believed if others find out
- Question whether or not reporting will help
- Anticipate further trauma or harassment for reporting
- Concerns about impact on career or military service
- Fear others will see them as weak or unfit for duty
- Difficult working or living near the offender
- Want to 'move on' with their life and career

Some possible reactions and changes in yourself after a sexual assault

The following summarizes some of the possible responses and changes that sexual assault victims may experience in the aftermath of a sexual assault. Remember, there is no right or wrong way to respond to this type of trauma. Not everyone experiences all of these concerns or responses. You may notice that some of these apply to you and others do not. However, if any of these issues are having a significant impact on your life or your ability to function (such as, sleeping, appetite, work, socializing), you may want to talk to a counselor or your doctor about what you can do to address these symptoms.

Psychological or emotional concerns

The psychological (mental) impact of a sexual assault can have short or long-term effects. Initially, reactions might include shock, disbelief or confusion. After days or maybe a few weeks, most victims will make a deliberate effort to get on with their lives. However, some symptoms may come back weeks, months or even years later, such as: mood swings, irritability, crying spells, depression, anxiety, sleep difficulties, fears, or a hard time making decisions. A delayed response is common since certain events and circumstances might trigger memories of the trauma.

Reminders of the trauma

While you are trying to move on with your life you might encounter some direct or indirect reminders of the trauma (situations, smells, familiar sights). These "triggers" remind you of the sexual assault or the offender and can cause you to experience some emotional distress. This can happen even if the trauma was months or years ago. The type of distress can vary from a mild, uncomfortable memory to a more vivid flashback or a physical reaction of anxiety or panic. A common example might occur on the anniversary date of the assault. While some people experience only mild distress when reminded of the trauma, others may have more alarming responses to the triggers. Most survivors will learn how to recognize and to cope with their "triggers" particularly with the assistance of a therapist or support group.

Post Traumatic Stress Disorder (PTSD)

Post Traumatic Stress Disorder (PTSD) can affect people who have experienced a life-threatening trauma, such as rape or war. Over one-third of all sexual assault victims will likely develop Post Traumatic Stress Disorder. Some MST survivors develop a shorter form of PTSD when the symptoms last only up to one month after the trauma. Some sexual assault victims will experience significantly more distress after the trauma--sometimes months or years later. These responses might include: preoccupation with the rape; unwanted, intrusive, thoughts or feelings about the trauma; flashbacks; repeated nightmares; efforts to avoid any reminder of the trauma; sleep difficulties; concentration difficulties; intense fear or anxiety, feeling numb and detached, having physical symptoms or generally feeling unwell or uneasy. These are some of the symptoms of posttraumatic stress disorder.

PTSD is a mental health diagnosis associated with the trauma. Qualified mental health professional including psychologists, counselors, psychiatrists, and social workers can make the diagnosis of PTSD. Counseling from a mental health professional (or medications) can help to treat PTSD or to lessen some of the symptoms. If you notice any of these reactions in yourself, consider talking to a counselor to help you to cope with the effects of the trauma.

Anxiety and Panic Attacks

Some trauma survivors experience anxiety that is not PTSD but can be just as distressing. There are several other kinds of anxiety disorders including: generalized anxiety; panic attacks (sudden, unexpected responses which often result in physical symptoms such as a rapid heartbeat, sweating, dizziness, lightheadedness, shallow breathing and a fear of dying); and phobias, (fear or anxiety associated with certain situations, events, social encounters or specific objects). Anxiety can be treated with counseling. In particular, cognitive behavioral therapy has very positive results based on the research. For some people, anti-anxiety medications or other alternatives, such as relaxation training or meditation can be very effective.

Depression

Another common psychological response to sexual trauma is depression. It can be mild and short term or it may last longer and more severe with thoughts about suicide. Some of the key symptoms of depression can include: tearfulness, sadness, decreased motivation, sleep disturbances, changes in appetite, decreased social interest, withdrawal, difficulty concentrating, decreased sexual desire and decreased energy. Some people, men in particular, might experience irritability or angry outbursts as a symptom of depression.

If depression is more severe, some people have thoughts about suicide or make efforts to end their life. Persons who have a depression that persists or continues to come back and interfere with normal daily functioning (such as relationships, job or school) or with suicidal thoughts might have a more serious type of depression called Major Depressive Disorder. It is most important that you contact a mental health professional or your physician if you have a depression that does not go away or if you have thoughts about hurting or killing yourself or someone else. Good counseling, and in some cases anti-depressant medication, can make all the difference in your recovery and healing from the trauma.

Physical and medical conditions

Your body may respond to the continued emotional and psychological stress with physical symptoms. You might have sleep difficulties, headaches, stomach distress, or other illness. Changes in sleep patterns are one of the most common after a trauma. Some survivors have recurrent physical symptoms that will become chronic if left untreated, such as inflammatory illnesses, fibromyalgia, headaches, some gynecological disorders, chronic pain or tiredness. Someone with long-term emotional effects of sexual trauma may also experience an impact on their physical health. Consider medical attention if your symptoms persist since many of these conditions will not go away on their own.

Relationships, intimacy and sexual concerns

Sexual assault can affect your relationships with friends, family and other loved ones. Although the trauma happened to you, it can also affect the people around you. They might have different ideas of how you should respond or when you should be "over it." You may want to suggest they read this information to understand better what you are going through.

Your intimate and sexual relations may also be affected. You may need time before you are fully comfortable having physical closeness, touching or sexual contact again. You may not want to do certain sexual activities or to be touched in certain places or ways because it reminds you of the trauma. This is common for many victims of sexual assault.

Some women also experience pain associated with intercourse due to anxiety or to other physical conditions. Similarly, some male survivors experience sexual difficulties, such as early ejaculation or difficulties getting or keeping an erection. These symptoms may be related to the trauma or memories of the sexual assault even if you do not have direct associations with the trauma. If you are having these difficulties or pain associated with sexual activity, tell your doctor who can help you to assess the issue.

Some sexual trauma survivors think of sex as a way to validate them self to feel they are still loved and accepted by their partner. Others seek comfort or reassurance through sexual activity in ways that might not be healthy, such as having sex with random partners, unprotected sex or high-risk experimentation. Some survivors go through a time of being promiscuous or sexually active with many partners. They may feel like sex does not matter anymore, or they may use sex as a way to feel in more in control. These important issues can be addressed in counseling to help survivors feel better about themselves and their bodies and to recognize they deserve healthy, loving relationships. If you are experiencing any concerns about your sexual desire, relationships or sexual behaviors since the assault, consider speaking with a qualified mental health counselor experienced in sexual trauma treatment issues.

Trust your instincts about what is right for you in your sexual recovery and remember, intimacy is not the same as sex. Be clear with your partner about what you need or want as you continue healing. Go at your own pace.

Safety and trust concerns

Many sexual assault survivors have concerns about safety or trust after an assault. The assault was an unexpected event that upset the balance of your life. You were vulnerable no control over what happened. You may have feared for your life if your attacker threatened you or your family. You might question your own instincts about trusting people, especially if your offender was someone known to you. Regaining a sense of safety, trusting your instincts and feeling in control of your life are important aspects of healing and recovering from the trauma.

Some additional considerations for sexual assault victims, family and loved ones

If you were a victim of MST, consider these options:

- Tell someone you can trust.
- Talk to a counselor who specializes in sexual trauma recovery.
- Get as much information as you can about your options.
- Contact a SAPR Victim Advocate or the Safe Helpline.
- Know the two reporting options and know what to expect from each option.
- Tell the police or make a report especially if you were threatened or have fears that the person will hurt you again.

- Consider requesting a legal 'no contact' order or protective order.
- If the offender is in your unit, talk to Command about your options for a transfer for you or the offender.
- Consider medical treatment, prevention for pregnancy and prevention of sexually transmitted infections.
- Know your rights. Go to www.myduty.mil for more information.
- Remember, you do not have to deal with this alone.

If you know someone who was the victim of MST, keep the following in mind:

- Believe them. If you have any doubts, keep them to yourself. It will not help the victim if you share your doubts.
- Give them information about their options. Ask what they need or want to do.
- Do not give advice. Empower and encourage the victim to make the decisions that are best for them.
- Be supportive and non-judgmental. Do not blame the victim no matter what the circumstance or situation.
- Remind them it was not their fault. No one ever deserves to be hurt in this way.
- If the victim was involved in an abusive relationship, it may be difficult to understand why they stayed in the relationship. Do not ask why or blame them for not leaving.
- Understand that victims often feel they have no power. The abuser was in control and is to blame for what happened. Victims may still feel a connection to the offender. Although this can be difficult to understand, it is important to be patient and supportive.
- Give them the numbers for the Safe Helpline, SAPR program or other resources.
- Talk to an advocate, counselor or call the Safe Helpline if you have questions.

Other warning signs to tell someone

Tell someone if you experience any of these warning signs or if you notice any of these behaviors in your colleague, friend or loved one. Do not keep it to yourself. Tell a counselor or call a crisis helpline. You do not have to deal with any of these by yourself.

- A depression that does not go away or gets worse
- Suicidal thoughts and plans or regular thoughts about death
- Serious thoughts or a plan to hurt or kill someone else
- Harming yourself on purpose (e.g. cutting or burning yourself)
- Physical symptoms or pain that won't go away

- Significant weight loss in a short time or a lack of appetite
- Nightmares or flashbacks about the trauma
- Excessive alcohol or other drug use

A final message on coping after a sexual assault

Whether it has been weeks or years since the sexual assault, coping with what happened to you will be a process with some challenges. This was a disruptive event in your life perhaps further complicated by how others responded to you or if you still encounter the offender.

Your healing journey is your own but you do not have to deal with this by yourself. The following are some examples that survivors have used to cope with their trauma and to move forward with their lives at a pace that was right for them.

- Therapy such as individual counseling, support groups, or couples counseling
- Medication (as needed for depression, anxiety, PTSD or other conditions)
- Reading and learning more about healing and recovery
- Meditation and relaxation such as breathing exercises or walking meditation
- Physical activities such as yoga, walks, exercise or sports
- Hobbies or other activities such as gardening, reading or writing
- Finding meaning by helping others such as volunteering or donating your services
- Spiritual practice such as religious activities, prayer, community or faith events
- Social support and relationships such as children, grandkids, friends or social groups

It may be helpful to have several coping strategies and to use the one that is right for you when you need it. For example, there may be times when you need to talk about the trauma and you decide to attend a support group; or, there may be times when you want to do something that will help you to refocus on other areas of your life, such as volunteering at a local food pantry or a senior center. Coping does not always have to be about the trauma. Whatever you decide to do, remember, there are many people who are available to support you on your healing journey. You are not alone.

Addendum II

FOR MILITARY LEADERS AND PROFESSIONALS
RESPONDING TO SEXUAL ASSAULT IN THE MILITARY

T HE FOLLOWING SECTION was developed by Sugati Publications. It is available as a leadership guide and a resource for persons working with military sexual assault victims.

All military leaders need to know how to respond to sexual assault allegations when
brought to their attention—whether by the alleged victim, the accused, or another Service
member. The following information can serve as a quick reference guide and resource for
military leaders as well as other professionals who work with military victims of sexual
assault.

Responding to Sexual Assault in the Military offers an overview about sexual assault, sexual
offenders, victim responses and options for victims on reporting and seeking care or advocacy. It also includes an overview of the DoD Sexual Assault Prevention and Response
(SAPR) policies and references to the Uniform Code of Military Justice relative to sexual
offenses.

This resource is not a comprehensive instruction although it does offer extensive information about sexual assault. In addition, it does not provide medical, legal or psychological
advice. Individuals should seek professional consultation if needed. Additional resources
and policies are included for further reference.

The original booklet in the series was developed as a national resource with the assistance and expertise of many individuals and organizations across the United States and
with a grant from the Violence Against Women Office, Office of Justice Programs, U.S.
Department of Justice. Points of view do not necessarily represent the position of the U.S.
Department of Justice or the Department of Defense except where specific laws or DoD

policies or directives have been cited. All references and existing policies are cited accordingly and were current based on availability at the time of publication but are subject to change and regular updates. For more information and updates about the DoD SAPR policies, go to the SAPR website at: www.sapr.mil.

This section is also available via Sugati Publications for individual or bulk copies.

Facts all military leaders should know about sexual assault

Sexual assault affects many people. It can also affect the mission and the unit's morale by creating divisiveness if not handled appropriately by leadership. In addition, it can have lasting effects on the victim and the accused. As the DoD SAPR motto states: "Sexual Assault-- hurts one, affects all."

Sexual assault can happen to anyone—no matter what his or her background, gender, rank or situation. Victims of sexual assault include women, men, enlisted, officers, and persons from all ages, sexual orientations, racial and cultural backgrounds. Anyone can become the target of a sexual offender.

Service members in new situations are at greater risk for sexual assault. Persons who are new recruits, trainees or newly deployed are much more likely to be at risk. They are potentially more vulnerable because of their younger age, inexperience in the military, or due to the rank differential and potential abuse of power.

Sexual assaults occur in many different situations, including any of these scenarios or locations:

- On a date with someone the victim knows
- Under the influence of alcohol or other drugs
- Off duty, on duty, on base, off base, on a ship
- At the victims' home by a spouse, partner or a stranger
- At the barracks by an NCO, supervisor, or an officer
- In a forward deployed environment by someone in the unit

No matter what the situation, it is never the victim's fault. Just like any other crime, the offender is responsible and to blame for the crime of any sexual offense. No one deserves to be sexually assaulted no matter what the situation.

Most sexual offenders are individuals that you would not have expected to commit this crime.

The majority of sexual offenders seem like very 'normal' and healthy individuals with successful lives and/or military careers. Some of them may even be married or high ranking officers. We do not think of these individuals as sexual offenders, which is why they are called "undetected rapists." [1] They are less likely to be suspected, reported, charged or convicted. Yet, they are the most common type of sexual offender.

All victims deserve support after a sexual assault. As a leader, Service members look to you for guidance. Your response to an alleged victim and the climate you set in your command affects the victim's recovery and how, or if, a case proceeds. There are many resources available to assist you in your role including the Sexual Assault Response Coordinator (SARC) and the Victim Advocate. Your response can make all the difference to victims, to the accused and to others serving under your guidance.

The Department of Defense (DoD) Policy and Directives on SAPR

The foundation of the DoD Sexual Assault Prevention and Response (SAPR) policy and program is based on the 2004 "Care for Victims" Task Force Report and these four guiding tenets:

1. Sexual assault is a criminal act.
2. There will be zero tolerance for sexual assault.
3. Offenders will be prosecuted to the fullest extent of the law.
4. Victims will have access to appropriate assistance and treatment.

Over the past decade, updates to the SAPR program and policies reflect the identified needs of the community and a more comprehensive response to address this issue. The following provides a quick reference of some of the prominent changes since its inception. The timeline is not intended to be comprehensive of all changes but it does highlight some key improvements and modifications during the first ten years of the SAPR policy and program.

Timeline and History of Sexual Assault Prevention and Response (SAPR)

2004   A joint task force was created to develop a sexual assault policy

2005   A total of 14 DTMs were issued as the basis for DoD SAPR policy

2005   DoD Directive 6495.01 DoD SAPR Program was approved and initiated

2006   DoD Directive 6495.02 SAPR Procedures approved

2010   Uniform Code of Military Justice updated Article 120

2011   New provisions added as Directive-Type Memorandums

2012   DoD Directive 6495.01 was updated 1.23.12 including new policies on:
   - Advocate-victim privileged communication

---

1 David Lisak, Ph.D. (March, 2002) "The Rape Fact Sheet."

- Expedited transfers
- Guideline on retention of forensic evidence
- Prevention training requirements

2012 Strategic Direction to the Joint Force on SAPR issued 5.7.12

2012 Uniform Code of Military Justice Article 120 updated effective 6.28.12

2013 Update to DoDI 6495.02 SAPR Program Procedures 2.12.14 including:
- Development of a record system of all unrestricted sexual assault reports and dispositions of cases maintained for 20 years from the date of the report.
- SAPR training within 14 days of active duty for all personnel

2013 National Defense Authorization Act (NDAA) signed into law with several new provisions including the following:
- Prohibit recruiting of anyone convicted of a sex offense
- Mandatory separation of convicted sex offenders
- Insurance coverage for abortions in cases of rape or incest for service women and military family members
- Retention of restricted report documentation for 50 years
- Creation of Special Victims Units to improve investigation, prosecution and victim support in child abuse, domestic violence and sexual assault cases
- Required prevention training in pre-command and command courses for officers
- Annual command climate assessment surveys to track individual attitudes toward sexual assault and sexual harassment
- Improved data collection and reporting by the military on sexual assault and sexual harassment cases

2014 National Defense Authorization Act (NDAA) signed into law with several new provisions including the following:
- Any and all decisions by a convening authority not to refer a sexual assault offense to court-martial will be reviewed by a superior competent authority.
- Commanders who do have disposition authority can no longer consider the general military character of persons accused under UCMJ.
- Significant amendments to the Uniform Code of Military Justice regarding to rape and sexual assault cases (addressed in a later section.)

2015 Updates to DoDD 6495.01 effective 1.20.15 (addressed in the following section.)

2015 Establishment of Special Victim Investigation and Prosecution (SVIP) Capability within the Military Criminal Investigative Organizations (MCIOs).

SAPR Program Goals

- Ensure sensitive and comprehensive treatment for victims
- Create a climate encouraging victims to report without fear of reprisal
- Establish sexual assault prevention training and awareness
- Create a climate to reduce sexual assaults
- Ensure leaders understand their roles and responsibilities and take appropriate administrative and disciplinary action

Initial SAPR Key Policy Provisions based on the original 14 DTMs in 2005

1. Victim support and assistance
2. Response capabilities (establishment of SARCs and Victim Advocates)
3. Confidentiality policy for victims of sexual assault (restricted reporting)
4. Evidence collection and preservation under restricted reporting
5. Collateral misconduct (consideration for sexual assault victims)
6. Administrative separation (involving victims of sexual assault)
7. Commanders' Checklist (when responding to sexual assault allegations)
8. Collaboration (within the military and civilian community)
9. DoD definition of sexual assault (for training/education purposes)
10. Training responders (Commanders, law enforcement, healthcare)
11. Training all Service members (mandatory annual training)
12. Pre-deployment training (for all Service members)
13. Essential training for a sexual assault response capability
14. Data Call (Quarterly and annual reports to track sexual assault reports)

DoD Directives 6495.01 and 6495.02: Key Provisions[2]

The Department of Defense implemented its' first Sexual Assault Response Program (SAPR) in 2005 with DoDD 6495.01 and DoDD 6495.02. The comprehensive SAPR policy is based on the original 14 DTMs approved by all Service Secretaries as noted previously. The updates to DoD Directive 6495.01 occurred in January 2012 and most recently in 2015; updates to the DoD Instruction 6495.02 occurred in March 2013 and 2015 with several key changes. The four overarching areas delineated in DoDD 6495.01 and DoDI 6495.02 are:

1. The DoD SAPR Office is the central oversight of SAPR.

---

2 DoD Directives 6495.01 (Jan. 2012 and 2015) and 6495.02 (Mar. 2013).

2. All Service Branches have a SAPR Office.
3. Victims have access to appropriate assistance and treatment.
4. Commanders have specific responsibilities under SAPR.

Updates to DoD Directive 6495.01[3]

The focus of this Directive and Reference is on the victim of sexual assault. The DoD shall provide support to an active duty Service member regardless of when or where the sexual assault took place. [4]

The SAPR Program Directive DoD 6495.01 was reissued with updates on 1.20.15. The following section summarizes the key points of this directive. Refer to the policy in full at http://www.dtic.mil/whs/directives/corres/pdf/649501p.pdf

Applicability: Per Section 2, DODD 6495.01 effective 1.20.15, this policy applies to:

1. *OSD, the Military Departments, the Office of the Chairman of the Joint Chiefs of Staff and the Joint Staff, the Combatant Commands, the Inspector General of the DoD (IG DoD), the Defense Agencies, the DoD Field Activities, and all other organizational entities within the DoD*
2. *National Guard and Reserve Component members who are sexually assaulted when performing active service and inactive duty training.*
3. *Military dependents 18 years of age and older who are eligible for treatment in the military healthcare system, at installations in the continental United States (CONUS) and outside of the continental United States (OCONUS), and who were victims of sexual assault perpetrated by someone other than a spouse or intimate partner.*
4. *Service members who are on active duty but were victims of sexual assault prior to enlistment or commissioning. They are eligible to receive full SAPR services and either reporting option.*

IMPORTANT NOTE: The Family Advocacy Program is the resource that provides services to victims of intimate partner violence and sexual assault by someone with whom they have an intimate partner relationship or dependents under the age of 18 years old.

Limited Eligibility of SAPR Services [5]

To ensure complete accuracy regarding eligibility, the following section is from DoD 6495.01, Section 2:

---

3 DoD Directive 6495.01 (January 20, 2015) http://www.dtic.mil/whs/directives/corres/pdf/649501p.pdf

4 DoD Directive 6495.01, January 20, 2015, Section 4n (page 6)

5 DoD Directive 6495.01, January 20, 2015, Section 2.

The following non-military personnel are only eligible for LIMITED healthcare (medical and mental health) services in the form of emergency care unless otherwise eligible to receive treatment in a military medical treatment facility. They will also be offered the LIMITED SAPR services of a Sexual Assault Response Coordinator (SARC) and a SAPR Victim Advocate (VA) while undergoing emergency care OCONUS. These limited healthcare and SAPR services shall be provided to:

(a). DoD civilian employees and their family dependents 18 years of age and older when they are stationed or performing duties OCONUS and eligible for treatment in the military healthcare system at military installations or facilities OCONUS.

(b). U.S. citizen DoD contractor personnel when they are authorized to accompany the Armed Forces in a contingency operation OCONUS and their U.S. citizen employees

Updates Affecting SAPR under the National Defense Authorization Act6

In addition to the updates to the SAPR policy, there were several significant provisions passed by Congress in the FY2014 and FY2015 National Defense Authorization Acts (NDAA) affecting both SAPR and the Uniform Code of Military Justice. The changes regarding sexual assault offenses pertain primarily to investigation, victims' rights and victims' care. Below is a summary of each of the new amendments that military leaders should be aware of and be prepared to implement if applicable.

Article 32 Preliminary Hearings

- Article 32 hearings will model preliminary hearings in the federal criminal system.
- Article 32 hearings will be conducted by a preliminary hearing officer (Judge Advocate)
- Victims (military and civilian) have the right not to testify at this hearing.

Military Rules of Evidence (MRE) Amendments

- Victims may exercise their rights through their legal counsel to be heard at all proceedings.
- Special victims' counsel shall receive adequate notice of hearings, trials, and other proceedings.

---

6 National Defense Authorization Act 2015 http://www.gpo.gov/fdsys/pkg/CPRT-113HPRT92738/pdf/CPRT-113HPRT92738.pdf

- If the victim believes the military judge made an incorrect ruling regarding rape shield evidence (MRE 412) or psychotherapist-patient privilege (MRE 513), the victim may petition for a writ of mandamus to the Service court of criminal appeals.
- The existing privilege between a psychotherapist and patient shall include other licensed mental health professionals under MRE 513.

Convening Authority Decisions

- A superior competent authority shall review all decisions by a convening authority not to refer a sexual assault offense to court-martial (NDAA FY 2014).
- The chief prosecutor of the Service may direct the Service Secretary to review any case where a convening authority decides not to refer a sexual assault for court-martial.
- Commanders who do have disposition authority can no longer consider the general military character of persons accused under UCMJ (NDAA FY 2014).
- Consideration of general military character during the findings phase of courts-martial proceedings is strictly prohibited except for a limited number of enumerated offenses.

Care for Victims Amendments

- Sexual assault victims have the option to request the military or the local prosecutor try their case. If the victim wants the case to go to the local prosecutor, the convening authority must ensure the prosecutor is aware of the victim's preference. The convening authority must inform the victim about the prosecutor's decision whether to prosecute the case.
- Sexual assault victims who received a less than honorable discharge may now challenge the type of discharge on the grounds that it was an adverse affect (or retribution) of being the victim of a sex-related offense. Service Secretaries must develop a confidential review process utilizing boards to consider the correction of military records as requested by victims of sex-related offenses.

Special Victims' Counsel
Victims have the option of free legal counsel to represent them during the entire investigation through the completion of courts-martial proceedings. It is the victims' option

whether to choose a Special Victims Counsel as their representative. The Secretary of Defense ordered this directive in 2014 and Congress affirmed it in NDAA 2015.

Special Victim Investigation and Prosecution (SVIP) Capability within MCIOs[7]
DoD Instruction 5505.19 released in February of 2015 establishes the development of Special Victim Investigation and Prosecution (SVIP) within the Military Criminal Investigative Organizations (MCIOs).

The Instruction directs MCIOs to implement a special victim capability. Each Military Service is required to develop this capability to be more responsive to victims of certain crimes, including sexual assault. Teams will include specially trained MCIO investigators, judge advocates, paralegals, and victim witness personnel.

Other key points about the SAPR program

- The focus is on the victim and the victim's recovery.
- SAPR shall provide gender-responsive, culturally competent care.
- Sexual assault victims are emergency cases.
- An immediate, trained sexual assault response capability shall be available for each report of sexual assault in all locations, including in deployed locations.
- The Sexual Assault Response Coordinator (SARC) is the single point of contact coordinating care for victims. SARCs supervise the SAPR Victim Advocates (VA).
- The Victim Advocate provides crisis intervention, support, information and referrals to victims of sexual assault. The advocate is not a counselor.
- The roles and responsibilities of Command, law enforcement and criminal justice procedures are within the SAPR policy.
- Victims of sexual assault shall be protected from coercion, retaliation, and reprisal in accordance with DoDD 7050.06.

Victims' Reporting Options
The most central mandates of DoDD 6495.01 pertain to reporting options. The two reporting options (unrestricted and restricted) have been a part of the SAPR program since the inception. However, the a significant change was added to DoDD 6495.01 effective 1.20.15 in accordance with the National Defense Authorization Act for Fiscal Year 2014: "Victims must be informed of the availability of legal assistance and the right to consult with a Special

---

7 DoDI NUMBER 5505.19 (February 3, 2015) http://www.dtic.mil/whs/directives/corres/pdf/550519p.pdf

Victims' Counsel (SVC)/Victims' Legal Counsel (VLC)." [8] The two reporting options remained unchanged with the addition of this additional option for victims of sexual assault.

The following section delineates Unrestricted and Restricted Reporting as well as the DoD dual objectives with regard to sexual assault reporting.

Unrestricted Reporting

Unrestricted reporting is one of the two reporting options available for sexual assault victims. With unrestricted reporting, the appropriate authorities will receive the report of alleged incident and all information about the incident (including the identity of the alleged victim and accused) for the purpose of investigation.

Key Points of Unrestricted Reporting

- DoD policy favors unrestricted reporting to allow for an investigation.
- Command and investigative services notified.
- Victims of sexual assault can receive:
    - Medical treatment
    - Sexual Assault Forensic Examination
    - Advocacy services and/or counseling services
    - Legal (JAG, law enforcement) involvement
    - Special Victims Counsel or Victims' Legal Counsel

Benefits of Unrestricted Reporting

- Ensures the widest range of rights and protections to the victim
- Makes Command support available to victims (such as Military Protective Orders, separation from offender, deferred collateral misconduct)
- Increases possibility for offender accountability
- Enhances community safety and may encourage others to report.

Limitations of Unrestricted Reporting

- Others will know about the report (possibly affecting victim's privacy).
- Investigation and court proceedings can be stressful and lengthy.
- Investigation may not result in a conviction or punishment of offender.

---

8 DoDD 6495.01 (January 20, 2015) Section 4L, page 6.

Restricted Reporting

Restricted reporting is the other reporting option available. It gives all victims the option of confidentially seeking medical care and assistance in the aftermath of a sexual assault without initiating a criminal report. It allows victims time to gain information and to consider all of their options.

Definition of Restricted Reporting [9]

Reporting option that allows sexual assault victims to confidentially disclose the assault to specified individuals (i.e., SARC, SAPR VA, or healthcare personnel) and receive medical treatment, including emergency care, counseling, and assignment of a SARC and SAPR VA, without triggering an official investigation. The victim's report provided to healthcare personnel (including the information acquired from a SAFE Kit), SARCs, or SAPR VAs will NOT be reported to law enforcement or to the command to initiate the official investigative process unless the victim consents or an established EXCEPTION applies in accordance with Reference (c). The Restricted Reporting Program option applies to Service members and their military dependents 18 years of age and older. Only a SARC, SAPR VA, or healthcare personnel may receive a Restricted Report, previously referred to as Confidential Reporting.

Key Points of Restricted Reporting

- Allows victims to confidentially receive:
  - Medical treatment
  - Sexual Assault Forensic Examination
  - Advocacy services and/or counseling services
- Victims can change their restricted report to unrestricted.
- Senior Commander notified within 24 hours of the alleged incident with no personal information that would identify the victim.
- Investigative services are not notified.

Applicability: Restricted Reporting Option is Available to:

- All active duty Service members
- Guard/Reserve on active status or inactive duty training
- Military dependents 18 years of age and older

---

9 DoDD 6495.01, January 20, 2015, Glossary, page 20. http://www.dtic.mil/whs/directives/corres/pdf/649501p.pdf

Personnel Authorized to Accept a Restricted Report

- Sexual Assault Response Coordinator (SARC)
- SAPR Victim Advocate (VA)
- Healthcare personnel authorized to accept a restricted report

Chaplains are NOT authorized to receive a restricted report but do have privileged communication (confidentiality) under Military Rules of Evidence. In December 2011, Victim Advocates were also granted privileged communication under MRE Rule 514.

Investigations of the allegation can occur in the following situations:

- The Commander learns about the sexual assault from another source.
- The victim tells another active duty Service member about the sexual assault (other than a SARC, Advocate, Healthcare Provider or Chaplain) and the person reports it under the mandatory reporting requirements.
- If anyone outside of the specified officials knows about the sexual assault and notifies Command or the authorities, it may lead to an unrestricted report and an investigation. This can happen regardless of whether the victim reported the incident or made a restricted report.

Benefits of Restricted Reporting

- Allows victims to receive medical treatment, advocacy, and counseling
- Provides victims time to consider options and begin the healing process.
- Empowers victims to seek relevant info and support to make more informed decisions about participating in a criminal investigation
- Victims have input regarding the release of their personal information.
- Victims get to decide whether to initiate investigation.
- Non-identifying personal information gives Senior Commander basic information about sexual assaults occurring in the command.

Limitations of Restricted Reporting

- Offenders remain unpunished and likely to commit the crime again.
- Victims cannot receive protective order (MPO)/No Contact Order.

- Offenders will still have access to their victims and may contact them.
- Over time, evidence from crime scene or the offender may be lost affecting a potential conviction.
- Victims cannot tell other Service members due to mandatory reporting.

Exceptions to Restricted Reporting

The exceptions to restricted reporting (when disclosing this protected information is allowable) are very specific. Disclosing information about a restricted sexual assault report is allowable only in these circumstances:

- The victim specifically consents to the disclosure in writing.
- It is necessary to disclose the information to prevent serious and imminent threat to the victim or to another person, as in situations involving violent threats or suicidal or homicidal ideations.
- Disclosure by a Healthcare Provider is required to the Disability Retirement Boards and officials to assess fitness of duty for disability retirement determinations only.
- For supervision or oversight of victim services (limited to: Healthcare Personnel, SAPR Victim Advocates and SARCs).
- If ordered by military or civilian Federal or State judge or required by federal or state statue or US International agreement.

The SARC will determine if an exception applies. If needed, the SARC may consult with the Staff Judge Advocate of the Senior Commander without disclosing any identifying information. If there is still uncertainty, the Senior Commander will be the deciding authority as to whether an exception applies.

IMPORTANT NOTE: Exceptions to restricted reporting do not permit full disclosure. Only the information that is absolutely necessary to satisfy the exception can be disclosed to another person. Violations of this policy with improper disclosure of confidential information can result in disciplinary action under UCMJ or other adverse personnel or administrative actions.

DoD Dual Objectives [10]

The following recognizes the dual objectives of the DoD regarding sexual assault prevention and response. The DoD Directive 6495.01 is as follows:

---

10 DoD Directive 6495.01, January 20, 20152, Section 4(2)(b) page 5.

- *The DoD is committed to ensuring victims of sexual assault are protected; treated with dignity and respect; provided support, advocacy, and care.*
- *The DoD supports effective command awareness/prevention programs.*
- *The DoD also strongly supports applicable law enforcement and criminal justice procedures that enable persons to be held accountable for sexual assault offenses and criminal dispositions, as appropriate.*

To achieve these dual objectives, DoD preference is for unrestricted reporting of sexual assaults to allow for the provision of victims' services and to pursue accountability. However, unrestricted reporting may represent a barrier for victims to access services, when the victim desires no command or law enforcement involvement.

Victims' Rights

Victims of crime are entitled to specific rights under Federal Law "The Crime Control Act: Title V, Victims' Rights and Restitution" from 1990. In addition, active duty Service members have rights under the DoD Victim Witness Assistance Program and the DoD Victims Bill of Rights (which is comparable to the Federal law on victims' rights). For more information, refer to DoD Directives 1030.1, 1030.2, and DD Form 2701.

DoD Victims' rights

1. To be treated with fairness and respect for the victim's dignity and privacy
2. To be reasonably protected from the accused offender
3. To be notified of court proceedings
4. To be present at all public court proceedings related to the offense, unless the court determines that testimony by the victim would be materially affected if the victim heard other testimony at trial
5. To confer with the attorney for the government in the case
6. To receive available restitution
7. To be provided information about the conviction, sentencing, imprisonment and release of the offender.

In addition, victims may have the option of preparing a Victim Impact Statement for court-martial convening authorities as well as for clemency and parole boards. These boards may also consider restitution to the victim.

Command Roles and Responsibilities

Initial disposition authority of sexual assault cases is withheld from any officer below 0-6 level (colonel or Navy captain) and who does not hold special court-martial convening authority.

The following offers a quick reference to the key policy changes affecting Commanders as ordered by Secretary of Defense Panetta in 2012 and as noted in DoDI 6495.02 SAPR Program Procedures.

Key changes relative to Command authority:

1. Unit commanders at the company or squadron level no longer have the authority to decide whether to take further action in reported cases of attempted rape, forcible sodomy or sexual assault. All of these reported cases are referred to a higher authority for review and disposition (e.g. referral for court-martial).

2. Unit commanders must forward all reports of attempted rape, forcible sodomy or sexual assault up the chain of command to a colonel-level special court-martial convening authority.

3. Any appearance, suggestion or threat of potential retaliation should be referred to the same higher-level authority for review and disposition. Unit commanders will not have decision-making authority in these cases either and are required to refer them to a colonel-level special court-martial convening authority.

4. Unit commanders must immediately refer any unrestricted reports to the appropriate MCIO. The Commander shall not conduct any internal investigation of the alleged offense nor should the Commander delay making the report to the MCIO.[11]

Other DoD Initiatives Affecting Military Leaders as of 4.26.12 include:

1. National Guard and Reserve personnel who are sexually assaulted can remain on active duty status to obtain all treatment available;

2. Sexual assault policies must be explained to all service members within 14 days of their entry into active duty;

3. Commanders must conduct annual organizational climate assessments to assess their culture of professionalism and zero tolerance;

4. A record of the outcome of disciplinary and administrative proceedings related to sexual assault shall be kept and retained centrally;

5. Training programs for sexual assault prevention will include training new military commanders on how to respond to sexual assault issues;

---

11 DoDI 6495.02 SAPR Program Procedures (12 February 2014).

6. A mandate to ensure wider public dissemination of available sexual assault resources, such as DOD's "Safe Helpline;

7. A Special Victims' Unit will be within each service to include specially trained experts in evidence collection, interviewing and working with victims.

Convening Authority Updates in 2014 and 2015[12]

The National Defense Authorization Acts for FY14 and FY15 (passed by Congress) include the following provisions affecting Commanders:

- All decisions by a convening authority not to refer a sexual assault offense to court-martial will be reviewed by a superior competent authority (FY14).
- The chief prosecutor of the Service may direct the Service Secretary to review any case where a convening authority decides not to refer a sexual assault offense for court-martial (FY15).
- Commanders who do have disposition authority can no longer consider the general military character of persons accused under UCMJ (FY14).
- Consideration of general military character is strictly prohibited during the findings phase of courts-martial proceedings except for a limited number of enumerated offenses (FY15).

Military Leaders' Key Roles and Responsibilities under SAPR

Military leaders have many administrative and ethical responsibilities to uphold the SAPR policy. The Commander's Checklist provides the most comprehensive information for Commanders. However, given the updates to DoDD 6495.01 and 6495.02, this checklist may also be updated to integrate new provisions.

Key Command Responsibilities under the SAPR program

1. Be familiar with SAPR Policy (DoD Directives 6495.01 and 6495.02).
2. Know the SARC and SAPR Victim Advocate and their contact information.
3. Know how to respond if someone tells you that he or she was sexually assaulted.
4. Know how to intervene if someone under your charge is accused.
5. Report all sexual assaults to a special court-martial convening authority.
6. Learn about the resources available to assist you and to assist victims.
7. Complete the required annual sexual assault prevention training.
8. Conduct an annual organizational climate assessment of your command.

---

12 National Defense Authorization Act 2015 http://www.gpo.gov/fdsys/pkg/CPRT-113HPRT92738/pdf/CPRT-113HPRT92738.pdf

Other Important Roles and Responsibilities for Commanders

- Be familiar with the Commander's Checklist and have it readily available.
- Establish working relationships with the SARC, Victim Advocates, and other members of the SAPR team in your military community.
- Be aware of and have a copy of the DoD Victims' Bill of Rights.
- Ensure victims' safety using a Military Protective Order (MPO) if needed.
- Determine the best course of action for separating the victim from the offender, including possible transfer. Consider the victim's needs and request in accordance with the directive on expedited transfers.[13]
- Refer victims for counseling or other services as indicated.
- Determine how best to defer issues of victim collateral misconduct.
- Ensure victims receive monthly reports regarding status of the case.
- Appoint and oversee SAPR VA (victim advocates) in your unit.
- Ensure everyone in your command completes required SAPR trainings.

Strategic Direction to the Joint Force on SAPR14

The Joint Chiefs and the Commandant of the Coast Guard issued a 32-point direction in May of 2012 for all commanders and military leaders. This guidance is a framework for commanders relative to sexual assault issues. The following comments are directly from the Joint Chiefs and the Commandant of the Coast Guard:

This Strategic Direction is written for commanders and leaders to improve awareness of sexual assaults, operationalize our commitment, and facilitate dialogue and open communications across our formations.[15]

As a matter of standard procedure, we will operationalize sexual assault prevention and response. This is not just about a program it is about leadership. Sexual assault prevention and response must be inculcated into our every-day planning, training and mission execution.[16]

The Strategic Direction addresses two primary areas: 1.) Lines of Effort and 2.) Overarching Tenets. The following delineate each these guidelines. Refer to the Strategic Direction to the Joint Force on Sexual Assault Prevention and Response issued on 5.7.12 for more specific instruction on the LOEs and the Overarching Tenets.

---

13 DoD Instruction 6495.02, March 28, 2013, Enclosure 5 "Commander and Management SAPR Procedures" Section 5, pages 37-40.

14 Strategic Direction to the Joint Force on Sexual Assault Prevention and Response (5.7.12)

15 Ibid (page 2).

16 Ibid (page 6)

The LOEs are organized into five SAPR program activities:

1. Prevention
2. Investigation
3. Accountability
4. Advocacy
5. Assessment

The Overarching Tenets include five areas necessary to ensure a professional culture and positive climate and environment:

1. Leadership
2. Communication
3. Culture/Climate Environment
4. Integration
5. Resourcing

Command Responsibilities to Mission Support and Organizational Climate

It is up to you, as commanders and leaders, to safeguard our core values and Service cultures by promoting a climate and environment that incorporates SAPR principles as habitual and inherent characteristics of our commands. [17]

One of your most important tasks as a military leader is to lead by example. Others turn to you for guidance and look to you as a model of what is right and acceptable. That is why your role is so important to the mission of SAPR Program. You have the power to influence the climate, attitudes and behaviors in your command—whether it is a platoon, a company, or an entire installation. In short, your leadership style and willingness to address these issues can significantly affect support, cohesion and the effectiveness of your organization.

Annual Organizational Climate Assessment

Commanders must conduct annual organizational climate assessments to determine if they are meeting the Department's goals related to their culture of professionalism and zero tolerance of sexual assault. The Defense Equal Opportunity Management Institute (DEOMI)

---

17 Ibid

now includes SAPR questions related to organizational climate as a part of the DEOCS survey as announced on 3.27.12. [18]

Respondents will answer questions about SAPR climate at their worksite, including:

- Their perception of leadership support for SAPR
- Their knowledge of SAPR reporting options
- The potential barriers to reporting a sexual assault
- The potential for bystander intervention in high risk situations

This information will assist military leaders to gauge the effectiveness of SAPR trainings as well as the climate within their unit.

The DEOCS is a management tool for commanders to assist them in more accurately assessing organizational climate factors, which can impact the mission, cohesion and effectiveness of the unit. According to DEOMI, "It is a confidential command requested organizational development survey that is used to assess the shared perceptions of an organization's members as related to equal opportunity and organizational effectiveness."

In addition to the annual command climate assessment, Commanding Officers are also responsible to ensure a climate free of retaliation for persons who report a sexual assault. Failure to do so can result in relief from command positions. Senior officers are responsible to conduct annual reviews to ensure their subordinate commanding officers are in compliance with this policy and have established a climate free of retaliation. This information will be included in records used for assignment and promotion selection boards.[19]

Consider the following example about leadership intervention and organizational climate:

An unrestricted report comes to your attention. Both the alleged victim and the accused are under your command. You are also aware of some gossip, conflict and divisiveness in the unit about this report. The rumors about the allegations are prominent in your command. Both the alleged victim and the accused are noticeably distracted in their work. As a result of the divisiveness and splitting within the unit, there is increased tension, harsh words, name-calling and even some threats. The entire unit seems to be involved and it is now a significant distraction. Since the case is being investigated, it will be awhile before there is any resolution. You are concerned about the impact on your unit's ability to fulfill their mission and to work together as a cohesive team.

---

18 Defense Equal Opportunity Management Institute (3.27.12) Sexual Assault Prevention and Response Climate Questions, Organizational Climate Survey (DEOCS) Release No. 12-03.08.

19 National Defense Authorization Act 2015, Section 1751 http://www.deomi.org/EOAdvisorToolkit/documents/FY14_NDAA_CCS.pdf

How do you respond? Consider which options are the best courses of action.

1. Do not address the issue and trust that it will resolve in time on its own.
2. Ask one of your subordinates to take care of the situation.
3. Talk to the victim and suggest the victim reconsider the report.
4. Talk to the accused and suggest the accused turn himself in.
5. Have a joint meeting with the victim and the accused to try to resolve it.
6. Transfer the victim to another location.
7. Transfer the offender to another location.
8. Talk to the SARC about your options and consider the suggestions.
9. Address your unit (WITHOUT disclosing confidential or critical information about the allegations or those involved) and provide the unit with clear guidance on what is acceptable and not acceptable given a pending investigation. Give them clear examples of what will NOT be tolerated under your command (harassment, name-calling, intimidating the alleged victim, acts of violence...). Inform them that anyone who is involved in retaliatory or harassing behaviors will be referred to a higher-level special court-martial convening authority for disciplinary action.

In the past, some commanders may have thought that options 1-7 would be sufficient and/or appropriate. We now know that the most acceptable responses to this situation are actions 8 and 9. Any of the other responses would be insufficient or potentially harmful to the victim, the accused, the investigation or to the mission. Although it is possible that you will eventually transfer either the victim or the accused in accordance with DoD 6495.02[20] a transfer alone would not sufficiently address this issue. In addition, you should use this as an opportunity to educate your command about sexual assault by inviting the SARC to provide a mandatory training on SAPR to all members of your Command. Moreover, the allegation should be referred to an O-6 or higher special court-martial convening authority for review and further disposition.

Fostering an Effective Command Culture and Climate
The following distinctions between culture and climate are from DODI 6495.02, under Commander and Management of SAPR Procedures:

• *Culture represents inherent aspects of professionalism and core values that promote social responsibility, team cohesion and trust.*

---

20 DoD Instruction 6495.02, March 28, 2013, Enclosure 5 "Commander and Management SAPR Procedures" Section 5, pages 37-40.

- *Climate/environment represents those actions by commanders to integrate unit members, build team cohesion, and provide seamless oversight to reduce high-risk behavior (e.g., responsible drinking and social activities that contribute to risk and vulnerability).* [21]

Tips to foster an effective culture and climate under your command:

- Be a leader that others respect.
- Model accountability and respect for other Service members.
- Offer an open door policy so that you will be more approachable.
- Give clear messages about what is acceptable and not acceptable.
- Refer to a higher-level special court-martial convening authority anyone who engages in unacceptable, harassing or retaliatory behaviors.
- Walk the talk. Uphold zero tolerance of sexual harassment and assault.
- Comply with the SAPR Policy and ensure your command complies.
- Develop a positive relationship with the SARC and victim advocate.
- Use SAPR resources to educate others about preventing sexual assault and intervening if someone is at risk of victimization or offending.
- If someone under your command is sexually assaulted, let him or her know about their rights and the resources available to them including a Military Protection Order.

Information obtained via RESTRICTED REPORTS[22]

Commanders may NOT initiate investigations based on information in restricted reports provided by the SARC or Victim Advocate. The non-identifying personal information from a restricted report is intended to give the commander basic information about the number and types of assaults.

Commanders may use the information to:

- increase preventive measures
- enhance the education and training of their personnel
- scrutinize their organization's climate and culture for contributing factors

Commanders may NOT use the information for investigative purposes or in a manner that will discover, disclose, or reveal the identities of those involved.

---

21 Strategic Direction to the Joint Force on Sexual Assault Prevention and Response, page 5 (5.7.12)
22 DoD Instruction 6495.02, March 28, 2013.

Command Responsibilities to Victims
Summary of Primary Responsibilities to Victims of Sexual Assault

- Ensure the victim's safety and the need for a Military Protective Order.
- Offer a SAPR victim advocate, chaplain or other support person.
- Provide referrals for emotional and medical care as indicated.
- Encourage victims not to destroy or tamper with any possible evidence.
- Inform the victim of the option to transfer to another duty location, unit, or living quarters in accordance with expedited transfer procedures.
- Ensure victims receive monthly reports regarding the status of their case.
- If possible, defer decisions on collateral misconduct and notify the victim.
- Report all alleged or suspected sexual assaults to a higher authority.

Collateral Misconduct [23]

I was afraid to report it because I might get in trouble. My Commander told me I did the right thing by reporting the assault and that I was not in trouble.

—— A VICTIM OF SEXUAL ASSAULT ON ACTIVE DUTY

Many sexual assaults involve instances where the victim may have engaged in some types of misconduct. The misconduct may be minor, but it is an offense under UCMJ (such as public intoxication). Collateral misconduct is often a barrier to reporting sexual assaults. Victims are concerned about discipline for their own actions at the time of the assault. Under SAPR policy, Commanders have guidance on how to handle these situations.

- Unit commanders have authority how to respond to alleged misconduct.
- SAPR policy encourages commanders to defer the decision until after sexual assault investigation is completed.
- With the victim's cooperation and willingness to report, Commanders are better able to conduct an effective investigation and disposition of the case.
- Victims will be more likely to come forward to report a sexual assault under your command if they are not fearful of repercussions.

23 DoD Instruction 6495.02, March 28, 2013, Enclosure 5 "Commander and Management SAPR Procedures" Section 7 Ibid "Collateral Misconduct in Sexual Assault Cases" (pages 41-42)

Commander's Checklist for UNRESTRICTED Reports of Sexual Assault [24]

It was common knowledge that my Commander did not like to deal with sexual assault cases. You wouldn't believe what happened to the last woman who reported someone in our unit. The Commander called an emergency formation and said that 'someone' reported an alleged rape. He suggested that she was lying and no one should report someone for rape unless they actually did it because it could ruin his career. She was humiliated and ended up leaving the military on a medical discharge. Everyone thought she was 'crying rape' because of what the Commander said. I would never report what happened to me, so I kept it to myself for years. Things have changed since then—I hope.

This tool assists commanders in ensuring the rights of the victim and of the accused. It has been reformatted here as a checklist for easier use. This information is subject to change as the DoDD 6495.01 and 6495.02 are updated over time.

Victim's Commander

1. Ensure the physical safety of the victim—determine if the alleged offender is still nearby and if the victim desires or needs protection.
2. Determine if the victim desires or needs any emergency medical care.
3. Notify the MCIO concerned, as soon as the victim's immediate safety is assured, and medical treatment procedures elected by the victim are initiated.
4. To the extent practicable, strictly limit knowledge of the facts or details regarding the incident to only personnel who have a legitimate need-to-know.
5. Take action to safeguard victim from any formal or informal investigative interviews or inquiries, except those conducted by authorities with legitimate need-to know.
6. Ensure notification of the SARC immediately.
7. Collect only the necessary information. Do not pressure the victim for more information.
8. If the sexual assault recently occurred, advise the victim of the need to preserve evidence as much as possible (such as: not bathing, showering, having anything by mouth, voiding bladder, or washing garments) until the forensic evidence is collected at the hospital.
9. If needed, assist with or provide immediate transportation for the victim to the hospital or other appropriate medical treatment facility.
10. Ensure the victim understands the availability of victim advocacy and the benefits of accepting advocacy and support.

---

24 *"Commander's Sexual Assault Response Checklist" Commander Response Protocols for Allegations of Sexual Assault; See also: DoDI 6495.02, enclosure 5 "Commander and Management SAPR Procedures."*

11. Ask if the victim wants a friend or family member to support them immediately after the assault. Advise the victim this support person may have to testify as a witness if the case goes to trial.

12. Ask if the victim would like a chaplain and notify accordingly.

13. Throughout the investigation, consult with the victim, listen and engage in quiet support, as needed, and provide the victim appropriate emotional support resources.

14. To the extent practicable, accommodate the victim's desires regarding safety, health, and security, without compromising a critical mission or investigation.

15. Continue to monitor the victim's well-being, particularly if there are any indications of suicidal ideation, and ensure appropriate intervention occurs as needed.

16. If needed, confer with victim's healthcare professional and consider the need for convalescent leave or other leave options as policy permits.

17. Determine if the victim desires or needs a "no contact' order or "Military Protection Order" to be issued, particularly if the victim and the alleged offender are assigned to same command, unit, duty location, or quarters.

18. Coordination with other commanders may be necessary if the alleged offender is assigned to a different commander.

19. Determine the need for temporary reassignment to another unit, duty location, or living quarters on the installation of the victim or the alleged offender being investigated, working with the alleged offender's commander if different than the victim's commander, until there is a final legal disposition of the sexual assault allegation, and/or the victim is no longer in danger. Consider the victim's needs when making any reassignment determinations.

20. Ensure the victim understands the availability of other referral organizations staffed with personnel who can explain the medical, investigative, and legal processes and advise the victim of his or her victim support rights.

21. Emphasize to the victim the availability of additional avenues of support; refer to available counseling groups and other victim services.

22. Attend the monthly case management meeting as appropriate.

23. Ensure the victim receives monthly reports regarding the status of the sexual assault investigation from the date the investigation was initiated until there is a final disposition of the case.

24. Consult with servicing legal office, as needed, to determine when and how best to dispose of the victim's collateral misconduct, if any.

25. Absent extenuating or overriding considerations which, in the commander's judgment, make it inappropriate to delay taking action, the commander should

consider deferring discipline for such victim misconduct until all investigations are completed and the sexual assault allegation has been resolved. Keep in mind the implications on speedy trial and/or statute of limitations.

26. When practicable, consult with the servicing legal office, MCIO, and notify the assigned VA or SARC prior to taking any administrative or disciplinary action affecting the victim.

27. Avoid giving an automatic suspension or revocation of a security clearance and/or Personnel Reliability Program (PRP) access, understanding that the victim may be satisfactorily treated for his/her related trauma without compromising his/her security clearance or PRP status. Consider the negative impact that suspension of a victim's security clearance or PRP may have on building a climate of trust and confidence in the Military Service's sexual assault reporting system. Make final determination based upon established national security standards. (See DoD 5210.42-R (Ref. (ad) for specific requirements.)

Commander's Checklist for UNRESTRICTED Reports of Sexual Assault [25]
Alleged Offender's Commander

1. Notify the appropriate MCIO as soon as possible after receiving a report of a sexual assault incident.

2. Avoid questioning about the sexual assault allegation with the alleged offender, to the extent possible, since doing so may jeopardize the criminal investigation.

3. Any contact with a Service member suspected of an offense under Chapter 47 of Reference (b) may involve rules and procedures that ensure due process of law and are unique to the military criminal justice system. Therefore, before questioning or discussing the case with the alleged offender, commanders and other command representatives should first contact the servicing legal office for guidance. However, if questioning does occur, you must advise the Service member suspected of committing a UCMJ offense of his or her rights under Article 31 of Chapter 47 of Reference (b).

4. Safeguard the alleged offender's rights and preserve the integrity of a full and complete investigation, to include limitations on any formal or informal investigative interviews or inquiries by personnel other than those by personnel with a legitimate need-to-know.

---

25 *"Commander's Sexual Assault Response Checklist" Commander Response Protocols for Allegations of Sexual Assault; See also: DoDD 6495.02, enclosure 5 "Commander and Management SAPR Procedures."*

5. Strictly limit information pertinent to an investigation to those who have a legitimate need-to-know.

6. Ensure procedures are in place to inform the alleged offender, as appropriate, about the investigative and legal processes that may be involved.

7. Ensure procedures are in place to inform the alleged offender about available counseling support. As appropriate, refer the alleged offender to available counseling groups and other services.

8. With the benefit of the SARC, VA, legal, and/or investigative advice, determine the need for a "no contact" order, or an MPO, DD Form 2873.

9. Monitor the well-being of the alleged offender, particularly for any indications of suicide ideation, and ensure appropriate intervention occurs if indicated.

Other Command Responsibilities to the Accused

- Follow the Commander's Checklist for specific guidance.
- Notify the military criminal investigative office (MCIO) immediately.
- Ensure the rights of the accused are enforced.
- Limit disclosure of information to strict "need-to-know" basis.
- Refer the accused for counseling as indicated.
- Determine the need for a Military Protective Order or transfer.

Commander's Checklist for Unrestricted Reports of Sexual Assault [26]
Commander for both the alleged offender and victim

1. Discourage members from participating in barracks gossip or speculation about the case or investigation. Remind everyone to wait until all the facts and final disposition of the allegation has occurred before reaching conclusions.

2. Remind members that discussion of a possible sexual assault incident might compromise an ensuing investigation

3. Emphasize that the alleged offender is presumed innocent until proven guilty.

4. Advise full cooperation during the investigation of those who may have knowledge of the events leading up to or surrounding the incident.

5. Consider some form of unit refresher training; or have an outside expert address the unit regarding preventive measures, as well as some of the emotional or

---

26 *"Commander's Sexual Assault Response Checklist" Commander Response Protocols for Allegations of Sexual Assault; See also: DoDD 6495.02, enclosure 5 "Commander and Management SAPR Procedures."*

psychological feelings that may manifest themselves, affect the unit, and require the unit's response during the course of the investigation.

6. Monitor the unit's overall climate to ensure neither the victim and/or the alleged offender is being ostracized and to prevent organizational splintering.

Other Considerations for All Concerned

As a Commander, there will be additional challenges if both the alleged victim and the accused are under your leadership. This will require your full awareness and sensitivity to opposing issues that could affect both parties. The following must be addressed as priority issues, in addition to the steps in the Commander's Checklist:

- Ensure safety. Determine if the victim desires or needs a "no contact' order or a DD Form 2873, "Military Protection Order (MPO)." [27] If the situation warrants either of these orders, it is your duty to take action.
- Assess the need for temporary reassignment to another unit, duty location, or living quarters on the installation to ensure the alleged victim's safety and wellbeing. Consider what the victim wants/needs when making reassignment determinations in accordance with the expedited transfer directive. In some situations, it might be best to relocate the accused.
- Limit disclosure of any information about the allegations to a strict "need-to-know" basis. Address any intimidation or harassment towards the alleged victim or the accused without hindering the investigation.
- Ensure zero tolerance of any harassment or sexual assault.

The climate in your command is the best indicator by others if you tolerate any form of harassment or abuse. Service members under your charge know exactly where the line is by your example and how you respond when allegations are brought forth. They look to you for leadership on this issue.

Additional Command Responsibilities and Considerations Under SAPR

In a forward deployed environment

There are many factors to consider in a forward deployed environment. Most important, victims of sexual assault are entitled to receive the appropriate care and advocacy under DoD SAPR policy regardless of their assignment or duty location. Responding to a sexual

---

27 DoD Directive 6495.02, March 28, 2013, Enclosure 5 "Commander and Management SAPR Procedures" Section 6 "Military Protective Orders" pages 40-41.

assault allegation in a forward deployed environment may present additional challenges, such as:

- Fewer resources will be available to victims than in CONUS.
- The SARC may not be as accessible to VAs creating supervision and oversight difficulties.
- It can be more complicated to separate the offender from the victim due to mission priorities or limited options.
- Protecting the victims' privacy may be more difficult. Others might find out due to closer quarters.
- The presence of embedded reporters could bring distraction or attention to the issue.
- Victims' may have heightened emotional reactions with the added stress of combat and limited access to support systems or family.
- Victims may have additional safety and privacy concerns in a deployed environment.

I was sexually assaulted while in theater. I was afraid to go anywhere alone—including to the latrine. It made doing my work impossible. I had to leave the military I so loved. – A veteran who was raped while serving in Afghanistan.

Suggestions for military leaders in forward deployed environments

- Refer all victims to an advocate. This will help you and the victims.
- Be responsive to victims' needs and mental health issues in this stressful environment following a sexual assault.
- Be aware of available resources for added support to victims (such as phone calls to CONUS, computer access, chaplains, transfer)
- Know your limits and call others for information or assistance, including SARCs, advocates, chaplains and mental health or healthcare providers.
- Support the VAs and SARCs in their duties.

Administrative Separations Involving Victims of Sexual Assault

It might become necessary to consider an administrative separation of a sexual assault victim if the situation warrants this as the best option or if the victim has indicated an ability to perform his/her duties subsequent to the assault (e.g. due to extreme emotional distress as with post traumatic stress disorder). In addition, Commanders may need to make decisions regarding administrative separation of the offender or an accused offender.

The disposition authority for sexual assault cases and authority for review of administrative separations involving victims of sexual assault is outlined below as reference in DoDD 6495.02 Enclosure 12. Commanders should seek additional guidance on this issue to ensure the rights of the victim as well as the needs of the mission.

Selection and oversight of victim advocates and coordination with SARC
Commanders have an added responsibility of ensuring the selection and oversight of victim advocates. The SARC can be of great assistance in this area. In addition, each Service has guidelines and further instructions applicable to their Service, including sample VA/ SARC appointment letters as well as the DD Form 2909 "VA and Supervisor Statement of Understanding." For more information and guidance, contact your Service SAPR Office.

Command's Role in Sexual Assault Prevention and Education [28]
The Commanders' Checklist also addresses sexual assault prevention and education. However, the key responsibilities for military leaders regarding sexual assault prevention are as follows:

- Establish a climate based on mutual respect valuing all members.
- Know the organization's climate and respond to any negative issues.
- Model respect by not using or tolerating any demeaning or harassing language, behaviors, gestures, photos, e-mails or computer images.
- Enforce a "zero tolerance" policy with a swift and certain response.
- Support the SAPR program by inviting the SARC and advocate to address your unit and to provide education SAPR.
- Ensure all Service members attend the required SAPR trainings.
- Promote and model bystander intervention that encourages Service members to intervene if they notice someone is at risk or in a vulnerable state. Bystander intervention is an effective prevention strategy used throughout DoD. The message is simple: Leave no other person behind or in danger. This approach is consistent with military values of honor and integrity.

Other Key SAPR Roles in the Military Community
Sexual Assault Response Coordinators Key Roles and Responsibilities:

- Acts as a single point of contact for coordinating response and victim care

---

28 "DoDI 6495.02, March 29, 2013, Enclosure 5 "Commander and Management SAPR Procedures" Section 8 "Commander SAPR Prevention Procedures" page 42

- Oversees SAPR program at the installation including training/education
- Supervises advocates in their collateral duty under SAPR
- Conducts case management review meetings
- Tracks and reports sexual assault cases
- Assists Command with SAPR information, education and resources
- Acts as liaison with civilian community resources

Victim Advocates Key Roles and Responsibilities:

- Provides non-clinical crisis intervention and support to victims
- Offers information and resources to victims about: reporting options; medical care options; criminal justice options; and victims' rights
- Accompanies victim through medical, legal or criminal justice process
- Offers safety planning and referrals if indicated
- Provides case information to SARC for supervision and oversight
- Provides monthly case status updates

Healthcare Personnel Key Roles and Responsibilities:

- Provides emergency medical treatment with victim-centered care
- Provides emotional support and contacts victim advocate or SARC
- Offers prevention options for sexually transmitted infections/ pregnancy
- Collects and preserves forensic evidence (with victim's consent) for sexual assault forensic evidence exam (SAFE) consistent with Department of Justice protocol.
- Completes DD Form 2911 Sexual Assault Medical Forensic Exam Report

Chaplains Key Roles and Responsibilities:

- Offers spiritual support or guidance
- Informs victim of availability of advocate
- Offers confidential spiritual counseling (privileged communication)

Law Enforcement Key Roles and Responsibilities:

- Secures the crime scene
- Identifies any known suspects
- Collects evidence

Military Criminal Investigative Offices (MCIO) Roles and Responsibilities:

- Investigates the crime
- Identifies and questions witnesses
- Prepares the case in conjunction with SJA/JAG
- Apprises victim of the case status

Judge Advocates (JAGs) Key Roles and Responsibilities:

Judge Advocates (JAs) may have any number of roles that interface with the SAPR Program. The responsibilities of the JAs will depend on their specific job as noted below:

- Prosecutor
- Defense counsel
- Military judge
- Appellate defense or government counsel
- Legal assistance attorneys provide consultation on domestic relations law in domestic violence cases

SAPR Related Documents and Forms

The DoD has developed useful forms to assist Commanders and other military leaders in fulfilling their SAPR duties. This section addresses the key forms for Commanders working with victims. However, this section does not cover Command responsibilities relative to the Defense Incident-Based Reporting System. This important reporting requirement is addressed in detail in the DIBRS Manual Number 7730.47-M, Vol. 1, December 7, 2010 available online at http://www.dtic.mil/whs/directives/infomgt/forms.

The key documents Commanders need to be familiar with when intervening with sexual assault victims are:

- Victim Reporting Preference Statement (VRPS) (DD Form 2910)
- Military Protective Order (DD Form 2873)
- Witten Information for Victims of Crime (under VWAP)

Each of these documents is summarized below. Samples of these forms are available online at: http://www.dtic.mil/whs/directives/infomgt/forms/formsprogram.htm

Victim Reporting Preference Statement (VRPS) DD Form 2910

All victims of sexual assault, regardless of whether they make a restricted or unrestricted report, will be asked to sign the "Victim Reporting Preference Statement" by the Sexual Assault Response Coordinator (SARC) or SAPR Victim Advocate. This form specifies the victim's decision about reporting. It is also referred to as the Victim Preference Statement.

Victims of sexual assault have the option of changing their restricted report to an unrestricted report at any time—even after they have signed the VRPS. Any changes must be documented by The SARC must document any changes to the document or report and notify a change of status to unrestricted to the Command.

Key points about the VRPS:

- The VRPS indicates the victim's awareness of the reporting options.
- The form explains both options and the limits of restricted reporting.
- Advocates give the original to the SARC and a copy to the victim.
- Victims are encouraged to keep their copy of the form.
- Victims have the option to change a restricted report to an unrestricted report at any time.

Military Protection Orders (MPO) DD Form 2873 [29]

A military protection order is similar to a civilian protection order. It is usually a written order, signed by a Service member's unit commander or another commissioned or non-commissioned officer with authority over the SM requesting protection usually after an incident of violence or harassment. It directs the Service member to have no contact with the specified person.

Commanders may give the order verbally in person, over the telephone or in any written form. The preferred method for issuing an MPO is by using a standard format, and listing standard provisions that have been previously reviewed for legal sufficiency (DD Form 2873).

An MPO may direct a Service member to refrain from contacting, harassing or touching the specified person. They may direct a Service member to stay away from certain areas such as base housing or schools or to refrain from certain acts or activities.

---

29 DoD Directive 6495.01, January 23, 2012, Enclosure 5 "Commander and Management SAPR Procedures" Section 6 "Military Protective Orders" pages 40-41.

Key Points about MPOs:

- Assessing the victim's safety and assisting with safety planning should be your priority when a victim is seeking a protective order.
- The victim should be informed in a timely manner of their option to request an expedited transfer.
- When an MPO is issued, the appropriate civilian authorities should be notified if any of the individuals involved do not reside on the military installation or when any changes occur in the MPO.
- MPOs are in effect until the commander terminates or re-issues the order.
- Civilian protection orders are honored on all military installations. However, a MPO is NOT enforceable by civilian authorities off base.
- Any violation of a MPO should be reported to law enforcement immediately.

Ensure that the person seeking the MPO is advised that the MPO is not enforceable by civilian authorities off base, and victims desiring protection off base should be advised to seek a civilian protective order in that jurisdiction pursuant to section 562 of Reference.[30]

Written Information for Victims of Crime through VWAP [31]

The Victim and Witness Assistance Program (VWAP) assists victims through the criminal justice process from the time of initial contact with the justice system through the confinement or release of the perpetrator. In addition, VWAP ensures the role of crime victims in the criminal justice process is protected and that victims are accorded their rights.

DoD developed six forms for victims and witnesses of crime service-wide. Each form has a specific purpose to assist and inform victims and witnesses at every level of the criminal justice process. They are available at vwac.defense.gov/vwres.html.

DD FORM 2701: Initial Information for Victims and Witnesses of Crime

- If You Are Threatened or Harassed
- If You Were Injured: State Crime Victims Compensation
- If You Were a Victim of Spouse or Child Abuse
- If You Need Assistance with Your Employer or Command
- If an Arrest Is Made

---

30 DoDD 6495.01, 1.23.12, Enclosure 2 "Responsibilities" page 13
31 Victim Witness Assistance Program website: vwac.defense.gov

DD FORM 2702: Court-Martial Information for Victims and Witnesses

- Court-Martial Information/Preferral of Charges
- Pre-Trial Conference/Article 32 Hearing
- Court-Martial/Testimony/Pointers While Testifying
- Sentencing/Punishment

DD FORM 2703: Post-Trial Information for Victims and Witnesses of Crime

- Clemency and Parole Consideration
- Notification Rights/How to Exercise Your Rights

DD FORM 2704: Certification and Election Concerning Inmate Status

- Certification of advice to victims and witnesses re: inmate status
- Election to be notified of changes in confinement status

DD FORM 2705: Victim/Witness Notification of Inmate Status

- Inmate status/Inmate eligibility
- Change in inmate status

Records and SAFE Kit Retention [32]

This policy delineates the requirements for retaining records of sexual assault reports by Service members. It is important to be aware of this requirement as it relates to both restricted and unrestricted reporting.

There are two schedules based on the type of report: Restricted or Unrestricted as defined in DoD Directive 6495.01. This allows for the confidentiality of victims who file a restricted report. In addition, if a victim of sexual assault later needs to verify a report (such as, a disability claim with the Department of Veterans Affairs) these records are retained as noted below in the summary of the policy.

Unrestricted Reports

- All sexual assault investigative reports by Military Criminal Investigative Organizations (MCIOs) will include "DoD Sexual Assault Forensic Examination (SAFE) Report" (DD Form 2911).

---

32 DoD Instruction 6495.02, March 28, 2013, Enclosure 8 "Safe Kit Collection and Preservation."

- The MCIO records will be retained for 50 years from the date the sexual assault investigation was closed. This does not include final disposition of the SAFE kit.
- The "Victim Reporting Preference Statement" (DD Form 2910) will be entered by the SARC as an electronic record in the Defense Sexual Assault Incident Database (DSAID) or the DSAID-interface Military Service system.
- This electronic record will be kept for 50 years from the date on the DD Form 2910.

Restricted Reports

- The SAFE Kit (including forensic evidence and the DD Form 2911) will be retained for 5 years.
- The SARC office will keep a hard copy of the DD Form 2910 in compliance with DoD guidance for the storage of personally identifiable information.
- The five year limit starts the day the victim signed DD Form 2910

Understanding Military Sexual Trauma Sexual Assault and Sexual Harassment

Military Sexual Trauma is the term used by the Department of Veteran Affairs and other professionals to refer to any type of sexual assault or sexual harassment towards a Service member. Military sexual trauma includes any type of sexual assault or sexual harassment that happens on active duty. It can occur during peacetime, wartime and training exercises. In fact, some research has found that the occurrence of sexual assault and sexual harassment is higher during wartime, possibly in part due to the increased stress associated with war while deployed.

Who is affected by MST?

Anyone serving in the military can be a victim of military sexual trauma. This includes women and men, officers and enlisted and persons from all races, backgrounds, religions and any sexual orientation. The offender could be someone of the opposite or the same gender as the victim. However, when someone sexually assaults another person of the same gender (such as when a man rapes another man) it does not mean this was a homosexual act. In fact, both the victim and the offender might be heterosexual. Sexual assault is an act of power and control. It is not a method of expressing sexual desire or intimacy. Similarly, sexual harassment is also about degrading, humiliating and controlling the victim—regard-less of the victim's gender or sexual orientation. However, it is a hate crime and is punishable by federal law if someone is sexually assaulted or harassed because of their sexual orientation, race or religion.

Any type of military sexual trauma can have a negative effect on the victim, the unit and the mission.

Sexual Assault and Sexual Harassment

The DoD does not use the terminology "Military Sexual Trauma" as defined by the VA. The DoD uses the terms *sexual assault* and *sexual harassment* in accordance with their policies. The following section highlights the key differences and provides the current DoD definitions as applied service-wide. However, in the military there can be overlap between sexual assault and sexual harassment. This is primarily because both can occur between persons in a chain-of-command (such as a supervisor who commits an offense against someone under their rank or authority).

What are the differences?

- Sexual assault always involves some type of unwanted, physical, sexual contact.
- Sexual harassment can include a variety of unwelcome behaviors of a sexual nature, including verbal remarks, gestures, pictures and pressure for sex.
- It can also be considered a sexual assault when harassment includes unwanted physical contact of a sexual nature (touching, kissing, any sexual contact),
- Sexual assault can occur in any location--and not necessarily related to work or work relationships.
- Sexual harassment generally pertains to persons with a working relationship or in the context of a work or school setting—often involving a person in a supervisory role.

Sexual Harassment

In 1988, the Secretary of Defense directed all services to incorporate the following definition of sexual harassment into their regulations:

Sexual harassment is a form of sex discrimination that involves unwelcome sexual advances, requests for sexual favors, and other verbal and physical conduct of a sexual nature when:

1. *submission to or rejection of such conduct is made either explicitly or implicitly as a term or condition of a person's job, pay, or career, or*
2. *submission to, or rejection of, such conduct by a person is used as a basis for career employment decisions affecting that person, or*
3. *such conduct interferes with an individual's performance or creates an intimidating, hostile, or offensive environment.*

Any person in supervisory or command position who uses or condones implicit or explicit sexual behavior to control, influence, or affect the career, pay, or job of a military member or civilian employee is engaging in sexual harassment.

Similarly, any military member or civilian employee who makes deliberate or repeated unwelcome verbal comments, gestures, or physical contact of a sexual nature is engaging in sexual harassment.

There are two types of sexual harassment: quid pro quo and hostile work environment.

Quid pro quo is when a person in a line of authority makes threats or stipulations on a person's career (e.g. promotion, security clearance) in exchange for sexual favors (such as, an NCO offers an excellent job review in exchange for oral sex.)

Hostile work environment can occur if a person is subjected to a workplace in which there are offensive, unwanted, and unsolicited comments and/or behavior of a sexual nature (such as, sexually provocative or pornographic photos or language permitted at the workplace.)

Key points about sexual harassment

- Sexual harassment is NEVER the victim's fault.
- The harasser's conduct is unwelcome and uninvited by the victim.
- If possible, the victim should inform the harasser that the conduct is unwelcome and the behaviors must stop.
- The distinction between welcome and unwelcome behavior is essential because sexual conduct becomes unlawful when it is unwanted.
- If possible, victims should use the chain of command, EEO (Equal Employment Opportunity), MEO Military Equal Opportunity) or any other support systems.

Sexual Assault

The terms sexual assault and rape are often used interchangeably, but they do not always refer to the same type of offense. For example, under the SAPR program, sexual assault is an umbrella term used to describe all types of sexual offenses including rape.

Sexual assault is a crime that can occur regardless of gender or spousal relationship or age of victim. However, if the victim is a minor, it may also be considered sexual abuse of a child. The following is the definition of sexual assault under the SAPR Program for education purposes, followed by the specific types of sexual offenses as listed in the UCMJ.[33]

Sexual assault is defined as intentional sexual contact, characterized by:

---

33 DoDD 6495.01

- use of force
- threats
- intimidation
- abuse of authority
- when the victim does not or cannot consent*

Sexual assault includes:

- rape
- forcible sodomy (oral or anal sex)
- other unwanted sexual contact that is aggravated, abusive, or wrongful (to include unwanted and inappropriate sexual contact or sexual touching)
- any attempts to commit these acts

Examples of sexual assault include:

- Touching a person's breast, vagina, penis or buttocks without permission
- Making someone give (or receive) oral sex by force, coercion or pressure
- Threatening or coercing someone to have sex
- Using an object to touch a person's breasts, vagina, penis or anus (on the inside or outside of their body) against their wishes or without consent
- Having sex with someone who is unable to give or to deny consent due to the person being mentally incapable, drugged or severely intoxicated with alcohol (such as., in a blackout with little or no memory of the event).

Consent refers to:

- Words or overt acts by a competent person that indicate an agreement to the sexual conduct.
- An expression of lack of consent through words or conduct means there is no consent.
- Lack of verbal or physical resistance or submission resulting from the accused's use of force, threat of force, or placing another person in fear does not constitute consent.
- A current or previous dating relationship by itself or the manner of dress of the person involved with the accused in the sexual conduct at issue shall not constitute consent.

Absence of Consent

Sexual assault occurs when consent is not given for the sexual contact. Lack of consent should be assumed regardless of whether a victim resists physically. Consent is also not given when a person uses force, threat of force, coercion or when the victim is asleep, incapacitated (due to drugs, alcohol) or unconscious.

Other sex-related offenses are defined as all other sexual acts or acts in violation of the Uniform Code of Military Justice (UCMJ) that do not meet the above definition of sexual assault, or the definition of sexual harassment in DoD Directive 1350.2

Sex Offenses under the Uniform Code of Military Justice (UCMJ)

The Uniform Code of Military Justice (UCMJ), enacted by Congress, contains the substantive and procedural law governing the military justice system. The President prescribes the procedural rules and punishments for violations of crimes in the Manual for Courts-Martial (MCM).[34] Rape, sexual offenses and other sexual misconduct are prescribed under Article 120, TITLE 10. ARMED FORCES, SUBTITLE A. GENERAL MILITARY LAW, PART II. PERSONNEL, CHAPTER 47. UCMJ, SUBCHAPTER X. PUNITIVE ARTICLES. This article was amended with significant changes effective 6.28.12.

The 2012 amendments to Article 120, Rape, Sexual Assault, Aggravated Sexual Contact and Abusive Sexual Contact, have reorganized the sexual offenses into these four specific offenses. For training purposes, the terms "sexual assault" or "the crime of sexual assault" refer to these four offenses plus Forcible Sodomy (Article 125) and any attempts to commit these offenses (Article 80).

The following summarizes Article 120 with regard to crimes against adults:[35]

IAW Article 120(b), UCMJ, Sexual Assault, any person subject to this chapter who—

1. *commits a sexual act upon another person by —*
    (a) *threatening or placing that other person in fear;*
    (b) *causing bodily harm to that other person;*
    (c) *making a fraudulent representation that the sexual act serves a professional purpose; or*
    (d) *inducing a belief by any artifice, pretense, or concealment that the person is another person;*

---

34 www.defenselink.mil/vwac

35 Uniform Code of Military Justice, Article 120, Rape, Sexual Assault, Aggravated Sexual Contact and Abusive Sexual Contact (6.28.12)

2. *commits a sexual act upon another person when the person knows or reasonably should know that the other person is asleep, unconscious, or otherwise unaware that the sexual act is occurring or*

3. *commits a sexual act upon another person when the other person is incapable of consenting to the sexual act due to—*

   (a) *impairment by any drug, intoxicant, or other similar substance and that condition is known or reasonably should be known by the person; or*

   (b) *a mental disease or defect, or physical disability and that condition is known or reasonably should be known by the person;*

   ...is guilty of sexual assault and shall be punished as a court-martial may direct.

This information is included as an overview of the UCMJ related to sexual offenses. It is not meant to provide a full reference to Article 120 of the UCMJ. For more information, consult the MCM, the UCMJ or your local JAG/JA.

The Use of Force in Sexual Assault

Most sexual assaults involve some type of force, but force does not have to involve physical violence (such as hitting or using a weapon). Force can happen in many different ways and most courts recognize that proof of injury is not necessary to prove sexual assault. In fact, the majority of sexual assaults do not include other physical injuries to the victim. Here are some examples of different types of 'force':

- Using threats to scare or intimidate
- Manipulating or coercing (offering a promotion or threatening career, reputation or security clearance)
- Overpowering someone physically due to their body size
- Giving alcohol or other drugs (with or without the person's knowledge) to limit their memory or impair their judgment
- Using their position of authority and trust (such as a supervisor or a higher-ranking person) to get the person to agree to do something sexual with them by using their power to make the person submit to their demands
- Taking advantage of someone or their vulnerability (such as, someone new to the unit, intoxicated, lower rank, or in a deployed setting)

The following is the definition of force per Article 120 of the UCMJ.[36] *The term force means action to compel submission of another or overcome or prevent another's resistance by—*

---

36 Uniform Code of Military Justice, Article 120—Rape, sexual assault and other sexual misconduct, 2012

(a) *The use or display of a dangerous weapon or object;*

(b) *The suggestion of possession of a dangerous weapon or object that is used in a manner to cause another to believe it is a dangerous weapon or object or*

(c) *Physical violence, strength, power, or restraint applied to another person, sufficient that the other person could not avoid or escape the sexual conduct.*

Alcohol and Other Drugs in Sexual Assault

Some offenders rely on a method other than force to subdue or control their victims: alcohol or other drugs. Alcohol is the number one drug used to commit sexual assault. It is why so many sexual assault cases involve an alcohol component. The use of intoxicants by offenders is addressed further in the section on drug-facilitated or drug-assisted rape.

Alcohol and drug use by the offender and/or the victim is one of the most common factors contributing to sexual assault, particularly between acquaintances. In fact, the majority of sexual assaults of young adults involve alcohol or other drugs with either the offender and/or the victim under the influence at the time of the crime.

However, even if a person willingly used alcohol or other drugs, they do not deserve to be taken advantage of while in this impaired state. Being vulnerable under the influence of alcohol or drugs is neither an invitation nor an entitlement to sex. Using an excessive amount of alcohol does increase the risk for harm including sexual assault. It can also lead to black outs, passing out or lethal alcohol poisoning. Victims who passed out or were in a black out will not remember any or parts of the assault which can make reporting the incident even more difficult. However, an impaired memory due to alcohol or drugs does not mean a sexual assault did not occur.

Any person subject to this chapter who causes another person of any age to engage in a sexual act by administering to another person by force or threat of force, or without the knowledge or permission of that person, a drug, intoxicant, or other similar substance and thereby substantially impairs the ability of that other person to appraise or control conduct is guilty of rape and shall be punished as a court-martial may direct. [37]

Drug-facilitated Sexual Assault

Drug-facilitated or drug-assisted sexual assault is when someone provides alcohol or another drug (either openly or surreptitiously) to impair another person's response, judgment or appraisal of an event with the intention of having sex with that individual. Some offenders give alcohol or other drugs to their target with the specific intention of taking

---

37 Uniform Code of Military Justice, Article 120—Rape, sexual assault, and other sexual misconduct, 2012

advantage and sexually assaulting the person. 'Drugging' someone to impair a person's ability to respond for the explicit purpose of having sex is illegal and considered felony rape in most states. It is also a violation of the UCMJ and considered rape.

Other drugs used for this purpose are incorrectly referred to as 'date rape' drugs because they are often used in the course of a date or by someone the victim knows. Common drugs used to commit sexual assault include Rohypnol (known as "roofies"); GHB (known as "G" or "easy lay"); and Ketamine (known as "special K" or "Bump"). Many of these drugs are colorless and odorless when put into a drink and they cause the person to pass out and not remember what happened. Using alcohol or other drugs to impair someone for the purpose of having sex with that person is a method used by persons known to the victim as well as strangers who target a potential victim.

There are several warning signs that someone may have been drugged with the intention of a sexual assault. The key indicators sexual assault victims may recall which may indicate that have been drugged and be the possible victim of a drug-facilitated sexual assault include:

- Suddenly and unexpectedly becoming very tired or drowsy
- Feeling very jittery or nervous for no reason (such as: increased heart rate)
- Having hallucinations (seeing or hearing things that aren't really there)
- Suddenly getting sick or throwing up soon after having a drink of any kind
- Not being able to remember pieces of time from the day or night before
- Snap shots of memories of something happening (such as, waking up to pain)
- Waking up from sleep and not remembering what happened hours earlier
- Having snippets of memory or recall about the sexual assault occurring

Given that the majority of sexual assaults involve alcohol and other drugs, it is imperative to be informed on the topic and be prepared for this complicating dynamic to be a part of the cases that you may be involved.

Sexual Assault Victims

Considerations and Barriers to Reporting   Telling someone about a sexual assault is often very difficult for victims especially disclosing to someone who oversees their job, such as a supervisor or a person in their chain-of-command. Sexual assault is a very personal physical and psychological violation. Victims may not want their work involved with their personal lives. Yet, it is difficult and sometimes impossible to separate these boundaries on active duty.

Fortunately, there are many reasons that victims do tell someone and report the sexual assault. As military leaders, it is important for you to be aware of the reasons why victims do report as well the reasons why victims do not report the crime. This section will highlight each of those areas to help you to be a more effective and responsive leader if a sexual assault occurs under your command.

The items noted in the following section are based on feedback from victims in military from the DoD surveys on sexual harassment and sexual assault as well as other research. [38] [39]

Top reasons victims DO report or tell someone

- Concerned about safety for themselves, their family or others
- Seeking justice for the wrong committed against them
- Wanting the offender to know he/she did something wrong
- Wanting the offender to be held accountable
- Trying to prevent the offender from hurting others
- Responding to pressures from others to report the crime

Reasons victims report to their chain-of-command

- For the offender to be disciplined so it will not happen to someone else
- To protect others in the unit/command from the offender
- For the offender to be hurt for sexually assaulting and hurting them
- For the offender to know what he/she did was wrong
- To be able to carry on with their job without threats or fears
- For the good of the unit—a sense of duty and obligation to others

Concerns about reporting

Victims of sexual assault often have concerns about reporting. If they know the person, victims may be concerned about repercussions for telling. In addition, if the victim works with the offender (or if he is in their chain of command) there will likely be other complications which will impact reporting. The following is a list of some of the top concerns expressed by military victims about reporting their sexual assault.

---

38 Report on Sexual Harassment and Violence at the Military Service Academies (December 2011), available at: www.sapr.mil/index.php/annual-reports and Department of Defense 1995 Sexual Harassment Survey at http://oai.dtic.mil/oai/oai?verb=getRecord&metadataPrefix=html&identifier=ADA323942.

39 For Love of Country: Confronting Rape and Sexual Harassment in the US Military, TS Nelson (2002) at Sugati Publications.com

- Feeling ashamed, guilty or blaming themselves
- Fear of further repercussions by the offender
- Worried about repercussions on the job or by a superior
- Concerned about not being believed if others find out
- Questioned whether or not reporting will help
- Anticipated further trauma or harassment for reporting
- Did not want 'to get the offender in trouble'
- Wanted to 'move on' with their life and not think about it

Gender-specific concerns expressed by women

- Worried that others will not see them as a 'team player' if they report someone in the unit, especially someone well-liked or respected
- Concerned about being labeled 'sexually promiscuous'
- Afraid to testify in court (being the target of the defense)
- Mixed feelings due to prior relationship with offender
- Concerned that others will not see them as fit for duty
- Fear that the offender will hurt/intimidate them again

Gender-specific concerns expressed by men

- Concerned that others will see or treat them differently
- Fears about being labeled a homosexual or as weak
- Self doubt and blame for not stopping the sexual assault
- Heterosexual men might worry being labeled homosexual
- Homosexual men might fear the impact of being 'outed' before they have done so or are ready to be open about their homosexuality

Additional concerns for victims in the military about reporting[40]

- Confidentiality and privacy concerns
- Uncertainty regarding the Commander's response
- Culture/climate in the unit (further harassment or indifference)
- Live or work with the perpetrator in close proximity

---

40 For Love of Country: Confronting Rape and Sexual Harassment in the US Military, TS Nelson (2002) at Sugati Publications.com

- Social impact (in unit, among coworkers)
- Fear of repercussions on career or job impact
- Psychological barriers (self blame, shame, embarrassment, and more)

Other Military-Specific Issues for Victims

There are issues specific to the military that victims of sexual assault may encounter due to the nature and demands of serving on active duty as well as the importance of the mission. Some of these issues are addressed in the next section, including: confidentiality and restricted reporting; mental health care and security clearances; collateral misconduct; and expedited transfer requests. The applicable and current policies on these topics are addressed and cited for further information.

Confidentiality

For many military victims, one of the most important aspects of dealing with a sexual assault is their concern about confidentiality and privacy. The Department of Defense recognized the magnitude of this issue and made significant changes to policies concerning reporting sexual assault. As a result, in June, 2005, DoD developed a restricted reporting option to offer confidentiality for victims of sexual assault. Sexual assault victims on active duty have the explicit right to get care and treatment without initiating an investigation about the sexual assault.

Key points about Confidentiality and Restricted Reporting

- Allows victims of sexual assault to report the crime to specified individuals and to receive medical care, treatment and counseling without notifying command or law enforcement officials
- Allows victim to disclose in confidence to designated individuals
- Individuals authorized to receive a restricted report are: Sexual Assault Response Coordinator, SAPR victim advocates and healthcare personnel
- Gives victims time to consider unrestricted reporting option

Exceptions or limitations to Confidentiality and Restricted Reporting [41]

- When disclosure is authorized by the victim in writing
- When disclosure is necessary to prevent or lessen a serious and immediate threat to the health or safety of the victim or another person

---

41 DoDD 6495.02

- If the case goes to a legal proceeding and testimony is court ordered by Federal or state law, providers can be compelled to testify
- To Disability Retirement Boards and officials when disclosure is required for fitness for duty for disability retirement determinations.
- When commanders have a "need to know" because fitness for duty is of concern. For example, if a victim is coping with physical or emotional conditions that might inhibit their ability to fully execute their duties or could potentially cause harm to the unit or the mission.

Victim Advocate-Victim Privilege [42]

Victims of sexual assault in the military can now confidentially seek information, support and assistance from a Victim Advocate regardless of the type of report (restricted or unrestricted) since communication with an advocate is considered "privileged communication" in the Manual for Court-Martial. Victim advocates will not disclose information unless the victim has specifically given the advocate permission to do so or if one of the exceptions to this rule applies as noted below.

Exceptions to privileged communication

- If the victim is deceased
- When Federal or state law or service regulation imposes a duty to report the information;
- The communication clearly contemplated the future commission of fraud or crime or...to enable/aid anyone to commit/plan to commit...a crime/fraud
- To ensure the safety and security of military personnel, dependents, military property, classified information, or the accomplishment of a military mission
- To ensure the safety of any other person (including the victim) when an advocate believes the victim's mental or emotional condition is a danger
- When required by the constitution

This rule allows victims to communicate with advocates with an additional safety net and security regarding confidentiality. A victim has a privilege to refuse to disclose and to prevent any other person from disclosing a confidential communication made between the

---

42 EXECUTIVE ORDER 12.13.11 effective 1.12.12 "Rule 514 Military Rules of Evidence, Amendments to the Manual for Courts-Martial." This order is available in entirety at www.sapr.mil

victim and a victim advocate, in a case arising under the UCMJ, if such communication was made to facilitate advice or supportive assistance to the victim. [43]

Reasons victims may want to talk confidentially to a counselor or victim advocate

- Speak about the sexual assault with someone other than family or friend
- Keep the situation separate from their work or duty assignment
- Receive support and guidance about their options from an unbiased party
- Address concerns about the offender, safety, repercussions, impact on job
- Receive treatment from a mental health professional for any other effects (such as, depression, anxiety or sleep difficulties)

Mental Health Counseling and Security Clearances [44]

Counseling and treatment for mental or physical health, in and of itself, is not a reason to deny or revoke a security clearance. In fact, many types of mental health counseling and treatment, to include treatment, which results from being the victim of a crime, such as rape or sexual assault, are usually not a concern with regard to security clearances.

No negative inference concerning eligibility for access to classified information may be made solely based on mental health counseling. [45] If a victim of sexual assault seeks counseling or treatment, it is not sufficient reason to revoke or suspend a security clearance. However, adjudicators must follow federal guidelines when assessing an individual's fitness for security clearance.

FAQ from OSD Memorandum on Security Clearances/Mental Health Treatment [46]

Q: *If I seek mental health counseling or treatment for a condition that is not excluded from being reported on question 21 of the Standard Form 86 Questionnaire for National Security Positions, how will it affect the decision whether to grant or renew my security clearance?*

A: *Your decision to seek counseling or treatment is viewed as a positive sign that you recognize a problem may exist and are willing to take steps towards resolving it. Early intervention is often a key to successful resolution. On the other hand, letting your mental health problem grow until your behavior endangers security may lead to a negative decision on your clearance.*

---

43 MRE, Rule 514

44 Office of the Secretary of Defense Memorandum (11.20.09) available in entirety at www.sapr.mil

45 Executive Order 12968 "Access to Classified Information"

46 Office of the Secretary of Defense Memorandum (11.20.09) available in entirety at www.sapr.mil

Q: *If I have received counseling or treatment from a mental health professional for reasons other than the exclusions listed on question 21 of the SF 86, what happens when I am investigated or reinvestigated for my security clearance?*

A: *You will have to report the counseling or treatment on your personnel security questionnaire. During an interview, the background investigator will ask standard questions about the length and reasons for your mental health counseling or treatment and its outcomes*

Collateral Misconduct 47

Collateral misconduct is when a sexual assault victim was involved in an activity or behavior that is non-compliant with the UCMJ at or around the time of the assault. Examples for collateral misconduct are generally personal offenses, such as: underage drinking, drug use, curfew violation, fraternization or adultery. The misconduct may or may not have been directly related to the sexual assault. For example, if an underage trainee is drinking alcohol, but later passes out and is raped, although the drinking was directly related to the rape, the victim did not cause nor intend the sexual assault to occur.

When victims of sexual assault are involved with misconduct at the time of a sexual assault, they are likely feeling uncertain or afraid to report the assault for fear of punishment of the other behavior in which they willingly engaged. Unfortunately, the potential of disciplinary action becomes a barrier to reporting the crime or seeking medical treatment for many victims.

With the implementation of the SAPR program, the collateral misconduct policy ensures victims' misconduct is not the focus of an investigation if/when a sexual assault is reported. It is the commander's discretion as to whether the collateral misconduct will be addressed after the conclusion of the sexual assault investigation. More importantly, the victim's safety and well being should be considered a priority above collateral misconduct.

This policy was developed specifically to protect victims from undue disciplinary action at the time of a sexual assault report and to encourage the reporting of sexual assaults and the appropriate treatment of victims. With this policy, victims can seek treatment and report the sexual assault without fear of imminent disciplinary action.

Expedited Transfer Requests 48

Any Service member who makes an unrestricted report (or who changes their restricted report to unrestricted on DD Form 2910 (Victim Reporting Preference Statement) is eligible

---

47 DoDI 6495.02, March 28, 2013.

48 DoD Instruction 6495.02, March 28, 2013, Enclosure 5 "Commander and Management SAPR Procedures" Section 5 "Expedited Victim Transfer Requests" pages 37-40.

to request an expedited temporary or permanent transfer from their assigned command or base to a different location within their command. The local Commander has 72 hours to respond to the request. If it is denied, the victim should be informed of the option to take it to the first flag or general officer in the chain of command who also has 72 hours to reply.

Key points about this policy

- Service members (SM) must be notified of this option at the time of making an unrestricted report or as soon as practical.
- Expedited transfer requests apply to those in the UCMJ Ch. 47, Title 10 and those defined for SAPR purposes.
- Transfer requests should be made to a commanding officer by SM.
- If approved, the request may result in: a permanent change of station, permanent change of assignment, or unit transfer.
- SM's dependents or spouse will also be transferred (if applicable).
- If disapproved, SM has the right to request review by first general or flag officer in their chain of command, or an SES equivalent.
- Reviews of denials must be made within 72 hours of request

Role of the Commander

- Document the date and time the request is received
- Consult with Military Criminal Investigative Organizations re case
- Make a decision within 72 hours from time of request

Reserve and National Guard Components

- Considered with regard to available resources and authorities.
- Access by alleged offender to SM who made the report is restricted.
- Options may include:
  - separate training on different times from the alleged offender
  - assignment to a different unit in the home drilling
  - transfer of alleged offender

A presumption shall be established in favor of transferring a Service member who initiated a transfer request following a credible sexual assault report.[49]

---

49   ibid

For Victims of a Sexual Assault: Deciding what to do and who to tell

Two of the most important decisions a victim will make is what to do and who to tell. Telling someone about the sexual assault can be very difficult. Often, victims are reluctant to do so because they have some worries about telling. Sometimes it is because they blame themselves or they might think they will not be believed. Some rape victims feel too ashamed to tell anyone. These are all very normal and common concerns.

Helpful tips for military leaders that will encourage victims to come forward:

- Foster a climate of respect for all Service members under your leadership.
- Model behaviors of strong leadership and dedication to military values.
- Promote esprit de corps. Challenge gossip affecting cohesion.
- Develop a cooperative and ongoing relationship with VA and SARC.
- Offer and attend regular trainings on SAPR under your leadership.
- Openly encourage Service members to come to you (or to the Victim Advocate) if they experience any type of sexual assault.
- Follow SAPR directives regarding expedited transfers, Military Protective Orders, confidentiality and all other relevant policies.
- Enforce zero tolerance of any type of harassment or sexual assault.

There are many issues for victims to consider when deciding what to do. Victims' options about what to do will depend on whether the sexual assault was reported to command or to the police for investigation (by someone other than the victim). The following are the primary options available to victims of sexual assault:

- Medical treatment (with or without evidence collection)
- Victim advocacy or counseling for information and support
- Restricted reporting to an authority (health care provider, chaplain, victim advocate, or SARC).
- Unrestricted Reporting (command, law enforcement, health care provider, chaplain, victim advocate, or SARC).

Helpful tips for leaders when you learn about a sexual assault allegation

- Meet with the victim to discuss his/her options and offer a victim advocate.
- Assess the victim's safety and whether a MPO is needed.

- Ensure the victim's medical and psychological needs are addressed.
- Follow the Commander's Checklist (as noted previously) to ensure the wellbeing of the victim, the mission and the safety of others.
- Respect the sensitive nature of this issue for the victim and for the purpose of an ongoing investigation. Never disclose information unless a need-to-know exists.
- Intervene promptly if there is any inappropriate gossip or harassment.
- Seek consultation from a superior, JAG, or SAPR as needed.

Common responses by victims and appropriate interventions

There are a wide range of reactions and responses that victims of sexual assault may experience. Victims may have many different feelings and reactions from the time of the sexual assault until weeks, months or even years later. Initially, they might feel as though nothing will ever be the same and they will find it hard to move forward. Or, they might be trying to get on with their life seeming as though nothing happened. People have different ways of responding to trauma including sexual assault. There is no right or wrong way to react. The following are some of the more common responses that victims of sexual assault have experienced.

- Shock, denial or disbelief that it actually happened
- Ashamed, embarrassed or guilty feelings (blaming them self)
- Angry, irritable or short-tempered
- Feeling a loss of control in their life
- Anxiety and self-consciousness about who knows and how people will
- Difficulty with concentration, attention and memory
- Changes in sleep (insomnia, over-sleeping, nightmares)
- Flashbacks about what happened or intrusive thoughts
- Changes in appetite (eating more or less)
- On-guard, jumpy and easily startled
- Anxious, nervous, scared or fearful of the offender
- Feeling numb or having difficulty expressing emotions
- Less trusting of others, more cautious
- Changes in sexual desire (from no interest to promiscuous)
- Concerns or ambivalence if the offender was someone they trusted
- Sadness, crying spells or feeling depressed
- Self-injury as a way of coping (e.g., cutting, burning)
- Using alcohol or other drugs as an escape or to cope

- Thinking about suicide or wanting to get away
- Angry at them self, the offender, command, or the military
- Hurt or betrayal, especially if the victim knew and trusted the offender
- Fear the offender will hurt them again

Victims of sexual assault or sexual harassment may experience any of these reactions days, weeks, months or years later. These uncommon responses (and delayed onset) are not uncommon for sexual assault victims.

If the victim or accused experience a depression that will not go away or has thoughts about harming them self, harming someone else or about suicide, it is imperative that you ensure the Service member is referred immediately for a mental health evaluation to ensure safety and wellbeing of the individual and of others.

Mental health responses

At least one-third of sexual assault victims will experience a significant depression, post-traumatic stress disorder or self-destructive behaviors. The following are the two most common types of mental health responses to sexual assault: Post Traumatic Stress Disorder (PTSD) and Depression.

Post Traumatic Stress Disorder (PTSD)
Post Traumatic Stress Disorder symptoms can include: preoccupation with the trauma; unwanted, intrusive, thoughts or feelings about the trauma; flashbacks; nightmares; sleeping difficulties; hyper-vigilance or hyper-startle response; or feeling numb and detached. PTSD is a mental health diagnosis considered a type of anxiety disorder. A physician or mental health professional (psychologist, counselor, social worker, or psychiatrist) can diagnose PTSD. Counseling from a licensed mental health professional (and/or medication) can help to treat PTSD or to lessen some of the symptoms. PTSD can be acute, chronic or, in some cases, resolve with treatment. For some people, however, without treatment it can get worse and lead to depression, alcohol or other drug abuse, or other complications.

Depression
Symptoms of depression can include tearfulness, sadness, less motivation, sleeping disturbances, appetite changes, decreased socializing, withdrawal, concentration difficulties, decreased sexual desire and decreased energy. Some people have thoughts about suicide or may try to end their life. Persons who have a depression that persists or comes back might have a more serious type of depression called a Major Depressive Disorder.

If someone has a depression that does not go away especially with thoughts about suicide, contact a licensed mental health professional. Good mental health care can make all the difference in treating PTSD or depression.

Warning signs

Contact a licensed mental health professional if you notice any of these signs in someone.

- A depression that doesn't go away and seems to get worse
- Intentional self-injury (such as., cutting or burning)
- Nightmares or flashbacks about the sexual assault
- Staying in an abusive, controlling or violent relationship
- Drug or alcohol use as a means of coping with the trauma
- Suicidal thoughts or plans or regular thoughts about death
- Serious thoughts or plans to hurt the offender or anyone else

Domestic violence, interpersonal violence and marital rape

If someone is in an abusive relationship whether by marriage, partnership or dating, sexual assault may very likely be a part of the abuse. Forced sexual activity may become an extension of physical violence or controlling behaviors. For the victim, it can become another problem to fear or to endure in the relationship.

It is possible that the victim will not leave their partner because they may still love the abuser (despite the violence). The majority of domestic violence victims do not leave their abuser after an initial incident, or two. For some victims, it may be after years of abuse before they leave their abuser, if they leave at all. Your role is not to help them to leave the relationship but to offer information, support and consideration of their wellbeing and their safety options including a Military Protection Order. Domestic and interpersonal violence is a very serious and potentially lethal dynamic. When victims try to leave, they are at the greatest risk of serious harm or murder by their abuser.

Interpersonal violence can include gay and lesbian couples as well as heterosexual couples. If you aware someone in your command is in an abusive, controlling or harassing relationship, it is important that you understand the implications of interpersonal violence and domestic violence before you try to intervene. The Family Advocacy Program is an excellent resource with information about domestic and interpersonal violence.

Contact the Family Advocacy Program Victim Advocate for assistance in cases involving interpersonal violence and domestic violence.

Allegations of false reports: Unfounded reports and misinformation

It is important to understand the differences between inconsistent information, unfounded reports, and false allegations of sexual assault. Some people incorrectly believe that if a victim provides inconsistent information, that she/he is lying and therefore it must be a false allegation. As a military leader, you should know how to respond if this issue arises to ensure fairness to all concerned and not summarily dismiss an actual sexual assault as a false allegation.

The differences between unfounded reports, false allegations and recantation

It is important to know that some victims of sexual assault will provide inconsistent information or fail to provide some information in their initial report. This does not mean they are making a false allegation. Providing inconsistent information may be a result of memory disorganization due to the trauma, alcohol or other drugs, discomfort talking about the sexual details (leaving out information), or a fear of being doubted or blamed. When a victim gives inconsistent information or leaves out important details, you may question their report or wonder whether they were sexually assaulted. It is much more likely that they are experiencing a normal reaction to the remembering or re-telling details about this traumatic event. This is not uncommon among victims of trauma.

Three other issues that you may encounter which need to be clarified and better understood are unfounded reports, false allegations and recantation. The term unfounded is used by investigative or law enforcement to indicate there is not enough evidence to suggest that a crime occurred. It does not mean a sexual assault did not occur. It is an administrative term used to clear the case and close the investigation. A false allegation is a deliberate lie that led to a sexual assault report. Recantation is when a victim later denies all or part of the original report. It is not indicative of whether a sexual assault occurred however.

There are many reasons why someone might provide a false report or misinformation or recant all or part of a sexual assault report. In rare cases, it is because sexual assault never occurred. Usually, it is due to one of the following:

- Fear of retribution or further harm from the offender or others
- Fear of not being believed or being stigmatized by others
- The desire not re-experience the trauma in a trial
- Pressure from persons in authority to withdraw the report

- Pressure from persons who want to protect the perpetrator
- Pressure or intimidation from others to withdraw the report
- Ambivalence about their past or current relationship with the offender
- A need to 'get on with their lives' and move forward without a pending trial or court case

Tips for leaders regarding recantations, misinformation or false allegations

1. Do not assume that a recantation or misinformation is a false allegation.
2. Meet with the alleged victim to address your concerns and ask a Victim Advocate to be present (if the victim consents).
3. Consult with the Victim Advocate or SARC about your questions but understand they may not be able to provide you with specific details due to victim-advocate privilege.
4. Remember, if a victim is expressing doubt about going forward with a report, it does not mean the sexual assault did not happen.
5. Create an opportunity for the victim to speak with you about their reporting concerns. Remind the alleged victim that if she/he is experiencing any harassment or retribution for reporting, that victims of sexual assault shall be protected from coercion, retaliation, and reprisal in accordance with DoDD 7050.06.
6. If the victim indicates there was coercion or retaliation, you must act in accordance with DoDD 7050.06 and address the responsible party.
7. Carefully recommend counseling or assessment if you are concerned about the misinformation, accusations of false allegations or recanting.
8. Address your concerns and respond accordingly upon assessment of the Service member and consultation from the SAPR Office, JAG or superior.
9. Never, under no circumstance, should you tell an alleged victim that you think he/she is lying or making a false report.
10. You should refer your concerns accordingly but not take direct action against the complainant (alleged victim).

Remember, the vast majority of sexual assault reports are true and the majority of sexual offenders deny the allegations. This is by far the more likely scenario you will encounter. If in doubt, consult with the SARC or the command authority authorized to address the sexual assault allegation.

Sexual assault prevention and response is more than a program and more than mandatory training. It must be an extension of each of us, intuitive in the way we think, plan and operate.

—Joint Chiefs and Commandant of the Coast Guard, Strategic Direction to the Joint Force on SAPR (5.7.12, page 18)

A Closing Message: What to Expect with Military Sexual Assault Cases

Responding to a sexual assault allegation is inevitable for all military leaders. Therefore, it is imperative that you are prepared before it happens since these cases often involve complex and complicating factors. To do so, you will need to be highly familiar with the SAPR policies and knowledgeable about sexual assault. Reading this Leadership Guide is a great start. The following summary will better prepare you when a sexual assault allegation is presented to you. Note, for simplicity in the example, female pronouns were used to refer to the victim and male pronoun refers to offenders. However, men and women may be victims or offenders of sexual assault.

The most common type of sexual assault in the military involves someone the victim knows such as a coworker or person in their unit or perhaps someone they recently met at a social function such as the NCO club or a party. The victim does not think that someone she knows (and possibly trusted) would commit such a violation against her. Since she felt comfortable with him, her guard was understandably down. She did not expect him to hurt her, to take advantage of her, or to violate her in any way, especially since she was in a vulnerable state being intoxicated and not fully able to comprehend what was happening. She believed he would help her if she needed it (to get home safely, for example)—not to hurt her.

Sexual offenders use and manipulate this underlying trust and safety within the relationship as a way to reach their victims or to get what they want. He may not even consider that what he was doing was sexual assault since they are friends and she likes him, right? He may have distorted perceptions, beliefs or thinking errors that lead him to believe she actually wants this to happen. He may even convince himself that this is true despite what she said (*"No, I don't want this"*) or what she did (crying, kicking, pleading, or simply lying there still and frozen unable to respond.)

When it is over, he may have little, if any, insight into what just happened. That is why he may kiss her goodnight, call her again for another date, or act as if nothing happened. He just does not get it. He certainly does not see himself as a rapist. It may never enter his mind that what he just did was a sexual assault. If it does, he may easily rationalize what happened (*She was asking for it*); minimize it (*It wasn't that bad*); or deny it (*She wanted it and was into it*).

This is the one thing that offenders and victims may actually have in common—clouded insight about what happened and why it happened. For victims, it is very different though. Yes, she may initially question if it was rape (in part due to her shock and disbelief) but she knows very clearly that *she did not want this to happen—not then, not with him, not in that way.* Her clouded insight, is also present because of her brain's reaction to the trauma and/or alcohol (which may very likely include a black out with actual gaps in her memory and ability to recall details). Mostly, however, the clouded insight and self-doubt comes from this underlying and complicating fact: She trusted her own judgment by trusting this person. She may doubt or blame herself about *why* it happened. She may ask herself: *How could I have gotten it wrong? How did I miss the warning signs that he would do this to me?*

Not only is her insight and memory clouded about exactly what happened and why, but this event has changed how she feels about trust, safety and relationships—at least for now. Things do not make sense anymore since her world was turned upside down by this event. She doesn't want to believe it is true—someone she trusted has sexually assaulted her. She has to make decisions about what to do or who to tell even though she never expected this kind of thing would ever happen to her. She may need time to think or time to consider her options. She may wonder what people will say if she does report it. This decision—whether or not to report what happened—is huge. She knows it will change lots of things. She wonders if it is worth it or if she should just try to get on with her life. Something just happened that she didn't want, didn't ask for and didn't think would ever happen to her. Now she has to figure out what she's going to do. If she does decide to tell, will you be ready?

It is very likely that you will encounter a case like this in your military career. It may be further complicated if the victim and accused had a prior or ongoing sexual relationship. Whatever the relationship or history between the two, no one ever has the right to sexually assault another person—even if both persons were under the influence of alcohol or other drugs, and even if they had consensual sex any time prior to the alleged sexual assault. Ironically, it is trust in the relationship that allows the offender to get close to the victim and to sexually assault her. The victim is left wondering how someone she trusted could betray and violate her in that way.

Although this is the most common type of sexual assault, it is one of the most difficult because it presents numerous challenges for victims, offenders, commanders, and investigators. It is further problematic since alcohol was involved, especially if the victim was in a black out and cannot remember all of the details. Even without the alcohol, it may have been so traumatic that the victim's ability to recall details was affected. The brain has a way of protecting us when we're experiencing a crisis. For some people, this may mean they don't remember all of the details or they have sensory triggers that create flashbacks or extreme anxiety. The information you receive may be messy, unclear, confusing and full of gaps or contradictions between the victim's allegation and the accused's denial. For some victims, they may be quite clear and calm—ready to tell you everything they remember. For others, it is blur and they may do or say things that are contradictory or counterintuitive (such as spending the night with the offender after the rape.) Sometimes people do things after a traumatic event that just doesn't make sense.

In these cases, you may find yourself questioning if a sexual assault occurred or wondering how this could have possibly happened. Your role as a Commander is *not* to determine if a sexual assault occurred. Your most important role is to be fully educated about SAPR and sexual assault including these complex dynamics that are actually typical in sexual assault cases. Then, you must follow SAPR policy and the Commander's Checklist to ensure the accused has due process and the victim gets prompt, sensitive and appropriate treatment.

With a solid and accurate foundation of knowledge about sexual assault, you will be better prepared to respond to sexual assault allegations and to ensure a climate of zero tolerance. What you do and say can make all the difference.

Change in the military culture will only happen one leader at a time. There are many people counting on you to lead the way.

For questions about the SAPR program, policies, training or related issues, contact your Sexual Assault Response Coordinator or Victim Advocate. Additional information is also available at the DoD SAPR website at www.sapr.mil.

Addendum III

For All Concerned
Additional Information and Resources

T HE RESOURCES INCLUDED here provide additional and relevant information on SAPR policies, military sexual trauma, and other organizations that are well known for their work in this area. Although this list covers a wide range of sources, it not intended to be a comprehensive inventory or a referral recommendation. The information was current at the time of publication but may change over time. Please contact the source for the most up-to-date policies or go to www.sapr.mil.

Military and Veterans' Resources

- **Center for Women Veterans**
  http://www.va.gov/womenvet

- **Department of Defense (DoD) Sexual Assault Prevention and Response Office** (SAPRO) http://www.sapr.mil

- **DoD SAPRO/My duty.mil**
  http://myduty.mil

- **DoD SAPR toolkit from DoD SAPRO** http://sapr.mil/index.php/dod-policy/sapr-toolkit

- **Air Force SAPRO**
  http://www.afpc.af.mil/library/sapr/index.asp

- **Army SAPRO/SHARP**
  http://www.sexualassault.army.mil

- **Coast Guard, Office of Work-Life** http://www.uscg.mil/worklife/rape_sexual_assault.asp

- **Marine Corps SAPRO**
  http://www.usmc-mccs.org/sapro

- **National Guard SAPRO**
  http://www.ng.mil/jointstaff/j1/sapr/default.aspx

- **Navy SAPRO**
  http://www.cnic.navy.mil/CNIC_HQ_Site/WhatWeDo/
  FleetandFamilyReadiness/FamilyReadiness/FleetAndFamilySupportProgram/
  SexualAssaultPreventionandResponse

- **Military One Source**
  http://www.militaryonesource.com
  Stateside: 1-800-342-9647
  Overseas: 00-800-3429-6477

- **SAFE HELPLINE** for the DoD Community and sexual assault victims
  Call: 877-995-5247
  Click: www.SafeHelpline.org
  Text* 55-247 (INSIDE U.S.) 202-470-5546 (OUTSIDE U.S.)
  *Text your location for the nearest SARC

- **Safe Help Room** online moderated and secure chat room for victims only www.safehelpline.org

- **US Department of Veteran Affairs**
  http://www.va.gov

- **US Department of Veteran Affairs Military Sexual Trauma** http://www.mentalhealth.va.gov/msthome.asp

- **US Department of Veteran Affairs National Center for PTSD** http://www.ptsd.va.gov

- **Victim Witness Assistance Program (VWAP)** http://vwac.defense.gov

Military Policies and Regulations

- **Army Policy AR 600-20 Army Command Policy** http://www.sapr.mil/media/pdf/directives/r600_20-1.pdf

- **US Army MEDCOM40-36 Medical Facility Management of Sexual Assault** www.sapr.mil/media/pdf/directives/Policy_Army_MEDCOM40-36.pdf

- **Marine Corps Policy** MCO 1752.5A Sexual Assault Prevention and Response www.sapr.mil/media/pdf/laws/mco1752.5a-final.pdf

- **Navy Policy Sexual Assault Victim Intervention Program BUMED 6310.11** www.sapr.mil/media/pdf/directives/SAPR_BUMED%206310_11-dtd-23Jun09.pdf

- **Air Force Policy Directive 36-60** www.sapr.mil/media/pdf/policy/afpd36-60.pdf

- **Air Force Instruction 36-6001** http://www.sapr.mil/media/pdf/policy/afi_36.pdf

- **Coast Guard Policy Instruction 1754.10C** www.sapr.mil/media/pdf/policy/ci_1754_10c.pdf

- **Uniform Code of Military Justice**

- **Article 120** Rape, Sexual Assault, Aggravated Sexual Contact, Abusive Sexual Contact www.sapr.mil/media/pdf/directives/article_120.pdf (6.28.12)

- **Article 125** Sodomy
  www.sapr.mil/media/pdf/directives/article_125.pdf

- **Article 134** Conduct Unbecoming an Officer and a Gentleman www.sapr.mil/media/pdf/directives/article_134.pdf

National Civilian Resources

- **Military Rape Crisis Center**
  http://stopmilitaryrape.org

- **National Center for Domestic and Sexual Violence**
  http://www.ncdsv.org

- **National Domestic Violence Hotline**
  800-799-SAFE (7233) or 1-800-787-3224 (tdd)
  http://www.ndvh.org

- **National Online Resource on Violence Against Women** (VAWNET.org)
  Special Collections on Sexual Violence in the Military http://www.vawnet.org/special-collections/SVMilitary.php

- **National Sexual Violence Resource Center (NSVRC)**
  http://www.nsvrc.org

- **NSVRC Sexual Violence in the Military** http://nsvrc.org/publications/nsvrc-publications-guides/sexual-violence-military-guide-civilian-advocates

- **Protect Our Defenders**
  http://www.protectourdefenders.com

- **Rape, Abuse & Incest National Network**
  National hotline 800-656-HOPE
  www.rainn.org

- **Service Women's Action Network (SWAN)**
  http://www.servicewomen.org

Other resources available from Sugati Publications

- Coping with Trauma Work and Vicarious Trauma: A Guide for Professionals (40 page booklet)

- Coping with Military Sexual Assault: A Guide for Active Duty Service Members (60 page booklet)

- Coping with Military Sexual Trauma: A Guide for Veterans, Their Loved Ones and Professionals (40 page booklet)

- Responding to Military Sexual Assault: A Leadership Guide (60 page booklet)

- How to Help a Friend who was Sexually Assaulted (12 page pamphlet)

- If it's been Awhile Since the Sexual Assault (12 page pamphlet)

- Military Sexual Trauma: What Every Active Duty Service Member Should Know (12 page pamphlet)

- Military Sexual Trauma: For Veterans, Their Loved Ones and Professionals (12 page pamphlet)

REFERENCES

The following references are from the first edition of the book. Updated references in the second edition are cited as endnotes for easier reference to the most recent policies changes.

Aaron, Ron (1996) Editorial. *USA Today,* November 15, p. 15A.

ABC News (1997a) *Primetime Live* (Interview with SGM Brenda Hoster), February 6.

ABC News (1997b) *This Week* (Interviews with SGM Brenda Hoster, Secretary of the Army Togo West, Senators Olympia Snowe and Rick Santorum), February 9.

Abrams, Irwin (1995) *The Words of Peace: Selections from the Speeches of the Winners of the Nobel Peace Prize.* New York: Newmarket Press.

Adde, Nick (1998) "Harassment Suit Against Navy Not Settled" *Navy Times,* December 7.

Ahn, II Soon (n.d.) "Great Army, Great Father: Prostitution and the American Army in Korea" in *Great Army, Great Father: Militarized Prostitution in South Korea, Life in GI Town* East Asia-U.S. Women's Network Against Militarism, pp. 12-16.

"Air Force Colonel Faces Court-Martial for Sexual Harassment" (1997) *Feminist News,* January 24.

"Air Force Discloses Sexual Harassment Complaints" (1996) *Feminist News,* November 15.

Air Force Judge Advocate (1997) Statistics on sex cases presented at the 105th Annual Convention of the American Psychological Association. Unpublished raw data. Chicago. August.

American Psychiatric Association (1994) *Diagnostic and Statistical Manual of Mental Disorders,* Fourth Edition (DSM-IV). Washington, DC: American Psychiatric Association.

Angell, Susan A. (1994) "Acute and Chronic Symptomatology of Sexual Trauma: Treatment Issues" *NCP Clinical Quarterly* 4(3/4).

"Annual Sexual Assault Data for USN" (1997) Navy data on sexual assault presented at the 105th Annual Convention of the American Psychological Association. Unpublished raw data. Chicago. August.

"Army Investigation Reports Widespread Abuse of Women" (1997) *Feminist News,* September 12. "Army Men Retire, Move, Get Discharged" (1997) *Feminist News: Feminist News Stories on Sexual Harassment, Assault and Discrimination in the Military.* June 3.

Barrett, Stephen (1996) "DoD Orders Services to Review Sexual Harassment Training" Armed Forces Press Service, November 14.

Bastian, L.D., Lancaster, A.R., and Reyst, H.E. (1996) *Department of Defense 1995 Sexual Harassment Survey* (Report No. 96-104). Arlington, VA: Defense Manpower Data Center.

Boehmer, George (2000) "Hearing Reopens for Ohio Army Sergeant" *Hamilton Journal News,* April 11, p. A5.

Bowser, Betty Ann (1996) "Improper Conduct—Sexual Harassment in the Military" *Online Newshour,* Public Broadcasting System, December 26. <http:// www.pbs.org/newshour/ bb/military/army_1226.html>.

Bradley, Barbara (1996) "Army Panel" *All Things Considered,* National Public Radio, November 22.

Brinkley, John (1992) "Air Force Official Discredits Rape Claims" *Rocky Mountain News,* Washington Bureau, September 18, p. 2.

Browne, A. (1993) "Violence Against Women by Male Partners: Prevalence, Outcomes, and Policy Implications" *American Psychologist,* 48, pp. 1077-1087.

Brownmiller, Susan (1975) *Against Our Will: Men, Women and Rape.* New York: Simon & Schuster.

Bureau of Justice Statistics (BJS) (1994) *Violence Against Women,* Washington, DC: U.S. Department of Justice, Office of Justice Programs.

Bureau of Justice Statistics (BJS) (1996) "National Crime Victimization Survey: Criminal Victimization 1994" (NCJ 158022) U.S. Department of Justice, April, pp. 1-8.

Bureau of Justice Statistics (BJS) (1997a) *Criminal Victimization in the United States, 1994: A National Crime Victimization Survey Report.* Washington, DC:

U.S. Department of Justice, Office of Justice Programs. Bureau of Justice Statistics (BJS) (1997b) "Criminal Victimization, 1973-95" (NCJ 163069) U.S.Department of Justice, April, pp. 1-8.

Burlas, Joe (2000) "Report Finds Incidents of Misconduct Toward Kosovars" Army Link News. Army News Service. September 22. <http://www.dtic.mil/armylink/ news/ Sep2000/a20000922kforabuse2.html>.

Butterfield, Marian I., McIntyre, Lauren M., Stechuchak, Karen M., Nanda, Kavita, and

Bastian, Lori A. (1998) "Mental Disorder Symptoms in Veteran Women: Impact of Physical and Sexual Assault" *Journal of American Medical Women's Association* summer, 53(4), pp. 198-200.

Cammermeyer, Margarethe and Fisher, Chris (1994) *Serving in Silence.* New York: Viking. Castaneda, Carol J. (1996) "Trainees Feel Betrayed by Abuse of Power" *USA Today,* November 15, p. 4A. Center for Women Veterans (2001) Department of Veteran Affairs Official Web site: <http://www.va.gov/womenvet/page.cfm?pg=23>.

Charen, Mona (2000) "A Military Gone Soft" From the Desk of Mona Charen. *Hamilton Journal News,* April 10, Section A. Chavez, Linda (1996) "Tailhook Lessons for the Army" *USA Today,* November 13, p. 15A.

"Checklist/Backlash Against Rape Awareness, The" (1992) *Anchorage Daily News,* Section B 6. September 21. Cloud, John (1998) "Sex and the Law" *Time Magazine,* March 23, pp. 48-54.

"Combating Sexual Harassment" (1997) Public Affairs United States Army. *USAREUR News Release 970325-2* Heidelberg, Germany, March 25, 1997.

Coyle, Bonnie S., Wolan, Diana L., and Van Horn, Andrea S. (1996) "The Prevalence of Physical and Sexual Abuse in Women Veterans Seeking Care at a Veterans Affairs Medical Center." *Military Medicine,* 161(10), pp. 588-593.

Delk, Lorrie (1997) "Former Aberdeen Drill Sergeant Guilty of Rape" Army Link News, April 30. <http://www.dtic.mil/armylink/news/apr1997/a19970430simpson. html>.

Department of Defense (DoD) (1992) "Tailhook '91: Part One: Review of the Navy Investigations" Department of Defense, Office of the Inspector General. September.

Department of Defense (DoD) (1996) "Defense Incident-Based Reporting System (DIBRS)" Directive 7730.47. October 15.

Department of Defense (DoD) (1998) *Manual for Defense Incident-Based Reporting System.* DOD 7730.47-M. Washington, DC: Undersecretary of Defense for Personnel and Readiness.

Department of the Air Force (1992) "Sexual Harassment Prevention Program Review" Office of the Chief of Staff, July 29.

Department of the Air Force (1993) "Sexual Harassment Awareness Education Handout," June 1.

Department of the Army, Public Affairs (1996) "Army Investigates Allegations of Sexual Misconduct and Rape in Training Command" U.S. Army News Release No. 96-78. November 7.

Department of the Army (1998) "Policies on Equal Opportunity and Sexual Harassment" Chapter 6, AR 600-20, Army Command Policy. Revision, February 16.

Department of the Navy (1993) "Memorandum on Sexual Harassment Policy," cover letter enclosed with Department of the Navy policy (SEC NAV INST 5300. 26B).

Dickey, Connie (1998) "Sergeant Major of the Army Shares Views, Observations," *Army LINK News,* February 11, pp. 1-2.

Dishneau, David (1997a) "Drill Sergeant Guilty of Raping Army Trainees" *The Cincinnati Enquirer,* April 30, pp. A1, A6.

Dishneau, David (1997b) "'Gangster' Sergeant Thrown Out of Army" *The Cincinnati Enquirer,* p. A1

Dishneau, David (1997c) "Women Watching Third Army Case" *The Cincinnati Enquirer,* March 31, p. A1.

Ebbert, Jean and Hall, Marie-Beth (1999) *Crossed Currents: Navy Women in a Century of Change.* Washington: Brassey's.

Editorial (1999) *Chicago Tribune,* Febrary 10, Sec. 1, pp. 22.

"EEOC Judge Recommends Army Pay $300,000 to Sexually Harassed Employee" (1997) *Feminist News,* February 5, p. 1.

Enloe, Cynthia (1983) *Does Khaki Become You? The Militarization of Women's Lives.* London: Pandora Press.

Enloe, Cynthia (2000) *Maneuvers: The International Politics of Militarizing Women's Lives.* Berkley: University of California Press.

Eskenazi, Martin and Gallen, David (1992) *Sexual Harassment: Know Your Rights!* New York: Carol and Graf Publishers.

Farrell, Warren (1993) *The Myth of Male Power.* New York: Simon & Schuster.

Federal Advisory Committee on Gender-Integrated Training and Related Issues (1997) "Report of the Federal Advisory Committee on Gender Integrated Training and Related Issues to the Secretary of Defense." Washington, DC, December 16.

Federal Bureau of Investigation (FBI) (2000) "Crime in the United States, 2000" Washington, DC: Federal Bureau of Investigation, U.S. Department of Justice.

Fisher, Bonnie S., Cullen, Francis T., and Turner, Michael G. (2001) *The Sexual Victimization of College Women.* U.S. Department of Jusice. National Institute of Justice and Bureau of Justice Statistics.

Fitzgerald, Louise F. (1993) "Sexual Harassment: Violence Against Women in the Workplace" *American Psychologist,* 48(10), pp. 1070-1076.

Fitzgerald, Louise F., Drasgow, Fritz, Magley, Vicki J., and Waldo, Craig (1997) Sexual Harassment in the Armed Forces: A Test of an Integrated Model. Paper Presented at the 105th Annual Convention of the American Psychological Association. Chicago. August.

Fitzgerald, L.F., Swan, S., and Magley, V.J. (1997) "But Was It Really Sexual Harassment? Legal, Behavioral, and Psychological Definitions of the Workplace Victimization of Women." In W. O'Donohue (Ed.), *Sexual Harassment: Theory, Research, and Therapy* (pp. 5-28). Boston: Allyn & Bacon.

Foa, Edna and Rothbaum, Barbara Olasov (1998) *Treating the Trauma of Rape, Cognitive Behavioral Therapy for PTSD.* New York: The Guilford Press.

Fontana, A. and Rosencheck, R. (1998) "Duty-Related and Sexual Stress in the Etiology of PTSD Among Women Veterans Who Seek Treatment" *Psychiatric Service,* 49(5), pp. 658-662.

Francke, Linda Bird (1997) *Ground Zero: The Gender Wars in the Military.* New York: Simon & Schuster.

Frankel, Bruce, Biddle, Nina, Williams, Kelly, and Ballard, Michaele (2000) "A Family's Grief" *People,* March 6, pp. 103-106.

Frayne, S.M., Skinner, K.M., Sullivan, L.M., Tripp, T.J., Hankin, C.S., Kressin, N.R., Miller, D.R. (1999) "Medical Profile of Women Veterans Administration Outpatients who Report a History of Sexual Assault Occurring While in the Military." *Women's Health Gender Based Medicine,* 8(6), pp. 835-845.

Frost-Knappman, Elizabeth and Cullon-DuPont, Kathryn (1997) *Women's Rights On Trial.* Detroit: New England Publishing Associates, Gale Research.

Gearan, Anne (1998a) "Former Top Army Officer Denies Harassment—Accusers Seeking Revenge, He Says" *Cincinnati Enquirer,* Fort Belvoir, March 4, p. A2. Gearan, Anne (1998b)

"Mckinney Guilty of Obstructing Justice—18 Charges Don't Stick to Soldier" *Cincinnati Enquirer,* Fort Belvoir, March 4, p. A2.

General Accounting Office (GAO) (1992) "DoD's Policy on Homosexuality" GAO/NSIAD-92-98. June. Washington, DC.

General Accounting Office (GAO) (1995a) "DOD Service Academies: Update on Extent of Sexual Harassment" GAO/NSIAD-95-58. March 31. Washington, DC.

General Accounting Office (GAO) (1995b) "Equal Opportunity: DoD Studies on Discrimination in the Military" report GAO/NSIAD-95-103, April 7.

General Accounting Office (GAO) (1998) "Gender Issues: Analysis of Methodologies in Reports to the Secretaries of Defense and Army" letter report, GAO/ NSIAD-98-125, March 16, Washington, DC.

General Accounting Office (GAO) (2000) "Military Dependents: Services Provide Limited Confidentiality in Family Abuse Cases" GAO/NSIAD-00-127. April. Washington, DC.

Gilmore, Gerry J. (1996) "McKinney Visits Aberdeen to Talk to Troops" Army Link News. Nov. 21.

Gilmore, Gerry J. (1997) "Simpson Receives 25 Year Sentence at Aberdeen Court-martial" Army Link News, May 7. <http://www.dtic.mil/armylink/news/may 1997/a19970509recruiti.html>.

Glenn, Mike (1999) "Harassment Hotline Calls Are Dropping" *Air Force Times,* February 1, p. 7.

Glover, Charles W. (1997) "It Boils Down to Mutual Respect" Commentary, Army News Service, Hanau, Germany, March 14.

Goodman, Lisa A., Koss, Mary P., Fitzgerald, Louise F., Russo, Nancy Felipe, and Keita, Gwendolyn Puryear (1993) "Male Violence Against Women: Current Research and Future Directions" *American Psychologist,* (48)10, pp. 1054-1058.

Greenfeld, L. (BJS) (1997) *Sex Offenses and Offenders: An Analysis of Data on Rape and Sexual Assault,* Washington, DC: Bureau of Justice Statistics. U.S. Department of Justice, Office of Justice Programs.

Gruenwald, Juliana (1997) "Army Defends Record on Sexual Harassment" *Congressional Quarterly Weekly Report,* 55(n6), p376(1).

Gutek, B. (1985). *Sex and the Workplace.* San Francisco: Jossey-Bass.

Hankin, C.S., Skinner, K.M., Sullivan, L.M., Miller, D.R., Frayne, S., and Tripp,

T.J. (1999) "Prevalence of Depressive and Alcohol Abuse Symptoms Among Women VA Outpatients who Report Experiencing Sexual Assault While in the Military" *Journal of Traumatic Stress,* 12(4), pp. 601-612.

Haws, Dick (1997) "The Elusive Numbers on False Rape" *Columbia Journalism Review,* November/December. <http://www.cjr.org/year/97/6/rape.asp>.

Headquarters Department of the Army (1985) "Chapter 18: Sex Offenses" in *Law Enforcement Investigations Field Manual,* 19-20. November 25. Washington, DC. <http://www.adtdl. army.mil/cgibin/atdl.dll/fm/19 20/Ch18.htm>.

Healy, Melissa (1998) "Harassment Verdict Pleases No One" *The Sydney Morning Herald, Los Angeles Times,* March 16. Herman, Dianne (1984) "The Rape Culture" in Freeman, Jo (Ed.), *Women: A Feminist Perspective,* Third Edition. Palo Alto, CA: Mayfield Publishing Company.

High, Gil (1997) "Combating Sexual Harassment" *Soldiers* 52(2), pp. 4-5.

Hutcheson, USAF Maj. Keith (1996) "The Discipline Crisis" *Armed Forces Journal International,* March.

John Marshall Law School (2001) "High Court Refuses to Examine Sexual Harassment in Military Says John Marshall Professor" PRNewswire, March 26. <http:// www.PRNewswire.com?>.

Johnmeyer, Connie J. (1997) "The Road to 'Zero Tolerance' and Beyond: A History of Sexual Assault Services at the United States Air Force Academy." Presented at the 105th Annual Convention of the American Psychological Association. Chicago. August 16.

Johnston Haas, Ann (1994) "Sexual Trauma in Military Problem Before Tailhook" *Cincinnati Enquirer*, November 11, p. D4.

Jones, Greg (1998a) "Hoster Testifies at McKinney Court-Martial" Army Link News, Feb. 18.

Jones, Greg (1998b) "McKinney Testifies at His Court-Martial" Army Link News, March 4.

Jowers, Karen (1997) "Taking a Stand on Privacy, Officers Quit Over Confidentiality of Patients' Records" *Air Force Times*. Oct. 13.

Kanin, Eugene J. (1994) "False Rape Allegations" *Archives of Sexual Behavior*, (23)1, pp. 81-90.

Kelly, R.J. (1998) "Assault Reports Distress Pacific's Leading Admiral" *Pacific Stars and Stripes*, May 13. p. 1.

Knight-Ridder/Tribune News Service (1996a) "A Two-Part Sunday Series: Rape in the Military" p6, 14K6154, June 14.

Knight-Ridder/Tribune News Service (1996b) "Army Won't Disconnect its Hot-line" *Cincinnati Enquirer*, November 19, p. A2.

Koss, M.P. (1993) "Rape: Scope, Impact, Intervention and Public Policy Response" *American Psychologist*, 48(10), pp. 1062-1069.

Koss, M.P., Goodman, L.A., Browne, A., Fitzgerald, L.F., Keita, G.P., and Russo,

N.F. (1994) *No Safe Haven: Male Violence Against Women at Home, at Work, and in the Community*. Washington, DC: American Psychological Association. Koss, M.P. and Harvey, M. (1991) *The Rape Victim: Clinical and Community Ap proaches to Treatment*. Lexington, MA: Stephen Greene Press.

Larimer, Tim (2001) "Incident in Okinawa" *Time Magazine*, July 9, p. 34.

Larsen, Kathie G. (1998) "Raped by the System: Sexual Traumatization of Women in the Military" *Treating Abuse Today*, 8(2), pp. 8-14.

Lombardi, Chris (1996) "Violence From One's Own Comrades is a Fact of Life for Military Women," Knight-Ridder/Tribune News Service. p9,18K5446, September 18.

MacKinnon, Catherine A. (1979) *Sexual Harassment of Working Women: A Case of Sex Discrimination.* New Haven, CT: Yale University Press. Madigan, Lee and Gamble, Nancy (1991) *The Second Rape: Society's Continued Betrayal of the Victim.* New York: Lexington Books.

Manchester, William (1978) *American Caesar: Douglas MacArthur, 1880-1964.* Boston: Little Brown and Company.

Marine Corps Commandant (1995) "Marine Corps Equal Opportunity Survey" (ALMAR Number: 145/95) May 2. Washington, DC.

Martin, L., Rosen, L.N., Durand, D.B., Knudson, K.H., and Stretch, R.H. (2000) "Psychological and Physical Health Effects of Sexual Assaults and Nonsexual Traumas Among Male and Female United States Army Soldiers." *Behavioral Medicine,* 26(1), pp. 23-33.

McAllister, Bill (1997a) "Charged with Harassment, 7 Top VA Officials Retired" *The Washington Post,* April 18, A23.

McAllister, Bill (1997b) "Senior VA Hospital Officials Disciplined for Harassment" *The Washington Post,* February 28, A1.

McCoy, Frank (2000) "Listening to the Victims" *U.S. News and World Report,* April 24, p. 31.

Mercier, Rick (1997) "Way Off Base—The Shameful History of Military Rape in Okinawa" *On the Issues,* Winter, pp. 29-31.

"Midshipman's Pleas in Rape Case Approved" (2001) *The Washington Post,* March 15, p. B3.

"Military Court Convicts U.S. Army Sgt. in Germany of Rape" (1997) *Feminist News,* June 12.

Morris, Celia (1994) *Bearing Witness: Sexual Harassment and Beyond—Everywoman's Story.* New York: Little, Brown and Company.

Murdoch, Maureen and Nichol, Kristin (1995) "Women Veterans' Experiences with Domestic Violence and Sexual Harassment While in the Military" *Archives of Family Medicine,* May 4(5), pp. 411-418.

National Academy of Public Administration, NAPA (1999) *Adapting Military Sex Crime Investigations to Changing Times Summary Report.* Washington, DC: NAPA.

National Victim Center (NVC) (1992) *Rape in America: A Report to the Nation.* Arlington, VA: National Victim Center.

"Naval Lt. Commander Faces Court-Martial for Rape" (1996) *Feminist Daily News Wire,* May 24. <http://www.feminist.org/news/newsbyte/uswirestory.asp?id=3499>.

Newman, Richard J. (1997) "Did We Say Zero Tolerance?" *U.S. News & World Report,* March 10, pp. 33-34.

O'Donohue, William, Downs, Kala and Yeater, Elizabeth A. (1998) "Sexual Harassment: A Review of the Literature" *Aggression and Violent Behavior,* 3(2), pp. 111-128.

Office of the Judge Advocate General, United States Army (1997) USACIDC Sex Crimes Investigations—FY 1996 (Female Soldier Victims) presented at the 105th Annual Convention of the American Psychological Association. Unpublished raw data. Chicago. August.

Palmer, Elizabeth A. (1994) "Harassment Tales Raise Doubt About Pentagon Reforms" *Congressional Quarterly Weekly Report,* March 12, 52(10), p. 614.

Pardue, Douglas and Moniz, Dave (1996) "Military Can Count Bullets but Not Servicewomen Raped." *The State,* Columbia, SC, June 16, p. A8.

Perry, William J. (1996) Press conference by Secretary of Defense William J. Perry on sexual harassment, November 13.

Ponce, Phil (1997) "War on Harassment—Sexual Harassment in the Military." Interview with members of the Army's Senior Review Panel, from transcript. *Online Newshour,* September 11. <http://www.pbs.org/newshour/bb/military/ julydec97/harassment_91. html>.

Popovich. Paula M. (1988) "An Examination of Sexual Harassment Complaints in the Air Force for FY 1987" (Report #: DEOMI-88-5) The Defense Equal Opportunity Management Institute. Patrick Air Force Base, FL.

Priest, Dana (1997a) "Army Finds Wide Abuse of Women: Panel Report Faults Leaders' Commitment" *The Washington Post,* September 12, p. A1.

Priest, Dana (1997b) "Military Faces New Sex Probes" *The Cincinnati Enquirer,* May 31, p. A3.

Pryor, John B., Giedd, Janet, L., and Williams, Karen, B. (1995) "A Social Psychological Model for Predicting Sexual Harassment" *Journal of Social Issues,* 51(1), pp. 69-84.

Pryor, J.B., LaVite, C., and Stoller, L. (1993) "A Social Psychological Analysis of Sexual Harassment: The Person/Situation Interaction" *Journal of Vocational Behavior* (Special Issue) 42, pp. 68-83.

Rennison, Callie (2001) *Criminal Victimization 2000, Changes 1999-2000 with Trends 1993-2000* Washington, DC: Bureau of Justice Statistics, U.S. Department of Justice.

Rhem, Kathleen (2001) "Services Move to Lower Instances of Rape in the Ranks" *Armed Forces Press Service,* April 5. Arlington National Cemetery, Women in Military Service for America Memorial.

Ricks, Thomas E. (2000) "Cohen Confirms Probe Into Sex Harassment of General" *The Washington Post,* March 31, p. A6.

Roig-Franza, Manuel (2001) "Women's Past an Issue in Academy Rape Case" *The Washington Post,* March 6, p. B1.

Roos, John G. (1996) "The Enemy Within—If You're Concerned About Military Discipline, You're Already a Step Ahead of Pentagon Officials" *Armed Forces Journal International,* March.

Rosen, L.N. and Martin, L. (1998) "Psychological Effects of Sexual Harassment, Appraisal of Harassment, and Organizational Climate Among U.S. Army Soldiers" *Military Medicine,* 163(2), 63-67.

Sadler, A.G., Booth, B.M., Nielson, D., and Doebbeling, B.N. (2000) "Health-Related Consequences of Physical and Sexual Violence: Women in the Military" *Obstetrics and Gynecology,* 96(3), pp. 473-480.

Scarborough, Rowan (1998) "Pentagon Finds Less Harassment; Officers Cite 'Fear' of Women" *The Washington Times,* December 10, p. A1.

Schafer, Suzanne (1997) "Study: Army Riddled with Harassment: Misconduct Crosses All Ranks, Lines" *Cincinnati Enquirer,* September 12, p. A1.

Schafer, Suzanne (1998a) "Army Charges Retired General for Improper Sexual Relations" *Seattle Times,* December 10.

Schafer, Suzanne (1998b) "More Army Sex Woes—Ex-General Under Inquiry for Relationship" The Associated Press, Washington, March 28.

Schafer, Suzanne (1998c) "Review of Hale Case Goes to Army" The Associated Press, June 25.

Schmitt, Eric (1996a) "Military Grapples with New Public Enemy: Illicit Sex" *Cincinnati Enquirer,* November 17, p. A12.

Schmitt, Eric (1996b) "Training Program Prevents Abuses by Drill Sergeants" *The Patriot Ledger,* November 28, p. 37.

Schmitt, Eric (1997) "A Mean Season at Military Colleges: Beleaguered, Embarrassed, Marching On" *Education Life,* April 6, pp. 24-30, 38.

Schneider, Dorothy and Schneider, Carl (1992) *Sound Off! American Military Women Speak Out.* New York: Paragon House.

Schulhofter, Stephen (1998) "Unwanted Sex" *The Atlantic Monthly,* October, pp. 55-66.

Schulte, Brigid (1992) "AF Rape Checklist Outrageous" *Denver Post,* September 18. Scully, Diane and Marolla, Joseph (1984) "Convicted rapists' vocabulary of Motive: Excuses and Justifications" *Journal of Social Problems,* 31(5), pp. 530-544.

Secretary of the Navy (1993) "Department of the Navy (DON) Policy on Sexual Harassment" SECNAV INSTRUCTION 5300.26B, January 6.

Seppa, Nathan (1997) "Sexual Harassment in the Military Lingers On" *American Psychological Association Monitor,* 28(5), pp. 40-41.

"Sexual Harassment in Army Not Only Result of 'a Few Bad Apples'" (1997) *Feminist Daily News Wire.* February 10.

Shilts, Randy (1994) *Conduct Unbecoming: Gays & Lesbians in the U.S. Military.* Fawcett Books.

Shortt, Debra (1996) "Charges Preferred in Three Cases" *Army Link News* Web site, November 8.

"Stop Bigoted Leadership" (2000) Editorial. *Air Force Times,* January 3, p. 44.

Suris, A.M., Davis, L.L., Kashner, T.M., Gillaspy, J.A. Jr, and Petty, F. (1998) "A Survey of Sexual Trauma Treatment Provided by VA Medical Centers" *Psychiatric Services,* 49(3), pp. 382-384.

Testa, Karen "Army Courts-Martial Begin in Sex Case—Sergeant Admits Misconduct." *USA Today,* November 13, p. A6.

Thomas, Evan and Vistica, Gregory L. (1997a) "A Question of Consent: In an Army Barracks, Where Sex and Power Intersect, a Woman's Sergeant Can Be Both Mentor and Tormentor" *Newsweek,* 129(17), p. 41(1).

Thomas, Evan and Vistica, Gregory (1997b) "At War in the Ranks" *Newsweek,* August 11, pp. 32-33.

Thompson, Mark (1994) "The Living Room War" *Time* Magazine, 143(21), p. 48.

Thompson, Mark (1997) "A Farewell to Arms" *Time* Magazine, 150(14), p. 46.

"Three Sailors Charged with Gang Rape" (1996) *Feminist News,* December 11, p. 1.

"Two Senators Call for Suspension of Top Army Official Accused of Sexual Harassment" (1997) *Feminist News,* February 10, p. 1.

Uniform Code of Military Justice, UCMJ (2001) "Rape and Carnal Knowledge, Sec. 920. Art. 120" (10 USC 920) Washington, DC: Government Printing Office. <http://www. access.gpo.gov.uscode/title10/subtitles_partii_chapter47_ subchapterx_.html>.

United States Marine Corps (1997) USMC rape and sexual assault database presented at the 105th Annual Convention of the American Psychological Association. Unpublished raw data. Chicago. August.

United States Marine Corps (1998) Official Web site <http://www.marines.com>. "U.S. Army Europe CSM Relieved, Charged with Sodomy" (1999) *Army Link News,* Oct. 21. <http://www.dtic.mil/armylink/news/Oct19991022csmcharged.html>.

U.S. Army Research Institute for the Behavioral and Social Sciences (1999) "Trends in Attitudes Toward Women in the Army" (Report No. 2000-08).

"U.S. Army Trainers Charged with Rape" (1996) Reuters, November 7. <http:// www. yahoo.com/headlines/961107/news/stories/rape_2.html>.

U.S. Merit Systems Protection Board (MSPB) (1981) "Sexual Harassment in the Workplace: Is It a Problem?" Washington, DC: U.S. Government Printing Office.

U.S. Merit Systems Protection Board (1987) Sexual Harassment of Federal Workers: An Update. Washington DC: U.S. Government Printing Office.

U.S. Supreme Court (1950) *Feres v. United States,* 340 U.S. 135, Certiorai to the United States Court of Appeals for the Second Circuit Court: Washington, DC. Van Sant, Peter (1997) Interview with Joan Furney and Vietnam veteran nurses. *Public Eye with Bryant Gumble,* March 24.

Warner, Margaret (1997) "Conduct Unbecoming: Harassment in the Military" *Online Newshour,* Public Broadcasting System, February 4. <http://www.pbs.org/ newshour/bb/ military/jan-june97/harassment2-4.html>.

Warshaw, R. (1988) *I Never Called It Rape.* New York: Harper & Row.

West, Togo and Reimer, Dennis J. (1997) "There's a Problem, and We Mean to Fix It" *Defense Issues,* 12(7), February 4.

West, Woody (1996) "Can We Emasculate the Military Culture?" *Insight on the News,* 12(49), p. 48.

White, USAFR Major General Jerry E. (1996) "Personal Ethics versus Professional Ethics" *Airpower Journal,* 10(2), pp. 30-34.

Widnall, Sheila and Dorn, Edwin (1995) "To Stop Harassment, Leaders Must Lead" *Defense Issues,* 10(64), May 12. <http://www.defenselink.mil/speeches/ 1995/s19950512dom. html>.

Wolfe, Jessica (1996) "Posttraumatic Stress Disorder in Women Veterans" *Women's Health Issues,* 6(6), pp. 349-352. Zimmerman, Jean (1995) *Tailspin: Women at War in the Wake of Tailhook.* New York: Doubleday. Zoll, M.H. (1999) "Sexual Harassment: One Woman Officer's Perspective" American News Service, January 21.

ABOUT THE AUTHOR

TERRI SPAHR NELSON is a national consultant, educator, author and psychotherapist with expertise in sexual assault and sexual trauma in the US military. She received her Master's degree in Social Work at the University of Texas at Austin and her military training in Behavioral Sciences at the Academy of Health Sciences while on active duty in the US Army. She was twice awarded the Army Commendation medal during her four years in the military.

Spahr Nelson served as a Subject Matter Expert for the Department of Defense on the development of their sexual assault program from 2004-2005 and consulted with the US Marine Corps to develop and write their initial SAPRO training curriculum. She was one of the first Sexual Trauma Counselors with the Department of Veteran Affairs, opening the Cincinnati Vet Center Sexual Trauma Counseling Program.

In addition to *For Love of Country*, originally published in 2002, Spahr Nelson has several other published works including a series of booklets on trauma and recovery for active duty Service members, veterans, professionals and for victims of crime. She is the author of a chapter on vicarious trauma in the 2015 book *Treating Military Sexual Trauma* (Springer Publisher) and an essay about rape in the US Military in the 2006 book, *Abuse Your Illusions*. She has appeared as a subject matter expert on sexual assault in the US Military in national and international media including CNN, NPR, 60 Minutes, BBC, Al Jazeera, Asia Times, Newsweek, The Village Voice, and others.

The author's recent related work and honors include the following: chosen by Joining Forces (a project of the White House) and the National Association of Social Workers to provide a national webinar on military sexual trauma for professional audiences; selected as consultant of the month by the National Center for Victims of Crime; named Alumna of the Year from the University of Texas School of Social Work in 2015; and her company was awarded the national "Impacting Veterans" award by Citi and the Institute for Military Veterans and Families in 2014. In addition to her military-related expertise, Ms. Spahr Nelson is also the author of a forthcoming (2016) book *51%: Women and the Future of Politics.* She is currently Director of the Undergraduate Social Work Program and on faculty at Miami University, Oxford, Ohio. She can be reached at nelsont@miamioh.edu.

Treat all sexual assault victims the way you would want your loved one to be treated if it happened to them——with respect, compassion and dignity.

www.SugatiPublications.com

Made in the USA
Coppell, TX
31 August 2020